SEA  ENGLAND

50 COASTAL PADDLING ADVENTURES
FROM MAINE TO CONNECTICUT

Michael Daugherty

Appalachian Mountain Club Books
Boston, Massachusetts

AMC is a nonprofit organization, and sales of AMC Books fund our mission of protecting the Northeast outdoors. If you appreciate our efforts and would like to become a member or make a donation to AMC, visit outdoors.org, call 800-372-1758, or contact us at Appalachian Mountain Club, 5 Joy Street, Boston, MA 02108.

outdoors.org/publications/books

Distributed by National Book Network.

Front cover photograph © Jerry and Marcy Monkman, ecophotography.com
Back cover photograph © Michael Daugherty
Interior photographs © Michael Daugherty, unless otherwise noted.
Maps by Ken Dumas © Appalachian Mountain Club
Cover design by Athena Lakri
Interior design by Abigail Coyle

Library of Congress Cataloging-in-Publication Data
  Names: Daugherty, Michael, 1964-
  Title: AMC's best sea kayaking in New England : 50 coastal paddling adventures from Maine to Connecticut / Michael Daugherty.
  Other titles: Best sea kayaking in New England
  Description: Boston, Massachusetts : Appalachian Mountain Club Books, [2016]
   | "Distributed by National Book Network"--T.p. verso. | Includes index.
  Identifiers: LCCN 2015046287| ISBN 9781628420067 (paperback) | ISBN
   9781628420074 (ePub) | ISBN 9781628420081 (Mobi)
  Subjects: LCSH: Sea kayaking--New England--Guidebooks. | New
   England--Guidebooks.
  Classification: LCC GV776.N35 D38 2016 | DDC 797.122/40974--dc23 LC record available at
   http://lccn.loc.gov/2015046287

The paper used in this publication meets the minimum requirements of the American National Standard for Information Sciences-Permanence of Paper for Printed Library Materials, ANSI Z39.48-1984. ∞

Outdoor recreation activities by their very nature are potentially hazardous. This book is not a substitute for good personal judgment and training in outdoor skills. Due to changes in conditions, use of the information in this book is at the sole risk of the user. The authors and the Appalachian Mountain Club assume no liability for accidents happening to, or injuries sustained by, readers who engage in the activities described in this book.

Interior pages contain 30% post-consumer recycled fiber.
Cover contains 10% post-consumer recycled fiber.
Printed in the United States of America,
using vegetable-based inks.

20 19 18 17 16   1 2 3 4

We're fortunate that over the last century, people have recognized the importance of public access to the ocean and public ownership of the places that give us that access.

In hopes that more paddlers will take care of these places as their own, this book is my humble thanks to those people who have shared their land, money, and time to preserve these places, and continue to do so.

Whether you're packing out garbage, clearing trails, or wrangling for rights, your work makes it possible for us to get out there.

Thank you. This book is dedicated to you.

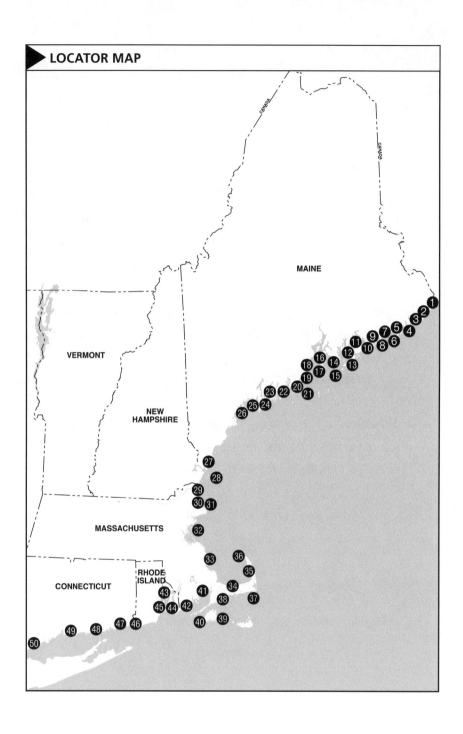

LOCATOR MAP

▶ CONTENTS

Essays

▶ AT-A-GLANCE TRIP PLANNER

trip number, trip name		primary launch	distance
DOWNEAST MAINE			
1	Dennys and Whiting Bay	Dennysville, ME	up to 15.0 nm
2	The Bold Coast: West Quoddy to Moose Cove	Lubec, ME	14.0–16.0 nm
3	The Bold Coast: Cutler to Moose Cove	Cutler, ME	8.0–9.0 nm
4	Machias Bay	Machiasport, ME	10.0–12.0 nm
5	Englishman Bay	Roque Bluffs, ME	4.0–14.0 nm
6	The Great Wass Archipelago	Beals, ME	8.0–10.0 nm
7	Bois Bubert Island	Stuben, ME	7.0–15.0 nm
THE ACADIA REGION AND PENOBSCOT BAY			
8	East Frenchman Bay	Sorrento, ME	8.0–16.0 nm
9	The Porcupines	Bar Harbor, ME	6.0 nm
10	The Cranberry Islands	Northeast Harbor, ME	10.0–13.0 nm
11	Placentia, Black, and Gott Islands	Tremont, ME	7.0–13.0 nm
12	Bartlett Island	Mount Desert, ME	8.0 nm
13	Swans Island	Brooklin, ME	21.0–25.0 nm
14	The Stonington Archipelago	Stonington, ME	6.0–14.0 nm
15	Isle au Haut	Stonington, ME	up to 23 nm
16	Pond, Great Spruce Head, and Butter Islands	Cape Rosier, ME	10.0–15.0 nm
17	The Fox Islands	Cape Rosier, ME	18.0–46.0 nm
18	South of Islesboro	Lincolnville, ME	10.0–20.0 nm
19	Muscle Ridge	Owls Head, ME	12.0–14.0 nm
THE MIDCOAST AND CASCO BAY			
20	Muscongus Bay	Friendship, ME	5.0–16.0 nm
21	Damariscove Island	East Boothbay, ME	9.0 nm
22	Georgetown Island	Phippsburg, ME	up to 20.0 nm
23	Sebascodegan Island	Brunswick, ME	up to 18.0 nm
24	Upper Casco Bay	Harpswell, ME	11.0–13.0 nm
25	East Casco Bay	Harpswell, ME	4.0–16.0 nm
26	West Casco Bay	Portland, ME	2.0–17.0 nm

water type	trip highlights	fee	skill	work boats	lighthouse	camping
protected	Abundant birds, wildlife, and solitude	$	(ALL)			▲
open ocean	Steep, wild, rugged coastline		⚠			▲ (nearby)
open ocean	Towering cliffs and steep, rocky shoreline		⚠		lighthouse	
open ocean	Grassy islands with great views; sheep and bird sightings				lighthouse	
protected/open	Ocean views; interior passages through the archipelago	$				▲
open ocean	Wild, exposed shoreline plus plentiful wildlife			work boat	lighthouse	▲
open ocean	Classic New England route: cobble beaches, cliffs, channels				lighthouse	▲
protected/open	8-mile island chain; sheltered or bayside routes		⚠			▲
open ocean	Steep, cliffy shores of Frenchman Bay islands			work boat		▲ (nearby)
open ocean	Long beach (possible surfing); marsh paddling; lighthouses				lighthouse	▲ (nearby)
open ocean	Sculpted pink granite on uninhabited shores				lighthouse	▲
protected/open	Public access and camping on mostly wild shoreline					▲
open ocean	Wild shores plus island villages		⚠		lighthouse	▲
protected/open	Dense collection of granite, spruce-topped islands		(ALL)	work boat		▲
open ocean	Miles of undeveloped shoreline; Acadia National Park	$			lighthouse	▲
open ocean	Penobscot Bay archipelago; hike to the best view around					▲
open ocean	Single- and multiday options far from the mainland				lighthouse	▲
open ocean	Wild islands beneath the backdrop of the Camden Hills	$			lighthouse	▲
open ocean	Granite archipelago with lighthouses, old quarries, osprey	$			lighthouse	▲
protected/open	Handrail an island chain to open ocean; possible puffins		(ALL)	work boat	lighthouse	▲ (nearby)
open ocean	Wild, steep-sided islands steeped in history				lighthouse	▲ (nearby)
sheltered/open	Rocky coast; sandy beaches; rivers; marshes	$			lighthouse	▲
sheltered/open	Open ocean; rivers; finger-like coves	$				▲
sheltered/open	Slate cliffs overlooking pocket beaches					▲
open ocean	Idyllic islands with historic sites; multiday possibilities	$		work boat		▲
open ocean	Maine's busiest harbor; Civil War fort; quiet, remote coves	$	⚠	work boat		

(ALL) = good for novices; ⚠ = expert only
▲ = camping on-route; ▲ = camping nearby

trip number, trip name	primary launch	distance
KITTERY TO BOSTON		
27 Gerrish Island	Kittery, ME	7.0–8.0 nm
28 Isles of Shoals	Rye Harbor, NH	14.0–18.0 nm
29 Plum Island	Plum Island, MA	17.0–18.0 nm
30 Castle Neck	Ipswich, MA	8.0–9.0 nm
31 Cape Ann	Gloucester, MA	up to 20 nm
32 The Boston Outer Islands	Hull, MA	11.0–13.0 nm
CAPE COD AND MARTHA'S VINEYARD		
33 Duxbury	Duxbury, MA	14.0–15.0 nm
34 Barnstable Harbor	Barnstable, MA	2.5–12.0 nm
35 Wellfleet	Wellfleet, MA	up to 9.0 nm
36 Provincetown	Provincetown, MA	2.4–14.5 nm
37 Monomoy Islands	Chatham, MA	17.0 nm
38 Waquoit Bay	East Falmouth, MA	3.0–14.5 nm
39 Chappaquiddick Island	Edgartown, MA	13.0 nm
40 Gay Head Cliffs	Menemsha Basin, MA	5.0–7.5 nm
BUZZARDS BAY TO LONG ISLAND SOUND		
41 West Island	Fairhaven, MA	8.0 nm
42 Westport River	Westport, MA	7.0–12.5 nm
43 Prudence Island	Portsmouth, RI	16.0 nm
44 Newport	Newport, RI	13.0–14.0 nm
45 Jamestown	Jamestown, RI	7.0–10.0 nm
46 Little Narragansett Bay	Stonington, CT	6.0 nm
47 Mystic	Mystic, CT	up to 15.0 nm
48 Old Lyme	Old Lyme, CT	5.0–9.0 nm
49 Thimble Islands	Branford, CT	4.0–5.0 nm
50 Norwalk Islands	Norwalk, CT	9.0–10.0 nm

water type	trip highlights	fee	skill	work boats	lighthouse	camping
sheltered/open	Wave-pounded shores; winding creeks; historical sites	$			lighthouse	
open ocean	Lonely islands full of history and bold scenery	$	⚠		lighthouse	
sheltered/open	Barrier island refuge for 300 species of birds				lighthouse	
sheltered/open	Sheltered creeks winding through salt marshes					
protected/open	Famed Blackburn Challenge circumnavigates Gloucester	$			lighthouse	▲
open ocean	Camp within sight of Boston's skyscrapers			boat	lighthouse	▲
protected/open	Paddle through a marsh and past beaches				lighthouse	△
mostly protected	Sheltered paddle to Sandy Neck and campsites			boat	lighthouse	▲
mostly protected	Bluffs, dunes, and beaches		ALL	boat		
protected/open	Three lighthouses and a view of Provincetown			boat	lighthouse	△
protected/open	Thousands of seals and birds at a wildlife refuge		⚠	boat		
protected/open	Camp in an estuarine reserve after a short paddle		ALL	boat		▲
protected/open	Five miles of undeveloped beach				lighthouse	△
open ocean	Colorful cliffs and sandy swimming beach				lighthouse	△
protected/open	Circumnavigate salt marshes and rocky shores		ALL			
protected	Sheltered, pastoral river and an ice cream store	$	ALL			△
open ocean	Circumnavigate miles of undeveloped shoreline			boat	lighthouse	
open ocean	Newport mansions and dramatic ledges		⚠	boat	lighthouse	
open ocean	Cliffs, rocks, ledges, a surfing beach, and lighthouses			boat	lighthouse	△
sheltered/open	Salt marsh, sandy beach, and boats in Watch Hill Cove	$	ALL	boat		
sheltered/open	Historic boats of Mystic Seaport and mechanical bridges			boat		
mostly sheltered	Marshes, tributaries, abundant birdlife			boat	lighthouse	△
sheltered/open	Pink granite islands			boat		
open ocean	Camp on-route and catch a view of Manhattan	$		boat	lighthouse	▲

ALL = good for novices; ⚠ = expert only
▲ = camping on-route; △ = camping nearby

▶ ACKNOWLEDGMENTS

While this is a book about places, the landscape is inextricably linked in my mind to the people with whom I've been fortunate to paddle.

I started sea kayaking in the Stonington archipelago with Todd Devenish, who helped inspire me to write a blog and begin taking notes for a guidebook. I think Todd imagined that he would lurk in the background of half of the guidebook's photos, mooning the camera. Sorry, Todd.

It didn't take long before I felt I knew a little about what I was doing. Fortunately, Todd dragged me to Bar Harbor for classes with Mark Schoon, who eventually suggested I take a surf class down at Popham Beach with John Carmody. At Mark's pool sessions, Melinda Rice coached me through the finer points, and there I met Nate Hanson, who has been an inspiration and close paddling partner ever since. Bill Baker thought I ought to guide at Old Quarry Ocean Adventures, so Rich MacDonald guided me through guide training. Todd Wright coached me toward instructor certification, and eventually took me under his wing as a long-term student, giving me numerous opportunities to coach and be coached, introducing me to Peter Casson and Carl Ladd who gave me valuable insights.

Many paddlers have generously shared their time and knowledge about their favorite places, including Carl and Samantha Ladd, John Hough, Chris Audet, Jim Connors, Matt McCambridge, Tim Gleason, Tim Motte, Ron Gautreau, Cat Radcliffe, Doug Mogill, and the paddlers of Rhode Island Canoe and Kayak Association (RICKA), Connecticut Kayak Association (ConnYak), and Northeast Seacoast Kayakers. Peter and Marilyn Fuchs and Barb Todd have accompanied me on many adventures, near and far. Diane and Ian Walker loaned me their entire collection of *Atlantic Coastal Kayaker*; thanks also to Tamsin Venn and countless ACK contributors who have shared their paddling enthusiasm over the years. I'm also indebted to bloggers like *Penobscot Paddles* and writers of trip reports for enthusiasm and information.

To those I have guided or taught, or just paddled with, as well as the few but valued readers of *Sea Kayak Stonington*: I'm grateful for the privilege to spend time on the water with you, viscerally or vicariously. Thanks to those who have extended hospitality, opened their homes, let me sleep on a couch, fed me, or invited me along on their excursions. And to those whose offers I haven't yet redeemed, I hope to do so soon.

Special thanks to John Carmody and Nate Hanson for their honest feedback, advice, and encouragement, and to Peter Tyson, Victoria Sandbrook Flynn, Leti Taft-Pearman, and Shannon Smith at AMC Books for making this book a reality.

But of course the most extra-special thanks are due to Rebecca Daugherty for paddling away with me all those years ago, even though we had no idea where we were going.

▶ INTRODUCTION

This book will inform and inspire you to take to the water with your sea kayak along the extensive, wild coast of New England. You could paddle straight from New York to the Canadian border in about 600 miles, but exploring the entire saltwater shoreline of New England—with its bays, estuaries, and islands—would require a trip ten times that distance. Beyond that, every stretch of shoreline is prone to daily and seasonal changes with the tide, the weather, and the season. And as kayakers out for a paddle, we see it through our own lens, colored by the company we keep and the mood through which we filter it. "You can never step into the same river twice," goes the ancient Greek proverb.

All of this considered, the "best" trips in New England are tricky to define: one paddler's favorite route could easily be a nightmare or a bore for another. While I was better prepared than most for the daunting task of choosing routes for this book, I continue to be humbled by the scope of paddling possibilities along the New England coast. I wish I could claim to have personally inspected all 6,000-plus miles of coast to distill it into these 50 best routes, but like most people wanting to make the most of their paddling days, I gravitate to the places that look as though they might have something special or unusual to offer. What makes a place special? Sometimes it's obvious features: big cliffs, sea caves, or remote, ends-of-the-earth islands. Other times there's something more subtle, perhaps hard to name . . . maybe just a feeling you get about a place.

Quite a few excellent stretches of shoreline are privately owned, and as you paddle along them you become more of a connoisseur of architecture than nature. While enjoying what people have made is its own attraction, most of us get our share of it in our everyday lives, so I've favored routes that will take you into less developed places. Opportunities to observe wildlife or experience historical remnants first-hand add another layer to any trip, as does the ability to craft circuitous, aesthetically pleasing routes over "there-and-back" routes, though I've certainly included a few of the latter. This isn't the first sea kayaking guidebook to cover these areas, and while some routes have been covered before, I've tried to bring something new to the table, or expand the route to include further possibilities. Some routes are omitted only because they seem obvious enough. Some excellent places are also omitted if a similar enough route was included nearby, since variety was a goal.

Good public access—including a launch (or two), somewhere to park, places to land along the way, and potential nearby camping facilities—was a major factor in determining which routes I included. Where launches tend to become overcrowded or where parking areas quickly fill, I've tried to include alternative launches to minimize impact.

It will be quickly apparent that I favor coastal exploration over long crossings (see "The Merits of Following the Shore" on page 72), though I've included a few locations that require substantial open water crossings. And though there are many exceptional paddling locales tucked away in areas that might be less exposed to the elements, I've favored the places that don't let you forget you're on the ocean.

I've also tried to accommodate sea kayakers of all levels by including routes that may be shortened to their more sheltered parts or completed in their entirety. I hope I've shed light on these areas in ways that help those with the ability to safely enjoy the challenging routes, and encourage others toward less risky places until they improve their skills.

The difficulty in being a novice paddler is that you don't know what you don't know. Monikers like "intermediate" and "advanced" can also be misleading terms, having more to do with paddlers' feeling about their abilities than their mastery of particular skills or overall seamanship. Paddling organizations like the American Canoe Association (ACA) have a tiered system of standards and a corresponding path of instruction that can help paddlers develop their abilities, and to understand where those abilities should lead them or not. Whether you're just starting out or hoping to add a new skill, there is no substitute for in-person, on-the-water instruction from a qualified instructor. I have, however, tried to include enough information in this book's front matter to provide you with an idea of what there is to learn.

I have often described the view from a kayak as "privileged," and the more I paddle, the more I understand how true that is. In a kayak we can inhabit that space between shore and deeper water where few others may venture. We go there for many reasons: to recharge, to reconnect, to loosen our bonds with a chaotic world on shore, and to find some peace in the watery part of the world. With a little practice and skill, we can maneuver among the rocks or through winding salt marsh creeks with the sort of animal-like grace that might make us feel we belong in these environments, perhaps even more so than in the places we call our homes. But we return home with an increased appreciation for the planet and our place on it. The New England coast is full of these places. Yes, it is a privileged view, but it is there for the taking. My hope is that this book will help enable you to take it.

▶ HOW TO USE THIS BOOK

While at first glance the routes in this book might appear to be solid, unwavering lines over the water that we must precisely follow, they are really just suggestions. The dynamic and fickle nature of the ocean and every paddler's preferences and skill make it likely that anyone would paddle an area differently from one day to the next. If you're looking for help choosing a route and starting the preliminary planning, read through the chapter introductions as a starting point. If you're already familiar with a particular part of the New England coastline, you can also use the At-a-Glance Trip Planner to narrow your options.

Rather than use a "novice to advanced" rating system, this book provides information and leaves it up to the paddler to understand his or her own strengths and limitations. While some areas may always be appropriate only for advanced paddlers (given a caution icon), there are no places that are always appropriate for the novice. Too many variables come into play, including but not limited to conditions, tides, weather, skills of paddlers in your group, and equipment. (For more about this, see "Trip Planning and Safety.") To help you evaluate the known elements on the routes, each trip highlights key information.

Icons shown in each trip and on the At-a-Glance Trip Planner will give you an idea of an individual route's highlights and cautions. You'll see indications where fees are charged for some or all parking and launches; for novice-friendly trips ("All") and expert-only routes (caution symbol); where other boat traffic can be a significant issue (though it can always be a concern); and for routes with lighthouses and campsites on the water. The At-a-Glance Trip Planner also highlights some basic route stats to help you narrow down what routes you'd like to consider before you delve into the full descriptions.

Mileage given is always in nautical miles, rather than statute miles. A nautical mile equals 1.15 statute miles or 1.852 kilometers. For tidal range and direction or places where it might cause hazards or opportunities, review Tidal Planning. Cautions lists particular hazards rather than every potential problem that the ocean could bring your way. This is where you should look for information about which areas are only suitable for those with strong skills or where wind, currents, and fog are known issues.

Where possible, multiple launch sites are listed, but the route described generally leaves from the launch that will be easiest for the most people. Charts and Maps are listed as a reminder that they are necessary (please don't strap this book onto your deck). The National Oceanic and Atmospheric Association (NOAA) no longer sells charts, but print-on-demand companies do, or you can download and print your own charts. Most paddlers prefer compact Waterproof Charts that rely on several NOAA charts to make a more useful hybrid edition.

When planning routes, keep on the lookout for bailouts, rest stops, and camping: use the information provided in Public Access and throughout the route descriptions and mark these potential pit stops on your chart. Land trusts own and manage far more properties than is easily apparent in charts, maps, and even these descriptions. In some cases I have included routes with more access than is apparent in the book. Maine and Massachusetts have different laws than other states regarding the area below high-tide line (see "Who Owns the Intertidal Zone?" on page 142). Since the Maine Island Trail Association (MITA) relies on privately owned property with use guidelines that change from year to year, only publicly owned MITA islands are noted. A MITA membership enables paddlers to access many more places, so "other options available to MITA members" is a common refrain in this book. Not only is the membership a great deal, but it helps ensure that these places remain accessible.

The Route Description details both the location of the trip and the suggested itinerary itself. While some routes obviously work best with a particular approach, there's a bit of an art to route planning. If you are guiding people, you try to show them some variety while steering them along the safest path of least resistance, ideally with an anecdote or two to give the place some cultural depth. So where possible, route descriptions include a few historical tidbits or background about wildlife or other details that can add dimension to the experience.

Whether you're looking for a more strenuous day than the main route describes or need to plan for difficult conditions, the Alternatives section highlights the many options present for each trip. First, you'll find ways to extend the route, sometimes referring to a nearby route that may be linked. Suggestions for backup plans follow, including ways to shorten the route and even nearby dry-land activities for days when the safest choice is to make another plan entirely.

More Information is your source for route-specific contact information. Always check with land managers and harbormasters for the most up-to-date information about use restrictions, exact fees, and parking.

Much more goes into planning a safe, enjoyable trip. Use the "Trip Planning and Safety" section as a refresher of any paddler's best practices, good technique, and essential gear. In the appendices, you'll find resources for further guidance.

EDUCATION

On the water, you must be attentive to numerous small-picture details—life jackets are zipped, grab loops are outside of the sprayskirt, hatch covers are closed, everyone is warm—while simultaneously processing the big picture: monitoring boat traffic, keeping an eye on the weather, and knowing what the currents are doing and where they're taking you.

Unfortunately, it is impossible to gain this wisdom merely from reading about it, and it is rarely acquired quickly. Most sea kayakers gradually gain perspective by paddling with more experienced peers and getting coached by qualified instructors. It takes some real work and effort. According to most guides and instructors, paddlers usually overrate their abilities (although women tend to underrate their own skills). About 880 paddlers died in canoe, kayak, or raft mishaps between 2000 and 2010; nearly 80 percent of these fatalities were paddlers who had no known paddling or safety education. Clearly, there is something to learn.

While these early chapters are a foundational review of kayaking best practices and technique, do seek out hands-on experience through trusted sources if you are new to sea kayaking. The good news is that our region offers as many opportunities to learn to paddle as it does exquisite paddling destinations. Appendix A lists just a few resources in every state. The guidance of a good coach will help you ascend the learning curve quickly and safely. Pool sessions are an excellent way to learn, especially when repeated every week or two through the winter. Sign up for guided trips or paddle with experienced friends until you are confident in your own abilities. The results will be worth the effort.

▶ TRIP PLANNING AND SAFETY

The best and safest trip begins long before you launch your boat. It includes how you prepare for a trip, planning the route, monitoring the weather, choosing who paddles with you, and what gear you bring and the condition in which you bring it. It includes making sure you have enough to eat and drink and that you have warm clothes to wear if you get wet. Safe handling of yourself and your boat requires a layering of skills and experience that enables you to make quick decisions. Often enough, the most important decision you make is whether you want to be on the ocean or not based on all the information available. It is far preferable to be on land wishing you'd gone kayaking, than to be on the ocean wishing you hadn't.

RISK FACTORS ON THE WATER

Even with the best planning, risk is inherent to sea kayaking. We take small boats onto a large ocean, and despite the feeling that our boats turn us into amphibious creatures, we rely on our boats, gear, and ability to return us safely to dry land. Risk can be a good thing; it gives us that tingle in our nerves that makes us feel alive and reminds us what we have to lose. But we want to live to paddle another day, so we accept that the risk is inevitable and learn how to manage it.

Before you head out, consider the following risk factors for your trip.

Wind Everyone has a different sense of acceptable wind speeds for paddling, and wind interacts with other factors like tide and the availability of sheltered areas to change the experience of a paddle. Novice paddlers should have little or no difficulty in winds under 5 knots. Winds up to 10 knots are generally still acceptable for most paddlers, but novices may get frustrated as boats become harder to control. From 10 to 15 knots, a little more skill is necessary, while winds over 15 knots can become hazardous for less-skilled paddlers. Paddling into the wind tends to reduce your speed by about a knot for every 10 knots of wind.

The easiest way to mitigate wind risk is to avoid it. Launch only after you've checked the current weather forecast, and monitor the weather as you progress on your journey. In the summer, winds often increase in the afternoon, so you could plan on finishing your trip before then. You may choose not to paddle on windy days, or you may seek routes offering the most shelter. If the forecast calls for increased afternoon winds from the southwest, you may choose to start your day paddling against lighter winds, and return with the stronger winds in your favor. Be careful about heading downwind if you need to return against it.

Waves and Swell When waves hit a steeper shoreline, they bounce back, creating a confused state called clapotis, which can be quite challenging to negotiate. Avoid this hazard by paddling farther from shore where the waves tend to be more organized and are less likely to be breaking.

While waves are wind-dependent, swell marches across the ocean—sometimes for thousands of miles—of its own accord. While swell tends not to be as steep as waves and doesn't usually break in open water, underwater topography shapes the swell into a breaking wave. A gradual, shallow incline results in gradual, spilling waves; a steeper incline creates steep, dumping waves. When studying the chart before an excursion, look for areas with submerged rocks or ledges exposed to incoming swell. If the swell happens to hit a rock or a ledge, it may rise abruptly and break just as abruptly, expending its stored energy onto the obstruction—which could be devastating to a small boat. As you're paddling, watch for texture in the water surface that might indicate submerged obstacles and remember that there's always a bigger wave out there.

Keep in mind that the forecast and buoy measurements are for "significant wave height" (the average height of the highest one-third of the waves) in open ocean. When those open-ocean waves roll into shallower areas such as beaches and ledges, they will grow even higher. Conversely, protected areas will have smaller waves than the forecast or buoy readings.

Tidal Current Be aware of the tidal current movement on your route and predict places where it may create hazards. Plan ahead, not only to use current to your advantage, but to negotiate potentially rough areas at slack tides. Tide rips are sometimes identified on charts, but plenty are not. You will need to develop a sense of where tidal currents will accelerate, anticipate the possibility, and be observant as you paddle. When crossing open stretches of water, keep a range to monitor tidal drift and watch for telltale signs of strong current, like submerged buoys.

When wind opposes tidal current, the friction on the water surface creates or steepens waves. When wind and current move in the same direction, waves may be diminished, but a dramatic change may occur as quickly as the tide changes.

When paddling in an inlet, estuary, or a gap between islands, know that the water in the middle of a channel is the fastest, with slower water near the edges. Eddies may also form along the edges, spiraling back against the current; use these to paddle against the prevailing current or as a respite from conditions in the main current. In some cases, however, eddies may create rough conditions of their own as the two opposing currents collide.

NOAA maintains tide stations and creates computer-generated tide calculators for just about anywhere you need them, as well as current stations in the more obvious places where currents increase. The NOAA website (see Appendix A) has tide and tidal current predictions. Weather radios broadcast times and heights for high and low tides, and apps are available for smartphones.

Lightning There is no safe place on the water when lightning is near. If you can hear thunder, you're probably within striking distance. The most effective way to mitigate lightning risk is avoidance. Monitor weather forecasts and if possible, watch the weather radar at home or using a cell phone. As you paddle, keep an eye out for the tall, billowing, anvil-shaped cumulonimbus clouds that produce thunderstorms.

If you do hear thunder, get off the water. Once on land, if you cannot find shelter in an enclosed building or vehicle, avoid open areas and if possible, seek low, rolling terrain. Avoid caves or rocky overhangs where lightning may arc across the gap. When risk is higher, perch on a foam pad or a life jacket, assuming "the lightning position": crouching or squatting, feet together, arms wrapped around your legs, eyes closed. Space group members at least 50 feet apart to reduce chance of multiple injuries.

Hypothermia Preparedness, constant attentiveness, and some background knowledge are your best defenses against hypothermia. Often enough, hypothermia is subtle and goes unnoticed until the victim starts showing more advanced symptoms.

Symptoms of moderate hypothermia include shivering, impaired speech and movement, lowered body temperature, and drowsiness. Be on the lookout for what current hypothermia educators refer to as the *umbles*—stumbles, mumbles, and bumbles— which amount to a loss of agility, an inability so speak clearly, difficulty with knots and zippers, and similar issues that indicate a loss of control over normal muscular and mental functions. A victim should be given dry clothing and placed in a sleeping bag, if available, then given quick-energy food to eat and something warm (not hot) to drink.

To prevent hypothermia, dress for the water. For water in the mid-50 degrees Fahrenheit or lower, this usually means a wetsuit or a drysuit. In midsummer when the New England air temperature is considerably higher and you can reliably get back into your boat quickly, you might instead wear something lighter (if you overdress, however, you may risk hyperthermia, or overheating; read more on appropriate clothing in "Equipment"). Have extra layers and hats and gloves where you can reach them from the cockpit. A loose-fitting outer layer that goes over a life jacket can quickly help a chilled paddler. Add extra clothing before the chill becomes a problem. Keep snacks and water where you can get to them on the go. This fuel helps your body stay warm. Choose rest stops deliberately to avoid exposure to wind. Avoid prolonged exposure to cold water: while 60-degree air might feel comfortable, 60-degree water cools you 25 times faster than air. Learn rolling and rescues; you should be able to get out of the water in less than two minutes. Never paddle alone if you can't do a quick and reliable self-rescue.

Be attentive to others. Before you launch, make sure your group members have extra food and clothing where they can reach it. The group will function far better if you help each other attend to hunger, thirst, and cold before they become issues. Watch others for signs of cold or fatigue, and don't expect them to confirm your observations. The best way to get someone to put on an extra layer is to hand it to them and ask them to put it on. Have backup route plans if it becomes obvious that your goals are too far for someone in the group.

Remember, not everyone responds the same to the same conditions. Children and those with less body fat get chilled more quickly. Fatigue and poor morale can speed the onset of hypothermia. Also, some medical conditions (including diabetes and thyroid conditions) and medication or alcohol use can increase risk of hypothermia.

Cold Shock A capsize in colder water presents the risk of cold shock as well as a gasp reflex, which could lead to drowning. Sudden immersion in cold water increases blood pressure, heart rate, and adrenaline levels, which could lead to cardiac arrest. There is no reliable way to prevent this, but wearing warm enough clothing is a good start. Practicing immersion in cold water (with close supervision) might prepare you or help you put the risk into perspective. To avoid surprises, reality-check your rescues in the water in which you paddle.

Wildlife On the water, jellyfish stings are possible. Sharks, including great white sharks, are becoming more common in New England waters, but sightings are rare and usually well publicized. Shark sightings are becoming more prevalent near large seal colonies around Cape Cod.

ON-SHORE HAZARDS

With our focus on safety on the water, it's easy to overlook on-shore hazards and the higher consequences of an incident on a remote island. A misstep could easily end your trip or worse, so taking a few precautions is well worth the trouble. Here are a few of the more common hazards, and how to mitigate their risk and prepare for them:

▶ Falling on slippery rocks can easily result in broken bones, sprains, or messy, bacteria-ridden lacerations from the sharp edges of barnacles or shellfish. Point out slippery areas for those who are unfamiliar with the terrain, especially while carrying boats. Let someone help you carry your boat. (More on preparing for these injuries in "Equipment.")

▶ Keep track of whether the tide is rising or falling and leave your boat well out of its reach when you go exploring. In addition, you should have a sense of whether or not a big wave or the wake of a passing boat could reach your kayak. If in doubt, either carry your boat higher than you think you need to or tie it to something solid on shore. Stash any loose gear in the cockpit, and remember that lightweight paddles, if not broken down and stashed, may blow away in a gust. Keep communications gear with you rather than with the boat so if you do lose a boat you can at least call for help.

▶ Foraging or fishing for shellfish is not recommended, especially as paralytic shellfish poisoning is potentially fatal if the victim can't get professional and timely medical attention. If you do choose to eat shellfish, first call the Red Tide and Shellfish Sanitation Hotline (see Appendix A) for updates on closures. Never collect shellfish from floating debris. Knowing about established closures and choosing healthy-looking specimens, however, are no guarantee. There's no way to tell if shellfish are contaminated. Symptoms of paralytic shellfish poisoning usually occur within 30 to 60 minutes after eating toxic shellfish and include numbness, headache, nausea, vomiting, and diarrhea. Untreated, it may lead to paralysis or respiratory failure, and in 6 percent of cases (most of which don't occur on remote islands) death. In case of poisoning, the only prudent measure would be immediate evacuation.

▶ Poison ivy thrives in some areas. If you do come in contact with the plant, wash the affected area with soap and water as soon as possible.

▶ Deer ticks, hardly bigger than a pinhead and very common throughout New England, may carry Lyme disease. Long sleeves and pants and DEET-based insect repellant are recommended for preventing tick bites. Always check for ticks on your hair, clothing, and skin after a hike.

▶ On some southern Maine islands the browntail moth caterpillar causes respiratory problems in some people. Bee and wasp stings are always possible, but be sure to find if anyone in your group has allergies, and if so, where they keep an epinephrine autoinjector.

▶ Use care around camping stoves and keep burn medication in your first aid kit.

▶ Sunburn is even more common and is most easily avoided by wearing high-UPF clothing and making sure exposed skin has adequate and frequently applied sunscreen.

▶ In general, attacks from wildlife on the shore is uncommon in New England, but give the animals you do see a wide berth.

▶ For most, driving to and from the launch is probably by far the riskiest endeavor related to sea kayaking. Car-topping boats presents risks both to you and others on the road; secure boats and check connections regularly. The shorter the span between roof bars, the more important it is to secure both the bow and stern, but be sure to tie bow lines in such a way that if they come loose, you won't drive over them.

BAILOUTS, DIFFICULT LANDINGS, ESCAPE ROUTES

When planning a trip, be wary of areas with limited landing spots and be aware that conditions may make some landing areas difficult or dangerous to access. Identify possible landing areas on your chart in advance. The ability to land in some areas is dependent on skills; in a group, landings are limited by the abilities of the least skilled paddler. Be wary of routes that commit you to an area that you can't assess in advance, or if currents or conditions make it difficult to retrace your route rather than continuing into hazardous conditions. In a group, be aware that less-skilled paddlers may be unable or afraid to turn around in difficult conditions. It helps to have alternate routes in mind as well as an ever-changing sense of the nearest place where everyone may safely land.

COLLISION AVOIDANCE

The prospect of being struck by a larger boat is an ever-present hazard. Avoidance is the most common way to control that risk. Increasing visibility is also a good idea, but we can't rely on it.

The first rule of collision avoidance: assume that no one can see you.

Kayaks ride low in the water, sometimes disappearing behind small waves; usually do not appear on radar; and become even less visible when weather or time of day reduces visibility. Assume that captains of larger boats have numerous distractions competing for their attention. They often can't see over the bows of their boats. Sometimes a captain might step away from the helm for a moment while the boat continues onward. Right of way is completely irrelevant when you see a boat bearing down on you. Always defer to the "law of gross tonnage," and let the larger boat have its way.

The second rule of collision avoidance: avoid the paths of larger boats.

Minimize the time you spend in channels, understand the routes larger boats will take, and get to shallow areas if there's any doubt. In marked channels, make sure to visually line up buoys to understand the channel location and cross at a right angle. In channels or open areas, groups should maintain a tight formation to give boats plenty of operating space. Look for unmarked channels: paths of deeper water that bigger boats will obviously follow (see "Paddling Among Lobster Boats" on page 85).

To determine if you are on a collision course with a vessel, note the angle it makes on your bow and watch to see if that angle changes. If the boat moves forward of that angle, it will pass ahead of you; if it drops behind that angle, you will pass ahead of it. If the angle does not change, you are on a collision course and need to adjust your heading.

It can't hurt to increase visibility using bright colors, and in low light using lights and reflective materials. Moving your paddles is sometimes the only thing differentiating you from colorful lobster buoys. Though these efforts help, never assume that these measures are ensuring visibility.

Finally, don't assume that you, as a hand-powered vessel, have right of way over motorboats. The Rules of the Road (also known as the International Regulations for Avoiding Collisions at Sea or COLREGS) make no distinction between kayaks and motorized boats; they are both referred to simply as "vessels." You must keep out of the way of vessels engaged in fishing or under sail, which suggests that if you get yourself run over by a fishing boat, you may be legally at fault.

STAY IN TOUCH

Leave a written float plan with someone on shore before you launch. This plan should include details about group members, itinerary, specifics about when you will check in and expected time of return, and clear instructions to call the Coast Guard for help should you fail to check in or return when expected. (See Appendix B for a float plan form.)

Many paddlers now use cell phones on overnight trips to check in with someone at home. It's a great idea, but be sure to leave specific instructions about what to do if you

xxiv ▶ TRIP PLANNING AND SAFETY

fail to check in, keeping in mind that you might not have cell service everywhere you go. If the plan is to check in, don't fail to do so unless you want to be rescued. If you get stuck at your check-in time without cell service, contact the Coast Guard on your very high frequency (VHF) radio to relay a message home; they are more than happy to do this. (For more on VHF communication, see "Basic VHF Protocol.")

The increased reach of phone and Internet brings potential for staying in touch, but can also cause problems. If you snap a picture and post it online, be careful about what you write. One kayak camper recently joked on Facebook of being "stranded on a desert island," then turned off the phone. A concerned relative called the Coast Guard, which was obligated to check it out.

INCIDENTS ON THE WATER
Accidents happen; things go wrong. Coming through an accident in the best shape possible begins before you launch, but sometimes preparation isn't enough.

Before You Leave
- ▶ Practice and master rescue skills.
- ▶ Ensure that you are equipped with the appropriate safety gear and first aid, boat repair, and communication tools (see more in "Equipment"). These should be within easy reach of your seat.
- ▶ At a pre-trip briefing or discussion, clarify your group's protocol for different scenarios such as capsizing or getting separated. Establish a channel for VHF communication between group members other than channel 16 (for distress and hailing only).

On the Water
- ▶ Look after yourself first. You're not much help to anyone if you become cold and tired, or worse: incapacitated.
- ▶ Help anticipate others' needs and encourage preventative steps, including adding extra layers, frequent eating and drinking, and adhering to plans to rest.
- ▶ Don't lose sight of your surroundings, the elements, and what needs to be done to continue ensuring a safe trip.

If Something Goes Wrong
- ▶ Your personal safety comes first, then the needs of the group, then the needs of the victim. This protocol helps minimize the chance of additional injuries or accidents that will only a make a bad situation worse.
- ▶ Manage problems as early as possible, continue to monitor for complications throughout the paddle, and if necessary, summon help before the situation gets worse.

Making a Distress Call

▶ Latitude and longitude is the best way to communicate your location. Keep in mind that many islands and geographic features have duplicate names.

▶ The Coast Guard would rather be called and decide that they aren't needed than be updated on an incident late when their job is more difficult. Know that some less urgent situations (for instance, a lost kayak) may be better handled by the local harbormaster or other agencies. A 911 dispatcher doesn't always know how to quickly respond to an offshore emergency.

▶ You can call for help with your cell phone if you have a signal and the appropriate numbers (see Appendix A), or use channel 16 on your VHF.

▶ If you call for help on the radio but receive no response, it is possible that the Coast Guard heard your call—either directly or through other boaters' relays— but your radio isn't powerful enough or your batteries are too low to receive the response. Continue updating, noting that you are unable to hear a response.

▶ If your emergency is resolved, be sure to let the Coast Guard know, even if you have not received a response. Odds are, they will search until they find you.

TRIP PLANNING

A journey in a sea kayak begins before you leave the shore, and continues well after you return. After a trip, you look through photos and recount stories, reliving the parts that went well and those that didn't, and in the process you begin planning your next adventure. Start with a goal: the highlight everyone will remember. It could be a pristine beach, a cauldron below a towering cliff, or the opportunity to see wildlife. Balance goals with risks and the group's abilities and formulate a plan, keeping in mind the effects of tides and potential of changing weather. Arrive at the launch confident that you've thought through as much as possible, and that you're equipped to deal with whatever the day may bring.

GROUP PADDLING

The need for leadership skills can sneak up on you. One day you're the inexperienced paddler in the group, counting on others for guidance, and soon enough you may realize that people are looking to you to ensure their safety. This is certainly the case if you learn to paddle and then take your family out for a trip. To be an effective leader, you need to have solid enough personal skills to be able to focus your attention on your group members rather than yourself.

Small groups of similarly skilled, self-sufficient paddlers may decide each member is equally responsible for all group decisions. This may work with the right group, but there is a fine line between "everybody is responsible" and "no one is responsible." If everyone is truly dependent on no one else and with no expectations from the group, it makes perfect sense. If this is not the case, an effort to reach consensus about an important decision may undermine quick and efficient action. If you happen to be one of the more experienced members of the group, you may feel powerless to establish a safe and manageable routine, and if things get out of hand, no matter what anyone says about shared responsibility, it will still be your problem. Another approach is to choose a leader. Among small groups of two to three paddlers with similar skills, a loose, "co-leader" approach may work, but as the group gets larger, it will operate most effectively with one designated leader. Before you head out, know your fellow paddlers' preferences and your own comfort level with the leadership style to which you all agree.

Even with a group of friends, a good on-shore trip briefing helps establish how you'll function as a group. What are your goals for the trip? Will you paddle quickly or investigate features along the way? Is there a leader delegated to make decisions for everyone? Is everyone prepared with proper gear, drinking water, snacks, sunscreen, and extra clothing (see "Equipment")? Are there medical issues you should know about? How far apart from each other do you paddle? What happens if someone capsizes or if the group becomes separated? Who has a first aid kit and other emergency gear?

On the water, it can be a challenge to keep the group together. Occasionally groups spread over large distances, faster paddlers getting way ahead while others dawdle behind. There are times—perhaps while following a shoreline—where getting spread apart has low consequences, and might even be preferable. Most of the time though, sticking together makes the most sense. In open water or in channels, a tight group makes for a "smaller target" for powerboats and doesn't block channels. Ideally, your group should be close enough together to easily communicate without shouting.

SELF-SUFFICIENCY

While not everyone should paddle alone, having the ability to do so greatly increases your safety and confidence in every paddling experience. If you become separated from your group but were relying on others for skills or equipment, you're no better off than if you'd launched solo. If you do choose to rely on others, crucial questions ensue. Is the person you are relying on truly self-sufficient, or is he or she also relying on you? If that person is not hired as your guide or instructor, is he or she aware of your dependence?

For many, a sense of autonomy is an attraction of sea kayaking. You can carry in your boats everything you might need for a long journey and you can carry within yourself the knowledge and skills to make such a journey possible. Unlike larger boats, the sea kayak is most often designed for one person, small enough to be portable and big enough to allow the paddler to pack along the essentials.

Becoming a self-sufficient paddler, though, takes more than a well-packed boat; it is a gradual process of learning through formal instruction and through picking up bits and pieces of information, advice, and gear from friends and fellow paddlers. Those most able to paddle alone—by choice or chance—are those who realize that preparation and skill are always more reliable than luck.

Paddling alone can be quite different from sharing the experience with others. Stretches of ocean that might otherwise be dominated by talk turn quiet. There's no one to speed ahead or lag behind and you may alter your pace at will. By setting your own pace, you may be more attuned to sounds and smells and the subtle information coming to you in the feel of the water through your hull. Without the distraction of other people, you're more likely to notice the environment around you. With only yourself to rely upon, you should give risks more thought, asking yourself "what would I do if . . . ?" Thoughts play through your head, and without others to interrupt, the places those thoughts go may be as much a journey as the physical trek. As technology connects us to networks of constant sharing and information overload, this time alone seems even more valuable and rare.

Solo paddling isn't for everyone, even those who have become truly self-sufficient. You may not be comfortable with the risks you assume alone on the ocean. You may prefer the company of others, no matter the weather or the route. But having the skills to undertake a solo paddle is nonetheless important. Alone or together, the self-sufficiency we develop when we learn to handle ourselves well in a sea kayak may have value and implications that extend into other parts of our lives as well.

If you do choose to paddle alone, plan every element of your excursion with extra care. Plan to be off the water long before dark. Always leave your full and detailed float plan with someone on shore. Prepare yourself well with navigation tools including charts and a compass, and perhaps a GPS; emergency gear; bailout plans; and a way to contact help if you need it (see more in "Equipment").

BASIC VHF PROTOCOL

At first, using the very high frequency (VHF) radio may seem a bit mysterious, with unfamiliar etiquette and language. Add to that the notion that anyone could be listening, including the Coast Guard, and you could easily be intimidated by talking into this little device. With practice, talking on the VHF may come as easily as using the phone, but there is protocol to be followed.

- ▶ Use channel 16 only for hailing and emergencies. Any talk on 16 should be brief; if needed, switch to a different channel.

- ▶ Before pressing the transmit button to speak, listen and make sure the channel is free. After transmitting, wait a reasonable period for a response. You won't be able to hear a response if you are transmitting again.

- ▶ Engage the transmit button for a moment before you speak. Speak clearly, making an effort to enunciate each word. Say "over" when you are done speaking and disengage the transmit button.

- ▶ Keep calls brief, with no unnecessary talk.

- ▶ Aside from general communication, there are three types of calls you need to know how to make. Each is made on channel 16.

- ▶ **The Sécurité call** (pronounced "say-CUR-i-tay") is used to advise other vessels of your presence. Most commonly, paddlers use a Sécurité call before crossing a channel in the fog. An example might sound like this: "Sécurité, Sécurité,

Sécurité, this is sea kayak group Joe, located in Deer Island Thorofare near Dow Ledge. We're a group of six kayaks crossing to Russ Island, estimated crossing time five minutes. Standing by on one-six. Over." Wait to hear a response before you cross.

▶ **The Pan-Pan call** (pronounced "pahn-pahn") is used to alert other vessels of an urgent situation regarding the safety of a vessel or person. This might be used to request medical help, or if danger is not as imminent as that of a Mayday call.

▶ **The Mayday call** is a call for help in case of imminent danger that could result in loss of life or vessel. An example might sound like this: "Mayday, Mayday, Mayday, all stations. This is sea kayak group Joe. We have a paddler experiencing chest pain and require immediate rescue by a motorized vessel, in Stonington, off the east tip of McGlathery Island. We are a group of six kayaks. The casualty is 55 years old, and experiencing severe chest pain and trouble breathing. Standing by on one-six. Over."

Check the battery level on your VHF frequently and recharge as needed. Press the transmit button to see if the battery level drops. Take some time to become familiar with the radio and practice without transmitting. Listen to others to gain familiarity with radio etiquette.

▶ EQUIPMENT

To be safe and self-sufficient, you need the right gear, which may change according to the environment and the length of your itinerary. There isn't always an easy answer for what is right or wrong. The following pages list the gear necessary for a safe paddle. A solo paddler should bring everything. Groups may choose to only bring one of some items and to disperse group gear across members. This can be a help to novice paddlers who are acquiring gear, but remember that if you don't have a piece of gear in your boat, you are dependent on the group member who is carrying it, and vice versa.

PERSONAL EQUIPMENT

Every paddler should be equipped with this gear, even when paddling with a group.

Boat For most of the trips covered in this book, a touring sea kayak would be most appropriate, but there are other options that would also work. There is no perfect boat for all conditions and pursuits, but some boats do well in most circumstances.

If you have not yet purchased your kayak, the variety of boats can be overwhelming, but the field could be narrowed by what you hope to do in your boat. Try a few kayaks and see what you like. Take classes from an instructor who has a few different demo boats for you to try. Some shops will offer demo days or the opportunity to try boats before you buy them. Consider every potential kayak's flotation, dimensions, and shape, all of which affect the way it handles and the ways you can use it. None of these design and performance factors are cut-and-dried equations; there's still a bit of art and mystery about how design affects the handling of kayaks, and some just seem to have a near-magical ability to respond to the paddler's desires. Fortunately for the multitude of kayak manufacturers though, no one agrees on which boats are magic, and which are not. "What to Look For in a Kayak" is brief; consult fellow paddlers and instructors for additional advice before making a purchase. A good shop or outfitter should be able to recommend a boat that fits properly.

What to Look For in a Kayak

Most sea kayaks have airtight flotation chambers created by sealing the bow and stern with bulkheads and watertight hatch covers. For boats that lack airtight chambers, inflatable flotation bags can do the job, but if you're shopping for a sea kayak, consider the cost of flotation bags as well as the convenience and storage space of sealed compartments.

The dimensions of a boat determines its potential speed, tracking (tendency to go straight), cargo space, and ability to handle ocean conditions. In general, longer boats may be faster and track better than shorter ones, while shorter boats maneuver more easily, but other factors like hull shape figure largely into the picture as well. Boats with a lot of curve in their profile, with upswept ends (a bit banana-shaped) can turn easily when edged. A long, straight boat is less maneuverable, but may inspire you to get the most power and speed out of each stroke.

The shape of the boat's bottom determines how easy or difficult it is to get to that edge. A flat-bottomed, U-shaped hull would be difficult to turn by edging and will come to rest either right-side up or upside down. When a wave hits it from the side, it tends to flip it over rather than pass beneath it. Alternately, deeper hulls have a whole range of edging available to them.

The hull shape can be either rounded, chined, or a combination of the two. The shape of a hard chine hull comes from traditional kayaks, but also occurs in wooden "stitch and glue" hulls as well as a few plastic or composite hulls that favor the traditional shape. A hard chine makes it easier to hold that particular edge, while with a rounded hull, the balance point is more variable but slightly less solid. Both hull shapes can allow waves from the side to pass beneath them. Some hull designs blend these different shapes in different sections of the boat.

Looking at the shape of the boat from above or below, the most distinguishing factor is whether the shape is symmetrical or where the widest part occurs in relation to the cockpit. The "fish form" places more volume ahead of the cockpit, while the "Swede form" places it just behind the cockpit. The more buoyant bow of a fish form boat may handle better in following seas, while a Swede form hull tends to accelerate quickly and have a more stable, reassuring feel.

Sit-on-top boats are a bit of a different animal, but the same design characteristics apply. They're most popular and more appropriate in warmer areas with warmer water and some sheltered areas, since any waves are likely to douse you, but they are well-suited for fishing. The oft-touted "self-bailing" feature simply means that water runs right through the boat, rather than pooling inside it, and rescues are as simple as righting the boat and hoisting your torso onto the deck.

A tandem might be preferable at times. Most tandems have pedal controls for the rudder mounted in the stern compartment. Sometimes there is even a center hatch that can be removed for a passenger or pet. With two paddlers and longer waterline, a tandem has the potential to go faster, and one paddler has the option of resting or taking pictures while the other steers and keeps the boat going. Tandems can be a good option when one paddler is less confident about solo paddling, or for children, and the cost is probably a little less than that of two fully outfitted single kayaks. While tandems may feel more stable than smaller boats, they're certainly capable of capsizing, and the need for rescue skills is not lessened. Furthermore, two people in a tandem lose the safety advantages gained by two people in singles who can rescue each other if necessary.

Many kayaks are equipped with either a skeg or a rudder. Both help control the boat when a beam wind causes weathercocking, or unintended swinging into the wind. Some boats weathercock more than others, and the way the load is balanced or not can affect the effects, but without a skeg or rudder, you may have little choice but to edge and perform repeated sweep strokes on one side. Dropping a skeg or a rudder helps anchor the stern, minimizing weathercocking.

Of course, the rudder is also used to turn the boat. Some fitness and expedition paddlers argue that a rudder minimizes effort, therefore allowing them to expend their energy propelling the boat forward. Others feel a rudder makes sharp turns and precise maneuvering difficult at best. It is possible to have a ruddered boat that turns well by edging, leaving the rudder up (disengaged) until needed in open areas or in wind.

Skegs may also get jammed, especially if you pull the boat onto the shore with the skeg down and rocks and other debris get jammed into the skeg box. Some skegs are more reliable than others, and some easier to fix, but few seem to be trouble free, and they divide the cargo space in the stern, making it more challenging to pack for a longer trip. Still, many paddlers prefer the option of having a skeg on a boat that can perform well without engaging it.

Closely related to design, fit is extremely important. It's easy to find a boat for medium-sized people, but a small person will find it difficult to maneuver a full-size touring kayak, while a larger person may find a cockpit on a small boat too cramped and the boat too tippy. Several kayak manufacturers make low volume (LV) models specifically for smaller paddlers, as well as high volume (HV) models for larger paddlers. Depth and cockpit size are particularly important to larger paddlers. You need to be able to stretch out your legs and fit comfortably into the cockpit, and you need to be able to do a re-entry. For especially tall paddlers, many boats on the market don't fit, but a few manufacturers will customize bulkhead distance to suit the paddler. Check the manufacturer's specifications for ideal paddler weight on any boat and take whatever gear you'll carry into consideration, including camping gear and drinking water for potential overnights.

While it is difficult to gauge paddling performance, experienced paddlers generally prefer the stiffer feel of a composite (such as fiberglass or Kevlar) or wooden hull over others, but for most beginning paddlers, the difference in investment between these and plastic boats is probably more noticeable than the difference in performance.

Rotational molded (rotomolded) plastic boats dominate the kayak market. Not all plastics are the same; resin manufacturers have patented formulas with different properties that can result in varying weight, degree of flex, and rigidity. Plastic boats are generally heavier than their composite or wooden counterparts. Their hulls are more durable, but dents and scratches are more difficult to repair than on composite boats, especially in the long run. Repairing rotomolded boats, especially in the field, is a bit more involved than with composite boats, and care must be taken to avoid damage from excessive heat; a hot day can bend a plastic boat over a roof rack.

Thermoformed kayaks, built from laminated sheets of plastic, are becoming more popular. They're generally lighter and cheaper than comparable fiberglass boats, with a smooth hull surface that's harder to scratch. Scratches are easy to repair, and thermoform boat owners have numerous tales of their durability when dropped. Manufacturers, however, don't recommend them for situations that might result in puncture, including whitewater, rock gardening, or surf. Compared to rotomolded kayaks, thermoformed boats are pricier, stiffer, perhaps prettier, more resistant to UV damage, and less likely to deform on the rack due to heat. In addition, thermoformed plastics are compatible with adhesives, making more interior outfitting possible. At temperatures below freezing, though, these boats are more susceptible to damage.

Paddlers often gravitate to the shiny and colorful composite boats, which are also more likely to have sculpted curves and well-finished details. Fiberglass boats have a longer lifespan than plastic boats, usually weigh a bit less, and tend to have more cargo volume inside. Most repairs can be done in the field, and shallow scratches affect only the gelcoat finish, which may be fixed without too much trouble. Kevlar is more lightweight, a bit pricier than fiberglass, and more difficult to repair.

Wooden kayaks can be attractive, fun to build, require less financial investment, and can be lighter than composite boats. Kits with laser-cut panels greatly reduce labor and add very little, if anything, to the materials cost. Plywood stitch-and-glue models are popular and generally easier to build than their strip-built counterparts, which are more able to create a curvy hull shape. Usually these wooden hulls are then covered with fiberglass, essentially creating a wooden-core fiberglass boat. It takes the right personality to build a boat, not to mention precision and plenty of time. It's not the fastest way to start paddling, but it's exactly the sort of project that can get us through a long winter.

Folding kayaks are constructed on the same skin-on-frame principal of traditional kayaks, with a wooden, aluminum, or carbon fiber frame and a tough nylon skin that zips around it. The unassembled boat fits into a travel-friendly duffel bag or two and may usually be assembled in under half an hour with practice. The flexible feel of a skin-on-frame boat takes some getting used to, but paddlers have undertaken huge expeditions in folding kayaks, including Hannes Lindemann's 1955–56 Atlantic crossing in a Klepper, during which he mostly sailed. Since folding kayaks don't have sealed bow and stern compartments, flotation is necessary. Some have built-in inflatable sponsons along the gunwales, which should keep the boat afloat, but paddlers of folding kayaks should be sure to practice rescues in a controlled environment before venturing onto the open sea. Some manufacturers will custom build fiberglass boats in three-piece versions for travel.

Paddles Ask a handful of sea kayakers about what paddle to use and you're likely to get a handful of different opinions, each one confident that his choice is the best. No matter what paddle you use, it's only as good as your stroke, which has more to do with finesse and good form than it does the type of paddle or your strength. If possible, take a lesson with a good coach before a poor forward stroke is so engrained in your muscle memory that it's difficult to change. Choose an instructor with lightweight paddles you can try. As with boats, it's helpful to try a few different paddles before you buy.

Good paddles are not cheap, but it is money well spent. The lighter the paddle, the easier the paddling. At the end of a long day, you'll either be glad you have a lightweight paddle or be cursing a heavy one with each stroke. Here are a few things to consider if you're in the market for a new paddle:

- **Greenland paddles** are more traditional, simple tools with great capabilities. Their use has risen sharply, and the efficacy of these "skinny sticks" has been proven on long expeditions. Many people build or carve their own Greenland paddles, but they are commercially available, including extremely lightweight and buoyant two-piece carbon fiber versions.

- European-style paddles, or **Euro blades,** are most common, usually in a two-piece shaft that connects with an adjustable ferrule. Most Euro blades are designed for either a low-angle stroke (the upper hand traces near chest height) or a high-angle stroke (the shaft is nearly vertical as it passes the cockpit). There are strong advocates of each style. Some believe the low-angle stroke to be more forgiving and sustainable for long periods than the high-angle stroke, which may be more powerful and efficient, resulting in less side-to-side motion of the boat.

- Euro blades are usually made from wood, plastic, fiberglass, or carbon fiber. Plastic is often the cheapest, heaviest, and most durable, while carbon fiber is more expensive, lighter, and easier to break. If you use a carbon fiber paddle, it's a good idea to have a fiberglass spare to use around rocks or while practicing rescues that put stress on a paddle.

- **Bent** or **crank shaft paddles** were developed to prevent wrist injury, but the best defense against wrist injury is to learn good loose-gripped technique that keeps your wrists aligned with your forearms and your knuckles aligned with the top of the blade. A beginning paddler is better served by a straight-shaft paddle and some guidance to learn good technique.

- **Wing paddles** have more scoop to their blades. Built for racing or fitness paddling, wing paddles can increase efficiency (3 percent to 5 percent, say wing paddle enthusiasts) and speed in the hands of a skilled paddler, but are less versatile than flatter blades when it comes to non-forward strokes.

- Some people like to set their blades at an angle from each other, called **feathering,** so that while one blade is in the water, the opposite blade is slicing through the air or wind sideways, with the least resistance. Some believe this to be effective while paddling into the wind, but there is no evidence to support this notion. Others prefer to avoid the wrist-twisting motion this causes by leaving the blades on an even plane, which also simplifies bracing from one side to the other. The simplest advice is to simply go with unfeathered blades, but since most paddles are now two-piece with adjustable ferrules, you can experiment with both.

Optimum paddle length is dependent on the width and height of your boat, the type of paddling you do, and the shape of the blade. If your paddle is too long or too short it will be difficult to fully immerse the blade or rotate the torso. In addition, a longer paddle will feel clumsy when attempting various strokes, and may be more difficult to quickly get into the position you need. Paddlers of tandem kayaks usually require longer paddles to reach over the wider beam and are more apt to use a low-angle stroke. The status quo changes, but for a general purpose paddle, touring sea kayakers in boats with 21- to 24-inch beams are well served by paddles in the 205- to 225-centimeter range. Ideally, try different lengths while observed by an instructor, or get fitted by a knowledgeable shop.

The system used by one paddle manufacturer breaks it into size for high- and low-angle paddles. For the low-angle paddler under 6 feet, use a 220-centimeter paddle. For low-angle paddlers over 6 feet, that length goes up to 230 centimeters, and a boat with a 28-inch or greater beam adds an additional 10 centimeters. Werner recommends 210-centimeter paddles for high-angle paddlers under 6 feet tall, 215-centimeter for taller paddlers (high-angle paddlers tend to use narrower boats, so beam doesn't usually enter the formula).

Paddles sometimes break or float away, so at least one person in a group should have a spare paddle stored within reach on deck.

Personal Flotation Device (PFD) A life jacket is an extremely important piece of equipment, and like the paddle, is one that people tend to skimp on. Invest in a Coast Guard-approved type III or V life jacket with several adjustment points that fits you so well you love wearing it. When you sit in your cockpit, the jacket should feel snug. In the water it should stay put with no upward migration.

The most important thing about a life jacket is that you wear it. They're not much good tucked under the deck bungies. Each year the Coast Guard compiles statistics showing that less than 10 percent of those who drowned in boating accidents were wearing life jackets.

Tow Systems Short, quick tows are needed to get someone out of danger, while longer tows may be necessary to help an incapacitated paddler. A tow line needs to be quickly accessed and deployed, simple to detach from, and easy to stash out of the way when no longer needed. The most common among touring paddlers are tow belts: a pouch worn around the waist with a quick-release buckle. Inside the pouch is an attached floating tow line, usually around 55 feet, with a clip on one end. Some have both a short length and a longer length line, but most paddlers setting up a quick tow "daisy chain" the line into a shorter length, which may be unclipped to allow the line to unfurl to its full length.

Spray Skirt From paddle drips to breaking waves, there is ample opportunity for water to get into the cockpit. Depending on the boat and how it's loaded, merely edging it may drop the cockpit rim below the surface. Even if you capsize and roll, a spray skirt should keep most of the water out. If you hope to use the boat in the capacity for which it was designed, you'll wear a spray skirt. The grab loop at the front of the skirt, however, must be within easy reach to allow you to exit the boat easily. A looser-fitting nylon skirt is easier to remove than those made of neoprene, which tend to be tighter fitting and more water resistant.

Lights If there's any chance you might be out after dark (and there is always that chance), have lights and flares on board, both so you can see and be seen. The Coast

Guard requires kayakers to have a light and three flares after dark. Waterproof head-lamps and bright LED lights that mount to the deck with a suction cup (the higher the better) are good solutions. The emergency strobe that clips to your life jacket may have a non-strobe setting, but conserve those batteries for an emergency. It is illegal to use a flashing light on the water if not for an emergency. Reflective tape and deck rigging can also improve other boaters' ability to see you.

Water and Food For a day trip, bring more food or snacks than you think you'll need, in case you're out longer than expected or if you need to share with someone. Paddlers burn through a lot of calories. Keep high-energy snacks like energy bars or trail mix where you can reach them from the cockpit. Take a short break at least every hour to eat and drink well before the lack of food or water becomes an issue. For water, the rule of thumb is one gallon per person per day, but this varies according to heat, exertion, and whether or not you'll do any cooking.

Other Personal Gear A pump and a sponge are useful for emptying water from your cockpit. A paddle float can transform your paddle into an outrigger, making the boat stable enough to climb aboard without tipping—a backup when other rescue techniques fail.

CLOTHING
Dress for the water temperature of your trip, bearing in mind that full immersion in 60-degree Fahrenheit water saps us of heat 25 times faster than 60-degree Fahrenheit air. Still, you want to be comfortable and avoid overheating. There's no one-size-fits-all clothing solution, but there are plenty of options. So … what to wear? If risk of immersion is higher (tide races, limited landings, surf), dress warmer and more waterproof. It's better to be a little hot than not warm enough. If consequences of a capsize are minimal (hot sunny day, good rescue skills, easy landing nearby) you could go with less. If in doubt about the clothing you're going to wear kayaking, go for a swim with it and see how it feels. Every paddler should be wearing clothing to protect against the elements present at launch and have appropriate layers for varying conditions and emergencies packed in their own boats and within easy reach.

Wet Gear This is clothing that insulates in the water but doesn't keep you dry. Neoprene pants and tops come in varying thicknesses, usually from 0.5 to 1.5 millimeters, and fit tightly without restricting movement. Some have fleece lining, and it is possible to wear a thin base layer or rash guard beneath. Paddlesport-specific wetsuits are generally a bit thinner than diving wetsuits, but at 3 millimeters, thicker than other Neoprene layers. The "farmer John" (or Jane) covers legs and torso, leaving the arms bare, and may be combined with a wetsuit top (or other type of top). Once they are soaked with salt water, Neoprene tends to stay damp, and can turn a bit rank after a few days. While less expensive than drysuits and other waterproof clothing, light-weight wet gear is generally more appropriate for air and water temperatures in the

50s or above, and is less comfortable, especially when worn damp for long periods. A wetsuit might be perfect for short surf sessions, or while swimming among rocks that might damage a drysuit, but most paddlers prefer the convenience and comfort of waterproof outerwear.

Outerwear These are nylon shells with a few variations, including jackets, pants, and full one-piece suits, all with different levels of protection against water. Splash wear helps keep you dry until you take a swim, since it lacks wrist or neck gaskets. Semi-dry wear has gaskets to prevent water getting in, but may use Neoprene instead of latex, therefore letting some water in. Dry wear, including drysuits, is intended to keep you completely dry.

There is a broad price range, and a broad range of effectiveness and comfort, in outerwear. Although you might not use it in July and August in New England, there's nothing like a good drysuit to keep you dry, comfortable, and—with the proper layers beneath it—warm. There are many variables to drysuit design and construction, but most would agree that a relief zipper is well worth the extra cost.

Innerwear Keep in mind that a drysuit is merely a shell, and part of its advantage is that you can vary the layers underneath according to need. In 55-degree Fahrenheit water and warmer air, you might wear very little, but in 45-degree Fahrenheit water and air, you'll wear more. Layering thin to medium layers gives you flexibility, and they may also be worn on land. Merino wool and synthetics work well. Never wear cotton. Even though a suit should keep you dry, there is always a chance of leakage and sweating, both of which will render cotton a hypothermia hazard, even in summer.

Non-paddle-specific gear In a New England summer, you may be able to get by with shorts and T-shirt as long as you avoid cotton, have some warmer layers, and an outer wind- and rain-layer. A dry change of clothes in case of capsize is a must. If you're going far enough offshore that changing into dry clothes would be difficult, dress in paddling-specific gear instead.

Sun Gear In addition to the use of sunscreen, harmful exposure to sun can be lessened with long sleeve, high-UPF clothing that blocks ultraviolet rays. A hat with a visor can help block overhead rays from your eyes, while sunglasses (preferably polarized to help you see into the water) diminish glare from the water surface.

BEYOND PERSONAL GEAR

If you're in a group, this class of gear may not need to be duplicated in every boat, but it is essential that a solo paddler carries these items and that group members know who is carrying what.

Navigation A chart and compass and the skills to use them are essential before setting out on the water. Even if you know an area well, if the fog rolls in, you'll need a chart to find a bearing and a compass to stay on a straight line (See "Fog" on page 37).

A baseplate compass is versatile enough to help find bearings on your chart and to reference while following a bearing. A deck compass makes it easier to follow a bearing.

GPS units are no replacement for non-electronic navigation tools and skills. They may be nice to have, but batteries can run out and electronics can fail. If you carry a GPS unit, do so in addition to a chart and compass.

Communication A cell phone and a VHF (very high frequency) radio are the two most basic communication tools, each with its own benefits and limitations, but having both makes it likely that you'll be able to summon help should you need it.

Invest in a waterproof container or case to protect your cell phone on the water. Cell phones don't work everywhere, but coverage around New England is improving constantly. In addition to making calls and texting, many phones also double as GPS units, track weather and tides, and perform other useful functions.

Handheld, waterproof VHFs are inexpensive enough that no one should be without one. If you call for help on channel 16 on a VHF radio, odds are good that the Coast Guard will hear and respond, but closer boaters may also hear it and respond first. The signal is limited, but the Coast Guard uses repeater towers along the coast, so they will probably hear your call. In addition, the VHF may be used to communicate within a group and to access NOAA weather channels.

Satellite messengers are handheld devices capable of sending short text messages and coordinates to someone monitoring your trip, as well as an emergency distress signal. They rely on commercial satellite networks and emergency calls are routed through a private company. They only work if you've paid your subscription fees.

You may also summon help using a personal locator beacon (PLB). With the flick of a switch, a PLB will transmit a powerful (5 watt) personalized distress signal at 406 MHz, an internationally recognized distress signal, to a network of satellites monitored in the U.S. by NOAA and the Air Force Rescue Coordination Center (AFRCC). Most PLBs also transmit GPS coordinates to rescuers within five minutes, guiding rescuers to within 100 meters of the beacon. Unlike a VHF, cell phone, or satellite messenger, a PLB's batteries remain dormant until activated, and should transmit for up to 24 hours. Most models are waterproof, have a built-in strobe, and may be carried on the shoulder in place of a strobe. Some models have texting capability as well. There are no subscription fees for use of PLBs.

For most paddlers, VHF and cell phones offer enough of a safety net, especially when weighed against the cost of PLBs and satellite messengers. But for more ambitious and less predictable trips taking you farther from shore, one of these beacons could easily save your life.

In addition to two-way communicators, less high-tech means of communicating a distress signal should be at the ready. Have options that will help you be both seen and heard. Everyone should have a whistle tied to his or her life jacket to get attention within the group. In an emergency the sound of the whistle will carry much farther than your voice and with less effort. You can also get attention and bring rescuers to your position with small pencil flares that can be carried in a life jacket. Other tools to direct rescuers to your location include hand flares or smoke, signaling mirrors, sea dye, strobes, and reflective tape. A fog horn is useful to help call attention to yourself in the fog and legally required, but using it does not ensure that someone will locate you or avoid you.

Gear to Fix People More important than any gear, first aid training will prepare you for mishaps. Basic first aid is a start, while a two-day Wilderness First Aid (WFA) course will cover most of the basics you might need. This training needs to be updated at regular intervals. See the Appendix for information on classes.

A first aid kit in your day hatch should have, at a minimum, adhesive bandages, gauze and tape, sunscreen, nonprescription pain relievers, moleskin, and personal prescription medications. Since hypothermia is easily the most common form of care we might need, remedies including warm clothes should be quickly accessible. A storm cag (a poncho-like outer layer that fits over life jackets) is a quick way to stop the loss of heat. Snacks, water, and warm liquids are also a good first step for treating hypothermia.

Bring a stove and fuel to ensure that, when off the water, you can make hot beverages and food and boil water as necessary. Keep several lighters stored in separate dry bags, in case one gets wet. No matter what the situation, a bite of chocolate and a warm, sugary cup of tea can go a long way.

There are several emergency shelters and exposure bags available that can quickly warm a chilled person and also work as a temporary respite from the elements for a small group. A tent and a sleeping bag could be simple options. A few items of spare clothing (in addition to the minimum you need for the elements) can warm someone with wet or inadequate clothing of their own.

Items to Fix Boats A simple repair kit can save you a lot of trouble if your boat gets damaged. In groups, more than one repair kit may be helpful. Bring at least the following:

▶ electrical tape

▶ duct tape (make sure it's a type formulated to adhere while wet)

▶ flexible window flashing or epoxy putty to quickly cover a hole, even while you're on the water.

▶ for longer trips and significant holes, a fiberglass repair kit, complete with two-part epoxy and fiberglass cloth (or a similar epoxy repair kit for plastic boats).

▶ a large flotation bag to keep a boat buoyant when the compartments have been compromised. For those playing in rocks, inflate in advance.

▶ tools and parts to fix a skeg or rudder.

▶ STEWARDSHIP AND CONSERVATION

New Englanders have access to plentiful islands and coastal lands thanks to the people who have made it possible through conservation organizations, land trusts, state parks, national parks, the Maine Island Trail Association (MITA), and others. Access was never assured. We're fortunate that forward thinking individuals realized early on that our region's coast would eventually be bought and privatized if they didn't act. It is fitting to continue what they've started by supporting the existing organizations, both with membership or donations, and by volunteering our time. But we can also help by taking care of these places as though they belong to us. In a sense, they do.

Whether we're aware of it or not, sea kayakers have an impact everywhere we go. We may roll into a town, clearly identified by the boats racked atop our roofs, and our actions will reflect upon the next car to arrive with a rack full of kayaks. It is better to be remembered for eating in a local restaurant or staying at a local motel than it is to be remembered for blocking a ramp with boats and gear.

Having met with enough skepticism, some of us go out of our way to make a better impression. Give anglers and those making their living from the sea plenty of room, on land and on the water. Park in a legitimate spot—paid parking is usually a bargain, if only for the peace of mind. Show some interest in a town beyond the need for a bathroom and a parking spot, and don't take these things for granted. Many of our on-shore needs are addressed thanks to the tax money of coastal residents, whether they feel it's their civic duty to address them or not.

Like all outdoorspeople, sea kayakers can actively take care of our favorite places. One way is to get involved with local organizations like MITA and land trusts. Most of us pick up our share of garbage while we're paddling, but if we organize an island-cleaning trip and invite the public, our efforts will be more visible. And the more people who care about these places, the better our chances of preserving them.

LEAVE NO TRACE

The Appalachian Mountain Club (AMC) is a national educational partner of Leave No Trace, a nonprofit organization dedicated to promoting and inspiring responsible outdoor recreation through education, research, and partnerships. The Leave No Trace program seeks to develop  wildland ethics—ways in which people think and act in the outdoors to minimize their impact on the areas they visit and to protect our natural resources for future enjoyment. Leave No Trace unites four federal land management agencies—the U.S. Forest Service, National Park Service, Bureau of Land Management, and U.S. Fish and Wildlife Service—with manufacturers, outdoor retailers, user groups, educators, organizations such as AMC, and individuals.

The Leave No Trace ethic is guided by the following seven principles:

1. **Plan Ahead and Prepare.** Know about public access, campsite limitations, and areas that are closed for seabird nesting. Small groups have less impact on resources and on the experiences of other visitors.

2. **Travel and Camp on Durable Surfaces.** Many islands are vegetated thanks to a thin layer of soil that collected there over many years, despite the forces of wind and water working to erode it. Stepping on plants can kill them and compact the soil beneath, rendering it lifeless. Dunes are similarly fragile, held together by grasses that could easily be killed by human impact. Whenever possible, walk on durable surfaces such as granite ledges and cobble beaches. Follow established trails and camp in established sites. Good campsites are found, not made.

3. **Dispose of Waste Properly.** Pack it in, pack it out. Inspect your camp for trash or food scraps, even small bits of biodegradable waste. Leave your site cleaner than you found it. Cook in the intertidal zone if possible, or on a ledge if not. Soap is usually unnecessary to clean, which can be done with hot water and a handful of sand to scour pots. Urinate below high-tide line and pack out solid human waste and all toilet paper. It is illegal to dump it in the ocean, and the "cat hole" method favored by backpackers doesn't work on a small island with little soil. Commercially available systems make packing out human waste easy, but any method of securing the waste and removing it from islands and the water is acceptable.

4. **Leave What You Find.** Cultural or historical artifacts, as well as natural objects such as shells, rocks, and plants, should be left as found.

5. **Kindle No Fires or Minimize Campfire Impact.** Cook on a stove. Use established fire rings, fire pans, or mound fires. Aside from the threat of wildfires, campfires scar rocks and other features, leaving charred remains. Always check island regulations—whether it's private or public—before building a fire. If you build a campfire, keep it small, burn driftwood but not downed wood or wood from elsewhere, and build it in the intertidal zone. Allow a fire to burn down to the smallest coals and scatter them below the high-tide line when fully extinguished. If possible, pack out the remains.

6. **Respect Wildlife.** Observe wildlife from a distance, paddling quietly and using binoculars. Extra care should be taken near seals; read more about their behavior in "Seals" on page 56). Feeding animals alters their natural behavior. Store your rations and trash securely. Adhere to warnings—posted on islands, near the shore, or online—about nesting birds in season, roughly April 1 through August 31.

7. **Be Considerate of Others.** Be courteous, respect the quality of other visitors' experiences, and let nature's sounds prevail. Share boat ramps and launches graciously. Store boats and other gear inconspicuously. Use the smallest campsites available in case a larger group arrives.

AMC is a national provider of the Leave No Trace Master Educator course. AMC offers this five-day course, designed especially for outdoor professionals and land managers, as well as the shorter two-day Leave No Trace Trainer course, throughout the Northeast. For Leave No Trace information contact the Leave No Trace Center for Outdoor Ethics, 800-332-4100 or 302-442-8222; lnt.org. For a schedule of AMC Leave No Trace courses, see outdoors.org/education/lnt.

DOWNEAST

Back when lumber schooners made the frequent run downwind and east of Boston to the Maine coast, the coast stretching roughly from Mount Desert Island to Canada became known as Downeast. On this shore, the Gulf of Maine compresses into the Bay of Fundy, creating bigger tides and stronger currents. The superlatives continue: bigger cliffs, taller people . . . and perhaps taller tales.

This part of the New England coast is unlike its more southern counterparts. Washington County alone has more land area than the states of Rhode Island and Delaware combined, yet has only 32,000 inhabitants. The county boasts almost thirteen people per square mile, most of whom live in towns away from the shore, a steep contrast with the southern edge of this book's purview: Connecticut's Fairfield County, which packs in more than 1,467 people per square mile along a far more developed coastline.

Even paddling near Downeast towns can be relatively quiet. At the far east end of the state, Eastport was once a thriving port with 5,000 inhabitants—the site of the first U.S. sardine cannery in 1875. Since then, nearly 400 sardine canning facilities have opened and closed along the coast until the last one in Prospect Harbor shut down in 2010. Like most coastal Maine communities with boom-and-bust economies, Eastport has never quite returned to its former prosperity but is the site of a few innovative plans, like offshore tidal energy generators and shipping pregnant cows overseas.

Fishing continues to be the dominant and more visible economic factor in most Downeast towns, especially in Jonesport, one of the top lobster ports. You're likely to encounter fishing boats and shellfish and seaweed harvesters wherever you paddle. On the drive to the launch, you'll probably pass some blueberry barrens; 85 percent of the world's blueberries come from Washington County, and when blueberry season is done, many locals make Christmas wreaths, another major export. While there is a regular flow of tourists, the region attracts fewer visitors than the rest of the New England coast.

With Downeast's bigger tides come bigger currents, and with bigger currents, paddlers need more experience and stronger skills to contend with difficult conditions. Add to that steep shorelines, long stretches with limited bailouts, and a reduced ability to summon help and even the most experienced paddlers are advised to take extra care. Before you launch, carefully consider the weather forecast and tide and current predictions, and keep a good Plan B route in mind.

Downeast Maine isn't the best place for novice paddlers. Rather than look for less challenging routes in the area, novice paddlers would do better to either hire a guide or head west. Cobscook Bay (Trip 1), however, offers generally sheltered paddling if you can avoid Cobscook Reversing Falls, as does the area where petroglyphs may be found in Machias Bay (Trip 4). The routes along the Bold Coast (Trips 2 and 3) should only be undertaken by skilled, experienced paddlers with solid rescue skills and a good understanding of the area's dynamic tides and currents.

1
DENNYS AND WHITING BAYS

Birds, wildlife, and solitude are abundant on these small arms of Cobscook Bay. Enjoy the spectacle of Cobscook Reversing Falls whether you paddle near it or not.

Distance ▶ Up to 15.0 nautical miles, round-trip, at high tide; up to 2.0 miles exploring the coves in the state park

Tidal Planning ▶ Average tidal range of 17.9 feet in Whiting Bay. Slack tide at the Reversing Falls is brief, and most paddlers will want to avoid the area the rest of the time.

Cautions ▶ Large tidal range; be aware of the tide and what it is doing. Strong currents, especially around Falls Island; keep in mind that speed builds mid-tide; if you're taken downstream at peak flow, you may need to wait for the current to diminish or change direction to return.

Charts and Maps ▶ NOAA chart #13394

LAUNCHES

Cobscook Bay State Park, Dennysville Public concrete ramp with its own entrance; daytime parking picnic shelter; and a pit toilet. The park land extends over a mile south of the launch to Burnt Cove. From the junction of ME 189 and US 1 in Whiting, go north 4.0 miles and turn right (east) on South Edmunds Road. After 0.5 mile, the park entrance is on the east side. The launch is another 0.5 mile north. *GPS coordinates: 44° 51.446′ N, 67° 8.890′ W.*

Little Augusta, Dennysville Hand-carry launch with steps down the embankment to the water; small parking area; no facilities. The launch accesses the river-like southern end of Whiting Bay, much of which dries out at lower tides. From the junction of US 1 and ME 189 in Whiting, the launch is just more than 1 mile north on US 1. *GPS coordinates: 44° 48.226′ N, 67° 9.994′ W.*

Reversing Falls Town Park, Pembroke Hand-carry launch just west of the falls (100 yards) or beach launch to the east; plentiful parking; no facilities. Anyone paddling near the falls should have experience with current and the ability to gauge their abilities in rapidly changing conditions. At the junction of US 1 and ME 214 in West Pembroke, turn southeast onto Ayers Junction Road (directly opposite ME 214). Take a right on Old County Road and an immediate left onto Leighton Point Road. Follow signs south to the park for about 6 miles and take a right on unmarked Clarkside Road. In 1.2 miles, turn left onto Young's Road, and continue 1.4 miles to the park and Reversing Falls Road. Look for a hand-carry launch on the rocky shore west of the falls. Just north of the park, a rough dirt road leads through the forest to a gravel and rockweed beach, which is just east of the falls. The entire beach may be submerged at high tide; you may prefer to park in a small clearing in the woods just inland. *GPS coordinates: 44° 52.998′ N, 67° 8.001′ W.*

Other Public Access Much of the shoreline in Whiting and Dennys bays is encompassed by a 7,200-acre tract of Moosehorn National Wildlife Refuge (MNWR). Williams Island (Hallowell Island) is part of the wildlife refuge and is open to the public for day use; at high tide its shores are a mix of ledges and marshy areas, and at low tide, much of the island is surrounded by tidal flats. State-owned Commissary Point Wildlife Management Area in Trescott is a 438-acre tract with hiking trails at the southeast part of Whiting Bay.

ROUTE DESCRIPTION

Cobscook Bay is often spoken of in abundant, bold superlatives—biggest tide range, most biological diversity, highest density of nesting bald eagles—but it can also be the calmest and quietest, a massive estuary that can resemble a lake at high tide. Don't let the placid facade fool you. The bay is in a constant state of flux, a massive volume of water constantly moving either in or out, meeting one restriction after another that create hard-to-predict tidal falls, eddies, and boils that shift from one moment to the next. At its heart lies Cobscook Reversing Falls, where the current squeezes between Mahar Point and Falls Island and a mist hangs above the turbulent chaos. But out at the ends of Cobscook's many river-like fingers you'll find calm, wind-protected coves.

At 18.7 feet (up to 28 feet during a big spring tide), Cobscook Bay's mean tidal range is the highest in the U.S., a fact you are not likely to forget as you paddle along its shores. At low tide the water drains away from the many islets, baring rockweed-covered shores that rise well above the receded waterline. Shellfish harvesters ground their powerboats and scour the seaweed for "wrinkles" (a local term for periwinkles). Aside from a few recreational kayaks venturing into the coves at the state park though, you're unlikely to encounter much other boat traffic. At high tide, there may be less to explore as ledges are covered, but the shallow, farther reaches become easier to access, making it possible to spend long days and many miles following the shoreline.

As early as 10,000 years ago, native peoples established summer fishing villages along the bay's shores, sustained by the great abundance of marine life. The bay has an unusually rich and diverse ecosystem that has provided the economic base for the area.

By the turn of the twentieth century, Eastport was home to as many as eighteen sardine canneries operating around the clock, and by the 1920s, plans were under-

DENNYS AND WHITING BAYS

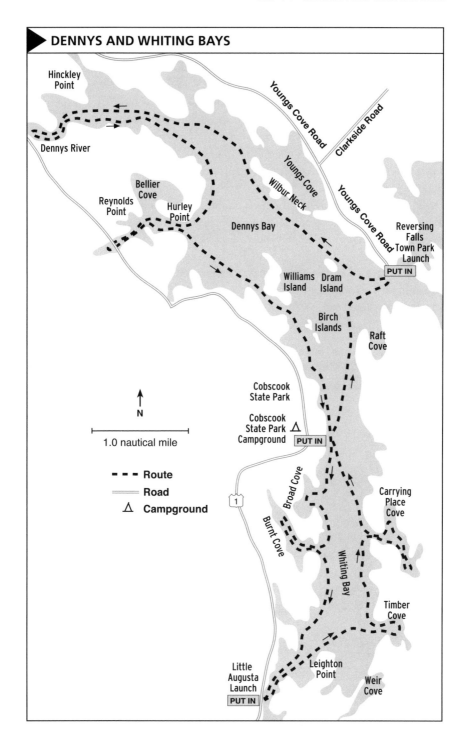

Hinckley
Point

Dennys River

Youngs Cove Road

Clarkside Road

Youngs Cove

Youngs Cove Road

Wilbur Neck

Bellier
Cove

Reynolds
Point

Hurley
Point

Dennys Bay

Reversing
Falls
Town Park
Launch

PUT IN

Williams
Island

Dram
Island

Birch
Islands

Raft
Cove

Cobscook
State Park

Cobscook
State Park
Campground △

PUT IN

Broad Cove

Carrying
Place
Cove

Burnt Cove

1

Whiting Bay

↑
N

1.0 nautical mile

- - - Route
——— Road
△ Campground

Timber
Cove

Little
Augusta
Launch

PUT IN

Leighton
Point

Weir
Cove

way to dam the mouth of the bay, which would have created jobs and ensured better long-term financial footing for the town. But by the 1930s the dam was discontinued for financial reasons, and while the bay is certainly better off in its natural state, the area has always been economically challenged. Like other parts of Maine, the prized species were overfished, one after another, and the sardine industry crashed in the 1950s. The last cannery in Eastport closed in 1983, while Lubec's last cannery hung on until 2001. Schemes to salvage the area economy—usually at the expense of the environment—have come and gone. A proposed oil refinery, a liquefied natural gas terminal, and aquaculture have all met with resistance by locals wanting to protect their strongest asset: the bay.

Dennys and Whiting bays are the most inland arms of Cobscook Bay, distinguished by the abundance of public access. Cobscook has many miles of shoreline and seemingly endless arms and coves, but the ease of access makes Dennys and Whiting a good place to start. In addition, the smaller bays can be paddled without going near Falls Island, where the most hazardous currents can be found.

Route choices for your trip will be largely dependent on tides, and while the bays are relatively sheltered compared to open ocean, winds certainly have an effect as well, particularly north or south winds, which can whip up some steep conditions when

Cobscook Bay's convoluted shore provides plenty of sheltered inlets to explore, like this arm of Bellier Cove where Hobart Creek runs beneath an old bridge.

opposing the current. You likely won't have the tide behind you for the whole trip, but starting on a rising tide from the state park boat ramp is generally a good strategy.

Dennys Bay

This description details the bay's eastern then western shores.

Head north from the state park or Little Augusta boat launches and pass the Birch Islands (MNWR; not open to visitors). You may want to cross over to Mahar Point, recognizable by the meadows above the shore. Here, you can pull your boat up plenty high on the shore and take a look at the reversing falls to the east. This is also the location of the Reversing Falls Town Park launches.

Continuing up the east shore, pass Dram Island and proceed toward Wilbur Neck. At the highest tides, Wilbur Neck is really a succession of islands that you may paddle through to get to Youngs Cove. At lower tides, the neck and the group of islets to the south tower overhead. At higher tides, you may prefer to explore the shoreline and the maze of small islands north of Wilbur Neck.

On a rising tide, you can follow one of the rivers to the north ends of the bay. The northernmost Hardscrabble River leads to Lower Dennysville. The Dennys River enters the bay from the west, taking a right-angle turn from the south, making the entrance barely visible until you're right in front of it. You can paddle below the US 1 bridge and a little farther, depending on tide and freshwater volume. You can probably get to a shallow bend in the river overlooked by a yellow colonial house that has at times been an inn and a restaurant. This is Dennysville. There's a bit more to town—a library and post office farther up the road—but not enough to suggest an afternoon on shore.

Follow the river back out, staying along the western shore. Rounding Hurley Point, spot Williams Island (Hallowell Island; MNWR) to the southeast. If you have the time, the inclination, and the tide in your favor, first follow the western shoreline into Bellier Cove. This shallow, islet-studded cove is fun to explore and will change rapidly with the tide, developing some swift currents where it turns shallow and constricted. One paddling friend saw a bear in this area. You can pass below an old bridge to the southwest, and then below the newer US 1 bridge upstream a short distance. Birds are often abundant in these sheltered waters.

Back out in the bay, head south for Williams Island (Hallowell Island). A white house sits atop a mainland bluff just south of the island. The gentle shoreline is a good spot for a break among the birches and other trees. From the sound end of the island, it's less than 1.5 nautical miles along shore to the launch.

Whiting Bay

Explore the southern end of Whiting Bay in any order you like, keeping in mind that only the 2.0 nautical miles south of the state park launch—as far as Gravelly Point and Freds Islands—is reachable at all tides.

The coves can be fun to explore. Much of Broad Cove is lined with campsites in the park, some with RVs, but if you're looking for a short paddle, the tiny islands there are easy to reach. In Burnt Cove, the campsites on the northeast side are less obvious, while the west shore is completely undeveloped.

On the east shore, Carrying Place Cove has only one obvious home overlooking it and is worth checking out, as is Timber Cove. The Freds Islands are undeveloped and forested.

Between Gravelly and Fields points, an inlet passes beneath a bridge (where, of course, currents increase). On the north shore is Tide Mill Organic Farm, a working organic farm that has been in continuous operation by the same family for eight generations.

ALTERNATIVES

Depending on paddler skills and tide height/current strength, Cobscook Reversing Falls and the area south of Falls Island may be negotiated in the short time before and after slack tide. The current builds quickly though, so be mindful not to get stuck on the wrong side of the falls unless you're ready for some turbulent paddling or a 6-hour wait until the next slack tide.

For an easier day, the ends of the many fingers of the bay can be sheltered places to paddle at high tide. Launch from Little Augusta to quickly reach the south end of Whiting Bay. There are also several short hikes, including the nature trail and an overlook in the state park.

MORE INFORMATION

Cobscook Bay State Park (parksandlands.com; 207-726-4412) is open year-round, 9 A.M. to sunset daily; a fee is charged at the gate. The park has more than 100 campsites, many of them on the water (although launching boats from campsites is frowned upon). Campsites are generally wooded and secluded, many with picnic shelters. Showers, pit toilets, and fresh water are available. Moosehorn National Wildlife Refuge (fws.gov/refuge/moosehorn; 207-454-7161).

THE BOLD COAST

Distinguished by its rugged, largely unpopulated coastline, the Bold Coast possesses an out-landish grandeur that is most fully experienced from the cockpit of a sea kayak. Much of the shore is tough to negotiate on foot, dominated by peat bogs and dense forests of fir and spruce, with jagged cliffs falling away into the sea. Hiking trails cross the four coastal preserves and one state park that protect about 12 of the 16.0 nautical miles of shoreline running between Cutler and West Quoddy Head. You may glimpse another human or two at one of the few enclaves of homes overlooking Grand Manan Channel, or in the protected harbor at Baileys Mistake; an occasional lobster boat, seaweed harvester in a skiff, or a recreational boater may cross your path but odds are good you will be completely on your own in the near-shore waters that few other vessels can safely navigate. From the water, enjoy stunning views of cliff after cliff, stretching far into the distance. If conditions allow you to land on the pocket cobble beaches, the ever-present plateau of Canada's Grand Manan Island will draw your eye across the 6- to 11-mile-wide Grand Manan Channel.

Like the scenery that inspires them, tales grow big on the Bold Coast and it's tough to sep-arate mythology from fact. One enduring tale traces the settlement of Baileys Mistake to an 1830s shipwreck when a Captain Bailey, piloting a lumber schooner in a thick fog, mistook this harbor for Lubec and ran aground on the ledges at the harbor's entrance. He and the crew salvaged the lumber, and rather than face the ship's owners back in Boston, built homes and settled here. Perhaps it was descendants of those shipwrecked sailors who later turned to "wrecking," giving this stretch of coast a reputation for lawlessness. In the winter of 1888, the schooner Flora wrecked at Boot Head, and while the captain went to Eastport for help, a gang of locals (apparently from Baileys Mistake) spent the night pelting them with stones in an effort to drive the stranded crew away so the ship could be looted. The captain returned the next day with the lifesaving crew from West Quoddy Head and the ship was saved.

But this stark beauty and fascinating lore comes with a price: the Bold Coast is also one of the most volatile stretches of New England water, subject both to open ocean conditions and currents accelerated by Grand Manan's chock stone effect on the sea rushing in and out of the Bay of Fundy. You need to know what you're doing here. Challenging conditions may develop with little warning, even in small seas. Most who paddle the Bold Coast opt for only the calmest days, but even then, be prepared for difficult conditions with little option for landing for long distances and be prepared to stay in your boat.

If all you want to do is get from one end of the Bold Coast to another, you can certainly ride the strong currents that develop offshore, but those currents often start as much as a mile out, separated from shore by an eddy going the opposite direction. From that far out, the Bold Coast is a distant shore. You'll experience it a little more intimately than the states you fly over in a jet, but you do get past it quickly, depending on tides and your boat and abilities. Keep in mind that with strong currents come volatile conditions. If that 5-knot wind from the east increases to 10 knots against a strong flooding current, you'll get some wind-driven waves that will slow you down and make paddling less comfortable. Add a little swell and you could find yourself in difficult conditions.

You can also plan your trip opposite of the dominant offshore current, anticipating that the eddies closer to shore are generally going the opposite direction. If you really want to see and experience the Bold Coast, this might be preferable, as long as conditions allow you to paddle close enough to shore to enjoy it. These near-shore waters tend to be more prone to disturbance than offshore. With the shallower water and variations in topography, both above and below the water surface, the current is more likely to create occasional stretches of rough water. Add to that whatever seas develop and clapotis from waves bouncing off steep shoreline, and it becomes obvious why this coastline has a reputation as being dangerous and formidable, no matter the size of your vessel.

This guide breaks down the Bold Coast into two trips: West Quoddy Head (Trip 2) to Moose Cove and Cutler to Moose Cove (Trip 3). Other possibilities include a one-way trip with a shuttle, or a long day paddling 15.0 miles with the tide one way until the tide turns and takes you 15.0 miles back the other—a daunting prospect for any paddler.

2
THE BOLD COAST: WEST QUODDY TO MOOSE COVE

Paddle a remote stretch of wild, rugged coastline not seen by many visitors, including the headlands outside of Hamilton Cove and the stretch from Boot Head to Jims Head, one of the wildest, steepest stretches of shoreline in New England.

Distance ▶ Up to 14.0 to 16.0 nautical miles, round-trip

Tidal Planning ▶ 18.35-foot range at Eastport. Floods to the northeast. Strong mid-tide currents. Planning for current-assist is crucial. Near-shore eddies tend to oppose dominant, offshore current.

Cautions ▶ Conditions may quickly change from serene to outright dangerous. Paddlers here must have advanced skills and judgment. The area is subject to open ocean conditions and swift tidal currents. In addition, reflecting waves and current interacting with eddies may create large areas of extremely confused and challenging seas. Long stretches of cliffs and steep shoreline make it difficult if not impossible to land in some areas. Landing potential is completely relative to conditions and a paddler's skills; be prepared to be in your boat for a while. If you're unsure of your abilities or conditions, do not attempt this route.

Charts and Maps ▶ NOAA chart #13394

LAUNCH

Carrying Place Cove, Lubec Undeveloped beach launch, mostly used by workboats; limited parking; no facilities. From the intersection of ME 189 and South Lubec Road in Lubec, follow South Lubec Road south. In 2.7 miles, shortly after the turn for Boot Cove Road, the road turns east and intersects Carrying Place Cove Road; turn right (south). After 0.2 mile, follow a rugged dirt road about 500 feet east to the beach. *GPS coordinates: 44° 48.443' N, 66° 58.903' W.*

Other Public Access Hamilton Cove Preserve, protected by the Maine Coast Heritage Trust (MCHT), has a cobble beach for day use. You could carry-over on the trail from the parking area to the beach (approximately 150 yards). MCHT's Boot Head Preserve has a gravel beach in Boot Cove, just north of Boot Head; it's nearly a mile to the parking area. The cliff-top trails between Brook Cove and Boot Head have spectacular views. In calm conditions, land at the cobble beach in Brook Cove. On the west side of Moose Cove, the trust's Bog Brook Preserve has some cobble beaches where you could land in calm conditions; the parking area is 1,100 feet away.

ROUTE DESCRIPTION

The Bold Coast is often described in strong, foreboding terms, seemingly intended to scare off anyone thinking of paddling there—and with good reason. The stretch of coast between Cutler and West Quoddy Head is remote and subject to unimpeded open ocean swells and a massive tide range creating formidable currents as the broader ocean funnels into the gap between Grand Manan Island and Maine. In even minor swells, waves hammer into the long stretches of steep, rocky shoreline, bouncing back

The shoreline of the Bold Coast is pocked with myriad chasms and passageways, accessible on calmer days.

into the current where they interact with eddies that swirl along the shore. The ocean can shift from calm conditions into a chaotic mess as quickly as the tide turns.

In any but calm conditions here, most paddlers will face an unwelcoming shoreline with limited landing opportunities. The most memorable stretches of the Bold Coast are steep and cliffy, with difficult if not impossible landings. But contrary to popular notions, opportunities for bailouts exist at frequent enough intervals elsewhere, depending on conditions and the paddler's skill. In addition to occasional cobble beaches and seaweed-covered rocks, there are even protected harbors.

Regardless of the weather forecast or how conditions appear at the beginning of the day, any paddler venturing into this area needs to be prepared for extremely difficult conditions; a lack of preparedness could easily be life-threatening.

That said, it can also be a fine place to paddle. Venturing beneath the bluffs or into the chasms along Boot and Jims heads is outstanding, and there are few if any areas along this route that don't have interesting, rocky features along the shore. When there is little or no swell you can paddle close to them, but the view from a hundred yards out is also over the top. And all the while, there's the big open ocean horizon to the south and the constant backdrop of Grand Manan's fissured, cliffy shoreline.

The 2.0-nautical-mile stretch south from Carrying Place Cove to Hamilton Cove is a good area to get a sense of the conditions before further committing yourself. The shoreline is generally gradual for the first mile or so along Wallace Cove until the boundary of the Hamilton Cove Preserve (MCHT). The bluffs lead to Lawrence Head, which gives a sneak peek, on a smaller scale, of things to come. If you don't like conditions here, turn around; things will only get rougher.

The cobble beach at the head of the Hamilton Cove is a good spot for a break. In the early 1800s, the cove was the site of a shipyard with a lumber mill on the stream.

A little more than a mile farther, Boot Cove has a rocky beach likely to be somewhat sheltered. The southern end of the beach is part of the Boot Head Preserve (MCHT) and is open for day use. The 1.5-mile stretch from Boot Head to Jims Head, all part of the preserve, is the epitome of Bold Coast clichés: the jaw-dropping scenery, the difficult landings, and the potential for rough seas. Boot Head in particular is about as cliffy as it gets. On days with any swell to speak of, the waves will thunder into the chasms and against the rocks, reflecting back into the channel where they interact with the main current and probably the eddies as well. It can be downright nasty (and get that way as quickly as the tide turns). But if it's calm enough, paddling close to the cliffs and into the large chasm is an amazing experience.

Brook Cove has some cobble beaches where, on calm enough days, landing is possible. For stunning vistas, take the short hike up to the cliffs. Jims Head is much like Boot Head, with similar conditions, but just west of it you have the option of ducking into Baileys Mistake. Aside from its colorful history, Baileys Mistake doesn't offer much except a temporary refuge from the open ocean. The inner harbor is residential, home to a few lobster boats, while hordes of seals favor the ledges that once wrecked at least one schooner.

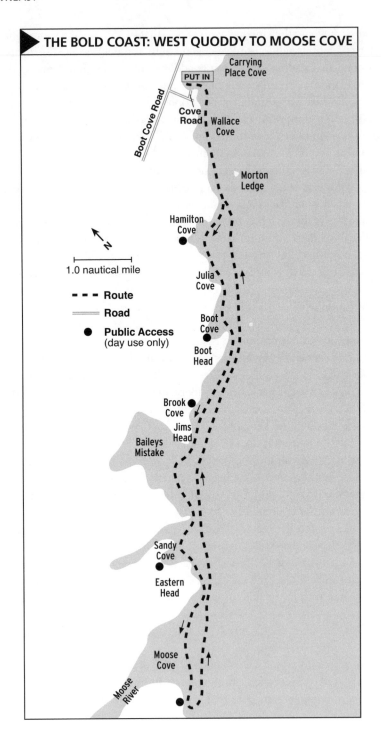

THE BOLD COAST: WEST QUODDY TO MOOSE COVE

Carrying Place Cove

PUT IN

Boot Cove Road

Cove Road

Wallace Cove

Morton Ledge

Hamilton Cove

N

1.0 nautical mile

- - - Route
═══ Road
● Public Access
(day use only)

Julia Cove

Boot Cove

Boot Head

Brook Cove

Jims Head

Baileys Mistake

Sandy Cove

Eastern Head

Moose Cove

Moose River

Haycock Harbor is another potentially quiet spot to duck into. At higher tides, you can paddle the narrow passage at the head of the cove almost a mile inland to the Pool. Just west of Haycock Harbor, Sandy Cove has a gradual sandy beach at its head that makes for an easy landing in calm conditions.

Though its shores lack the height and steepness of Boot Head, Eastern Head is another exposed headland with potentially wild conditions off its shore. Just west of the head, the shore curves north into Moose Cove in an area thick with rockweed-covered rocks and ledges, leading out to Eastern Head Ledges. Wind your way through these rocks for a break on state-owned Little Moose Island, or head across the cove to MCHT's Bog Brook Cove Preserve. In calm enough conditions, landing is possible at the cobble beach west of the point.

If you've arrived here at low tide and are heading back to Carrying Place Cove, be attentive to the tide change and how it affects conditions. As the current increases after the tide change you will get more tidal assist, but there is also greater potential for the current to complicate conditions. It may be prudent to get past the biggest headlands before mid-tide.

ALTERNATIVES

For a complete tour of the Bold Coast, add the stretch from Cutler to Moose Cove (Trip 3) to your itinerary. Suggestions for completing this very challenging route can be found in "The Bold Coast" on page 9.

If you're looking for a Plan B and are in the area, head to Dennys and Whiting bays (Trip 1), instead. For an on-shore option, grab your hiking boots and explore one of the many local coastal preserves.

MORE INFORMATION

Maine Coast Heritage Trust (mcht.org; 207-729-7366). Though it's not on the route, Cobscook Bay State Park (parksandlands.com; 207-726-4412) or commercial campgrounds in Lubec are nearby options.

3

THE BOLD COAST: CUTLER TO MOOSE COVE

Like its eastern counterpart, this route covers some of the wildest, least-developed shoreline in New England with long stretches of steep, rocky shoreline and towering cliffs.

Distance ▶ 8.0 to 9.0 nautical miles, one-way; round-trip mileage is variable

Tidal Planning ▶ 13.73-foot range at Cutler Harbor. Floods to the northeast. Strong mid-tide currents. Planning for current-assist is crucial. Near-shore eddies tend to oppose dominant, offshore current.

Cautions ▶ Conditions may quickly change from serene to extremely challenging, dangerous seas. Paddlers here must have advanced skills and judgment. The strong currents, exposure to open ocean, and steep shoreline sets the stage for chaotic conditions that can develop quickly, leaving paddlers in rough water, miles from the nearest potential bailout. If you're unsure of your abilities or conditions, don't attempt this route.

Charts and Maps ▶ NOAA chart #13326

LAUNCH

Cutler Town Ramp Shared with workboats and (on select days in season) puffin tour boat passengers; limited roadside parking near the ramp and along the road in town; no facilities. From the intersection of US 1 and ME 191, take ME 191 (Cutler Road) south for nearly 13.0 miles, then turn right onto Wharf Street. *GPS coordinates: 44° 39.462' N, 67° 12.488' W.*

Other Public Access Little River Lighthouse (littleriverlight.org) is located at the mouth of the harbor. The Cutler Coast Public Reserved Lands dominates the shore for 4.5 statute miles; a cobble beach landing may be possible north of Long Cove. The cobble beach at Bog Brook Preserve (Maine Coast Heritage Trust [MCHT]) lies at the east end of the route.

Boot Head is one of the more dramatic spots along the Bold Coast, and worth exploring on foot as well.

ROUTE DESCRIPTION

While the Bold Coast's northeast section boasts the tallest cliffs, the southeast portion is home to long stretches of rugged, undeveloped shoreline with only a handful of scattered cabins overlooking Grand Manan Channel. Much of the coast looks as it did when the first Europeans arrived.

Launching in the town of Cutler is a worthwhile experience in its own right. If conditions outside the harbor aren't promising, a tour of this idyllic harbor—from the upper reaches of the Little River on out to the aqua-trimmed lighthouse—is well worth the trip. There isn't much to do in town but enjoy the same view taken in by the cluster of homes overlooking the harbor. There's a lobster coop and wharves for the fishing boats, but not much else. You may see a few cruising boats laying over before making the trip to Grand Manan.

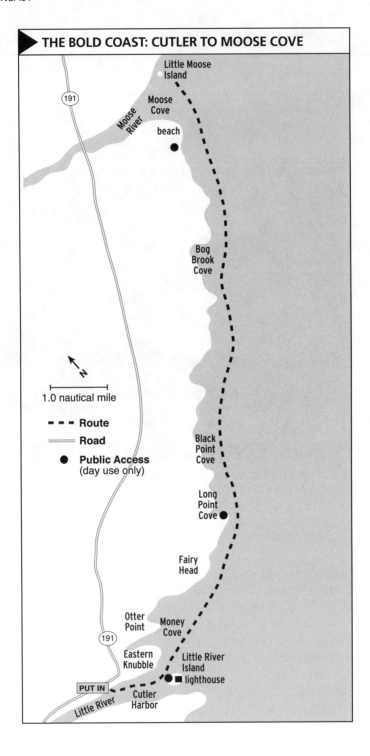

THE BOLD COAST: CUTLER TO MOOSE COVE

Little Moose Island

Moose Cove

Moose River

191

beach

Bog Brook Cove

N

1.0 nautical mile

- - - Route

Road

● Public Access
(day use only)

Black Point Cove

Long Point Cove ●

Fairy Head

Otter Point

Money Cove

191

Eastern Knubble

Little River Island

lighthouse

PUT IN

Little River

Cutler Harbor

At the mouth of the harbor stands the Little River Lighthouse on Little River Island, first built in 1847, with the present stone tower dating to 1876. Now owned by the New England Lighthouse Foundation, the lighthouse offers overnight accommodations in the old keeper's house (book well in advance).

Depending on the tide and conditions, you have two or three options for route strategy: eddy-hop up the coast, catch the Bold Coast Express offshore, or take a hybrid near-shore/eddy-hopping approach. If you're launching from Cutler on a rising tide, you'll probably encounter the least resistance either very close to shore, or well offshore. For a falling tide, expect the opposite.

If conditions allow, the most spectacular way to experience this section of the Bold Coast is the hybrid, near-shore approach. Explore rocky playgrounds where current is less noticeable, while occasionally paddling a little farther from shore in the eddy (flowing opposite of the dominant current). Occasionally, rocky constrictions will create small areas of increased current.

If you're paddling on a falling tide, against the dominant current, look for eddies along the shore where you'll have the current behind you. Be aware that conditions may occasionally be tricky where these eddies bunch up around headlands or brush against the dominant current.

If you choose the offshore route (the Bold Coast Express), paddle just beneath the lighthouse or even through the west channel behind the island, and point in the general vicinity of Grand Manan. Watch lobster buoys and the surface texture for clues to the current direction; it may be a mile or so out before direction changes. When you reach the dominant, eastbound current, the change in the water texture will probably be obvious and sometimes dramatic (steeper waves). Once in the current, keep an eye on the shore to get some sense of your speed; if you're not moving fast, you probably need to move farther offshore. Before mid-August, you may get lucky and see a puffin or two out here, maybe even a whale.

If conditions allow you to take the near-shore route, stick close to the shore all the way out to Fairy Head to avoid paddling against a large eddy that will most likely be spinning counterclockwise around the harbor. You may not be able to completely avoid it.

At Fairy Head, you may see hikers along the shore, on the cliff-top trails in the Cutler Coast Public Reserved Lands, where they keep an eye out for whales offshore and the 200-plus species of birds that have been spotted in the area. The Cutler Coast Public Reserved Lands encompass more than 12,000 acres with 10 miles of trails and 4.5 statute miles of shoreline. While there are campsites available, they are situated far from any easy landings and are not really viable for sea kayakers. The shoreline is rugged, with difficult access until Long Cove, where you might land on the cobble beach in smaller conditions.

As you approach the northern boundary of the reserve just south of Holmes Cove, the stark grassland barrens are visible inland, the result of fires in the 1850s. After Holmes Cove, the shoreline is private, with a few cabins for the next 1.5 miles. Starting just south of Bog Brook, Maine Coast Heritage Trust's Bog Brook Cove Preserve encompasses intermittent stretches of shoreline. There's a gorgeous cobble beach near the point just south of Moose Cove—a nice place for a break—but be aware that you may be sharing it with visitors who have taken the 1,100-foot trail down from the parking area. (It's worth mentioning that this is a fairly even, universally accessible path, which would be negotiable by kayak cart).

Moose Cove has a few lobster boats on moorings and a handful of homes on its shores. When tides allow, paddle up the shallow inner reaches of the Moose River. On the northeast side of the cove, Little Moose Island and an adjacent cobble beach, while privately owned, are undeveloped and have a maze of interesting rocks just offshore, which can be fun to explore. Time your trip back to Cutler with the tide, and be aware that a changing tide may bring changing conditions.

ALTERNATIVES

If time, tide, and conditions allow, you could continue on around Eastern Head, perhaps even explore Haycock Harbor or Baileys Mistake (see Trip 2).

If you're looking for a Plan B and are in the area, head to Dennys and Whiting bays (Trip 1) or explore Northern Machias Bay (Trip 4). For an on-shore option, grab your hiking boots and explore one of the many local coastal preserves.

MORE INFORMATION

Cutler Harbormaster (207-259-3645). Cutler Coast Public Reserved Lands (parksandlands.org; 207-941-4412); campsites here are not really an option for kayakers. Bog Brook Cove (mcht.org/preserves/bog-brook-cove.shtml; 207-422-1130). Nearby options include Cobscook Bay State Park (parksandlands.com; 207-726-4412) and commercial campgrounds in Lubec.

4
MACHIAS BAY

*Enjoy bold grassy islands with great views,
a lighthouse on South Libby Island, the
potential for outstanding rock gardening, plus
sheep and bird sightings.*

Distance ▶ 10.0 to 12.0 nautical miles, round-trip

Tidal Planning ▶ 12.76-foot tidal range at Cutler Naval Base. It will be easiest to plan on going south on a falling tide, and north on a rising tide. The gravel bar between Starboard Island and Point of Main and the area to the north flat out at lower tides. A large gyre circulates counterclockwise around the mouth of the bay. Regardless of general tide direction, the current will most often be moving southwest from Machias Bay toward Ram Island and the Scabby Islands. It is not easy to predict.

Cautions ▶ Aside from the predictable conditions from exposure to the open ocean, the mouth of Machias Bay presents some less-predictable hazards from tidal currents. The least pre-dictable is the gyre (see note in Tidal Planning) which results in a current that sometimes runs counter to and interacts with the usual tides, creating steep and confused conditions. Add wind and swell to that mix, and wild seas may ensue. Be particularly wary around the ends of islands, where currents converge and accelerate. Also, look out for the sheep. They are sometimes territorial, and you never know what they might want to eat. But if you don't land, they probably won't bother you.

Charts and Maps ▶ NOAA chart #13326; Maptech #42

LAUNCHES

Pettegrow Beach, Machiasport Town-owned cobble beach launch; daytime and overnight parking; portable outhouse. From the junction of US 1 and ME 92 in Machias, take ME 92/Elm Street east toward Bucks Harbor. In 3.0 miles, continue on

Port Road (ME 92 turns north here toward Machiasport). In another 5.7 miles, turn left (east) on Pettegrow Point Road and follow it 0.6 miles to the launch on the left. *GPS coordinates: 44° 38.354′ N, 67° 22.709′ W.*

Jasper Beach, Machiasport Town-owned cobble beach with short (steep) carry from small parking area; no facilities. From the intersection of Port Road and Pettegrow Point Road, continue on Port Road for 0.8 mile, through Bucks Harbor to Jasper Beach Road. The beach is at the end of this short road. *GPS coordinates: 44° 37.678′ N, 67° 23.377′ W.*

Starboard Cove, Machiasport Crude high-tide launch; several parking spots; no facilities. Continue past Jasper Beach Road for a little over a mile. *GPS coordinates: 44° 36.507′ N, 67° 23.840′ W.*

Seawall Point, Machiasport Hand-carry/crude ramp on Little Kennebec Bay; day and overnight parking; no facilities. From the intersection of US 1 and Kennebec Road in Machias, turn south onto Kennebec Road. In 0.9 mile, take the right fork for Roque Bluffs Road toward Roque Bluffs State Park. In the next 5.5 miles, this road becomes Kennebec Road then Roque Bluffs Road again; your route turns left at Roque Bluffs Town Hall onto Johnson Cove Road. Follow Johnson Cove Road until it ends in 2.8 miles. *GPS coordinates: 44° 36.855′ N, 67° 26.055′ W.*

Other Public Access This route is light on options for additional landings. Both South Libby (part of the Maine Coastal Islands National Wildlife Refuge [MCINWR]) and North Libby islands (state-owned) are closed for bird nesting season, April through August. Stone Island (The Nature Conservancy [TNC]) is a difficult landing except at low tides by experienced paddlers.

ROUTE DESCRIPTION

For those who enjoy paddling among rocks and ledges, gems abound in the mouth of Machias Bay, changing constantly with the tide. Starboard and Stone islands are both forested, but the stark outer islands are mostly treeless and grassy, the result of years of sheep grazing. The castle-like home on Foster Island is certainly out of place, but along with the grassy, sheep-dotted hills and the tidal races, it's easy enough to imagine that you may have been transported to Scotland.

It pays to be attentive to the tides in this area, since the currents are not easy to predict. In the 1.5-mile-wide gap between Foster and Libby islands, several distinct eddy lines may form, along which the conditions may easily become rough. Strong current with multiple eddy lines may also form off Point of Main and in Foster Channel. In some conditions it may be wise to forgo crossing to Stone or the Libby islands.

Because scarce public access is further limited by steep shoreline, conditions, and nesting season, be ready to be in your boat for a while. The area has its challenges, but for prepared paddlers, they are challenges worth facing. The shores of the Libby Islands in particular are riddled with dramatic clefts, even a small sea cave. And of course there's a lighthouse and plenty of history: Machias Bay was the site of one of the first naval battles of the Revolutionary War.

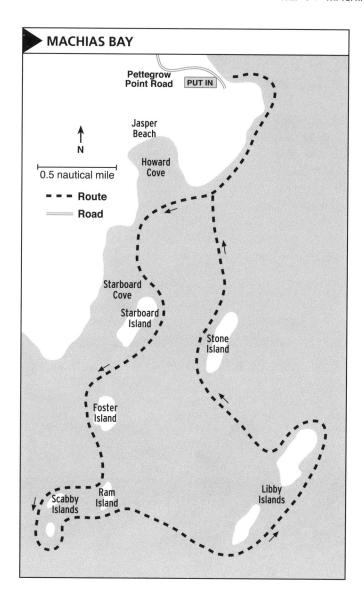

Ideally, launch from Pettegrow Beach on a falling tide. Round Bucks Head and mosey south along the shoreline past Jasper Head toward Howard Point. While this shoreline is looked over by a handful of homes, the rock-strewn shallows can be a maze of rockweed-covered passages, easily a destination in itself. Far less exposed than the islands at the mouth of the bay, it is a good sneak peek of conditions to come. If it feels big here, you might want to turn around and head north.

Unless it's foggy (which is common here), you can't miss the 26 radio towers dominating Cutler Peninsula, 3.0 miles across the bay. The towers, some of them nearly a thousand feet high, make up a U.S. Navy VLF (very low frequency) surface-to-submarine transmitter capable of reaching submerged submarines all over the Atlantic. The second largest radio transmitter in the world, it transmits at 1,800 kilowatts, making it one of the most powerful transmitters and one of the world's largest consumers of electricity.

West of Howard Point, Howard Cove juts inland to Jasper Beach. If you want to get out to the islands, save this detour for another time, but the shores of the cove are craggy and fun, the smooth cobble beach inviting closer inspection. The radar dome atop Howard Mountain is a landmark easily recognizable from miles away.

Head south to Starboard Island. At lower tides the gravel bar will be exposed, blocking passage along the shore of Starboard Cove. Predictably, when submerged that gravel bar can also create some waves and lively conditions that some may enjoy.

To the south, a castle-like home overlooking the rocky spit at the northwest end of privately owned Foster Island is easy to spot. Watch for sheep along the island's shores.

Maine Island Trail Association (MITA) membership provides access to far more places along the Maine coast, including this campsite on a private island in Machias Bay.

Ram and Scabby islands are both also privately owned sheep grazing islands, but neither has a home on it. At lower tides, their steep shorelines are skirted by intricate networks of exposed rocks and rockweed-coated hallways.

Before crossing over to South Libby Island (1.25 nautical miles from Ram Island), take a moment to observe the conditions and be sure to understand what the current is doing here. You may need to set a ferry angle and keep a range to stay on course. Be aware that those adjustments may change as you cross eddies. Miscalculations here could result in you being swept out to open ocean—and there's a lot of it to the south.

Libby Island Light was first established in 1817 as a wooden tower, then built from granite in 1823. A fog signal and a lifesaving station were added later, which required several families to live on the island, where in some years the fog signal sounded more than any other on the Maine coast. Despite this, at least 35 ships have wrecked off of South Libby Island with considerable loss of life. The light has been automated since 1974.

In most seas, you will probably want to maintain a little space from South Libby's steep, rocky shores, below which lie numerous boulders and ledges. Landing on the state-owned island is limited to non-nesting months (closed April through August); North Libby (MCINWR) is closed April 15 through August. The two islands are connected by a rocky bar at lower tides. North Libby has a gorgeous cobble beach encircled by steep bluffs on its eastern side—a great landing spot when conditions and birds allow. A tide rip sometimes forms just north of the island, while the steep western shore has plenty to explore, including a sea cave that extends 30 to 40 feet in from the face.

Before crossing over to Stone Island (about a mile from the north end of North Libby), take a moment to observe and figure out what the current is doing. If there's much current, you might be just as well off to leave from the south end of South Libby.

Landings on Stone Island (TNC) are difficult at best, probably part of the reason this significant blue heron rookery is otherwise uninhabited. The 89-foot high bluffs at the south end are particularly impressive, but at lower tides in calm seas, skilled paddlers could make the landing on rockweed-covered ledges.

Return via Howard Point, approximately a mile from Stone Island. If you have time, you might enjoy checking out the salmon pens near the north ends of both Stone and Starboard islands.

ALTERNATIVES

Add on a paddle through Englishman Bay (Trip 5) for an overnight or multiday trip. The trip north toward Machias could include a visit to the petroglyphs at Picture Rocks at Clark Point (Birch Point), or on the southwest shore of Hog Island and on the east side of the bay at Holmes Point (see "Ancient Rock Carvings in Machias Bay" on page 27).

For a Plan B, the inner/northern part of Machias Bay may be relatively calm when conditions at the mouth of the bay are not. The private islands just off Bucks Harbor are worth paddling around, while the western half of Salt Island is a preserve owned by The Nature Conservancy (closed March 15 to August 15). The Machias River, reachable by a launch on US 1 in Machias, is also a relatively sheltered paddle. Cobscook Bay (Trip 1) is about an hour's drive, as are the Bold Coast hiking trails.

MORE INFORMATION

Machiasport Town Office (machiasport.org; 207-255-4516); open 8 A.M. to 4 P.M. Monday through Friday. Maine Coastal Islands National Wildlife Refuge (fws.gov/refuge/Maine_Coastal_Islands; 207-594-0600). Maine Department of Inland Fisheries and Wildlife (maine.gov/ifw; 207-287-8000). The Nature Conservancy (nature.org/maine; 207-729-5181). Camping is not available except on a private island available for Maine Island Trail Association (MITA) members. If combining this route and a tour of Englishman's Bay, see Halifax Island (Trip 5).

ANCIENT ROCK CARVINGS IN MACHIAS BAY

The shores of Machias Bay are the site of the densest concentration of indigenous rock art in the eastern United States, but seeing these petroglyphs is not so easy as one might guess. There are at least nineteen known sites along Machiasport's shoreline, but their exact location is intentionally not mapped to reduce traffic and prevent degradation. And if the light isn't right, you could look right at the rock carvings and not know it. Maybe it's better that it takes some effort: when you've been searching for some time and the texture on the rock surface suddenly organizes itself into recognizable figures, it feels as if you've earned it.

Some of the petroglyphs date back 3,000 years. Their makers—Wabanaki ancestors of the present-day Passamaquoddy tribe—pounded the rock surface with another rock, texturing it into images of human and animal forms. No one knows the petroglyphs' true meanings for sure, but most theories suggest they were made as part of a shamanistic ritual.

Launching either from Pettegrow Beach in Bucks Harbor (Trip 4) or the Gates House in Machiasport (limited parking) puts you within short paddling distance of two locations open to the public: Picture Rocks on Birch Point or Long Point. Choose a sunny day, when shadows make the textures more pronounced. From the water, try to imagine where a prehistoric local would want to make rock art: a smooth rock surface near a good landing, just above high tide, perhaps somewhat angled so it can be seen from the side.

With luck, after you stare long enough, figures emerge from the chaos. You may wonder how you didn't see them before: animal figures with big antlers, a cross of Christian proportions, and beside it a Rorschach blob that (if you've done your homework) could vaguely resemble a European square-rigged ship from about 1605 (the French explorer DeMontz established a trading post on this point). Or it could be a Norse ship from the eleventh century. Maybe that's squinting too hard, but if you look long enough, the rough patches of rock certainly resemble *something*.

5

ENGLISHMAN BAY

Enjoy wide, open-ocean views from atop the bluffs on Halifax Island, sheltered interior passages through the Roque Island archipelago, and a mile-long sandy beach on Roque Island.

Distance ▶ 4.0 to 14.0 nautical miles, round-trip

Tidal Planning ▶ 12.76-foot tidal range at Cutler Naval Base. The current generally floods to the northeast. Launching on a falling tide and returning on a rising tide will provide the most current assist.

Cautions ▶ The southern side of these islands is exposed to open ocean and whatever conditions it may bring. In particular, the area south of Halifax Island, including Green Island and the Brothers, is likely to be rough, with increased currents interacting with those conditions. Be wary of the shallow bar north of Green Island.

Charts and Maps ▶ NOAA chart #13326; Maptech #42

LAUNCHES

Roque Bluffs State Park, Roque Bluffs Hand-carry beach launch; parking across the street in lot; lot is gated at night and when park is closed (see "More Information" for park schedule); small state park entrance fee. From the intersection of US 1 and Kennebec Road in Machias, turn south onto Kennebec Road. In 0.9 mile, bear right at Roque Bluffs Town Hall; the launch is immediately after the fork on the left with parking on the right. *GPS coordinates: 44° 36.684' N, 67° 28.952' W.*

Shoppee Point, Roque Bluffs Paved ramp; daytime parking. From Roque Bluffs Town Hall turn right on Shoppee Point Road and continue another mile or so until the road ends in the water. *GPS coordinates: 44° 36.934' N, 67° 29.770' W.*

Seawall Point, Roque Bluffs Hand-carry/crude ramp; day and overnight parking; no facilities. From Roque Bluffs Town Hall turn left onto Johnson Cove Road. Follow Johnson Cove Road until it ends in 2.8 miles. *GPS coordinates: 44° 36.855' N, 67° 26.055' W.*

Other Public Access Shoppee Island is closed during nesting season (February 15 through May 15, and possibly longer). Roque Island's beach on Roque Harbor has been, at times, closed to the public. Halifax Island (Maine Coastal Islands National Wildlife Refuge [MCINWR]) is open year-round. The Brothers (MCINWR) are closed April to August for nesting season; landings here are more challenging.

ROUTE DESCRIPTION

Roque Island is well known to sailors, who like to anchor off of its long, sandy beach and in the sheltered, narrow passages between the islands in the archipelago. It is likely that you will encounter a cruising boat or two as you paddle in the area. Roque, though privately owned, has a designated stretch of beach open to the public. The gradually inclined sandy beach (about a 3-mile paddle from Roque Bluffs State Park) is a rarity in this rockier part of Maine. You could easily spend days exploring the passages among Roque Island and its neighbors, all privately owned but generally wild and undeveloped. The rocks and ledges south of the islands are fun spots as well, with long passages among the shore rocks that appear at the right tide.

Halifax Island (MCINWR), a little more than 2.0 miles from the beach at Roque Bluffs, has a wild, distant feeling that belies its proximity to the launch. Halifax has a raised bog on the interior of its east end that is off-limits to visitors. Camping is allowed above the beach, with permission. A short walk is rewarded with magnificent views from an idyllic, grassy bluff.

If conditions allow, the Brothers may easily become the highlight of a trip. The pair of barred islands, also part of the MCINWR complex, are outlandishly gorgeous, with steep cliffs rising directly from the sea to grassy heights frequented by sheep and rare bird decoys.

Any of the three listed launches are good starting points for this trip, but the beach at the state park is the closest to Roque and Halifax islands. From here, you could easily paddle the 2.0 miles directly to Halifax Island, but the route described takes a leisurely 8.0-mile amble through the archipelago to get there.

From the beach, head southwest to Shoppee Island. Shoppee has at times been an eagle-nesting island. It is closed February 15 through May 15, and if eagles are nesting, through August 31 as well.

It's about a mile from the south end of Shoppee across Englishman Bay to Marsh Island (connected to Roque Island). Be attentive to the current here and follow a range to avoid getting set too far downcurrent. Follow the shoreline south to the opening between Marsh and Bar islands. If the tide is too low to get through, continue south around Bar and follow Lakeman Harbor to its western opening into Roque Harbor. From here you'll see the beach on Roque Island to the northwest.

Roque and the surrounding islands have belonged to the same family since the early 1800s, and at times public access has been permitted. As of 2015, a pole near the middle of the beach marks the eastern boundary of where the public is allowed to land and walk, while signs atop the beach request that visitors not advance any farther inland. A caretaker monitors the area.

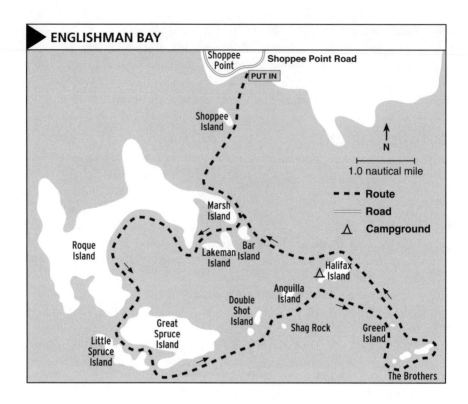

ENGLISHMAN BAY

When you're done marveling at the long stretch of sand, follow the shoreline south to the Thorofare, a narrow gap between Roque and Great Spruce Island. At low tides, the gap at the southwest end is narrow indeed, and current increases accordingly.

Head southeast in Bunker Cove, a very protected passage between the Spruce Islands, and wind around the east end of Little Spruce to exit into open water at Bunker Hole.

Depending on conditions, the southern shore of Great Spruce, Double Shot, and Anguilla islands (all private) can be a rocky obstacle course as you turn northeast. In bigger conditions, you may prefer the calmer waters on the north side. Watch for strong currents between the islands and make your way to Halifax Island.

The easiest landings on Halifax are on either the north or south coves where the island narrows near the southwest end. A small campsite (prior permission required) atop the beach stones overlooks the north-facing beach. Signs request that visitors not enter the raised bog to the northeast. A trail leads to the grassy bluffs at the southwest end.

Not all paddlers will want to venture into the more exposed waters surrounding the Brothers, but on a calm day, skilled paddlers could enjoy a visit to these dramatic islands. Perched on Eastern Brother's cliffs are numerous tern, puffin, and razorbill decoys, convincing enough to prompt unsuspecting paddlers to whip out their cameras and snap photos until they realize how still the birds stand. Real birds nest there as well, and the island is closed April through August. Landing on these islands is generally difficult, but the most likely take-out is near the bar, below the cabin on Western Brother that houses refuge employees. The south side of the Brothers is very exposed. Expect strong currents in Brothers Passage and over the bar north of Green Island.

From Halifax, head straight back to the beach at the state park, or take a slightly longer route to the northeast, via Bar and Marsh islands (both private).

ALTERNATIVES

This route may easily be combined with a trip through Machias Bay (Trip 4), particularly for a multiday trip; the campsite at Halifax Island is your best bet. Jonesport and the Great Wass Island (Trip 6) are only a few miles to the west.

If you're looking for easier options, Little Kennebec Bay north of Seawall Point could be a sheltered area, as could the Englishman River at higher tides.

MORE INFORMATION

Roque Bluffs State Park (parksandlands.com; 207-255-3475); open 9 A.M. to sunset daily, May 15 to October 30; an entrance fee is charged. In the off-season and during these same hours, visitors may enter the park on foot. Maine Coastal Islands National Wildlife Refuge (fws.gov/refuge/Maine_Coastal_Islands; 207-594-0600). For permission to use the Halifax Island campsite, contact the U.S. Fish and Wildlife office in Milbridge (204-546-2124). Other overnight options for MITA members are available on nearby routes.

In Englishman Bay, the Brothers have steep, craggy shorelines watched over by sheep and rare bird decoys.

6
THE GREAT WASS ARCHIPELAGO

*Explore the wild and exposed southern end
of Great Wass Island and its neighbors, plus
enjoy Moose Peak Light and plentiful seals,
eagles, razorbills, and other wildlife on
Freeman Rock.*

Distance ▶ 8.0 to 10.0 nautical miles, round-trip, with potential for much more

Tidal Planning ▶ 11.31-foot range at Milbridge. Current in Eastern Bay floods to the north. For maximum tidal assist, paddle south on a falling tide and north on a rising tide. North of Head Harbor Island the current begins to funnel into Moosabec Reach. Though not on the route, Moosabec Reach develops a strong current, flooding to the east.

Cautions ▶ Strong currents in Moosabec Reach; lobster boats. The area is known for its dense fog, which can descend unexpectedly. The south ends of Great Wass and neighboring islands are exposed to open ocean swell and can develop big conditions, especially when wind opposes tidal currents.

Charts and Maps ▶ NOAA chart #13326; Maptech #42

LAUNCHES

Great Wass Island All-tides gravel beach launch beside a busy fishing pier; a number of parking spaces, but plenty of seafood harvesters' pickup trucks to fill them; portable outhouse available in warmer months. From the intersection of US 1 and ME 187 in Columbia Falls, follow ME 187 south for 10.6 miles through Jonesport. Turn right on Bridge Street/ME 187 and, in 0.5 mile, cross the bridge to Beals Island. At the end of the bridge, turn left onto Barney's Cove Road and continue immediately south on Bay View Drive. In 1.2 miles, cross a small bridge onto Great Wass Island and take a left. Follow Alleys Bay Road as it curves back to the north and ends at the launch, which faces the west end of Pig Island 1.2 miles from the bridge. *GPS coordinates: 44° 30.56.9' N, 67° 35.24.3' W.*

Jonesport Municipal Marina Paved ramp; limited daytime and overnight parking. From the intersection of US 1 and ME 187 in Columbia Falls, follow ME 187 south for 11.6 miles through Jonesport. From Bridge Street, go another mile to a right onto Sawyer Square. *GPS coordinates: 44° 31.918' N, 67° 35.723'W.*

Moose Point, South Addison Gravel beach; a few parking spaces at the end of the road, plus another lot up the hill; no facilities. This launch is several miles away from this route, but it's a good start point for the add-on route described here. A narrow channel separates the beach from Tibbets Island, a Downeast Coastal Conservancy preserve. From the intersection of ME 187 and Wescogus Road in Addison, head southwest on Wescogus Road. In 1.4 miles, turn left onto East Side Road. Continue for 5.9 miles to a fork where Mooseneck Road leaves to the right. At the end of Mooseneck Road, about 1.5 miles from the previous turn, turn left (south) onto Narrows Road, which ends at the gravel beach. *GPS coordinates: 44° 29.848' N, 67° 42.767' W.*

Off of Great Wass Island, the salmon pens provide entertainment, especially at feeding time.

Other Public Access The Great Wass Island Preserve, owned by The Nature Conservancy (TNC), encompasses several islands on this route. The preserve dominates the southern part of Great Wass Island, including the shorefront south of Three Falls Harbor on the west side and Mud Hole Point on the east. A parking area just north of Black Duck Cove accesses two trails that, combined with a stretch of shoreside hiking, make up a 5-mile loop. The eastern shore can also be followed on foot to the southern end of the island. Mistake Island is also part of the preserve, with the exception of four privately owned acres around Moose Peak Light. At lower tides, a bar extends across the channel to Knight Island (also TNC-owned) and makes a convenient place to land. TNC also owns Little Hardwood Island in Eastern Bay (closed February 15 to August 15), Black Island just north of Steele Harbor Island, the Man Islands, and the point on Head Harbor Island.

ROUTE DESCRIPTION

The Great Wass archipelago's more than 40 islands stand apart from the rest of the coast as plainly as Tall Barney, an early Jonesport settler, stood above his peers. The island group extends farther into the ocean than any other land mass in eastern Maine, which helps explain its reputation as one of the foggiest places in the state. This exposure also puts the islands at the nexus of Gulf of Maine and Bay of Fundy waters, creating a cool marine climate where jack pines and rare plants thrive amid inland bogs.

At the south end of the island group, shorelines drop abruptly into the sea, plunging rapidly to great depths along a curiously straight line from Egg Rock to Black Head. Unsurprisingly, paddling anywhere along this dropoff is ruggedly gorgeous with the potential for wild conditions.

In Eastern Bay though, conditions from the open ocean are buffered by surrounding islands and it is often possible to find a sheltered route when it is dicey elsewhere. Thanks to TNC, the area has plenty of public access, concentrated at the southern end of Great Wass Island. Moose Peak Light, standing over the granite-lined channels on Mistake Island, rounds out the area's visual appeal.

The route follows a modest course through Eastern Bay to the lighthouse, with numerous options for add-ons, subject to conditions and paddlers' skills.

From the launch, head east through Pig Island Gut and turn south, past Alley Island. About a mile to the southeast a group of fish pens lies just west of private Spectacle Island. You can head for the island, but it may be interesting to check out the salmon, especially if you happen to arrive around feeding time.

Head south along Green and Mink islands before heading southeast to a second Green Island, this one in Mistake Harbor. State-owned Little Water Island lies southeast. The Maine Island Trail Association (MITA) maintains a public, first come, first served one-tent campsite on this fragile island, with access from the east side; no campfires are allowed. This area is thick with seals; give them a wide berth, especially during pupping season in the spring, and plan to visit during other seasons. The island is also very exposed, and would not be a good place to be in bad weather.

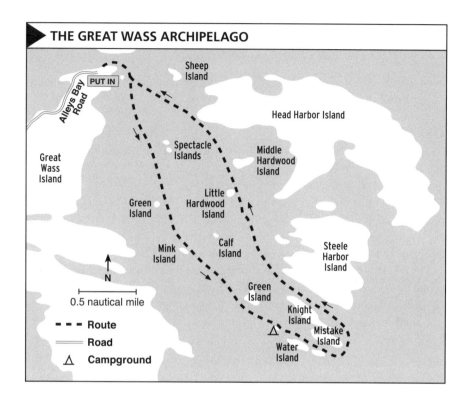

The channel between TNC-owned Knight and Mistake islands is just to the east. At lower tides a sandbar connects the two islands and provides a good place to land. At higher tides, landing near the boathouse on Mistake Island's east end is more challenging. A boardwalk starts just behind the boathouse and leads to the lighthouse, which is a wonderful place to stop for lunch and gaze out at the open ocean. In early summer months, Freeman Rock, to the southeast of Mistake Island, is home to a razorbill colony.

The return trip can be made via Little Hardwood Island to the northwest. From there, make your way back to Pig Island Gut. At lower tides you'll need to pick your way around the shallow areas; stay south of Sheep and Pig islands and watch for the channel markers leading back into the gut.

ALTERNATIVES

After your visit to the lighthouse, if conditions allow, head northeast along the eastern shore of Steele Harbor Island to Man Island, then wind through Head Harbor to rejoin the route at Little Hardwood Island. Or continue around the north side of Head Harbor Island back to Pig Island Gut. Or, you could continue to the east side of Great Wass Island or to the steep, rocky shoreline along the south end before heading back. Great Wass can also be circumnavigated, either as a day trip or with a stop on one of the camping islands; plenty of interesting paddling can also be found on the west side. The Roque Island group is nearby (see Trip 5) and it isn't far to the Bois Bubert area (Trip 7).

In rough weather, follow the Great Wass shore to Mud Hole, or take advantage of the hiking trails to explore the Great Wass Preserve on foot.

MORE INFORMATION

Great Wass Island Preserve, The Nature Conservancy (nature.org/maine; 207-729-5181). No pets are allowed in the preserve.

Besides the MITA-managed, first come, first served campsite on Little Water Island, there are a few other options along and near the route. MITA (mita.org, 207-761-8225) allows its members to camp on Stevens and Sands islands, both to the west of Great Waas. Halifax Island (camping for MITA members only) can connect this route to Englishman Bay (Trip 5). The town of Jonesport maintains Henry Point Campground (207-598-6479), a little over a mile west of the Beals Island Bridge; from the intersection of ME 187 and Kelley Point Road, take Kelley Point Road southeast for 0.4 mile then make a right onto Campground Road. The campground, dominated by RVs, is on the southwest point, and has direct water access.

FOG

Fog can be ethereal. With less to see, the remaining details stand out in sharp focus, and any color at all seems vivid. Our senses become attuned to subtleties: the slap of a wave against a granite slab or the hiss of tumbling stones on a beach. Paddlers tend to slow down in the fog, drifting through clouds that obscure and reveal our surroundings as impressionist landscapes, our thoughts trickling slowly, like haiku. Of course, paddling in fog is not always calming. Offshore, the approaching hum of a motor can turn the dream into a nightmare; crossings become even more dangerous, especially without the aid of strong navigational skills.

Fog, especially at sea, can form quickly during a perfectly sunny day, any time of the year, and it's not easy to predict. You may choose not to venture into the fog, but you can't make that choice if you're already out there when the fog appears. You can try to avoid it, but you also need to be prepared for it.

Fog forms when air completely saturated with water vapor lowers to its dew point and the vapor condenses on solid particles in the air. These "cloud seeds" could be almost anything: dust, ice, air pollution, salt from the ocean (especially where there are breaking waves), or even iodine released into the air by sun-heated kelp.

Land fog (radiation fog) usually forms at night when the air is clear and calm. Lack of cloud cover allows the heat from the land to dissipate, which cools the air closest to the ground. On the ocean, we're most likely to encounter radiation fog in the morning as it blows off the land. Land fog tends to burn off as the temperature rises.

Sea fog (advection fog) forms when warmer moist air condenses over colder water. This can happen when the water is brought to the surface by currents or brought closer to land by the tide. Perhaps more commonly, the warmer air blows over the cooler water. Unlike land fog, sea fog sticks around regardless of the day getting warmer. It can linger for days or even weeks.

The most immediate fog hazard to a kayaker comes from other boats. Despite several avoidance measures (a Sécurité call on the VHF, fog horns, and radar reflectors), you may never know if your attempts to be seen are working. A Maine Association of Sea Kayak Guides and Instructors (MASKGI) and U.S. Coast Guard study conducted in 2003 and 2004 by Natalie Springuel, Paul Travis, and Richard MacDonald found little difference between commercial radar reflectors and a tinfoil hat.

The only sure way to avoid collisions with other boats is to stay out of their way. If you get caught out in the fog, you may have little choice but to cross a channel, but more often you can make choices to avoid the situation: stay in shallow water, follow the shoreline, or wait. You should also be confident in your navigation skills before making a crossing in the fog.

7
BOIS BUBERT ISLAND

*Any paddler will be delighted by this route's
many classic New England sights, including
wild, exposed cobble beaches; seabirds
swarming steep cliffs; winding channels; an
arch to paddle though; and a lighthouse.*

Distance ▶ 7.0 to 8.0 nautical miles, round-trip, to circumnavigate Bois
Bubert Island; an additional 5.0 to 7.0 nautical miles to tour
the Douglas Islands, Jordans Delight, and Pond Island; an
additional 6.0 to 7.0 nautical miles for a Petit Manan Point–
Petit Manan Island loop from Little Bois Bubert Island

Tidal Planning ▶ 11.31-foot range at Milbridge. Currents flood to the north.

Cautions ▶ Currents are strong in this area; avoid paddling against
them or in opposing winds, which steepen the waves. The
south end of Bois Bubert is directly exposed to the open
ocean and whatever swells it may bring. The shallow areas
south of the island and Little Bois Bubert stretch out for
some distance, producing breaking waves. The crossing between Bois Bubert and Jordans Delight is similarly exposed
and might be best paddled toward slack tide. Plan to be at
Petit Manan Island around low tide for the most tidal advantage; slack tides should be the least dangerous time to
be near the Petit Manan Bar.

Charts and Maps ▶ NOAA chart #13324; Maptech #42

LAUNCHES
Pigeon Hill Bay, Steuben Town-owned ramp; limited parking on the road; no
facilities. From the intersection of US 1 and Pigeon Hill Road in Milbridge, take
Pigeon Hill Road south about 5.0 miles to ramp. *GPS coordinates: 44° 27.117′ N, 67°
53.018′ W.* An additional two parking spots are 0.25 mile north at the Pigeon Hill
trailhead (Downeast Coastal Conservancy).

Other Public Access While the northwest side of Bois Bubert Island is privately
owned with homes along its shore, the southern end is part of the Maine Coastal

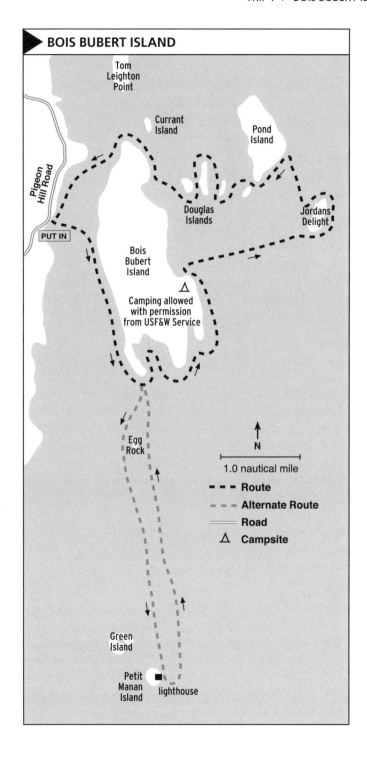

BOIS BUBERT ISLAND

Tom
Leighton
Point

Currant
Island

Pond
Island

Pigeon
Hill Road

PUT IN

Douglas
Islands

Jordans
Delight

Bois
Bubert
Island

△

Camping allowed
with permission
from USF&W Service

Egg
Rock

N

1.0 nautical mile

- - - Route
- - - Alternate Route
——— Road
△ Campsite

Green
Island

Petit
Manan
Island   lighthouse

Islands National Wildlife Refuge (MCINWR); a campsite is available with a prior reservation. Jordans Delight (closed April through August for nesting season) is also part of the MCINWR, while the small house atop the grassy hill still belongs to the family who donated the island. Petit Manan Point and Petit Manan Island are both part of the Petit Manan National Wildlife Refuge (a division of the MCINWR); the island is also closed April to August for nesting.

ROUTE DESCRIPTION

Bois Bubert Island lies at the south end of Narraguagus Bay, the 1,200-acre center of a neighborhood of stellar paddling locales that includes Petit Manan Island, Jordans Delight, and the Douglas Islands.

From the Pigeon Hill Bay ramp, a 0.5-mile crossing brings you to Bois Bubert Island. You can go either way around the island, depending on current and conditions. The conserved, southern end is wild and rocky, facing out to the open ocean where the swells roll in and turn to big waves as they hit the rock-strewn shallows. If conditions allow, landings are most likely in Little Bois Bubert Harbor and at the steep cobble beach at Big Head. Your route could continue eastward or westward from here.

Eastward Islands

Jordans Delight (MCINWR) lies almost 1.5 nautical miles east of the campsite on Bois Bubert Island's Seal Cove. Paddle directly there, or handrail along the Douglas and Pond islands. Paddling toward this 27-acre, steep-sided rock feels like the approach to a forbidding exile in a gothic novel. The west side is all vertical cliff, much of which drops directly into the ocean. The east side is more gradual, with rough, rocky shoreline and a small, north-facing cobble beach, which is the most likely landing spot (closed April through August for nesting). Just west of the beach is a stone arch that can be paddled through at higher tides: a childish pleasure, but a thrill nonetheless. Plan on being here within an hour or so of high tide.

The south shore of Pond Island (private) is bluffy and bold, usually washed by swell. The lighthouse at the east end is decommissioned and is now a private residence. The Douglas Islands are steep-sided and undeveloped but private. You can usually find a spot for a break on nearby ledges.

Westward Islands

Paddle west from Little Bois Bubert Island to reach Petit Manan Point, where the ocean floor rises rapidly from great depths to form a shallow bar that stretches southeast more than 1.5 miles to Green Island. The current, flooding northeast and ebbing southwest, becomes abruptly constricted here, both vertically by the bar, and horizontally, between the point and the islands, accelerating the water that then piles up on top of itself as it squeezes through. If that weren't enough, the prevailing southwest winds land squarely upon the bar as well, often opposing the ebbing tide. The result is an area known for rough water and rogue waves that can rise suddenly, seemingly from nowhere. On a calm day at slack tide, the bar is certainly navigable and at its least

Only a few miles from the launch, Petit Manan Island is a likely area to see puffins.

dangerous, but it is still a risky place to be. A channel is buoyed across the bar at about midpoint, but this is of little use to kayakers. Excellent skills and judgment are a must here; it would be an easy place to overestimate both and get into trouble.

Not everyone will want to venture anywhere near here, but Green and Petit Manan islands have birds you're not likely to see elsewhere, including puffins, which visit early summer to early August. And the Petit Manan Lighthouse, rising 123 feet above the water surface, draws the curious toward it just as surely as it warns of its dangers. Odds are, though, you can paddle past, but not land. Green Island is always closed to visitors, while Petit Manan Island is closed April through August.

It is possible to reach Petit Manan and Green islands from Little Bois Bubert Island by heading south past Egg Rock (closed April 15 through July 31), giving the bar from Petit Manan Point a wide berth (although on an ebbing tide you'll need to keep track of your position, to avoid getting pulled over the bar).

Whatever route you choose, plan to be at Petit Manan Island around low tide for the most tidal advantage.

ALTERNATIVES

When conditions deteriorate, the area north of Bois Bubert Island and the head of Pigeon Hill Bay is likely to be more sheltered. In particular, higher tides provide access to the tidal areas of Pigeon Hill Cove and Bobby Creek. If you have plenty of energy, plan an hour after your paddle for a hike up Pigeon Hill (trailhead 0.5 miles north from launch). You'll be rewarded with broad vistas of the Downeast coast.

MORE INFORMATION

Steuben, Maine, Town Office (207-546-7209). Maine Coastal Islands National Wildlife Refuge (fws.gov/refuge/Maine_Coastal_Islands; 207-594-0600). For permission to use the Bois Bubert campsite, contact the U.S. Fish and Wildlife office in Milbridge (207-546-2124).

THE ACADIA REGION AND PENOBSCOT BAY

West of Schoodic Point, Maine's coastline curves northward then west along the edge of Frenchman and Blue Hill bays. Between these bays lies Mount Desert Island, home to Acadia National Park, which welcomes 3 million visitors a year. From the ocean, Mount Desert Island is dominated by the glacially sculpted peaks that give the island its name, with 1,528-foot Cadillac Mountain visible for miles along the coast in either direction. The mountains create a stunning backdrop for several unique pad-

dling trips along some of the most dramatic shoreline in New England.

Once you're out of Bar Harbor (which can be quite busy, especially with a cruise ship in port), the Porcupines (Trip 9) tend to be fairly quiet and free of tour boats, especially close to shore. The cliffs along Ironbound Island's shore (Trip 8) can feel like another world, especially if the conditions are calm enough to venture into one of the sea caves. Just south of Mount Desert Island, the small communities on the Cranberry Isles (Trip 10) feel removed from the hustle and bustle. Enjoy the same, dramatic view of Cadillac and Sargent mountains as the century-old rusticator cottages lining the Cranberry shores. Stop to explore the communities on Great and Little Cranberry islands and Baker Island, where a lighthouse still stands over the remnants of a tiny village. Paddlers will find the quietest paddling off the western shore of Mount Desert Island, in the Gott-Black-Placentia island group (Trip 11) or around Bartlett Island (Trip 12). In the middle of Blue Hill and Jericho Bays, Swans Island (Trip 13) is yet another out-of-the-way microcosm, with its own towns and satellite islands.

Exuding rugged beauty and cultivated charm, the shores of Penobscot Bay tell a tale of settlement that began when the French built a trading post in Castine in 1613, seven years before the Pilgrims arrived in Cape Cod Bay. In the 1800s, logs traveled the Penobscot River from the Great North Woods, were milled in Bangor, and delivered by schooner to busy Penobscot Bay. Now you can paddle past the remains of granite quarries and resorts once serviced by steamships from Boston, their remnants existing side by side with lobster co-ops and businesses catering to visitors. Or for an even more rustic day, land on islands that feel about as wild as they did 400 years ago.

Deer Isle, reachable by a large suspension bridge, has a mix of pastoral and settled shoreline with a number of smaller islands just off its coast. At its southern end, the fishing town of Stonington (Trip 14) overlooks a dense archipelago of spruce-topped granite islands extending to Isle au Haut (Trip 15). These closely spaced islands are frequently described in a spiritual context: a paradise for paddlers, with plenty of public access and camping. Much of the 6-mile-long Isle au Haut is encompassed in a remote unit of Acadia National Park, where surf surges among the rugged cliffs at the southern end.

Occupying the mouth of Penobscot Bay, the Fox Islands (Trip 17) feel distinctly set apart from the rest of the world. More commonly known by their individual names—North Haven and Vinalhaven—the pair are challenging for most paddlers to get to, but it's a worthwhile trip. The islands' shores and the constellations of smaller island groups around them invite nearly endless exploration. One way to get there is along the island stepping stones in the Great Spruce Head Island neighborhood (Trip 16), another archipelago where the islands seem to draw you endlessly onward.

Yet another fashionable summer community established by Bostonians in the late 1800s, Islesboro and its harbors are still home to fleets of eye-catching sailboats. The islands south of it (Trip 18) make for some quieter paddling, with broad views of the bay and the Camden Hills rising above Camden Harbor, which appears almost spiny with sailboat masts. At its southern end, Penobscot Bay widens and the Muscle Ridge Islands (Trip 19) make up yet another idyllic archipelago, perhaps best visited late in summer when we are once again welcome on osprey nesting islands.

8
EASTERN FRENCHMAN BAY

A beautiful chain of large islands stretches 8 miles along the northeast corner of Frenchman Bay, with views of Mount Desert Island's mountains, choices of sheltered or bayside routes, the stunning cliffs along the southern side of Ironbound Island, and a few sea caves.

Distance ▶ 8.0 to 16.0 nautical miles, round-trip

Tidal Planning ▶ 10.56-foot mean tidal range in Bar Harbor. Current floods to the north, ebbs south. Stave Island Bar and parts of Flanders Bay flat-out at low tide.

Cautions ▶ Despite being somewhat sheltered from the open ocean by the mid-bay islands, the Sorrento-Dram-Preble area has enough fetch to the south to develop some big seas, and if the current goes against the wind, waves will steepen. An offshore wind (from the north) can be deceptively dangerous here. The Stave Island Bar develops mudflats at lower tides, and the Jordan Island Bar develops a strong current mid-tide. Watch for opposing wind and waves. Also expect strong currents between Jordan and Ironbound islands. Even on the calmest days, Ironbound Island is no place for the unprepared. Expect rough conditions and no bailouts. Paddlers here should have solid boat-handling and rescue skills.

Charts and Maps ▶ NOAA chart #13312; Maptech #42; Waterproof Chart #105

LAUNCHES

Sorrento Harbor Launch from a ramp, a floating dock, or the gravel beach adjacent to the small parking lot; about twelve parking spaces; portable outhouse and antique payphone. From the intersection of US 1 and ME 185 in Sullivan, take ME 185 south toward Sorrento. In 3.3 miles, continue ahead onto Kearsarge Avenue, then immediately merge right onto Ocean Avenue. Parking is on the left. *GPS coordinates:*

44° 28.310' N, 68° 10.900' W.

South Gouldsboro Concrete ramp; limited parking; no facilities. The parking area fills with vehicles owned by commercial harvesters (there's a lobster facility adjacent to the ramp), but later in the day or in the off-season you can quickly reach the Ironbound Island neighborhood from this ramp. From US 1, take ME 186 south for 3.4 miles to a right on Shore Road. Follow Shore Road 0.3 miles to a small parking area with the launch on the right. *GPS coordinates: 44° 25.950' N, 68° 6.987' W.*

Winter Harbor Town Landing Paved ramp; daytime on-street parking; no facilities. From US 1, take ME 186 6.5 miles to a right on Main Street. The ramp is on the left. *GPS coordinates: 44° 23.673' N, 68° 5.069' W.*

Other Public Access Dram and Preble islands are both owned by The Nature Conservancy (TNC), but are not reliable for easy landings. The south end of Stave Island is protected by a Maine Coast Heritage Trust (MCHT) preserve.

ROUTE DESCRIPTION

At the head of Frenchman Bay, occupying the narrow end of Waukeag Neck, the town of Sorrento is sheltered from the worst of open ocean weather by the mid-bay islands, yet has quick access beyond its sheltered harbor to a broad swath of the water, beyond which rise the mountains of Mount Desert Island. The Penobscots from the Bangor area who summered here left a few shell heaps (known as middens). Later, in the 1880s, the Hotel Sorrento and a steamship service lured wealthy rusticators to what became a grand resort town. Like most grand hotels, it eventually burned down, but the community was established, and the rusticators' influence is obvious not only in the stunning shingle-style cottages around town, but also in a way of life still maintained by the century-old Sorrento Village Improvement Association (VIA). The group ensures that modern-day rusticators have opportunities for croquet, tennis, competitive sailing, golf, and enjoying a saltwater swimming pool. Now the population is about half seasonal and half year-round, with a few fishing boats and recreational craft in the harbor.

Surpassing 800 acres with more than 4 miles of shoreline, Ironbound Island is large enough to encompass most of Bar Harbor, yet this privately owned island is far off the radar of most area visitors. In the late 1800s, artist Dwight Blaney (with the financial support of his wife, an heiress of the Eastern Steamship Company) bought Ironbound as their summer retreat. Over the years, they hosted a number of prominent artists at their home, including John Singer Sargent and others who inspired the greater public with their images of the Maine coast. Their family still summers on the island today. The best way for most of us to see it is from the cockpit of a kayak.

Launching from Sorrento Harbor gives some insight into the quiet side of Frenchman Bay. Across the water, Bar Harbor hums with a constant stream of tourists coming and going by land, sea, and air, a magnet drawing more than its share of visitors; here, however, the surroundings are relatively quiet. A chain of mostly unpopulated

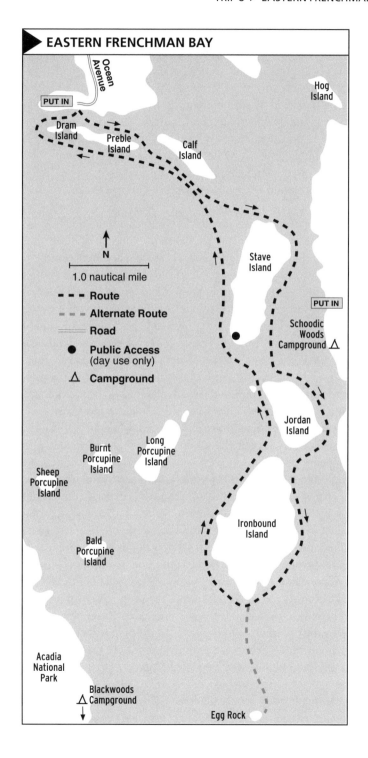

EASTERN FRENCHMAN BAY

Ocean Avenue

PUT IN

Dram Island

Preble Island

Calf Island

Hog Island

Stave Island

PUT IN

Schoodic Woods Campground △

↑ N

1.0 nautical mile

━ ━ ━ **Route**

━ ━ ━ **Alternate Route**

━━━ **Road**

● **Public Access**
(day use only)

△ **Campground**

Jordan Island

Burnt Porcupine Island

Long Porcupine Island

Sheep Porcupine Island

Ironbound Island

Bald Porcupine Island

Acadia National Park

Blackwoods
△ Campground

Egg Rock

islands stretches 8.0 miles from Sorrento south to the magnificent, wave-pounded cliffs of Ironbound Island, with Cadillac Mountain a constant backdrop.

Though the northern islands are somewhat sheltered by the mid-bay islands, there's still plenty of fetch and current to create lively seas. The contrast in conditions between the bay sides and more sheltered sides of the islands can be dramatic; you have the choice of paddling on either, tides permitting.

Public access is not great here. While TNC-owned Dram and Preble islands are open to the public, they don't abound in easy landings. South of Stave Island (MCHT), be ready to stay in the boat for a while. The south side of Ironbound Island has few landing opportunities even in calm seas; only experienced paddlers with solid rescue skills should paddle here.

There's a certain beauty in a route that progresses with the tide from sheltered Sorrento Harbor to the exposed cliffs of Ironbound Island, handrailing along the chain of east Frenchman Bay islands along the way. Try to reach Ironbound Island mid-trip and at low tide. If this can't be arranged, you can also launch from South Gouldsboro or Winter Harbor to go with the current or to more quickly reach Ironbound Island.

Cross Sorrento Harbor, and if the tide is high enough, pass along the north shore of Preble Island. Owned by TNC, limited access helps keep Preble and Dram islands wild, despite their proximity to town. The most likely landing on Dram is on the north side at lower tides. Preble has several cobble pocket beaches tucked among the rocks along the steep southern shore. Calf Island is the site of a former community, but is now privately owned with a house at the south end. Just to the south, Little Calf Island is a tiny uninhabited pile of eroding glacial till, topped by few trees.

The north end of Stave Island is privately owned, while an MCHT preserve occupies part of the south end. Along the inside route, the Stave Island bar flats out—that is, mudflats appearing as the tide goes out—at low tide. To the east of Stave, the village of South Gouldsboro sits on Bunker Cove, a utilitarian working harbor with more lobster boats than pleasure craft; there are no services for visitors nearby. Just west of the harbor, a pair of attractive islets form a small harbor just off a beach on Stave Island where MCHT has a sign. Lilacs and other domestic trees from a former period of habitation mix with the usual spruce that now dominate the island.

Yellow Island (private; previously Red Island) is named for its yellowish-red rock. A color-matched stone house blends in. Privately owned Jordan Island is sided with steep bluffs around the north end. On its east side, ocean depths rise up to the Jordan Island Bar, covered by only a few feet at low water; increased currents and lively conditions can stack up against southern wind or swell. A cabin is tucked into the woods near the southeast point, and another on the southwest side. To the south, the gap between Jordan and Ironbound islands is called Halibut Hole, another constriction where currents increase.

Aside from a couple stretches of cobble beach on its northeast end, the entire east side of Ironbound Island—almost 2 miles of shoreline—is composed of near-vertical cliffs rising right out of the water. The cliffs are rich with features, including multiple chasms with boulders sprinkled beneath the walls, and even a few small sea caves.

This is no place for inexperienced paddlers. The southeast end is exposed to the open ocean with depths quickly dropping to well over a hundred feet. Even a mild day's swell creates plenty of action among the rocks, and bailouts are scarce, especially in bigger conditions. There are few places to paddle in New England as exciting as this.

After you've followed the tall walls down nearly to the south end, there's an uncharacteristic break in the shoreline where Seal Cove pokes inward, often with calmer water inside. This is a good place to catch your breath.

Having paddled the east and south ends of Ironbound, some primeval urge to circumnavigate may tempt you to continue around the west side, along which you'll find a cove with a small dock and a few homes. If you liked the cliffs, you may as well head back the way you came.

ALTERNATIVES

One possible add-on for this trip is Egg Rock (closed April through August for nesting), over a mile south of Ironbound Island's southern end. Egg Rock is a nesting is-

Away from Bar Harbor's tour boats, the eastern side of Frenchman Bay offers plenty to explore, like this cobble beach on Stave Island.

land for gulls and eiders, and boasts an unusual lighthouse built in 1875, with the light tower rising from the peak of the keeper's building. Aside from the predictably bigger conditions you're likely to encounter here, the stretch of water south of Ironbound is a busy one, traveled by tour boats angling for a view of the cliffs, and the usual fishing boats, recreational boats, and the ferries that regularly run between Bar Harbor and Winter Harbor. Landings at this starkly gorgeous, far-out spot are easiest at lower tides at a cobble beach on the north side. The Porcupines (Trip 9) are just to the west. From Ironbound Island, it's about 14 miles east to Petit Manan Point and Bois Bubert Island (Trip 7).

At higher tides, Flanders Bay could be a sheltered area to explore.

MORE INFORMATION

Maine Coast Heritage Trust (mcht.org; 207-729-7366). The Nature Conservancy (nature.org/maine; 207-729-5181); no pets are allowed in the preserve. Mountainview Campground (flandersbay.com; 207-422-6408) in East Sullivan has waterfront campsites and cabins at the head of Flanders Bay.

9
THE PORCUPINES

*The rock-bound islands of Frenchman Bay
with their steep, cliffy shores are just a short
paddle from Bar Harbor.*

Distance ▶	6.0 nautical miles, loop around Long Porcupine Island; similar distance to finish via Bald Porcupine Island
Tidal Planning ▶	10.56-foot mean tidal range in Bar Harbor. Floods north, ebbs south.
Cautions ▶	Heavy boat traffic in the area includes cruise ships and tour boats. The usual southern swell and wind can create lively conditions, especially when it opposes increased current that funnels through the islands.
Charts and Maps ▶	NOAA chart #13312; Maptech #42; Waterproof Chart #105

LAUNCHES

Bridge Street, Bar Harbor Bar connecting Bar Island and Mount Desert Island can be driven on at low tides (be careful of driving on soft, wet sand); use this as a dropoff only and do not park here; parking available on West Street. From the junction of US 1 and ME 3 in Ellsworth, follow ME 3 to Bar Harbor. In 18.1 miles, turn left (east) on West Street and follow it 0.3 mile to Bridge Street to reach the bar launch. *GPS coordinates: 44° 23.527′ N, 68° 12.607′ W.*

Bar Harbor Town Ramp Ramp to water and beach; parking on town pier limited to 3 hours and may be scarce; bathrooms beside harbormaster's office. Be prepared to get some attention here from numerous visitors. *GPS coordinates: 44° 23.484′ N, 68° 12.249′ W.*

Other Public Access Bar Island, Sheep Porcupine Island (closed between February 15 and August 31 for eagle nesting), the Hop, and Bald Porcupine Island are all part of Acadia National Park and are open to the public unless otherwise noted. Long Porcupine Island, owned by The Nature Conservancy.

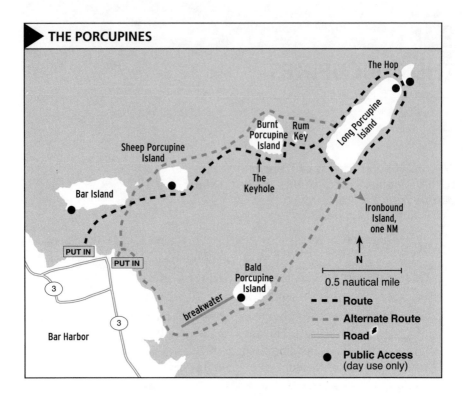

THE PORCUPINES

The Hop

Burnt Rum
Porcupine Key
Island

Long Porcupine Island

Sheep Porcupine
Island

The
Keyhole

Bar Island

Ironbound
Island,
one NM

PUT IN

PUT IN

N

Bald
Porcupine
Island

0.5 nautical mile

3

breakwater

3

- - - Route

- - - Alternate Route

——— Road

Bar Harbor

● Public Access
(day use only)

ROUTE DESCRIPTION

While Bar Harbor has a reputation as a tourist magnet choked with dense traffic
and hordes of cruise ship passengers swarming the small town's T-shirt and fudge
"shoppes," there's more to the place, especially if you have the wherewithal to paddle
a short distance from the downtown hubbub. And odds are, even in midsummer you
can get out to the Porcupines and have them more or less to yourself.

On the water, the commercial kayak tours tend to stay offshore and might venture as far as Rum Key. The larger tour vessels keep even more distance from the
shore—though you're likely to hear some narration about "the kayakers" over the
boats' loudspeakers. While paddling near large cruise ships may be intimidating,
the ships spend most of the day at anchor, with a steady stream of water taxis ferrying
passengers into town and back. The town posts an annual schedule of cruise ships
on its website so it is possible to avoid them or—if you find them interesting—to visit
when several are in town. Peak cruise season is in September and October when up
to four ships arrive at a time.

It's worth a hike or drive up to the top of Cadillac Mountain to have a look at
Frenchman Bay. From the summit, the Porcupines' unusual shape is evident: gently
sloping on the north, steep on the south. About 12,000 years ago, glaciers scoured
the northern sides of the islands into gentle slopes. On the southern ends, however,

the glaciers pulled out the bedrock, forming steep cliffs called *roches mountonnée* (fleecy rock).

Though the guided kayak tours skirt the edges of the Porcupines multiple times daily, do not take the islands lightly. On most days, swells from the open ocean bear down on their coasts and a considerable current develops as the tide squeezes between them. The shores have long, steep stretches with minimal landing opportunities. For skilled rocks and ledges enthusiasts, it's a playground with one enticing feature after another. Still, monitor conditions and choose your day accordingly—and keep an eye out for that monster wave.

For anything more than a 3-hour trip, it probably makes the most sense to launch from the end of Bridge Street. At lower tides, the beach beside the town pier may be preferable, but nearby parking is short term, there's a carry down to the beach, and you can expect an audience, watching and recording from the railing above the amphitheater-like beach. I've waited to launch while foreign visitors posed for photos beside my kayak as if it were a large fish they'd hauled in—all part of the fun.

From either launch, cross the harbor to Bar Island. Barred to a beach at the end of Bridge Street, Bar Island is a popular walking destination at lower tides. Rarely, at just the right tide, southern swells rolling toward the bar create well-formed surfing waves. During the 1800s, Bar and Sheep Porcupine islands were owned by the Rodick family, who pastured livestock there to supply their large hotel in town. Both islands are now mostly owned by Acadia National Park. When crossing to Bar Island, watch for increased current atop the shallow narrows and stay off Sheep Porcupine Island during eagle nesting season (February 15 through August 31).

Cruise ships sometimes anchor north of Sheep Porcupine, so watch for water taxis on the crossing eastward to Burnt Porcupine. Privately owned, undeveloped Burnt Porcupine Island's steep southwest shore has several interesting features, including the Keyhole. Depending on the tide height, this chasm turns narrow before widening on the inside to a tiny cobble beach where the clatter of wave-tossed stones echoes from the walls. At any of these features, watch a few wave sets before getting close.

Continuing east, tiny Rum Key (private, undeveloped) amplifies waves passing to either side of it. If you're looking for a place to land, you can usually find calm enough water on the backside or at a cobble beach nearby on Burnt Porcupine. A shallow area extends to the ledges just east, producing waves that usually break over a submerged ledge: these are often great surfing waves, but watch out for that ledge!

If you haven't already found a spot for a break, Long Porcupine Island, a TNC preserve, is not the easiest spot to take out. Like the other Porcupines, the exposed south side is steep and rocky. Aside from that, it is closed during nesting season. Northeast of Long Porcupine Island, the Hop is a small island owned by Acadia National Park and is a good spot for a break before starting back toward Bar Harbor.

For the return trip, you might opt to retrace the route, visiting features at a different tide. However, if you'd like a change of scenery or more sheltered paddling, make a loop by paddling along the gentler north sides of the islands. If you're returning to Bar Harbor late in the day, the cruise ships are probably getting ready to embark, so be

Even when a cruise ship is in port, paddlers can find their own secluded nooks in the Porcupine Islands.

cautious. Or, cross to Bald Porcupine Island (Acadia National Park) for a little variety. This 32-acre island is shaped much like the other Porcupines. Tall cliffs rise vertically from the ocean on the southern side, and a breakwater extends most of the way to the shore of Mount Desert Island. The most likely places to land are at beaches on the west side. From Bald Porcupine it's an easy paddle back to the harbor beneath the Shore Path.

ALTERNATIVES

Circumnavigating Ironbound Island (Trip 8) adds 5.0 to 6.0 miles if you loop back through the Porcupines to Bar Harbor.

On truly rough days on the ocean, the freshwater lakes of Mount Desert Island offer far calmer options. Launch at Hadley Point or Thompson Island in higher tides to explore Thomas Bay. You could also paddle Northeast Creek; the launch is off ME 3, just 2.0 miles east of the Mount Desert Island Narrows Bridge.

MORE INFORMATION

Bar Harbor (barharbormaine.gov; 207-288-1571 [harbormaster]); cruise ship schedules posted online annually. Acadia National Park (nps.gov/acad; 207-288-3338). The Nature Conservancy (nature.org/maine; 207-729-5181); no pets are allowed in the preserve.

There are no available campsites on-route. There are several nearby campgrounds on Mount Desert Island. Mountainview Campground (flandersbay.com; 207-422-6408) in East Sullivan has waterfront campsites and cabins at the head of Flanders Bay.

SEALS

While seals are safeguarded by the Marine Mammal Protection Act of 1972, they were not always so well loved and respected. Before the turn of the twentieth century, seals were largely blamed for competing with commercial interests for fish and lobsters, and as a result, state governments offered bounties for dead seals. Maine ended its $1 reward in 1905, but Massachusetts held out until 1962, possibly leading to the end of seal breeding in Cape Cod Bay.

Seals mostly eat fish and invertebrates. Their well-developed senses function best in the water. They can swim as fast as 8 miles per hour, dive beyond 1,200 feet, and submerge for up to 40 minutes before needing to resurface for air. Seals also "talk," making diverse, species-specific sounds.

Though they live in the water, seals also need to spend time on land to rest, pup, and molt. They aren't terribly graceful on land and they know it. When they sense danger, seals will rush to the water, even at risk of exhaustion. In their hurry, seals are also prone to injury and can abandon or crush pups. Though to humans our smaller, quieter vessels might seem to pose a lesser threat, seals are more fearful of kayaks than they are of fishing boats. When a seal spots the stealthy profile of a kayaker—even one attempting to be quiet and nonintrusive—an alarm goes up, and a panicked exodus into the water ensues.

Stay at least a hundred yards from seals; this is the law. Watch for signs that you might be too close for their comfort, even if you are more than the lawful hundred yards away. They often know you're there before you see them. Watch for raised heads, indicating that they are aware of your presence. Other signs that you are too close may include vocalization (seals seeming to grumble about your presence) and any change from their normal resting position (stretching, yawning, waving flippers).

If you come across a seal pup that has been left behind, do not intervene. Mothers leave their pups for long periods while they go out to hunt, so you may not know if the pup has truly been abandoned without observing for an extended period, and your scent may deter the mother from caring for the pup when she returns. While little can be done for an abandoned pup—they are not likely to survive long in captivity—call NOAA's Marine Animal Reporting Hotline at 866-755-6622.

In New England, we're most likely to see harbor seals, which are plentiful in some areas. This species spends most of its time in the Gulf of Maine, with the greatest concentrations occurring in Machias (Trip 4) and Penobscot bays (Trips 14 to 19) and off Mount Desert and Swans islands (Trips 8 to 13). In Connecticut, look for harbor seals around Hammonasset Beach and the Norwalk Islands (Trip 50). In Rhode Island, Rome Point in North Kingstown is a popular harbor seal haulout.

Adults average from 150 to 250 pounds and 4 to 5 feet long, and have some canine characteristics. In profile, their short muzzles and concave foreheads resemble those of small dogs, and their speech is often referred to as barking. They are easily distinguished from gray seals, but to be sure, look for the broad V of their nostrils, which almost meet at the bottom. Harbor seal mating takes place in the water from early May to August, while pupping occurs in late April to mid-June when the pregnant females seek protected islands and ledges in the upper reaches of bays and estuaries. Pups are nursed for 4 to 6 weeks. In late summer, they move offshore to deeper water. They may live as long as 35 years.

Imposing gray seals are less common in New England. Adult males grow to 8 feet and 800 pounds. When confronted, they are likely to stand their ground and may even be aggressive. If you invade their territory, they may follow you, sometimes for miles. And if an 800-pound gray seal jumps out of the water to give you a warning splash, you will certainly feel chastised. Gray seals tend to choose more exposed offshore haulouts than those of harbor seals. Most likely found from Frenchman Bay to Penobscot Bay (Trips 8 through 19), they may also range as far south as Nantucket, with a large colony on the Monomoy Islands (Trip 37).

Gray seals have broad, donkey-like snouts. When viewed from the front, their nostrils form a W. Males compete for breeding privileges, and the biggest, most aggressive specimens may horde four to six females for themselves. Competition may contribute to males' shorter, 35-year life expectancy, as opposed to females' 45 years.

Gray seal pups stay ashore for the 2 to 3 weeks that they nurse. Then they shed their white pup coat and enter the water, where they fend for themselves, often wandering far from their birthplace. About half of the pups die in their first year.

Harp and hooded seals are rare in New England, most often spotted on ice in winter. Both species are still commercially hunted in Canada, Norway, and several other countries. While they are mostly valued for their pelts, the seals' meat is also used, generally sold to Asian markets for pet food. Oil from the blubber is used as a fish oil supplement. In 2010, the price for a pelt averaged about $21. Fortunately, harbor seals and gray seals have little commercial value.

10
THE CRANBERRY ISLANDS

Enjoy two lighthouses, a long beach with sometimes surfable waves, and a marsh you can paddle through at high tide, all in the shadow of Mount Desert Island.

Distance ▶	10.0 nautical miles, round-trip, from the Little Cranberry Island launch; add 3.0 nautical miles to go around Baker Island
Tidal Planning ▶	10.56-foot mean tidal range in Bar Harbor.
Cautions ▶	Heavy recreational traffic. South sides of islands are exposed to full ocean conditions. Current in Western Way can be strong.
Charts and Maps ▶	NOAA chart #13312; Maptech #42; Waterproof Chart #105

LAUNCHES

Northeast Harbor Town Dock Paved ramp; ample parking; restrooms. After crossing the ME 3 bridge onto Mount Desert Island, continue straight onto ME 102/198 where ME 3 bears left. After 4.3 miles, turn left (east) at the light onto ME 3/198 toward Northeast Harbor. In 5.6 miles, continue straight on ME 198 for another 0.7 mile. Turn right on Harbor Drive, and follow signs to the town dock. *GPS coordinates: 44° 17'40.2" N, 68° 17'02.4' W.*

Southwest Harbor Town Ramp and Dock Paved ramp next to Coast Guard Station or town dock with an inconvenient carry; 3-hour parking only near ramp, and very limited longer term parking a short walk away; more parking, including 24-hour spots, available near dock; portable outhouse near dock. After crossing the ME 3 bridge onto Mount Desert Island, continue straight onto ME 102/198 where ME 3 bears left. Continue 10.7 miles on ME 102/198 into Southwest Harbor, then turn left on Clark Point Road. *GPS coordinates: 44° 16.608' N, 68° 18.808' W* (ramp).

Manset Public Ramp Beach launch adjacent to a paved ramp and dock with floats; gravel parking lot, with no overnight; portable outhouse. From Southwest Harbor, go south on ME 102. Turn left onto ME 102A. After 0.6 mile, turn left on Ocean House Road, then a right on Shore Road to the parking area. *GPS coordinates: 44° 16.155' N, 68° 18.650' W.*

Seal Harbor Sandy beach, long carry at low tide; parking lot; restrooms. After crossing the ME 3 bridge onto Mount Desert Island, continue straight onto ME 102/198 where ME 3 bears left. After 4.3 miles, turn left (east) at the light onto ME 3/198 toward Northeast Harbor. In 5.6 miles, turn left onto ME 3. Follow for 2.9 miles to a parking area on the left. *GPS coordinates: 44° 17.783' N, 68° 14.455' W.*

Other Public Access Great and Little Cranberry islands both have public landings. Most of Baker Island is in Acadia National Park and is open to the public. The Cranberry Shores Preserve, owned by the Maine Coast Heritage Trust (MCHT), is located on the south end of Great Cranberry Island but has limited access from the water.

ROUTE DESCRIPTION

Not far from the shores of Mount Desert Island, the Cranberry Islands occupy their own, quieter orbit in the Mount Desert galaxy. Life in these island communities passes at a far more relaxed pace than in the thriving tourist destination only 3 miles away. Named for the wild cranberries that grow in the marshes, both islands have small year-round populations that swell during summer months when classic boats once again occupy their moorings beneath century-old "cottages." Depending on conditions, you can paddle to the more settled north sides and explore the islands on foot, or venture into the exposed water south of the islands, where the swells are likely to break over the numerous ledges even on calm days. Bring insect repellent if you

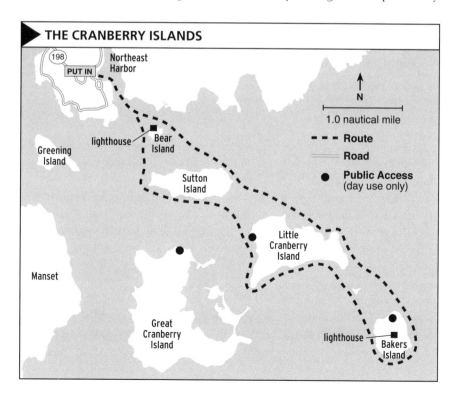

THE CRANBERRY ISLANDS

As you approach Sutton Island, look for a tall rock near the northwest point occupied by a decades-old osprey nest—probably one of the largest you'll see.

plan on walking: the islands have a reputation for fierce mosquitoes. It would be tough to squeeze in everything on a day trip to the Cranberries, and the only overnight accommodation is a small site for MITA members.

The area is dense with both fishing and recreational traffic, so be alert and minimize time spent in channels. Depending on where you launch, crossing either Western or Eastern Way is necessary. Launching in Northeast Harbor shortens channel crossings to more manageable lengths between Bear, Sutton, and Little Cranberry islands, and while the east-west current may be strong at times, you're less likely to find yourself paddling against it than in Western Way.

From the Northeast Harbor launch, cross the channel to the east side and head out to Bear Island. The harbor and its approaches are busy with boat traffic; avoid the channels. Bear Island is private, but the still-functioning lighthouse stands above a forested, elevated shoreline and is best viewed from some distance.

As you approach Sutton Island, look for a tall rock near the northwest point occupied by a decades-old osprey nest—probably one of the largest you'll see. A town dock at Fernald Point (on the west side) provides public access to this privately owned island. A network of boardwalks and trails lead to the seasonal homes that dot the shoreline. Much of the island is undeveloped. On the east end, great rocky fins and dikes extend into the water, creating chasms and passages through which you can paddle. The house formerly occupied by Rachel Field, a writer best known for the novel *Hitty, Her First Hundred Years* (1929), sits on the island's northeast side.

Little Cranberry Island is often referred to as Islesford after its western village of historic homes overlooking Cranberry Harbor. The harbor is a nexus of boat traffic, so be alert as you enter. Kayakers may land beside the town dock in Hadlock Cove to explore the town and its museum, restaurant, and galleries. Most homes on the 200-acre island cluster around the north and west sides; the rest of the island's shores are mostly undeveloped. South of town, a row of old fishing shacks have been converted into residences overlooking a beach. The southern point, known locally as the Maypole, juts into the Gut, a narrow passage between Great and Little Cranberry islands where currents increase.

Steep cobble beaches stretch over more than a mile of the southern side of Little Cranberry. While the beaches are exposed to the open ocean, a stretch of shallower water often saps the energy of incoming swells; depending on the tide, surfing waves can be found here, especially at the east end. A former Coast Guard lifesaving station, now a residence, stands upon Bar Point overlooking a shallow stretch of ledges leading almost a mile to Baker Island, where a lighthouse at the top barely pokes above the treetops.

Acadia National Park owns most of Baker Island, maintaining several of the buildings. Look for landing spots on either side of the ledges and follow a path up through the meadow to the lighthouse. White buildings are owned by the National Park Service, red ones are private. Settled in 1806 by Hannah and William Gilley, 123-acre Baker Island has been home to a lighthouse since 1828. The present 43-foot-tall tower was built in 1855, and stands 105 feet over sea level. A small building nearby hosts a display of photos and artifacts detailing the island's history. Most of the shoreline is dominated by rocks and ledges and is subject to wave action even in mild swell. On the south side, the Dance Floor or Dancing Rocks is a series of large, nearly flat slabs of granite where islanders held dances long ago.

Head back to Little Cranberry, following the eastern shore to Marsh Head. Almost another island, the head is separated by a marsh that can be explored at higher tides. This is a good place to watch for birds or to take shelter on windy days.

Ideally, the trip back to Northeast Harbor via Sutton and Bear islands would be done on a rising or slack tide. If not, it could take less effort to go directly to the Mount Desert Island shore and follow it back to the harbor in areas with less current.

ALTERNATIVES

A trip around Great Cranberry Island could add more than 5 nautical miles to a route. The island's homes are spread out, with numerous stretches of undeveloped shoreline. Land at the town dock in Spurling Cove on the north side, where there are public restrooms, two cafes, a historic museum, a public library, and a public hiking trail that leaves from Cranberry House. On Great Cranberry's east side, the Pool is a large, shallow basin, much of which flats out at lower tides. Keep this sheltered area in mind during rough conditions elsewhere. The south end of the island is generally rugged and steep, subject to swells from the open ocean. At Bunker Head, Cranberry Shores Preserve (MCHT) has a hiking trail overlooking its rugged shores. Plan for current in Western Way, where speeds increase over the shallower area between Seawall and Great Cranberry; accordingly, increased conditions may follow. A solo paddler in a recreational kayak drowned in this vicinity in 2009.

For more sheltered routes, consider Somes Sound, but note that it can get significant north–south winds. In Valley Cove, just north of the entrance on the west side, you can drift beneath the steep, dramatic flanks of St. Sauveur and Flying mountains. When it's rough on the ocean, a freshwater paddle on Long Pond may be an option

MORE INFORMATION

Mount Desert Harbormaster (Northeast Harbor, Seal Harbor; 207-276-5737). Southwest Harbor Harbormaster (207- 244-7913. Acadia National Park (nps.gov/acad; 207-288-3338). Cranberry Shores Preserve (mcht.org/preserves/cranberry-shores-preserve .shtml; 207-729-7366). The only on-route camping option is available only to MITA members. Blackwoods and Seawall campgrounds in Acadia National Park may also be convenient, but cannot be accessed from the water.

11
PLACENTIA, BLACK, AND GOTT ISLANDS

Sculpted pink granite dominates these wild,
uninhabited shores

Distance ▶ 7.0 to 13.0 nautical miles, round-trip

Tidal Planning ▶ 10.56-foot mean tidal range in Bar Harbor. Current over the Bass Harbor Bar floods west (into Blue Hill Bay) and ebbs to the east. Elsewhere in the islands the currents are complex, hard to predict, and can form tide rips and eddies.

Cautions ▶ Strong currents around all of these islands, especially over the Bass Harbor Bar. Heavy boat traffic. Watch for the Swans Island/Frenchboro ferry that docks on the east side of the harbor.

Charts and Maps ▶ NOAA chart #13312; Maptech #42; Waterproof Chart #105

LAUNCH

Tremont Town Landing Concrete ramp, which is primary access for commercial fishing vessels; limited parking; portable outhouse behind the harbormaster's office. You may need to drop off gear and park on Rice or Bernard roads. After crossing the ME 3 bridge onto Mount Desert Island, continue straight onto ME 102/198 where ME 3 bears left. Follow ME 102 for 13.2 miles. At the junction with ME 102A, stay right and take an immediate right to stay on ME 102 for another 0.9 mile. On the way, pass the bridge at the head of the harbor; turn left on Bernard Road then left on Rice Road in 0.6 mile. The landing is on the right. *GPS coordinates: 44° 14.400′ N, 68° 21.161′ W.*

Other Public Access Tremont maintains a town landing on Great Gott Island. The Maine Coast Heritage Trust (MCHT) protects Black and Little Black islands, and the Great Gott Preserve on that island's east side. Placentia Island is owned by The Nature Conservancy (TNC).

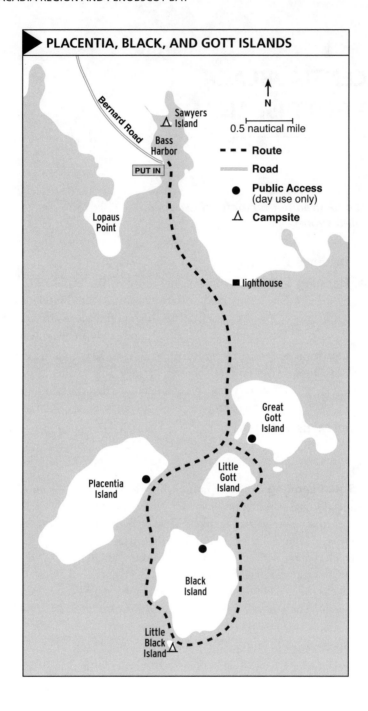

PLACENTIA, BLACK, AND GOTT ISLANDS

ROUTE DESCRIPTION

There is no perfect tidal timing for this route, but departing on a falling tide and re-turning on a rising tide will give you the most tidal assistance. That said, such a plan would also put you into potentially chaotic areas like the Bass Harbor Bar when cur-rents are running stronger. Some paddlers may welcome the interesting conditions, while others may prefer to avoid them, perhaps crossing in wider areas or at slack tide.

Launch at the town landing (be mindful of boat traffic here and on your crossing), and cross to the east side, following the shore out to Bass Harbor Head. A dredged channel runs close to the shore near the lighthouse on the head, where conditions will likely be tamer. (If you prefer to avoid the bar completely, follow the west shore out to Lopaus Point and make the longer, 1.75-nautical-mile crossing to Placentia Island.) The Bass Harbor Head Lighthouse, with its distinctive red light that flashes every 4 seconds, is one of the more-often photographed lights around; it's worth planning a photo break beneath it.

Be mindful of the current direction during the 1.0-mile crossing over to Great Gott Island (floods to the west). Start on the downcurrent side of the bar if you prefer not to be pulled over it. Otherwise, aim for the meadows on the north end of Great Gott and make your way around the west side to the village of Gotts Island and its town landing. Inhabited as early as the late 1600s, Gotts Island's population peaked around 1900 with more than 100 year-round residents. The year-round community dwindled in the 1920s and the homes were bought by summer residents. The exception was Mont Gott, who was born on the island in the 1880s and lived alone there from 1938 until 1960. Great Gott Island is featured in the novels of island native Ruth Moore. The gap between the bar at Little Gott Island develops strong currents until it flats out at lower tides. Assuming you're here on a falling tide, ride the current southeast and follow the shore to the south side of Little Gott Island (private) and its rounded granite bluffs exposed to the open ocean. A little swell can make conditions lively here. If you'd prefer quieter water, follow the west side instead.

Again, be mindful of the current as you cross between Little Gott to Black Island where tide rips may develop mid-tide. Like the east side of Little Gott, Black Island's east shore is sculpted from pink granite with numerous features, including a couple of slots worth paddling into in the right conditions. Several offshore ledges also develop lively conditions when any swell comes in.

MCHT owns the northern two-thirds of 451-acre Black Island, and a 120-acre parcel at the south end where it's barred to Little Black Island. Extensive quarrying took place on Black Island from 1884 to around 1910. Three granite companies op-erated near the island's northeast corner, where a narrow-gauge railway ran from a pier to the quarries. Stonecutters, some locally born and some recently arrived from Italy, manned the quarries. A boarding house and an on-island school supported their families.

Follow the south shore to Little Black Island, an MCHT preserve with two camp-sites. Higher-tide landings may take a little more effort, especially in bumpy con-ditions. A walk around the perimeter on smooth, pink granite ledge takes about 10 minutes, affording sweeping views out to the Duck Islands and Long Island. Continue along the west shore of Black Island, past a cove with a gravel beach, a good alternate rest stop if conditions make landing on Little Black difficult. Salmon pens dominate the water off of Black's west shore. At any point here, you could cross over to Placentia Island and follow the shore to the sandbar at the northeast end.

Uninhabited Placentia Island (locally pronounced "pla-sench") is owned by TNC. The 522-acre island, whose name is a corruption of the French *plaisance* (pleasure), is best known for its most recent inhabitants, Art and Nan Kellam, who lived there from 1949 to 1984, and left the island to TNC. The Kellams' tenure here is documented in the book *We Were an Island* by Peter P. Blanchard III. The island was also inhabited as early as Revolutionary times and farmed for more than 40 years in the early 1800s by Robert Mitchell and his family, who shared the island with 30 to 40 inhabitants. The northeast sandbar is an easy place to land. Just to the west,

Black Island's east shore is sculpted from pink granite with numerous features, including a couple of slots worth paddling into in the right conditions.

beside some TNC signs, a trail leads to the site of the Kellams' home and its bronze commemorative plaque.

To get back to Bass Harbor, head across to Little Gott and Gott Islands, retracing your route over the bar to the lighthouse, or head straight across to Lopaus Point.

ALTERNATIVES

For a longer route, take a trip to Swans Island (Trip 13).

At higher, rising tides, Bass Harbor Marsh and Marshall Brook are part of a large, grassy estuary stretching 1.5 miles inland. Sheltered from the open ocean, this serene, out-of-the-way stretch of water has several branches to explore. Be careful below the bridge: swift water develops here at all but slack tides.

MORE INFORMATION

Maine Coast Heritage Trust (mcht.org; 207-729-7366). The Nature Conservancy (nature.org/maine; 207-729-5181). Campsites are available on Little Black Island (MCHT) and Sawyers Island (town-owned, 0.3 nautical miles north of town landing). There are also several nearby campgrounds on Mount Desert Island.

12
BARTLETT ISLAND

*An easy-to-reach island with more than
11 miles of rocky, mostly wild shoreline
and nearby public access islands with
beautiful campsites.*

Distance ▶ 8.0 nautical miles, round-trip

Tidal Planning ▶ 10.56-foot mean tidal range in Bar Harbor. Floods to the
north, ebbs to the south.

Cautions ▶ The current in Bartlett Narrows can create choppy conditions when opposing wind or swell. The west and south
sides of Bartlett are exposed to a broad stretch of water and
subject to wind, swell, and the currents in Blue Hill Bay.

Charts and Maps ▶ NOAA chart #13312; Maptech #42; Waterproof Chart #105

LAUNCHES

Bartlett Landing, Mount Desert Paved ramp or gravel beach; very limited parking;
portable outhouse. This launch has a reputation for being crowded midsummer.
After crossing the ME 3 bridge onto Mount Desert Island, continue straight onto
ME 102/198 where ME 3 bears left. Follow ME 102 for 5.1 miles to its junction with
ME 102 N/Pretty Marsh Road. In 3.5 miles, turn right onto Indian Point Road, then
make a slight left onto Bartlett's Landing Road in another 0.3 mile. Follow Bartlett's
Landing Road 1.0 mile to its end. *GPS coordinates: 44° 20.592' N, 68° 25.014' W.*

Seal Cove Public Landing, Tremont Paved ramp or gravel beach; daytime and
overnight parking; portable outhouse. Follow above directions, but continue south on
Pretty Marsh Road/ME 102 N/Tremont Road another 1.6 miles and make a right on
Cape Road. The launch is 0.5 mile down Cape Road. *GPS coordinates: 44° 16.983'
N, 68° 24.514' W.*

Other Public Access Though private, several of Bartlett Island's western cobble
beaches are open for public landings (look for posted signs). The Hub and Johns
Island, both state-owned, each feature one public, two-person campsite managed by
the Maine Island Trail Association (MITA). Folly Island (day use only) is owned by
the Maine Coast Heritage Trust (MCHT).

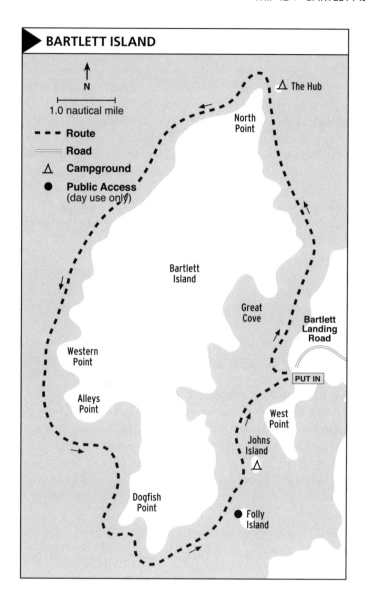

BARTLETT ISLAND

N

1.0 nautical mile

- - - Route
——— Road
△ Campground
● Public Access
(day use only)

The Hub

North Point

Bartlett Island

Great Cove

Bartlett Landing Road

Western Point

PUT IN

Alleys Point

West Point

Johns Island

Dogfish Point

Folly Island

ROUTE DESCRIPTION

Less than 0.5 mile across Bartlett Narrows from Mount Desert Island, Bartlett Island is more than 3 miles long with more than 11 miles of rocky, mostly wild shoreline. While the island is privately owned with several year-round homes on it, there are many undeveloped stretches of shoreline with public access and camping on some tiny islands nearby.

David and Peggy Rockefeller purchased 2,400-acre Bartlett Island in 1973 and began raising cattle in its inland pastures. They limited further development with conservation easements, and though camping and fires are prohibited, signs along the western shore don't discourage landing on its cobble beaches. Expect to share the area with a few others. Plenty of lobster boats moor in these harbors and plenty of recreational craft take to the water here, including flotillas of guided tandem kayak tours between Seal Cove and Bartlett Landing.

Though tidal planning is important, you're unlikely to have the current behind you the whole time. It would certainly be helpful to have it at your back in the narrowest part of Bartlett Narrows, where the currents may reach 2 knots. The current will matter less on the west side of the island. If you find yourself going against the current, move to the side of the channel and look for eddies or slower-moving water. This description proceeds counterclockwise, starting north through Bartlett Narrows on a flooding tide, but a clockwise circumnavigation would be just as enjoyable with the right current and conditions.

Just off the northeast end of Bartlett Island, the Hub is a big rock with a few trees atop it. The state-owned island has a two-person campsite maintained by MITA nestled in the trees; the site is open to the public and is first come, first served. The easiest landing is tide-dependent, but there are sandy areas at both the north and south ends that uncover at lower tides.

Around North Point, the rocks slope directly into the water, while the northwest shore gradually slopes down several gravel beaches. With the prevailing southwest winds, the conditions in this area give you a glimpse of things to come. You can always explore the Bartlett Narrows if it's rougher here than you'd like.

A series of rocky points separates cobble pocket beaches along the rest of the west shore. A boulder identifies Rock Point. A cabin overlooks the cove north of Western Point, the first sign of development as you head toward the year-round homes and expansive meadows around Alleys Point. Residences dwindle then disappear around Dogfish Point to Dogfish Cove, where the steep cliffs of Eastern Point drop straight into the water, with rockweed draped from overhangs at low tide. There's a nice beach at the head of this cove.

Hardwood Island (private) lies just south of Eastern Point. Continue around the south end of Bartlett, beneath the steep sides of Eastern Point and Old Field Hill. This is a good spot to head across to 7-acre Folly Island (MCHT), which is open for day use. According to one legend, it was named by a judge's displeasure over two Bartletts' dispute regarding a title to the tiny island. Used mostly for timber, oats, and sheep, Folly once had a house on its northern end. Just to the north, Johns Island sits just outside Pretty Marsh Harbor. One small MITA campsite—available to the public first come, first served—is perched amid the poplars on the grassy peak of the 1-acre island, within view of a few homes on Mount Desert Island.

Along Bartlett's eastern shore, Birch Cove is a pastoral respite from most sea conditions during higher tides; enter it at the entrance marked by Birch Island. A landing just north of the cove provides access for the island residents who cross the Narrows on a small car ferry.

ALTERNATIVES

Launching from Seal Cove adds about 6 miles to the route. If you launched from Seal Cove, you could paddle along Hardwood's shore on your return trip.

If conditions south or west of Bartlett are too rough, Bartlett Narrows might be sheltered enough to paddle, but be aware that the changing tide can turn the Narrows rough as well. At higher tides Mill Cove and Squid Cove, just north of Bartlett Narrows, can be sheltered, lovely routes, as can the islands north of High Head in Western Bay.

MORE INFORMATION

Maine Island Trail Association (mita.org, 207-761-8225). Maine Coast Heritage Trust Folly Island Preserve (mcht.org/preserves/folly-island.shtml; 207-729-7366).

In Dogfish Cove on Bartlett Island's southern end, steep cliffs drop straight into the water, with rockweed draped from overhangs at low tide.

THE MERITS OF FOLLOWING THE SHORE

Only a few quick miles from the launch, my mind was still so tethered to land-bound concerns that I nearly cruised past the cove entirely. By chance, my eye caught sight of icicles dangling from a frozen waterfall. I couldn't resist and turned toward shore. I paddled beside rocky cliffs, drifting past one majestic, ice-covered cascade after another, when I saw movement on the beach: a coyote pawing through washed-up rockweed. I didn't dare lift my paddle—its drips seemed suddenly loud—but the kayak drifted closer. The coyote looked up, maybe 40 feet away, then turned and loped away into the forest.

From a distance standpoint, my detour to see the icicles added a quarter-mile to my trip, but it was easily the best quarter-mile of the day. The question comes up all the time, both when planning ahead and making route decisions on the go: do you take the most direct point-to-point route, or do you curve inland a bit and see more shoreline?

While open water and larger crossings bring their own challenges and high points, close-to-shore routes have their own advantages—and they're not all about catching a glimpse of the wildlife.

In most places, sticking to shore keeps you away from the bigger boat traffic. And even without the surprises, you see much more along the shore than you would on open water.

When you track the curving shoreline, also known as contour paddling, your kayak can take you into a zone for which it is distinctively suited. As you get closer to the shore, you may discover that you can get in among those rocks, where you may find hidden chasms and passages. Challenges appear: can you make it through that gap? Could you get over those rocks on the crest of a wave? The answer isn't always "yes." We all leave our share of gelcoat behind, but we become better paddlers for it. As opposed to deep, open water, the tide here changes the landscape by the minute. You could paddle here every day and it would be different each time.

Even when paddling inshore, continue to be attentive to conditions offshore. Small seas can turn into big waves when they roll into shallows where there's more to run into, much of it very hard and covered with sharp barnacles.

There's a fine line between peacefully negotiating inshore passages and riding waves through them; many a contour paddler has evolved into a thrill-seeking "rock gardening" adrenaline junkie, but the consequences of making a mistake here can be high. If you go this route, getting some instruction is a good idea. Putting on a helmet doesn't make you invincible.

In the end, it's for you to choose. Do you merely wish to get from Point A to Point B? Or do you paddle for that moment of magic along the way? For most of us, the answer lies somewhere in between.

13
SWANS ISLAND

Explore miles of wild shoreline and several villages on this big island and its neighbors.

Distance ▶ 21.0 to 25.0 nautical miles, round-trip; add 3.0 to 4.0 miles, round-trip, to reach Little Black Island's campsites

Tidal Planning ▶ 9.86-foot mean tidal range. Strong currents in Jericho and Blue Hill bays, flooding north, ebbing south. Casco Passage floods east.

Cautions ▶ The areas of Jericho and Blue Hill bays that flank Swans Island develop strong currents and are exposed to open ocean conditions, creating the potential for very rough seas. Watch for boat traffic, particularly in Casco Passage. The south side of Swans is exposed to prevailing wind and swell from the south. The current between the Sister Islands increases and interacts with conditions, sometimes creating large standing waves.

Charts and Maps ▶ NOAA chart #13312; Maptech #42; Waterproof Chart #105

LAUNCHES

Naskeag Point, Brooklin A state-maintained gravel beach launch and ramp; ample parking; portable outhouses in summer. From the junction of US 1 and ME 15 in Orland, follow ME 15 south toward Blue Hill. In 12.4 miles, take a right on ME 15/172/176 and follow to the roundabout, where you will take the third exit left (southeast) onto ME 172/175. You'll have the Tradewinds grocery store on your right, the Dunkin' Donuts on your left. After 2.5 miles, turn right (east) onto ME 175 and follow 9.3 miles to Brooklin. Turn right (southeast) onto Naskeag Point Road and follow it 3.6 miles to the boat launch at the end. *GPS coordinates: 44° 13.752′ N, 68° 32.079′ W.*

Other Public Access Mahoney Island, part of the Maine Coastal Islands National Wildlife Refuge (MCINWR), is closed for nesting season, April through August. The Triangles and Crow Island are both state-owned, though Crow poses the better opportunity for a landing. Swans, Little Black (also Trip 11; two campsites), West Sister (closed when eagles are nesting), Frenchboro Long, Marshall (campsites by

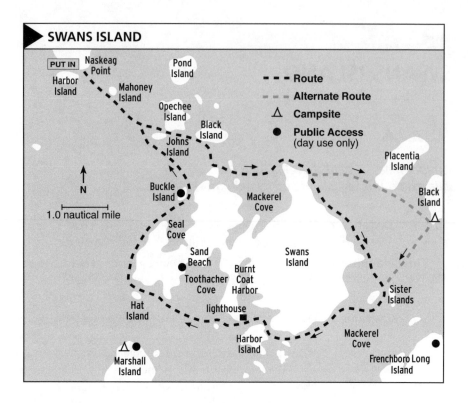

reservation), and Buckle islands are all homes to Maine Coast Heritage Trust (MCHT) preserves. Just off Naskeag Point, Hog Island (MCHT) as well as state-owned Little Hog and Sellers islands (managed by MITA) all have campsites.

ROUTE DESCRIPTION

Spanning some 7,000 acres and miles of contorted shoreline, Swans Island is a paddling destination much less traveled than surrounding areas. Swans lies near the mouth of Blue Hill and Jericho bays, splitting the waters between Deer Isle and Mount Desert Island. Most people get there on the car ferry that travels from Bass Harbor six times daily, but skilled paddlers might island-hop from Naskeag Point, Stonington, or Bass Harbor.

With a year-round population of around 350 that triples in the summer, Swans isn't big on amenities—in fact promotional blurbs seem to welcome those who can entertain themselves. (Kayakers will find ample opportunity for excitement in the miles of shoreline and the surrounding islands.) There are no stores or liquor sales, but a few take-out restaurants open in the summer, and a small year-round inn caters to visitors. Hiking trails crisscross the island, some contained in several preserves that are open to the public. There's a library, a small marine museum, a lighthouse with public grounds, and a quarry pond, open for swimming. Lobster fishing is the mainstay of the economy, with much of the activity based in Burnt Coat Harbor, between the villages of Swans Island and Minturn. The ferry arrives near the northern point at the village of Atlantic. Residences are spread around the island, but there are plenty of long stretches of undeveloped shoreline.

Paddling to Swans should only be undertaken by experienced paddlers, with an eye on the weather for the return trip since conditions may change drastically. Launching from Naskeag Point requires a 2.0-mile crossing.

From the launch, this route crosses Jericho Bay and circumnavigates Swans Island. It could be done as a day trip or as an overnight, paddling either 9.0 miles around the north side of Swans to camp on Little Black Island or Marshall Island, or 14 or so miles around the south side, doing the other half on the second day. A trip this long could get a bit tedious if you don't have the current behind you. Ideally, head south on a falling tide, north on a rising tide. Potential for rough conditions while crossing either bay is lessened if undertaken around slack tide.

Another multiday option: camp at one of the islands just off Naskeag Point, near the launch. Hog Island (MCHT) has campsites at the head of either large cove near the island's midsection. Nearby Little Hog and Sellers islands are state-owned with campsites managed by MITA.

From the launch, follow a line southeast: past the end of Harbor Island, past the steep rocky hump of Smuttynose Island, and on to Mahoney Island. Mahoney is part of the MCINWR and is off-limits during nesting season (April through August), but it's a good spot to pause a moment and savor the stink of guano before proceeding. Continue on the same bearing about 1.5 miles to the gap between Opechee and Johns islands (at lower tides, go south of Johns). The ledges continue for a ways to the east. Graze the southern shore of Black Island and cross Casco Passage, a popular thoroughfare where you're likely to see some traffic. The easiest place to start a quick crossing might be just north of Orono Island. The current here floods to the east, ebbs west. Continuing east, both the Triangles and Crow Island are state-owned, treeless, and uninhabited. Crow Island has a ground shell beach on the west side at low enough tide, not a bad spot for a break.

East of Crow Island look for the north–south channel leading into Mackerel Cove, and watch for the ferry rounding Swans Island's North Point on its way to the dock near Fir Point. You can land at the small gravel beach beside the ferry dock and walk into the village of Atlantic, or head around North Point and follow the shore southeast along the beach to Burnt Point.

Cross here if you're headed to the campsites on Little Black Island (MCHT; Trip 11), especially if the tide is still falling. For a range (lining up two objects to determine your right or left movement), line up Staple Ledge (marked by green can #1) with the west end of Plancentia Island (also Trip 11); the ocean squeezes into the gap between Swans and Placentia and considerably increases current here. The charts list tide rips to the north, but this whole area is likely to produce interesting and not entirely pre-dictable currents.

From Little Black Island, aim for Swans's East Point or the Sister Islands. West Sister is an MCHT preserve that may have nesting eagles. The funnel-shaped gap between the Sisters points inward to a shallow bar—a recipe for tide rips, which occur on the ebb and the flood.

The northeast shore of Swans has a few scattered homes, but the stretch between Red Point to Stanley Point remains undeveloped. From here, you could detour about a mile and a half south to Frenchboro Long Island. A year-round fishing community clusters around Lunt Harbor at the north end, but much of the island is encompassed by a 1,159-acre MCHT preserve with more than 5 miles of shoreline. Depending on conditions, land at the cobble beaches on one of the southeast coves to take in the wildly gorgeous scenery. As of 2016, camping is allowed in designated sites.

Marshall Island, another worthy detour just a few miles southeast from Swans, does have overnight options (call for reservations). At 985 acres, Marshall is the largest undeveloped island on the eastern seaboard. A deserted airstrip remains from development plans abandoned before the island became an MCHT preserve with well-maintained trails and campsites. Drinking water is available from a well with a hand pump near the west end of the airstrip (near the island's north end); fires are only allowed by permit.

If you're not taking a detour, follow the shore of Swans north of the Baker Islands through the passage between Harbor Island and Stanley Point, and into Burnt Coat Harbor. Early French explorers called Swans *Brûle Côte* (burnt coast) probably due to a recent fire. By 1754 British charts had Anglicized the name to Burnt Coat, a name that stuck to the harbor. North of the point is a public landing. From here it's only a short walk to a swimming quarry, and a bit farther to the village of Minturn and its general store. In the water, proceed west, south of Hockamock Head Lighthouse to the mouth of Toothacher Cove. To the northwest, Fine Sand Beach, a town park, sits at the head of Sand Cove. The beach makes a good spot for a break.

Otherwise, set a course for Irish Point and round the mostly undeveloped southwest corner of Swans, inside of Hat Island and around West Point. Pass a few homes along shore on your way toward Swans Island Head and Buckle Island beyond, which is another good spot for a break. To the east of Buckle, Buckle Harbor is a popular anchorage, flanked by MCHT preserves on Buckle and Swans islands.

By this point, if you've circumnavigated the island in a day, you're probably ready to get back to Naskeag as directly as possible. From the north end of Buckle it's almost a straight shot along Johns, Mahoney, and Smuttynose, and it will certainly help if you have the flooding tide behind you.

Be careful crossing Casco Passage: the channel splits, sending the southern boats south, sometimes making a sharp turn toward Buckle Harbor. The conditions are likely to pick up a bit here as well, as the deeper water of Jericho Bay floods into the shallower area at the east of the passage.

Lobster fishing is the mainstay of the economy on Swans Island, with much of the activity based in Burnt Coat Harbor, between the villages of Swans Island and Minturn. Early French explorers called Swans *Brûle Côte* (burnt coast) probably due to a recent fire. By 1754 British charts had Anglicized the name to Burnt Coat, a name that stuck to the harbor.

ALTERNATIVES

Two additional launch points could vary this trip. An experienced paddler attentive to the currents in Jericho Bay can get to Marshall Island from a Stonington launch in 2 or 3 hours. It's about 7 miles from Stonington to Marshall, including a 3.0-mile crossing of Jericho Bay. From Marshall Island it's about 3 miles to Burnt Coat Harbor. You could also make a direct, 3.0-nautical mile crossing from Bass Harbor to North Point or take a more sheltered route through the Gott-Placentia island group (see Trip 11). Finally, you could launch at Seal Cove (Trip 12), cross to the Tinker Island group, and make your way through the Pond-Black group to Swans.

Depending on conditions, paddling out of Stonington (Trip 14) could be an alternative when conditions are too big on Swans. Or, launch from Naskeag Point and head to the islands just south and across Eggemoggin Reach, which could be sheltered when Swans is not. The Swans Island Ferry departs from Bass Harbor daily. You could choose to avoid the 2.0-mile crossing from Naskeag Point and simply launch from the

island instead. For fees, schedules, and other information, visit maine.gov/mdot/ferry/
swansisland.

MORE INFORMATION

Maine Coastal Islands National Wildlife Refuge (fws.gov/refuge/Maine_Coastal
_Islands; 207-594-0600). Maine Coast Heritage Trust (mcht.org; 207-729-7366). Call
ahead for reservations on Marshall Island (MCHT); camp only in established sites;
fires allowed at MCHT campsites sites only by permit through the Maine Forest Service in Old Town (800-750-9777). Other on-route camping options include Little
Black Island (MCHT), Hog Island (MCHT), Sellers Island, and Little Hog Island
(MITA), and other sites for MITA members only.

14
THE STONINGTON ARCHIPELAGO

Paddle a dense collection of granite, spruce-topped islands with plenty of public access.

Distance ▶ 6.0 to 14.0 nautical miles, round-trip

Tidal Planning ▶ 9.86-foot mean tidal range in Oceanville. Aside from the predictable north–south/in-out tidal current, the tide in the archipelago generally floods to the east and ebbs to the west. A strong or constant wind, however, might turn it the other direction, so it is not always easy to predict.

Cautions ▶ Watch for lobster boats!

Charts and Maps ▶ NOAA chart #13315; Maptech #75; Waterproof Chart #104

LAUNCHES

Colwell Ramp, Stonington Busy, town-owned ramp; unload and park along Bayview Avenue or at Greenlaw's on Indian Point Road (fee); public restrooms at the fire station next to Hagen Dock. Traveling east on ME 15/Main Street from downtown Stonington, turn right (south) on Seabreeze Avenue (at the Methodist church). The ramp is at the end of the street. *GPS coordinates: 44° 9.249' N, 68° 39.601' W.*

Old Quarry Ocean Adventures, Stonington Boat fee and parking fee, but usually easier than parking downtown. From ME 15, look for signs at Oceanville Road, 3.5 miles south of Deer Isle village. Drive east on Oceanville Road for 0.9 mile and turn right onto the dirt road marked by an Old Quarry sign. Follow 0.6 mile to the office. *GPS coordinates: 44° 10.555' N, 68° 38.573' W.*

Other Public Access Publicly owned islands are plentiful in this area; land managers and permitted uses are noted in the description. Contact land managers for specific restrictions (see More Information).

ROUTE DESCRIPTION

The approximately 36 square miles of ocean between Stonington and Isle au Haut is packed with about 75 islands, some with miles of shoreline and thick interior forests and others barely large enough on which to pitch a small tent. After just a look, passages between the islands present themselves, drawing you on. Carved from a pinkish vein of

Deer Isle granite stretching from the mainland to Isle au Haut, the enticing archipelago is formed by submerged ancient mountain ridges poking above the water surface.
Spruce forests hold down a thin layer of soil, supporting fragile ecosystems littered
with erratic boulders left by the glacier. The islands make this an often sheltered place
for less experienced paddlers to learn. Like anywhere else, conditions may change as
quickly as the tide turns. Navigating such short stretches between islands might seem
easy, but the archipelago can be maze-like; a chart and compass are still essential.

While many of the islands are privately owned, public access is never far away. In
2016 there were around 30 islands with public access, including 11 where camping
is allowed. In addition, Maine Island Trail Association (MITA) members have access
to several more. Some islands have well-maintained trails or walkable shorelines, and
others have small, sandy beaches. Various tides expose countless pocket beaches.

Stonington also has one of the greatest densities of lobster boats you're likely to encounter. The town's fleet of commercial fishing boats usually numbers near 400, operating out of several coves, but mostly concentrated in Stonington Harbor. If you've
never seen lobster fishing in action, it may be interesting to observe the workers tending their traps, but be attentive and stay out of their way and take care during crossings. Stonington's granite boom in the late 1800s brought stonecutters from abroad,
boosting the town's population to nearly 5,000. Laborers commuted to quarries on
the islands, and angular grout piles of cast-off stone still mark the old sites. Rooming
houses sprung up to house transient laborers and the quarrymen brought Wild West-
like lawlessness. At the same time, Italian immigrants built the opera house, which is
still open over a hundred years later. As with most booms, the granite industry faded
and the population dwindled. Fishing became the most popular livelihood, as it still
is today, but the boom-and-bust pattern continues, most recently with the demand for
sea urchins in the 1980s.

The route possibilities in this area are staggering. The described approach is more
strategy than route. No matter where you launch, paddle 2 or 3 miles out and maintain
this distance while "arcing" through the archipelago. This could translate to a simple
6.0-mile out-and-back route, or a 14.0-mile journey with many stops. If you stopped at all
the public access islands mentioned, you might be in for a very long day, but you have
the freedom of many choices, in addition to several opportunities for camping. The
direction and itinerary you ultimately choose will likely depend upon wind and tidal
current, but plenty of paddlers have ignored both here with only minor consequences.

Launch at Colwell Ramp and head east through a large mooring area for lobster
boats. Be mindful of the heavy motorboat traffic just a short distance from the launch
and in the mooring field. You'll pass two lobster operations here, and there are often
plenty of boats coming and going, particularly in the afternoon or early morning.

Dow Ledge (private) is 0.7 nautical mile east of the launch. The ledge has a few
spruce trees atop it and is barred to Deer Isle at lower tides. To the south, the Chewonki Foundation's Russ Island lies beyond a 0.25-mile crossing of the busy Deer
Island Thorofare. This is one of the shorter places to cross with long lines of sight
toward approaching boats. Russ Island has a campsite on the south side near the east

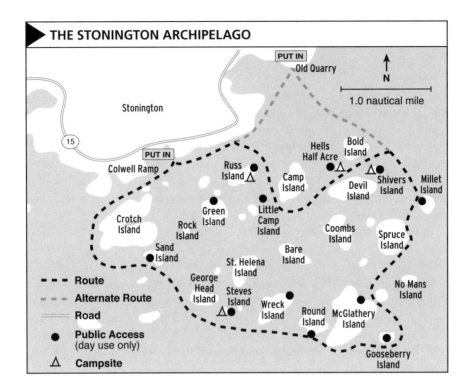

THE STONINGTON ARCHIPELAGO

PUT IN
Old Quarry
N

1.0 nautical mile

Stonington

15

PUT IN

Colwell Ramp

Russ Island

Hells Half Acre

Bold Island

Camp Island

Devil Island

Shivers Island

Millet Island

Crotch Island

Green Island

Rock Island

Little Camp Island

Coombs Island

Spruce Island

Sand Island

St. Helena Island

Bare Island

Route

Alternate Route

Road

Public Access (day use only)

Campsite

George Head Island

Steves Island

Wreck Island

Round Island

McGlathery Island

No Mans Island

Gooseberry Island

end. From the beaches on the south end, look for trails that lead to elevated meadows with fine views of Stonington and the islands, and blueberries to pick in season.

Just 0.25 mile southeast of Russ, Little Camp Island (unnamed on most charts) is owned by the Maine Coast Heritage Trust (MCHT), and open for day use. The beach on the east end makes for an easy, sheltered landing, but the southwest beach has quicker access to the spectacular view from the island's summit. Be wary of the gap between Little Camp and Potato Island just to the west: a popular lobster boat route runs through here, and the boats throw steep wakes in the shallow water that can wash away kayaks left too close to the tide line.

Follow the south shore of Camp Island (private) and pass between the Coots on your way to very popular Hell's Half Acre (state-owned). Hell's has a couple of campsites, one with tent platforms. There are easy landings on both the north side and the south, where a high-tide sandy beach looks about as idyllic as it gets. In the warmer months, you will probably not be alone here.

Hell's was probably so-named because of adjacent Devil Island (private). Devil may be named after Robert Merchant, who lived on Camp Island in the 1830s and '40s. One set of lore blames Merchant for the death of his two sons. Reportedly, a son died after a severe beating and the other drowned when Merchant knowingly sent him to fetch cattle from Little Camp as the tide rose over the bar. Another story has the sons dying of diphtheria and being buried, to avoid contagion, on Devil Island. To this day, most visitors wonder why such a nice place, often frequented by eagles and seabirds, has such a foreboding name. At low tide, pick your way carefully through the shallows north of Devil.

Just ahead, tiny, state-owned Shivers Island has an intimate campsite where you can watch the lights of Stonington twinkle to life in the evening.

A little more than 0.5 mile southeast, Millet Island is owned by the Island Heritage Trust (IHT) and is open for day use. Land at high tide on the sandy beach on the west side; at low tide you can pick your way over the rockweed. Walk the granite perimeter of Millet in less than an hour (the interior is dense forest) or simply linger on the beach. Following the described route, Millet is just more than 3.0 miles from Colwell Ramp. This is a good place to begin the arc westward.

Granite ledges slope into the sea along the southeast shore of Spruce Island (private) with glacial erratic boulders poised on the slope as if ready to tumble into the sea. It's probably safe to paddle beneath them: they've been there since the end of the last ice age. Landing here would be difficult and, depending on the swell direction, conditions may increase here. If your group is less experienced, pass north of Spruce and wind your way through a more sheltered part of the archipelago.

From Spruce it's about 0.5 mile to McGlathery Island, but look both ways: this is part of the same lobster boat highway mentioned earlier. Head for the big boulder on Little McGlathery Island. At the higher end of the tide cycle, you can pass to the north into a cove known informally as Lindy's Cove. Legend has it that Charles and Anne Lindbergh anchored their yacht here while escaping paparazzi on their honeymoon. McGlathery is owned by a private land trust and open to the public for day use. There's a beach here and one on the southeast side that make good landing spots.

It's not much more than 0.25 mile southeast to Gooseberry Island (MCHT; day use). At higher tides when the conditions are fairly calm you may land on a tiny sandy beach in a narrow cove on the south side. A playground of boulders top the ledges, and a broad view reaches toward the open sea.

Head back to the southeast shore of McGlathery. Like Spruce Island, McGlathery's granite ledges slope dramatically into the sea with boulders scattered here and there, and there's a stretch in which landing would be difficult. Even on a day with minor swell, you'll likely feel some of it here. It is an awe-inspiring place. From here, you have several choices for the continuing route, spanning about 9 to 14 nautical miles.

The Long Arc
If you're feeling energetic, maintain the arc from the ramp by crossing Merchant Row to Bills Island (MCHT; day use), about 0.75 mile away, then aim for Harbor Island (state-owned; campsites), past the end of privately owned Merchant Island toward Hardwood and tiny Ram Island (state-owned) before skirting the edge of Penobscot Bay along the archipelago's western islands. Sparrow Island, while state-owned, is off-limits for much of the summer due to nesting birds, and is best avoided other times as well due to the large seal population in the area. Mark Island (IHT) has some tricky

Route possibilities near Stonington are staggering, including this stretch along McGlathery Island where granite ledges slope dramatically into the sea, with glacial erratic boulders scattered here and there.

ledge landings, but it is possible to take a break there near the lighthouse before heading back toward the launch via the Deer Island Thorofare. This route covers about 14 nautical miles.

A More Direct Return

If, from the west end of McGlathery, you're inclined to make a shorter trip back to the ramp, head northwest toward the south tip of Round Island (IHT; day use) where there's sandy beach at higher tides. Wreck Island (IHT; day use) has an idyllic sandy beach at its east end, but if you're heading back to the ramp, paddle past its southwest tip, onward to tiny Steves Island (state-owned). Be alert here: the channel between Wreck and Steves is a popular lobster boat route. Popular Steves Island has four campsites overlooking sculpted granite ledges and intimate pocket beaches.

As described, this more direct route has brought you 3.5 nautical miles from Millet Island (total about 6.5 to 7 nautical miles). From Steves, you could take a fairly direct route that would get you back to the ramp in about 2 miles. Just head north, following the west shore of St. Helena Island (private; be very careful of lobster boats speeding from the channel to the gap between the George Head sandbar and St. Helena). If you're up for a swim, stop at the southeast cove on Green Island (MCHT; day use) for a freshwater dip in the quarry pond. Otherwise, pause at the ledges west of Scott Island and look both ways before crossing the Deer Island Thorofare back to the launch (total route about 9 nautical miles).

A Moderate Option

If you're up for a colorful sunset over Penobscot Bay and a total route of about 10 to 11 nautical miles, follow the route as described immediately above from McGlathery to Steves Island, then head west around George Head (private) and cross the busy channel northwest toward Sand Island.

Sand Island (MCHT; day use) is so named due to the gorgeous little beach on its west side, a great spot to take in the beginnings of a sunset. Follow the western shore of Crotch Island (private), which is easy to identify due to the tall structure rising over the active granite quarry and the mountains of cast-off stone rising from the water's edge. The island was inhabited before 1800 and has been actively quarried on and off since 1870. If they're cutting granite, you will hear it. At busy times, the cutting equipment fires up at 7 A.M. and continues non-stop through the day, clearly heard in Stonington.

Noise or not, the west side of Crotch makes for a lovely paddle along the rounded granite ledges. Look for the distinctive bluff known locally as the Old Man's Ass, a landmark visible for several miles. At the north end, turn into the Deer Island Thorofare and cross when you get the chance. Since you're likely to reach this point later in the day when workboats are returning, be very careful winding toward the launch. Pass Green Head Lobster and the entrance to the inner harbor; there is likely to be plenty of traffic.

ALTERNATIVES

Beyond making the long arc, possibilities for additions to this route are vast. Isle au Haut (Trip 15) is always an option if you want to explore more than the islands in this immediate area.

On a windy or foggy day with a rising tide, circumnavigate more sheltered Whitmore Neck. Launch from Colwell Ramp, Old Quarry, or the bridge in Hatch Cove. At higher tides, launch at Mariner's Park (off Sunshine Road in Deer Isle) to paddle in the sheltered water of Long Cove. Near the northeast part of Deer Isle, Reach Beach in Gray's Cove is an IHT preserve with quick access to Greenlaw Cove (best at higher tides).

MORE INFORMATION

Maine Bureau of Public Lands (maine.gov/dacf/parks/about/public_reserved_lands.shtml; 207-287-4960). Chewonki Foundation (chewonki.org; 207-882-7323). Maine Coast Heritage Trust Merchant Island Preserves (mcht.org/preserves/merchant-row-island -preserves.shtml; 207-244-5100). Island Heritage Trust (islandheritagetrust.org/visit .html; 207-348-2455). Fires on MCHT preserves allowed only by permit through the Maine Forest Service in Old Town (800-750-9777); fires not permitted on any Island Heritage Trust islands in this area.

PADDLING AMONG LOBSTER BOATS

When lobster harvesters get a chance to talk with kayakers, they're usually eager to share the cautionary advice and well-meant (if sometimes disdainful) suggestions that experienced paddlers have heard many times. The number one piece of information they all want to impart is the same: they can't see us. And they're right: kayakers simply need to stay out of the way of fishing boats. Here are a few tips:

▶ Assume nothing. Captains are prone to multitasking and may even step away from the helm; never assume you've been seen. Those hauling traps may be more focused on their immediate surroundings than where their boat is going. The rest are probably going somewhere fast. Lobster boats can travel at more than 50 MPH.

▶ Anticipate local traffic patterns. While lobster boats may go anywhere while tending traps, they get to their fishing grounds on established routes, usually on direct, deep-water passages between ports and fishing grounds. Identify these working highways with local knowledge and some common sense. Cross them quickly at right angles, keeping groups together in a tight pod.

▶ Learn how lobster boats move. There is a logic to setting and hauling traps. When someone at the stern gaffs a buoy, threading its line onto a motorized pot hauler, the boat begins a circle. The lobsters are removed, and the trap is rebaited and dropped overboard. By then, the boat is usually pointed in the original direction, toward the next buoy. Lobster boats are required by law to display their buoy colors, often in the form of a buoy mounted on the antenna. If you can make out the colors, you might be able to see which buoys the boat is headed to next.

Evidence of lobster fishing is abundant in New England. Here, lobster traps are stacked on a wharf on Beals Island, Maine.

▶ Always let workboats go first. If you're not sure where a boat is going, pause and let it go first, especially if you can't tell if the captain has seen you or not.

▶ Keep paddling, or at least keep your paddle moving. A wet, moving paddle catches the light, presents an easier-to-notice profile, and distinguishes you from colorful buoys.

▶ Make a small target. In open water, keep your group together and make it easy for workboats to avoid you.

▶ Don't rely on technology. In the fog, radar and radar reflectors may work, but not all boats monitor radar. Make Sécurité calls on the radio, but remember that not all boats monitor channel 16. Fog horns are unlikely to be heard over the roar of a motor. It can't hurt to use these devices, but avoid putting your faith in them completely.

▶ Avoid rush hour. Lobster boats tend to leave port a little before dawn and return any time from midafternoon until sunset. These are good times to avoid busy harbors and the channels that lead to them. In Maine, lobster fishing is prohibited at night and on summer Sundays, so these can be quieter times near fishing ports.

▶ Approach only on the "working side." If they're not too busy, lobster harvesters may sell lobster off the boat, but they often feel this isn't worth the trouble since they're taking time from hauling to sell lobsters they'd sell at port anyway. If you want to approach a boat, try hailing the crew on the radio first. Then, making absolutely sure that they've seen you, approach on the working side—the side equipped with a winch to haul the traps. If they want to sell you lobster, make a quick transaction and don't dicker over price: they're only doing it as a courtesy to you.

15
ISLE AU HAUT

*Miles of wild, undeveloped shoreline,
including the exposed southern end protected
by Acadia National Park, make this long
circumnavigation worth the effort.*

Distance ▶	10.0 to 23.0 nautical miles, round-trip
Tidal Planning ▶	9.86-foot mean tidal range in Oceanville, predictable north–south currents. For a circumnavigation, your day will be far easier if you can plan to paddle around the southern end at low tide.
Cautions ▶	Be alert for lobster boats. The areas south of Kimball Island and York Island are subject to open ocean and whatever conditions it may bring—usually at least a little swell on a calm day. The south end can be especially rough and committing with minimal bailouts in bigger conditions.
Charts and Maps ▶	NOAA chart #13315; Maptech #475; Waterproof Chart #104

LAUNCHES

Colwell Ramp, Stonington Busy, town-owned ramp; unload and park along Bayview Avenue or at Greenlaw's on Indian Point Road (fee); public restrooms at the fire station next to Hagan Dock. Traveling east on ME 15/Main Street from downtown Stonington, turn right (south) on Seabreeze Avenue (at the Methodist church). The ramp is at the end of the street. *GPS coordinates: 44° 9.249' N, 68° 39.601' W.*

Old Quarry Ocean Adventures, Stonington Boat fee and parking fee, but usually easier than parking downtown. From ME 15, look for signs at Oceanville Road, 3.5 miles south of Deer Isle village. Drive east on Oceanville Road for 0.9 mile and turn right onto the dirt road marked by an Old Quarry sign. Follow 0.6 mile to the office. *GPS coordinates: 44° 10.555' N, 68° 38.573' W.*

Other Public Access Publicly owned islands are plentiful in this area; land managers and permitted uses are noted in the description. Contact land managers for specific restrictions (see More Information). There's a gravel beach just south of the Isle au Haut town dock. Much of the southern end of the island is part of Acadia National Park, which offers public access (with a park pass) anywhere you can land, including the pier at Duck Harbor (rockweed landing just east of the pier).

ROUTE DESCRIPTION

Isle au Haut, almost 5 miles off Stonington, is its own world, quite separate from the goings-on not so far away. It isn't difficult to reach—thousands make the trek via mail boat every summer—but staying for more than a few hours takes some planning and effort. There's only one campground, at Duck Harbor, and to stay in one of its Adirondack shelters usually requires a reservation months in advance. Inns have come and gone, but they are generally small and pricey. There are nearby camping options, and the island can be circumnavigated in a long day trip from Stonington (Trip 14), but you'll get only a fleeting tease of the laid-back, otherworldly ambiance of Isle au Haut.

There's not much to "do" on Isle au Haut for those looking to be entertained: a general store, a chocolatier/café, and a few other shops keep intermittent hours in midsummer. The town has a few sights of interest, including the old shingle-style town hall or the church; perhaps try to soak in how the 40 or so year-round inhabitants live. For many outdoorspeople, the wild southern end of the island is the attraction. Acadia National Park occupies 60 percent of Isle au Haut, maintaining 18 miles of trails over some spectacular terrain, such as Western Head's bold cliffs and mossy forests.

Other than the landing, the rest of the town's shoreline is private, but the park provides over 9 miles of wild shoreline, open to anyone with a park pass. Of course, actually landing on that shoreline can be another matter. Much of it is rough and rocky, exposed to the open ocean, which usually has some swell rolling in. The shore south of Duck Harbor is dotted with rocks and offshore ledges, while the rugged cliffs of Western Ear and Western Head drop steeply into ledge-strewn ocean, which tends to thunder with roiling whitewater even on calm days.

Getting around Isle au Haut takes some effort. A round-trip from Stonington is over 20.0 miles. From a campsite on Harbor or Wheat islands, you'll still paddle at least 14.0 miles to circumnavigate the big island. Staying at Duck Harbor with early planning puts you close to the action and makes it easier to explore on foot. Or arrange to be dropped off or picked up by Old Quarry's excursion boat (see Alternatives).

For the circumnavigation, launch 3 or 4 hours before low tide for ideal tidal timing. From Colwell Ramp, head straight for Steves Island. Cross the Deer Island Thorofare and follow the west shore of Green Island and continue west of St. Helena Island before arriving at Steves (state-owned; camping). From there, cross Merchant Row, aiming either for Harbor or Bills islands. Harbor is state-owned with campsites, while Bills is a Maine Coast Heritage Trust (MCHT) island open for day use.

At this point, if you are circumnavigating Isle au Haut, decide which direction to take. Since winds often increase in the afternoon, frequently from the southwest, traveling clockwise as described here puts those winds behind you as you head back.

Wheat Island (state-owned; camping) could be a good spot for a break if you haven't taken one. The east side of Isle au Haut is largely private, and depending on conditions, it may be a few miles to the next easy take-out. Continue on roughly the same bearing, passing Burnt Island and Richs Point. For the next 12.0 to 16.0 miles, just keep Isle au Haut on your right.

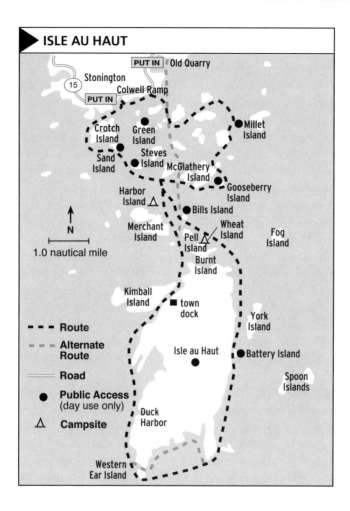

▶ ISLE AU HAUT

PUT IN Old Quarry

Stonington
15
Colwell Ramp
PUT IN

Crotch
Island   Green
Island

Millet
Island

Sand
Island
Steves
Island McGlathery
Island

Harbor
Island △

Gooseberry
Island

Bills Island

N

Merchant
Island
Wheat
Island
Fog
Island

1.0 nautical mile
Pell
Island

Burnt
Island

Kimball
Island

town
dock
York
Island

Isle au Haut

Battery Island

- - - Route

- - - Alternate
       Route

——— Road

● Public Access
   (day use only)

△ Campsite

Spoon
Islands

Duck
Harbor

Western
Ear Island

Just northwest of York Island, tiny Doliver Island (state-owned; campsite) is grass-covered, with a single, wind-battered spruce. The island is very exposed, both to the elements and to the homes on Isle au Haut and York Island. There is a probable landing on the northwest side.

York Island (private) was inhabited intermittently from Revolutionary times until the 1840s. Then from the late 1800s into the early 1900s, in the age of fishing from sailboats, the island became a base for Stonington workers who spent their weeks here, selling their catch to a fishing smack from Rockland. As motorized vessels replaced sailboats, the need for such outposts diminished.

Continuing down the east side of Isle au Haut, assuming you've planned for the tides, you'll have a little current behind you, especially a little farther from shore. Paddling near shore is more interesting but takes longer; farther out is faster but may be less interesting. Keep your total distance and pace in mind when you decide which you prefer.

Just past the York Island Narrows, Battery Island (state-owned) lies a short distance from shore—a good spot for a break, with the most probable rockweed landing on the north side (a challenging landing in conditions). A little farther south, Horseman Point (private) has a cobble beach on both sides and can be a good spot to duck out of wind or swell. Assess the conditions here. Whatever you're experiencing will likely be magnified on the island's south end.

Ahead there's a passage between Eastern Head and Eastern Ear Island where the shore turns very rugged and rocky as it curves westward. Look for a tall chasm called Thunder Gulch. At this point, you've traveled 9.0 to 11.0 miles. Hopefully, you're within an hour or so of low tide, so you'll be getting some push on the way back. Finishing the circumnavigation and getting back will take at least 12 more miles of paddling; pace yourself and your explorations accordingly.

From Eastern Head, Western Ear is 1.5 miles away by a direct route. A close exploration of the shoreline would take about 4 miles. It would seem a shame to paddle all the way out here and not paddle along the cliffy east side of Western Head, one of the more spectacular stretches of shoreline in New England. Not only is the shore superlative, but any amount of swell makes for some lively paddling.

For the detour, paddle north from Eastern Head into Head Harbor. Despite the harbor's proximity to open ocean, a sandbar near its mouth helps keep it relatively calm. The harbor is just far enough from town to be its own community, which had a store in its heyday but is now usually very quiet. On the harbor's west side is MCHT's Head Harbor Preserve, which has trails, an old fishing shack, and allows day use. Landing here might be easiest at lower tides, when there is room beneath the granite seawall. Merchant Cove, Barred Harbor, and Squeaker Cove (all contained within Acadia National Park) have cobble beaches at their heads; if conditions permit these could offer pit stops, but be prepared for potentially larger swells and difficult landings.

The cobble beach at the head of Deep Cove (Acadia National Park) is the next likely landing spot. This is the end of Western Head Road, where it is joined by the Cliff Trail and the Goat Trail. It's well worth taking a short hike up to the point just south on the Cliff Trail, which has spectacular views of the rocky shoreline.

In 1814 the American sloop of war *John Adams*, captained by Charles Morris, ran aground in the fog on a ledge near here, known as Morris's Mistake. The crew floated the ship off the ledge as the tide rose and made it up the Penobscot River to Hampden for repairs, where it was scuttled when the British attacked. Just south of this amphitheater of rocks and ledges lies a tiny cobble beach in a gorgeous rocky cove that might sometimes be sheltered.

At higher tides, cut through the gap north of Western Ear, or carry over if you wish to avoid rough conditions south of the Ear, another dramatic and potentially lively spot.

On the west side of Isle au Haut, the cove north of Western Ear and several cobble beaches to the north—all within Acadia National Park—make good spots for breaks. At Duck Harbor, the camping shelters (reservation only) are on the hillside on the south side of the cove. There's a place to land beside the pier. Water is available at a hand pump, 1,600 feet east beside a dirt road that skirts the harbor.

On Isle au Haut's rugged and remote southern end, much of the shoreline is encompassed by Acadia National Park, like this stretch on Western Head, below the Cliff Trail.

Just north is Eben's Head, a tall, rounded lump of rock with several cobble beaches just past it. Head across the mouth of Moores Harbor to Moores Head and Trial Point. Nestled between these promontories is a narrow cove called the Seal Trap.

Robinson Point Light soon appears ahead, just before the thorofare narrows into the gap between Kimball Island and Isle au Haut. If you planned well for the tides, you'll be thanking yourself now. If not, try the edges of the channel for less current.

If you have time, you might want to pull out for a break in town, either at the ferry dock or, with permission, at the store just a little farther north.

At the north end of the thorofare, paddle past the old rusticators' enclave called Point Lookout. Started by landscape designer Ernest Bowditch in 1878, it began as an exclusive bachelors' retreat, but as those bachelors married, it grew into an elite summer colony for a few wealthy families who eventually donated their large parcels of land on the island to Acadia National Park.

Head past Flake Island, north toward Nathan Island (MCHT-owned; campsite). If conditions permit landing, Nathan is a good spot for a break before the last big push home.

Head north, past the sandbar on Merchant Island, and follow the shore toward Harbor Island. From Harbor Island's eastern end, it's almost a mile to Steves Island, and from there, under 2 miles back to the launch.

ALTERNATIVES

On a multiday trip, a visit to Great and Little Spoon islands (closed to foot traffic during nesting season) could take you to some spectacular scenery: rugged cliffs, grassy, treeless heights, and plentiful birds. Also, a trip around Kimball Island takes you past dramatic Kimball Head and Marsh Cove Head with plentiful rocks and ledges.

To shorten the route considerably, you could arrange for a drop-off and pick-up at Isle au Haut with Old Quarry Ocean Adventures (oldquarry.com; 207-367-8977). You could also choose to paddle the Stonington archipelago (Trip 14) for a shorter trip or when conditions are rough.

MORE INFORMATION

Maine Bureau of Public Lands (maine.gov/dacf/parks/about/public_reserved_lands.shtml; 207-287-4960). Maine Coast Heritage Trust Merchant Island Preserves (mcht.org/preserves/merchant-row-island-preserves.shtml; 207-244-5100); fires on MCHT preserves allowed only by permit through the Maine Forest Service in Old Town (800-750-9777). Acadia National Park (nps.gov/acad; nps.gov/acad/planyourvisit/duckharbor.htm [Duck Harbor Campground reservations]; 207-288-3338). Besides the sites and shelters mentioned in the description, several other overnight options are available to Maine Island Trail Association members.

16
POND, GREAT SPRUCE HEAD, AND BUTTER ISLANDS

This Penobscot Bay archipelago, set apart from towns or other islands, abounds with highlights, including migratory birds in spring and fall and a hike with the best view around.

Distance ▶ 10.0 to 15.0 nautical miles, round-trip

Tidal Planning ▶ 10.39-foot mean tidal range at Fort Point. Ideally, launch on a falling tide and return on a rising tide.

Cautions ▶ There are some wide-open stretches of water here with plenty of fetch to the south. Tidal current speeds up enough to make tidal planning worthwhile, keeping in mind that an ebbing tide will often enough oppose the prevailing southwest winds, producing a chop.

Charts and Maps ▶ NOAA charts #13302, #13305, and #13309; Maptech #74: Penobscot Bay; Waterproof Chart #104

LAUNCHES

Bakeman Beach, Cape Rosier Town-owned gravel-sand beach; park at the top of the beach (be mindful of the tide) or along the road (limited parking); no facilities. From the intersection of US 1 and ME 15 in Orland, turn southeast on ME 15. In 3.7 miles, turn right onto ME 199, then in another 5.0 miles, at the T intersection with ME 175, turn left. Follow ME 175 for 4.8 miles, then turn right on ME 175/176. (A bridge crosses Bagaduce Reversing Falls, a worthwhile example of tidal action.) In 1.1 miles, follow ME 176 as it splits right (north), then take an immediate left on Varnum Road. In 2.6 miles, turn left onto ME 176. Continue for 1.7 miles to Cape Rosier Road, which leads to the right. Follow Cape Rosier Road for 4.0 miles, then turn left on Weir Cove Road. The beach is 1.9 miles farther; if you reach Ames Cove Road, you've gone too far. *GPS coordinates: 44° 18.668' N, 68° 48.160' W.*

Betsy's Cove, Brooksville Town-owned ramp and dock in Bucks Harbor; drop off gear in summer (no parking); no facilities. Follow the directions above to the first junction of ME 175 and ME 176, before the bridge. Continue straight on ME 176 for

2.4 miles, then continue ahead on ME 15. In 2.9 miles, turn right on ME 175. The launch is 3.6 miles ahead on the left. *GPS coordinates: 44° 20.516' N, 68° 44.507' W.*

Other Public Access Great Spruce Head, Butter, and the northern Barred islands are all private with some public access, as noted below and usually posted on shore. Pond Island (campsites) is a Maine Coast Heritage Trust (MCHT) preserve. Eastern Barred Island, Colt Head, and Crow Island are state-owned. Bradbury Island is an Island Heritage Trust property.

ROUTE DESCRIPTION

The heart of this route is an unnamed area that some call the Great Spruce Head archipelago, a group of large, privately owned islands with a rich history and just enough public access to make a visit feasible. The islands are set off on their own, far from any busy harbor, but close enough together to feel like a neighborhood. Indeed, inhabitants of several islands have cooperated over the years, sharing the Eagle Island mail boat for access and supplies.

The neighbors are a distinguished bunch. Bear Island belongs to the family of R. Buckminster Fuller, who spent his summers here and credited the island caretaker Jim Hardy as an influence on his innovative thinking. Great Spruce Head Island is documented in photographer Eliot Porter's *Summer Island* and in his brother Fairfield's paintings that hang in many museums. The family still brings a number of artists to visit the island every summer. Descendants of Tom Cabot own Butter Island; in his lifetime Cabot acquired more than 60 islands and donated them to land trusts or the state. Eagle Island is the only island in the area with year-round residents, descendants of the original Quinn settlers who arrived in the early 1800s.

Even with a good deal of private land here, limited public access is available. Posted signs at beachheads on Great Spruce Head Island welcome visitors to the beaches and trails, but prohibit fires or camping. Desiring some privacy, the owners of Butter Island have designated a public access area on the eastside beaches, where visitors may then hike up Montserrat Hill; signs here and on the northern Barred Islands (also known as the Chain Links; not to be confused with Eastern and Western Barred islands north of Beach Island) are very specific about where visitors are welcome. Bear and Eagle islands are off-limits unless you rent one of the houses or cabins on them.

While the route described covers some 15 nautical miles, you could cover only part of the trip. For many, a short trip to Pond Island and its neighbors is plenty. Others opt to go as far as the Barred Islands. A paddle from the Bakeman Beach launch to Great Spruce Head is 4.0 to 5.0 miles; a trip to Butter Island and back from here adds 7.0 to 8.0 miles.

From Bakeman Beach, Pond Island (MCHT) is clearly visible a mile to the south. There are plenty of places to land on Pond, since most of its shores have gravel or cobble beaches. A meadowy hillside on the northwest overlooks the passage between Pond and Western Island, while the marshy tidal pond on the southeast is a pretty spot with campsites on either end. The mosquitoes like it too; on a windless day they are likely to follow you.

Look for the Barred Islands southwest from the west end of Pond Island, distinguishable by the narrow gap between them. It's a 1.75-nautical-mile paddle to get there, where you can pull up on the sandbar at all but the higher tides. Eastern Barred Island (state-owned) has a campsite; Western Barred is private.

Just southwest, the rocky, steep-sided Colt Head (state-owned; closed for nesting April through August) rises directly from the ocean. On the approach, it may be difficult to get a sense of its scale, but the hump rises around 60 feet from mean low water. While much of the grassy top is indeed grass, thick tangles of sumac trees and thorny bushes cover much of the island's flanks. It is not an easy island to land on, but for the intrepid few willing to seal-land and climb through dense foliage, it will probably feel worthwhile. The ledges to the southeast of Colt Head are generally covered with seals; give them a wide berth.

If you don't plan on landing on Colt Head, view it from a distance as you paddle directly from the Barred Islands to Great Spruce Head Island, a distance of 1.5 nautical miles. The stony beaches on Great Spruce Head's west side make a good spot for a break, as does the narrow double beach projecting from the island's southeast end.

Depending on weather and your desires, you could go either north or south of Butter Island. Going north allows you a close-up look at another group of Barred Islands,

Colt Head Island (closed for bird nesting April through August) is a grassy hump of rock rising some 60 feet above mean low water.

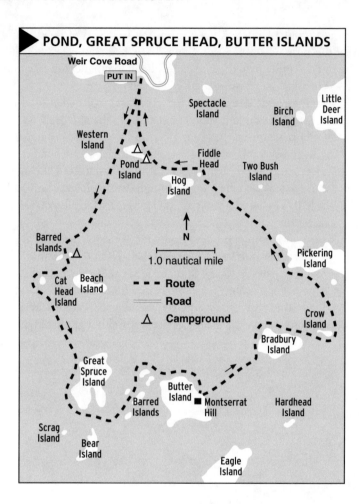

POND, GREAT SPRUCE HEAD, BUTTER ISLANDS

Weir Cove Road

PUT IN

Spectacle Island

Birch Island

Little Deer Island

Western Island

Pond Island

Fiddle Head

Two Bush Island

Hog Island

N

1.0 nautical mile

Barred Islands

Pickering Island

Cat Head Island

Beach Island

Crow Island

- - - Route

Road

△ Campground

Bradbury Island

Great Spruce Island

Butter Island

Montserrat Hill

Hardhead Island

Scrag Island

Barred Islands

Bear Island

Eagle Island

also known as the Chain Links (private) and their pretty, bluffy shorelines. On the east side of Butter Island, between Orchard and Nubble beaches, a trail leads up to 150-foot high Montserrat Hill, where a granite bench memorializes Tom and Virginia Cabot. The view is outstanding and well worth the hike. The public access area extends to the Nubble, the rocky southeast point.

It's about a mile from Butter to Bradbury Island (IHT; day-use), but be aware that mid-tide currents here will increase and have the potential to create rough conditions. A number of cobble and rocky beaches offer access to the island; the steep cobble beach at the southwest end is a particularly stunning spot for a break. The island's steep banks make exploring the densely forested interior difficult, but are a thrill to paddle below.

Just east, beyond a shallow area that can develop some lively currents, Crow Island (state-owned) is another good spot for a break; if eagles are nesting, it will be closed April through August. Many visitors have reported seeing petroglyphs on the north side. From Crow it's about a mile north to Pickering Island (private), which has a long history of careful public visitation. The island has a number of beaches and a steep, dramatic headland in the middle of its southern side. Paddle another 1.5 nautical miles northeast to Hog Island (private), which was farmed from the 1860s to the 1930s and took in summer boarders at a mansard-roofed house that still stands over its meadowy west shore.

Pond Island is only a short paddle from Hog, and if you launched from Bakeman Beach, you'll probably be able to see your car from the middle of Pond Island. Returning on a high tide makes carrying boats back to the car far less work.

ALTERNATIVES

This mid-Penobscot area is adjacent to plenty of other route possibilities, especially if you're planning a multiday excursion (or brutally long days). A 3.0- to 4.0-nautical-mile crossing to Pendleton Point links this route to Islesboro (Trip 18). This is an exposed crossing subject to strong currents, open ocean conditions, and occasional large ship traffic. From Crow, Butter, or Eagle Islands, cross to Deer Isle and follow its shore south to the Stonington archipelago (Trip 14). The area between the archipelago and Deer Isle (especially the Eagle Island-Hardhead Island-Dunham Point stretch) is subject to strong currents that may interact with wind and swell to produce dangerous conditions. North Haven (Trip 17) is just a skip and a jump along the islands to the south. From Bakeman Beach, a trip of about 14 nautical miles through Eggemoggin Reach brings you to Naskeag Point, the put-in for Swans Island (Trip 13). Launching at Betsy's Cove in Bucks Harbor provides fairly quick access to the finger-like harbors and coves east of Cape Rosier. In particular, winding, river-like Horseshoe Cove is a fun paddle on a rising tide.

The put-in for Holbrook Island Sanctuary State Park (parksandlands.com; 207-326-4012) in Harborside provides quick access to a relatively sheltered area at the mouth of the Bagaduce River that includes Holbrook and Ram islands, both with public access. With the right tide, you could even ride the tidal Bagaduce current inland and back (or set a shuttle at the Reversing Falls). If you prefer a day off the water, there are several hiking trails in the park, including John B. Mountain, which provides an excellent view of the stretch of ocean included in this route.

MORE INFORMATION

Maine Bureau of Public Lands (maine.gov/dacf/parks/about/public_reserved_lands .shtml; 207-287-4960). Maine Coast Heritage Trust (mcht.org; 207-244-5100). Island Heritage Trust (islandheritagetrust.org/visit.html; 207-348-2455). Fires on MCHT preserves allowed only by permit through the Maine Forest Service in Old Town (800-750-9777); fires not permitted on any Island Heritage Trust islands in this area. Besides the campsites mentioned in the description, another on-route overnight option is available for Main Island Trail Association members.

PRESERVING THE COAST

When they arrived in New England with their Old World views on the land they settled, what had been home to native peoples with abstract concepts of land ownership, Europeans soon carved the New England coast into huge tracts for a privileged few. Ownership aside, settlers put down roots where they wanted, or were given settler's rights by owners of large land grants. Later, the post-Revolutionary War government issued deeds to settlers for the lands they inhabited. A paddler traveling the New England shore in the early 1800s or even the early 1900s probably could have landed or camped almost anywhere. But bit by bit, the New England coast became privately owned, diminishing the commonly owned shorefront to a smaller and smaller percentage.

In the industrial heyday of the late 1800s, populations urbanized and some state governments preserved wild tracts of land. Despite the success of parks out west, the concept of public lands took hold slowly in New England. In 1876, a group of Bostonian hikers started the Appalachian Mountain Club, the nation's first conservation association. In 1891, at the proposal of Charles Eliot and his supporters, the Massachusetts legislature established The Trustees of Reservations to privately acquire and maintain land for public use. In 1898, AMC, The Trustees, and the Environmental League of Massachusetts (incorporated in 1898 as the Massachusetts Forestry Association) lobbied for the creation of the region's first state park at Mount Greylock. Rhode Island and Connecticut followed, founding their state park systems in 1909 and 1913, respectively. In 1919, Maine Governor Percival Baxter campaigned to preserve the wild lands around Katahdin as a state park, but found no help in the state legislature. Instead, he bought the land himself, and in 1930 donated 6,000 acres, including Katahdin, to the people of Maine. Baxter State Park was dedicated to him in 1931. New Hampshire, which had begun acquiring lands in the late 1800s but lacked the support for a publicly funded park system, organized its self-sustaining public parks in 1935.

In 1919, when Percival Baxter was working to preserve Maine's interior, Tom Cabot took his first sailing trip to Maine. He and a college roommate sailed Cabot's open-cockpit daysailer, not much longer than most sea kayaks, from Boston's North Shore as far as Frenchman Bay. Despite heavy fog for much of the voyage, Cabot fell in love with the islands he saw. By the 1940s, when he had a bigger boat and some money to spend, he began acquiring islands, which were not highly prized real estate at the time. Cabot became known for his willingness to pay $100 for any decent-sized island with trees on it. By the mid-1940s, he had bought 41 islands off the coast of Maine for less than $5,000. He had no plans for the land and acted out of an instinct to preserve them from development. Eventually, as the islands became more valuable, Cabot donated some to the state and federal government, which in turn made them available to the public, and began protecting the birds that nested on them.

Cabot was not alone in his impulse to acquire and protect islands. Sometime around 1960 at a cocktail party on Mount Desert Island, Peggy Rockefeller asked Cabot if he would sell her one of his islands. Instead, he helped her buy one, and soon she was hooked as well. By 1965, though, Rockefeller recognized that their efforts, though satisfying, preserved a very small portion of the coast, and she asked Cabot what else they could do. He proposed that they persuade landowners to put conservation easements on their lands. But when owners limited their properties' development potential, they would also lower their property taxes.

To help landowners with this process, Cabot and Rockefeller started Maine Coast Heritage Trust (MCHT) in 1970. Partnering with The Nature Conservancy, Acadia National Park, and others, the trust persuaded the Maine legislature to authorize the use of conservation easements, which could be tailored to meet the landowners' needs. The first such easement in Maine was for Cabot's own Butter Island (Trip 16). Within the year, MCHT protected 30 islands.

Working closely with private landowners, partner organizations, and government agencies, MCHT has conserved more than 143,000 acres in Maine, including hundreds of miles of shoreline and more than 314 entire coastal islands. But MCHT's reach goes farther than its own accomplishments. When the trust's early efforts gained momentum, MCHT started the Maine Land Trust Network, which encourages the formation of local land trusts and now lists nearly a hundred on its website.

17
THE FOX ISLANDS

*A whole world of paddling offers daylong
and multiday routes, far from the hustle and
bustle of the mainland.*

Distance ▶ 18.0 to 46.0 nautical miles, round-trip; numerous options for single and multiple-day routes

Tidal Planning ▶ 9.78-foot mean tidal range in Rockland. In the Fox Island Thorofare, tidal current floods east, ebbs west. Flooding tide meets between Iron and Zeke points. Elsewhere it generally floods to the north.

Cautions ▶ To cross to the Fox Islands from either side of Penobscot Bay requires a substantial crossing that should only be undertaken by experienced paddlers. Potentially rough seas, strong currents, and a gamut of boat traffic surrounds the islands. There are especially strong currents in Hurricane Sound. The entrance to the Basin develops whitewater during peak flow.

Charts and Maps ▶ NOAA charts #13305, #13308, and #13309; Maptech #74; Waterproof Chart #103

LAUNCHES

Bakeman Beach, Cape Rosier Town-owned gravel-sand beach; park at the top of the beach (be mindful of the tide) or along the road (limited parking); no facilities. From the intersection of US 1 and ME 15 in Orland, turn southeast on ME 15. In 3.7 miles, turn right onto ME 199, then in another 5.0 miles, at the T intersection with ME 175, turn left. Follow ME 175 for 4.8 miles, then turn right on ME 175/176. (A bridge crosses Bagaduce Reversing Falls, a worthwhile example of tidal action.) In 1.1 miles, follow ME 176 as it splits right (north), then take an immediate left on Varnum Road. In 2.6 miles, turn left onto ME 176. Continue for 1.7 miles to Cape Rosier Road, which leads to the right. Follow Cape Rosier Road for 4.0 miles, then turn left on Weir Cove Road. The beach is 1.9 miles farther; if you reach Ames Cove Road, you've gone too far. *GPS coordinates: 44° 18.668' N, 68° 48.160' W.*

Rockland Public Landing, Snow Marine Park, Rockland Paved ramp; day and overnight parking; facilities. From the junction of US 1 and ME 73 in Rockland, head south on ME 73 for 0.7 mile. Turn left onto Mechanic Street and follow signs, 0.2 mile, to ramp. *GPS coordinates: 44° 5.550′ N, 69° 6.326′ W.*

Other Public Access Publicly owned islands are plentiful in this area and a few private lands offer public access; land managers and permitted uses are noted in the description. Contact land managers for specific restrictions (see More Information).

ROUTE DESCRIPTION

North Haven and Vinalhaven, together known as the Fox Islands, are connected to Rockland by regular ferry service but are missed by all but those who make some effort to get there. For kayakers, the required effort is considerable. Either island could be circled in a long day trip in 20.0 miles or less, but that mileage doesn't begin to account for the innumerable options for exploration in the area, and you need to get there first.

Separated by a channel that narrows to about a half-mile, the two islands began as one township in 1785, but parted in 1846 as differences became evident. Benjamin Beverage wrote in the early 1800s: "No part of the state produces better beef, pork, mutton, butter, and cheese [than North Haven]." The farmers there also grew plentiful vegetables, corn, and grains. Vinalhaven, by contrast, had harbors and access to the open sea. By the mid-1800s, the southern island's fleet of fishing vessels was three times that of North Haven's.

As time passed, granite quarrying became the principal industry on Vinalhaven, and the island's character evolved accordingly. The Bodwell Granite Company, which began in 1871, employed more than 1,500 workers, many of whom came from Britain and Scandinavia. At the same time, fish processing flourished. Meanwhile, North Haven became popular with rusticators who built their retreats along the Fox Island Thorofare and whiled away their summers in stylish comfort. The visitors hired North Haven locals as builders, caretakers, and boatsmen, and supported local farms—a locavore tradition that has recently been revived. Today, many of the grand cottages still stand, and in the summertime, countless moored pleasure craft swing with the current in the thorofare.

This multiday route takes a northern approach, which is usually the least exposed, but depending upon your skills, ambitions, and conditions, you could launch from numerous put-ins around Penobscot Bay. Getting back to your launch in changing weather can be difficult thanks to these crossings. The calmest conditions are likely to be found around slack tide.

Day 1: Bakeman Beach to Little Thorofare Island, 11.0 nautical miles

From Bakeman Beach on Cape Rosier, cross to the Great Spruce Head Island area (see complete description in Trip 16), and continue south, past Sloop Island. Since tides flood to the north, head south on a falling tide.

At low tide, a sandbar connects the small, treeless pair of masses that form Sloop Island (state-owned). Popular with birds and seals, it could be a good spot for a break if you can do so without disturbing the wildlife. Continuing south, signs above the beach on Oak Island (private wildlife preserve) welcome visitors. Trails lead to several beaches

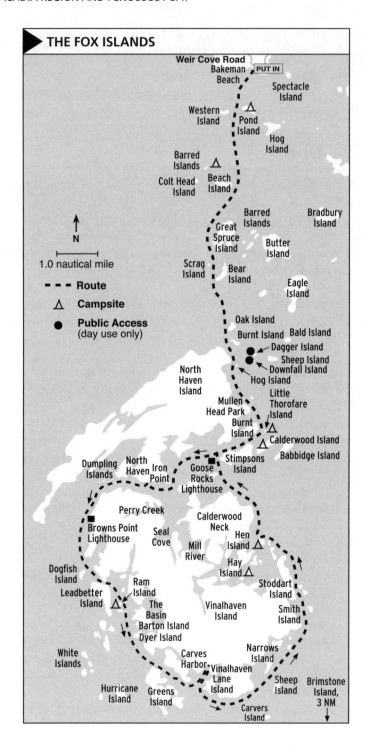

as well as a small cottage, which is available to rent. At mid-tide some confusing currents run east and west through this area, particularly south of Oak Island as you continue to Burnt Island (state-owned; closed for eagle nesting April through August).

Oak Hill, North Haven's northeast point, rises steeply from bluffs along the shore. Atop the hill, a house looks south over Marsh Cove. To the east are Dagger and Downfall islands (both state-owned). Dagger has a few trees on its elevated, grassy pastures, with the most obvious landing on the northwest side. Sheep Island (state-owned; closed for eagle nesting April through August) is even farther east. To the south, spruce and deciduous trees top the rocky bluffs on Mullen Head, a town park. Land at one of the several small cobble beaches to enjoy hiking trails and picnic areas. From Mullen Head, set a straight course past the eastern end of another Burnt Island (North Haven Conservation Partners [NHCP]; not to be confused with the one off Oak Point). This Burnt Island is a town park open for day use. The most likely landings are by the dock near the western end and the low-tide bar to Indian Point.

Continuing, the straight course brings you to the steep, rocky banks of Little Thorofare Island (state-owned) and its limited area for camping (one party; two campers). Carry boats and gear above the high-tide line; here that generally means lugging it all up some steep rocks. Judging from logbook entries, some campers might find the process too difficult. Still, it is a spectacular place to spend the night. Landing at lower tides on the sandbar to the west is fairly easy. At higher tides, launching and landing can be more of a challenge.

If you prefer more room, stay at Calderwood Island, a Maine Coast Heritage Trust (MCHT) preserve. Just south of Little Thorofare, this island has two designated camping areas. The site at the southwest tip requires lugging gear up and down the rockweed-covered rocks at lower tides, but has nice views toward Vinalhaven. The site atop the beach near the southeast end may be easier to negotiate. Trails wind through the juniper and tall grasses of the island's meadows, leading to a high area near the middle of the island with nice views.

Day 2: Little Thorofare/Calderwood Island to Ram Island, 9.0 nautical miles

Despite the relatively low mileage required of this segment, you could easily explore further, logging many more miles on the water or on land. Ideally, head west through Fox Island Thorofare on the ebb. This description details far more options than you could attempt in a day.

Go west through the channel known as Little Thorofare, past Stimpsons Island and Goose Rocks Lighthouse, which stands midstream and rises directly out of the water. At one time, the lighthouse keeper would arrive at this isolated outpost by dory and haul the boat up after him. No families were allowed, and the only place for recreation was the catwalk surrounding the tower, which the keeper needed to circle 88 times to walk a mile. Despite the spare accommodations, Goose Rocks was manned from 1890 to 1963.

Along the North Haven shore, Indian Point is forested and undeveloped; a few homes and an old farmhouse overlook Kent Cove's shores. Just east of Fish Point, Turner Farm produces organic vegetables, meat, and cheese, which you can sample in town at Nebo Lodge. Archeological work at the farm has unearthed artifacts from the Red Paint People and pre-Algonquins.

West of Fish Point, the narrow entrance of Waterman Cove leads to Cubby Hole. Some current develops at the entrance of the tidal basin, but with enough room along the edges to eddy-hop against the flow. The meadow at the head of Cubby Hole is privately owned, but with a conservation easement (NHCP) that allows hand-launching boats carried down from the parking area. A path at North Haven Golf Course follows Waterman Cove's west shore, crossing a small inlet via a pedestrian bridge. A large home in a neighborhood of old estates dominates Iron Point. The flooding tides meet between this point and Zeke Point on Vinalhaven, and the ebb flows in both directions. Expect strong currents.

The large old house on Zeke Point overlooks the granite pilings of the former dock of the *Governor Bodwell*, a ferry that ran from Boston to Bar Harbor. To the south are Mill River, Seal Cove, and Perry Creek. Much of Mill River dries out a couple of hours before and after low tide, but at high enough water you can paddle to its head, cross beneath the bridge, and enter Winter Harbor. Perry Creek is a favored anchorage, especially in poor weather when its waters remain calm. Its entire north shoreline and parts of the south are encompassed by Perry Creek Preserve, a Vinalhaven Land Trust (VHLT) property. Trails lead along the water, as well as to higher ridges with views.

In the summer, the Fox Island Thorofare is home to more than 200 boats, including a couple dozen fishing boats. Several docks line North Haven's waterfront. At the east end, a house with the features of an ornate galleon hangs over the water as if the ship sailed onto the shore and stayed there. Farther west is the dock for J.O. Brown and Sons, where sailors go for supplies and showers. Just west of the ferry landing is the town dock, the most likely place to land. It's a busy spot; try to stay out of the way and minimize the space you take. Just west of the town dock are some private docks off of Hopkins Wharf, and then the North Haven Casino, a private nonprofit yacht club with floating dinghy docks. Just west of that is a small, town-owned gravel beach, a place to land with difficult access to the road.

North Haven has a quiet, friendly feel. Residents' openness to outsiders seems to run deeper than their dedication to the success of their tourism economy. Most who pass you on the road will lift a hand in greeting, even if you're traipsing about in a drysuit. The year-round population of 350 to 400 triples in summertime. When you're in town, seek out ice cream or some other treat, and perhaps a walk to Ames Knob, which rises to the west on Ames Point. To get there, follow the roads west, probably a half-hour walk each way. The view from the 152-foot high hilltop takes in the thorofare and a good chunk of the Fox Islands.

Town visitation complete, drag yourself back to your boat and continue west. Pass the mouth of Browns Cove and continue on to Ames Point (Telegraph Point), where utility lines on land disappear before crossing beneath the thorofare. Ahead, the nine Dumpling Islands (Acadia National Park; day use) stretch about a half-mile westward, much of the chain barred together at lower tides. To the north of Pigeon Hill and Ames Knob, Southern Harbor's pastoral shoreline stretches inland to a boatyard. The increasingly narrow southwest end of North Haven curves southward, with only a

Separating Vinalhaven and North Haven, the Fox Island Thorofare is home to more than 200 boats and the town of North Haven's waterfront.

few homes upon its shore, to Crabtree and Stand-In points, beyond which lie ledges jutting southward toward Fiddler Ledge and a stone navigational monument.

The less exposed and more direct route forward crosses the thorofare from the Dumplings southward to Vinalhaven, past Fish Head toward Browns Head Lighthouse. First built in 1832, the lighthouse now belongs to the town of Vinalhaven, and is the office of its town manager.

Follow the shore of Crockett Point south to the mouth of Crockett Cove, another inlet that warrants exploration. Tip Toe Mountain stands over the north side of the cove (sometimes called a river), where you can expect some current moving in and out, creating some rapids before it reaches Whitmore Pond at its head. Continue south through Leadbetter Narrows; you will want the current in your favor here. Ram Island (state-owned; camping) lies less than a mile southeast (157 degrees magnetic). A pair of tiny islets connected by a bar at lower tides, Ram is a generally protected spot with a small campsite in the woods on the larger east islet.

Exploring the west side of Vinalhaven is reason enough to base-camp on Ram for an extra night, paddling out around the White and Hurricane islands. First, you could stop at the Basin, a shallow tidal pool sprinkled with rocks and tiny islets. Depths just beyond the entrance plunge to over a hundred feet, explaining the strong currents that develop there. At peak flow, the current reaches 6 knots, creating standing waves and a patch of whitewater that stretches for several hundred feet. According to local lore, schooners used to winter-over inside the Basin, and at least one of the contemporary schooner fleet has made the run through the narrows to reach the inside. The Basin's water tends to be calm, as does the wild, undeveloped shoreline that surrounds it. The northern arm provides a good view of the wind generators.

Elsewhere in the area, watch for the ferry that passes through Lairey's Narrows multiple times daily. West of Crotch Island (private) is an unnamed landmass often referred to as Spectacle Island (private). The charts are unclear as to which islands are "The Spectacles." Perhaps all of them are. Either way, most of the north end of this island has been quarried away, leaving a lopped-off mess, an example of the conse-quences of the process gone unchecked. By contrast, the rest of the island is beautiful, with huge views taking in Penobscot Bay's northwest shore.

Big Garden (the northernmost of the White Islands) and Big White (the southern-most) were donated to The Nature Conservancy by Charles and Anne Lindbergh and are open for day use. Their smaller counterparts are private. Little Hurricane Island (state-owned) offers possible landings in calm enough conditions.

Hurricane Island (private; some access) was once a major quarrying island. From 1870 until 1915, there were two large and a number of smaller quarries in operation, run by as many as 1,200 employees. Now the island is managed by the Hurricane Island Foundation as a center for education and research for Outward Bound. Hike on the northern end of the island after checking in with the steward at the top of the main pier and signing a liability form.

Day 3: Ram Island to Seal Bay, 12.0 nautical miles

From Ram Island, head south down Hurricane Sound near slack or on a falling tide due to strong currents. Hug Vinalhaven's shore through the Reach and into busy Carvers Harbor where there is a public dock at the head. Fishing boats and the ferry come and go here. Stay out of their way, but check out the town's several restaurants, grocery, gallery, and other shops. Numerous remnants of the granite industry endure, including carved water troughs for horses and an eagle sculpture near the landing.

South of the harbor, Lane Island has a town preserve at its southern end. The island was the site of native peoples' villages from around 4,000 B.C. to Colonial times, and is now joined to Vinalhaven by a causeway. About 2 miles to the southeast, the tallest of a group of stark, mostly treeless islands is the 112-foot grassy summit of Brimstone Island (closed April through August for nesting storm petrels), visible for miles around and known for its beaches of polished black stones. Just east of Arey Neck State Beach is a town park. From here it's about 4 miles to Seal Bay, so it might be a good spot to stretch your legs.

Vinalhaven's east shore is open to Isle au Haut Bay, with Isle au Haut making a distinct profile 5.0 miles away. The property along this stretch is all private, but not overly developed. Past Calderwood Point, wind through the numerous islets and rocks and follow the shore along Coombs Neck. Just past Deep Cove, if the tide is high enough, slip south of Neck Island and into Seal Bay. Otherwise, continue on around Bluff Head and past Hen Island to Little Hen, which lies just west. The Little Hens (state-owned) are a pair of small islands with campsites for four people on each; look for landings on the east side and be careful of poison ivy.

Sailors like the protected anchorages in Seal Bay and Winter Harbor, but much of the contorted, shallow shoreline is tough to reach in all but the smallest boats. If you're not in a hurry, it's a great place to meander. There's another campsite on state-owned Hay Island: a pretty spot, much of it covered in tall marsh grass. The best landing is on the northeast-facing cove. Just west of Hay, the Burnt Islands and about a half-mile of shoreline south of them are all part of MCHT's Huber Preserve.

On the north side of Winter Harbor, Starboard Rock rises 163 feet directly from the water, while just behind it, a tidal inlet called Mill Priviledge winds nearly a mile into Calderwood Neck past mostly wild shores. A little west of Mill Priviledge, Carrying Place Bridge connects Vinalhaven with Calderwood Neck. This stretch of water, which flats out at lower tides, connects Winter Harbor with the Mill River.

Day 4: Seal Bay to Bakeman Beach, 14.0 nautical miles

If you began the trip with midafternoon low tides, by now low tide should occur at the end of the day, with a midday high tide. This is perfect for the trip back north if you launch in the morning and aim to arrive back at Cape Rosier midday.

Head north along the shore of Calderwood Neck and cross the entrance of the Fox Island Thorofare to Stimpsons Island. For the shortest crossings, go north of Carver Cove and pass Widow Island (private), the former site of a U.S. Navy yellow fever quarantine hospital from 1885 to 1904, later used as a retreat for patients from the Augusta and Bangor psychiatric hospitals. Goose Rocks Light is just to the north. From here, Little Thorofare Island is to the northeast. Retrace your route from Day 1.

ALTERNATIVES

The route as described is set up for economy of miles, but there may be time to explore the various inlets and nearby islands, particularly on multiday trips.

To avoid the long crossing, you could car-top out to the islands on a ferry. You could also consider a paddle or hike at Holbrook Island Sanctuary State Park (parksandlands.com; 207-326-4012) if conditions aren't favorable (see Trip 16: Alternatives for more).

MORE INFORMATION

Maine Department of Inland Fisheries and Wildlife (maine.gov/ifw; 207-287-8000). North Haven Conservation Partners (northhavenconservation.org; 207-867-2113). Maine Bureau of Public Lands (maine.gov/dacf/parks/about/public_reserved_lands.shtml; 207-287-4960). Maine Coast Heritage Trust (mcht.org; 207-244-5100). Vinalhaven Land Trust (vinalhavenlandtrust.org; 207-863-2543). Nearby routes offer additional camping options.

18
SOUTH OF ISLESBORO

Paddle wild islands beneath the backdrop of the Camden Hills.

Distance ▶	10.0 to 20.0 nautical miles, round-trip
Tidal Planning ▶	9.78-foot mean tidal range in Rockland. Floods north, ebbs south.
Cautions ▶	Western Penobscot Bay has plenty of boat traffic, including the ferry between Lincolnville and Grindle Point. Keep an eye out for big ships, which move more quickly than they first appear. The current increases as it moves around Islesboro. The ebb tide frequently opposes the prevailing southwest wind and waves, creating rough conditions, sometimes soon after calm conditions. Be attentive.
Charts and Maps ▶	NOAA charts #13305 and #13309; Maptech #74; Waterproof Chart #103

LAUNCH

Lincolnville Gravel beach north of ferry pier; parking fee in summer at the pier; free 4-hour parking at Lincolnville Beach; parking adjacent to sandy beach south of pier is for Islesboro residents only; bathrooms inside ferry office. From the intersection of US 1 and ME 173 in Lincolnville, take ME 173/McKay Road south a few hundred feet to the beach. *GPS coordinates: 44° 16.828′ N, 69° 0.442′ W.*

Other Public Access Mark Island is owned by The Nature Conservancy (TNC); Goose Island and East Goose Rock are state-owned nesting islands, closed April through August, but otherwise open for day use. A town park sits just east of Pendleton Point. Warren Island State Park offers landings, trails, and campsites; see More Information for details. Public landings are available at Grindle Point, near the ferry dock and lighthouse.

ROUTE DESCRIPTION

The west shore of Penobscot Bay tends to be steep and lacking in obvious features. Long stretches of eroding shorefront are divided by various retaining walls, most supporting backyards of homes overlooking the water. There aren't many nooks in which to shelter or public access landings. But, the Islesboro archipelago, just to the west, offers a mix of wild, contorted shoreline and old upscale homes, with myriad route possibilities among the many islands.

Warren Island, Maine's only island state park, can provide a base camp for exploring the area. The islands stretching southward make for a good day trip, taking you to a place that truly feels "out there" but which is not far from the constant backdrop of the Camden Hills and the more distant shores of North Haven.

The Penobscot name for Islesboro meant "island that lies between two channels," while their name for Lincolnville roughly translated to "choppy seas." The first European settlers in 1769 were less imaginative, calling it Long Island Plantation, which eventually gave way to the present name. During the 1800s Islesboro housed the largest commercial shipping fleet in Penobscot Bay, but that changed after the Civil War when a resort community took hold and wealthy rusticators built large summer homes, many of which are still visible along Islesboro's shores.

Crossing from Lincolnville to Seven Hundred Acre Island may not be the shortest way to get across West Penobscot Bay, but it keeps you south of the diagonal path the ferry takes to Grindle Point. The current is likely to push you one way or another, so be sure to line up a couple of landmarks to keep a range. The most current-efficient approach to this route is to start on a falling tide, rounding Mark Island around low tide, and returning on the flood.

Aim just about anywhere on Seven Hundred Acre Island (private); there aren't a lot of distinguishing features. If you can discern the slightly different tone to the spruces on Philbrook Head, neighboring Philbrook Cove could be a good spot toward which to aim. There is a nice beach in the cove with a couple of homes near its west end. Follow the shore to the southern point and on to the Ensign Islands (private) about a half-mile south. To the east, the big island is Job Island (private), named for early settler Job Pendleton. Head for its southern end. A farmhouse and barn that once stood are both long gone, leaving only a cellar hole filled in by forest. About a half-mile south, gravel beaches on low, treeless Little Bermuda (town-owned) appear at lower tides, making landings easy. This is a good spot for a break, and in summer months, you're likely to share it with others.

Follow the chain of islands south. Low-lying Lime Island (private), named for lime kilns there in the 1700s, has a gradual shore and is barred to Lasell Island (private). Both were occupied for generations by inhabitants who farmed and fished. One legend has it that 30 or so British soldiers are buried on the eastern shore of Lasell, but there has been no sign of the graves for many years. Currently there are several houses on its west side and a large beach in the east-facing cove where a fisherman keeps traps on a floating dock. Forested Mark Island (TNC) lies about a mile southwest. The most likely landing area along its steep and rocky shores is a gravel beach at the northeast end; at the south end, ledges extend seaward and are likely to produce rough seas.

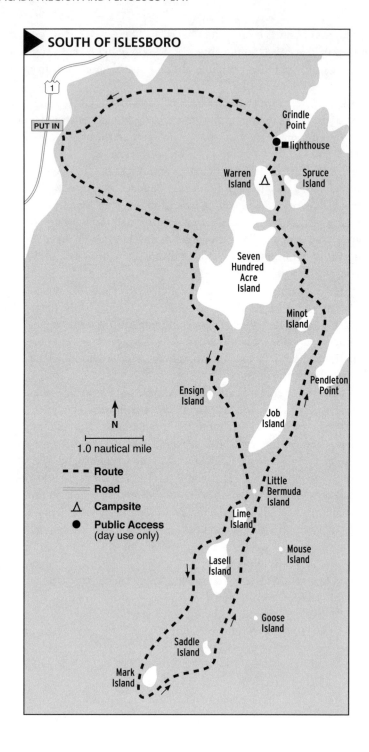

SOUTH OF ISLESBORO

PUT IN

Grindle
Point

■ lighthouse

Warren
Island

Spruce
Island

Seven
Hundred
Acre
Island

Minot
Island

Pendleton
Point

Ensign
Island

Job
Island

N

1.0 nautical mile

- - - Route
——— Road
△ Campsite
● Public Access
(day use only)

Little
Bermuda
Island

Lime
Island

Mouse
Island

Lasell
Island

Goose
Island

Saddle
Island

Mark
Island

Return north via the bluffy southern end of Saddle Island (private). Pass the gravel beach at the northeast cove and continue north. Goose Island (state-owned) is a treeless, rocky hump.

Follow the eastern side of Job Island to Islesboro's Pendleton Point, which has a town beach just to its east. Pass Middle Island (private; barred to Job) and Minot Island (private), and take a northwest course across Gilkey Harbor, back to Seven Hundred Acre Island.

Among other affluent rusticators, illustrator and *Life* magazine publisher Charles Dana Gibson summered on Seven Hundred Acre Island and his descendants now own much of it. The estate on the island's eastern point is Gibson's "Indian Landing." Just above the beach is a small, castle-like cottage that he built for his grandchildren in 1926. North of the point, Cradle Cove has a full boatyard.

Just ahead to the north is Warren Island (state park; camping). Tide permitting, follow the passage southwest of Spruce Island. A sandy area at Warren's south end makes a good break spot, or follow the eastern shore to a dock and a gravel landing area with a park kiosk. A fee is required to visit and walk the trails.

The Grindle Point ferry terminal is across a short, busy stretch of water. There's a museum and a café at the Grindle Point Lighthouse. To avoid the ferry on your trip

The Islesboro archipelago offers a mix of wild, contorted shoreline and old upscale homes, with myriad route possibilities among the many islands.

back to Lincolnville, take a northerly course, toward Spruce Head, at the north end of Ducktrap Harbor. As on the first leg of the trip, be aware of the currents. You may need to keep a range and set a ferry angle to stay on course.

ALTERNATIVES

Warren Island makes a great base camp from which to explore Islesboro. The short portage between Crow Cove and Islesboro Harbor is over private land. Muscle Ridge (Trip 19) is not far to the southwest, while Cape Rosier (Trip 16) is just a few miles east. From Mark Island, North Haven (Trip 17) is about 3 miles away.

To eliminate the initial crossing, car-top from Lincolnville via the ferry; on Islesboro, park along the road and launch near the ferry terminal or at other points on the island. This option isn't cheap, but could make sense if you're spending a few days on Warren Island or avoiding rough conditions. Shore paddles from Lincolnville are one option too, but the bay is likely to be as rough as areas around the islands. The Passagassawakeag River north of Belfast is likely to be sheltered on most days. Or take a day off from paddling and hike in the Camden Hills for stunning views of the area you could be paddling. The waves will look small from up there.

MORE INFORMATION

The Nature Conservancy (nature.org/maine; 207-729-5181). Maine Department of Inland Fisheries and Wildlife (maine.gov/ifw; 207-287-8000). Warren Island State Park (parksandlands.com; 207-446-7090 [May 15 to September 15] or 207-941-4014 [September 16 to May 14]); open Memorial Day through September 15; entrance fee charged. Reservations for campsites are recommended. Fresh water, outhouses. Some sites have shelters. Wheeled carts are available to haul gear. Nearby Camden Hills State Park has campsites, but they are not near the water.

19
MUSCLE RIDGE

Explore a stunning archipelago of granite islands with lighthouses, old quarries, and osprey.

Distance ▶	12.0 to 14.0 nautical miles, round-trip
Tidal Planning ▶	9.04-foot mean tidal range in Thomaston. Floods northeast, ebbs southwest. This route works best if you start on a falling tide, and the tide changes before you begin paddling back to the northeast.
Cautions ▶	A strong current runs through Muscle Ridge Channel. Be aware of conditions and how they will interact with the current, especially as tides change. The southeast shores of the outer islands are exposed to open ocean and even on mild days tend to have rough conditions.
Charts and Maps ▶	NOAA chart #13303; Maptech #74; Waterproof Chart #103

LAUNCHES

Birch Point State Park, Owls Head Hand-carry to a sand beach launch when park is open; daytime parking; outhouses. From the intersection of US 1 and ME 73 in Rockland, go south on ME 73 for 3.9 miles. Turn left (east) on Dublin Road and drive for 1.3 miles to Ballhac Road. Take a right and continue 0.4 mile, through the park entrance, to the beach. *GPS coordinates: 44° 2.350' N, 69° 5.840' W.*

Weskeag River Launch, South Thomaston Paved ramp; limited daytime and overnight parking. Area near ramp flats out at low tide. From the intersection of US 1 and ME 73 in Rockland, go south on ME 73 for 3.9 miles. The ramp is across the intersection of ME 73 and Dublin Road. *GPS coordinates: 44° 3.099' N, 69° 7.510' W.*

Merchants Landing, Sprucehead Island Boatyard with ramp (fees); daytime and overnight parking; water, supplies, and bathrooms. From the Weskeag River Launch, continue west on ME 73/Spruce Head Road. In 7.2 miles, turn left onto Island Road; it becomes Rockledge Road in 1.3 miles. The left turn for Merchants Landing is 0.3 mile beyond; follow the road for about 0.25 mile to the boatyard. *GPS coordinates: 44° 0.024' N, 69° 7.008' W.*

Other Public Access Landings here are most plentiful for Maine Island Trail Association (MITA) members, except during osprey nesting in the spring when all MITA islands are closed. For others, a few private islands allow public landings; always look for signs confirming permitted access. Dix Island has a northern-facing cove with a landing. High Island welcomes visitors to land at the beach and to use the trails. State-owned Two Bush Island is closed April through August.

ROUTE DESCRIPTION

The Muscle Ridge is an underwater mountain chain thick with mollusks. The first charts of the area were made by English cartographers, and in this case, their Old English spelling made it onto the modern charts; while there is a certain muscularity to the stout, rippling granite on the ocean side of this island chain, the spelling refers to the creature.

This idyllic group of islands is separated from South Thomaston by a stretch of open water and a channel that runs 8.0 miles between the lights at Owls Head and Whitehead Island. The bigger outer islands—Andrews, Hewett, Pleasant, and Graffam—buffer the effects of the open sea upon the smaller islands in their lee, and if the crossing from South Thomaston isn't too rough, you can usually find some sheltered paddling in this area. The southeast side can feel surprisingly rough though, even on otherwise calm days, so venture there only after assessing the conditions.

Quarries put these islands on the map back in the late 1800s, and you can see signs of this activity as you paddle. The area has quieted in the last century, but you're unlikely to be alone. The islands still support a few summer cottages and homes. Sailors like the anchorage between Dix and High islands, though most boats pass through the channel without exploring the numerous rocks and ledges among these islands.

Birch Point Beach is a fine place to launch during the park's hours of operation. If you prefer an earlier start or plan on enjoying the sunset, consider the other launches. The Weskeag River launch adds a couple of miles onto either end and makes going with the tide more important. Merchants Landing and Lobster Buoy Campsites (see More Information) are also on the route.

From the beach, take care to give swimmers plenty of room. Line up the green day marker on Otter Ledge with the red one on easily recognizable Otter Island and start the crossing. The current in Muscle Ridge Channel may push you; be attentive and adjust your ferry angle accordingly.

Otter Island, about a mile and a half from the launch, has a house on it with a private dock on the south shore. Head south past low-lying Little Green Island to Dix Island (private), which allows public landings in the north-facing cove; look for signs confirming the public is still welcome on the trails. Cast-off black and white-flecked granite fragments, some bearing the marks of quarrying tools, litter the beach. Over 2,000 workers once lived on Dix Island, where trails edge through the quarries' remains. The island had more than 150 buildings, including boarding houses and an opera house. Today, Dix is owned by the Dix Island Association, whose members seek

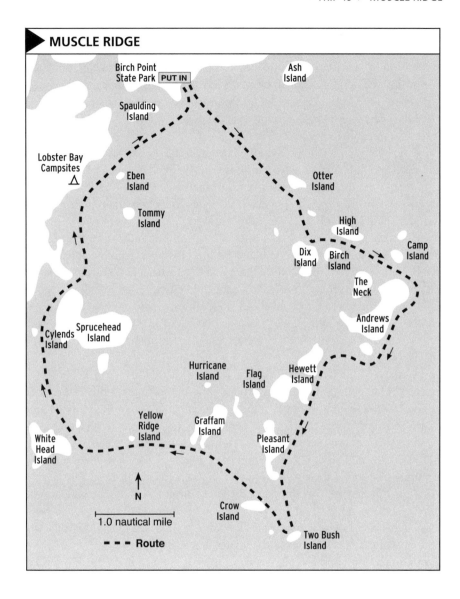

a self-sufficient lifestyle without electricity. They own the land in common, and their individually owned houses are built to blend with the landscape.

Continue past low, treeless Birch Island and the Neck to the north side of Andrews Island. Cottages line Andrews's north side, but almost a mile of the southeast shore is bold and steep with smooth, pink-orange granite bluffs dropping into the sea. There's a lot of fetch off to your left. Matinicus is a low smudge 10.0 miles to the southeast, while the Green Islands, 5.0 miles away, appear a bit right of it. This is not a place to be if you're not prepared: a little swell goes a long way here, the sea rolling in from

180-foot depths a half-mile out to pile up over rocky shallows. If the seas look big, take a more sheltered route along the northwest sides of the islands.

At Nash Point, the shore turns treeless and low, giving way to scattered rocks and ledges at the end. There's usually calmer water in the west-facing cove beyond the point, a good place for a breather. Arc northward along the shore of Hewett and Pleasant islands for a more interesting route that keeps you away from boat traffic; it adds 0.2 mile to a more direct route.

At low tide, ledges stretch out far to the northeast of Two Bush Island (state-owned; closed April through August for nesting). Reach the lighthouse here from the north side, or land at the gravel beach just north of the ledges. From the hilltop near the lighthouse, Matinicus and the Greens rise higher over the horizon, while Metinic Island, just 5.0 miles southwest, looks almost close.

Whitehead Island Lighthouse is a little over 2.0 miles north of Two Bush. You're more likely to encounter easier conditions for this crossing around slack tide. (To get through shallow Seal Harbor and the bridge to Sprucehead Island after Whitehead, you'll need the depths that come later than low tide.) Assuming you follow a perfectly straight line, a direct route to Whitehead is 2.2 miles; an arcing, near-shore route of 2.5 miles grazes Crow and Graffam islands before crossing the channel via Yellow Ridge Island. The longer takes the average paddler less than 10 extra minutes; the choice is yours.

The working Whitehead Light Station has guided mariners into Penobscot Bay since 1803. The grounds are also used for adult enrichment programs and rentals. A dock and boathouse are just north of the lighthouse. The rest of the island is private and parts are under a conservation easement held by the Maine Coast Heritage Trust.

Wind your way north along the ledges through Seal Harbor, passing tiny Cylends Island (pronounced "Slins"), which is private but gets plenty of visits from the local community. Assuming there's enough water to float your boat, head for the bridge connecting Elwell Point to Sprucehead Island. Beyond that, make your way past Tommy and Eben islands (both private), or toward Waterman Beach. If you're hungry, Waterman's Beach Lobster offers a beach landing and picnic table dining. North of Waterman Point, Lobster Buoy Campsites also has a stretch of beach.

Continue past the mouth of the Weskeag River and Spaulding Island. Birch Point Beach is just past Otter Point.

ALTERNATIVES
Head north around Ash Island (land trust-owned) or farther to Fisherman, Sheep, or Monroe islands. Or head south toward Tenants Harbor.

To shorten the trip, plan a 4.0- to 5.0-mile out-and-back to Dix Island. If conditions are rough, explore the Weskeag River via the Weskeag River launch.

Dix Island (private) allows public landings in the north-facing cove; look for signs confirming the public is still welcome on the trails that lead to the remains of a once thriving granite quarry.

MORE INFORMATION

Birch Point State Park (parksandlands.com; 207-941-4014); open 9 A.M. to sunset, Memorial Day to Labor Day. Maine Department of Inland Fisheries and Wildlife (maine.gov/ifw; 207-287-8000). Whitehead Light Station (whiteheadlightstation .org; 207-200-7957). There are camping options for Maine Island Trail Association members on the route. On shore, Lobster Buoy Campsites (lobsterbuoycampsites .wix.com; 207-594-7546) has tent and RV sites; launch directly from waterfront tent-sites or use the campground's launch area.

THE MIDCOAST
AND CASCO BAY

Following the course of Midcoast Maine's rivers on a chart without getting lost takes some effort. South of US 1, the rivers are all tidal estuaries, more influenced by the ocean than the influx of fresh water from the lands they drain. The Saint George and Medomak rivers feed into Muscongus Bay (Trip 20), where island ridges extend seaward, and eventually toward Eastern Egg Rock, where puffins congregate for much of the summer. To the south, Monhegan Island is a trip requiring greater commitment than most paddlers are willing to undertake, but it's certainly attainable in the right conditions. Just west of Muscongus, the Damariscotta River empties after a 19-mile journey from its source. Among the islands scattered southward at this drainage is Damariscove Island (Trip 21), where a cove sheltered a European settlement as early as 1604.

The Kennebec River, the region's largest, flows 170 miles from Moosehead Lake. Though several other rivers join the Kennebec before it meets the sea, it's tidal as far north as Augusta. Just east, the Sheepscot River also reaches southward and in between them flow lacework of the Back and Sasanoa rivers, joining at Hockamock Bay. The abundance of fish at this nutrient-rich meeting of rivers and ocean supported colonization earlier than other areas. English settlers built a fort and colony at the mouth of the Kennebec River in 1607, a short-lived, largely forgotten settlement overshadowed by the success of Jamestown and Plymouth. If you time your trip with the strong currents, you can catch a tidal push around Georgetown Island (Trip 22), taking in quite a lot of scenery and passing several campsites along the way. Paddlers know the Popham area for its surf and the standing waves that form in the mouth of the Kennebec—a fun place to play if you know what you're doing, a hazardous stretch of water if you don't.

Considering that more than a third of Maine's population lives near Casco Bay's southwest shore in Greater Portland, the bay usually feels relatively uncrowded. Maybe that's due to its numerous islands: depending on who you ask, they number anywhere from 136 to 222. At the east end of the bay, the New Meadows River, a 12-mile long estuary, flows past Sebascodegan Island (Trip 23) and out past Cape Small. To the west, the islands and necks turn more finger-like, alternating with corresponding slips of the ocean reaching inward to vast shallows. At the "fingertips," the ridges of land sink below the surface, but reemerge as long, narrow islands projecting southwest.

Public access to islands abounds in Casco Bay (Trips 24 to 26). Island camping here feels almost as remote as anywhere else on the Maine coast. And you can't go far without coming across reminders of the past. Casco Bay has been the site of six forts, most obviously Fort Gorges, and is marked with the remains of various concrete bunkers and gun emplacements on a number of the islands, some of which date back to the War of 1812.

Conditions in Casco Bay can be strikingly diverse. Seas on the south side tend to be more prone to open ocean conditions, while the island-sheltered northern areas can be a good place to paddle when seas pick up, particularly in the upper bay. Look out for the gaps between the islands where increased currents can turn seas rough.

20
MUSCONGUS BAY

*Handrail an island chain to the edge of open
ocean and visit the third-oldest lighthouse in
the state and possibly a puffin colony.*

Distance ▶ 5.0 to 16.0 nautical miles, round-trip

Tidal Planning ▶ 9.04-foot mean tidal range in Thomaston. Current floods both inland, toward the rivers, and to the east, toward Penobscot Bay.

Cautions ▶ Friendship is a busy fishing harbor; avoid boat traffic. Muscongus Bay is subject to open ocean conditions, especially as one leaves the shelter of the inner islands. Current going in and out of the Medomak and St. George rivers can complicate those conditions.

Charts and Maps ▶ NOAA chart #13301; Waterproof Chart #102

LAUNCHES

Bradford Point, Friendship Paved ramp and gravel beach leading to an area that flats out at lower tides (usually about a 100-foot walk over the mud); limited parking on east side of road, west side by permit only; no facilities. Residents of the Garrison may drive across flats; do not block the road. For parking options, some books list a bed and breakfast nearby that is no longer in business. This is not the same Bradford Point shown on charts to the northeast on the Meduncook River. From the junction of US 1 and ME 220 in Waldoboro, take ME 220 south for 9.3 miles. At the junction with ME 97, turn left for 0.2 mile and make a right on Bradford Point Road. The launch is at the terminus in 1.4 miles. *GPS coordinates: 43° 58.224′ N, 69° 19.661′ W.*

Friendship Town Landing Steps down to mud/gravel beach launch between fishing boats with about 100 feet of mud and debris to cross at low tide; plenty of parking, but popular for workboats and others; secluded town lot is just a 5-minute walk away, beside Harbor Cemetery; no facilities at either location. This is the heart of the town's fishing activity; expect a crowded harbor. From the junction of ME 220 and ME 97 in Friendship, go south on Harbor Road for 0.6 mile to Town Landing Road. Take a left; the landing is at the end in 0.1 mile. *GPS coordinates: 43° 58.418′ N, 69° 20.233′ W.*

Other Public Access Black Island (Chewonki Foundation [CF]) offers a small campsite and a possible landing. Franklin Island is part of the Maine Coastal Islands National Wildlife Refuge (MCINWR) and is closed April through July. State-owned Eastern Egg Rock is also closed for nesting April through August. Other options are available for Maine Island Trail Association (MITA) members.

ROUTE DESCRIPTION

Bordered by tidal rivers winding inland to the north and a broad mouth spanning 11 miles, Muscongus Bay offers ample route possibilities for paddlers of any level. The sheltered harbors and rivers are likely to be calm on most days, while chains of closely spaced islands lead south toward more challenging broader crossings, dotted with desolate, wave-swept ledges.

There could easily be a route for each of the three chains of islands and the rivers stretching north to south but this description focuses on the central island group, launching from Friendship. Previous paddling guidebooks have warned against this launch point due to congestion and the abundance of fishing boats in the harbors. These are always issues, but in recent years (perhaps due to those guidebooks or declining numbers of small boaters) paddlers have used Friendship's launch sites with few problems. As always, be considerate and consciously minimize your impact on and off the water.

Depending on whose translation you use, the Abenaki called the bay "Muscongus" to reflect either the abundance of fish or rocky ledges. While the fish population has dwindled since the Abenaki fished here, the bay's nutrient-rich waters—fed by two major rivers and several smaller ones—still support a thriving fishery. Both Friendship and Port Clyde house large fishing fleets, consistently among the top ten in the state for value of their annual catches.

Rocks and ledges are abundant here. Eastern Egg Rock lures birders (usually on tour boats) to view puffins, razorbills, and other uncommon species. The sparsely vegetated island exerts its pull on paddlers outside of nesting season as well. The 7-acre island lies about halfway between Pemaquid Point and Port Clyde, and whether you see birds there or not, a visit to Eastern Egg Rock satisfies that urge to get "out there." Once "out there," some paddlers will be taunted by the apparent nearness of Monhegan Island, which lies about 6 miles southeast; this long trip over a volatile stretch of ocean requires planning and preparedness.

Either Friendship launch starts this route off well. From the end of Bradford Point Road, the route passes the Garrison (private), barred to the point at lower tides. Settled in 1750, this island sheltered European homesteaders during the French and Indian War. In 1758, thirteen settlers were killed or captured in two separate raids in the area.

Follow either shore of Friendship Long Island. Just north of the Garrison and Long Island's northern point, Friendship Harbor—home to the local lobster fishing fleet and its share of recreational craft—bustles with activity. Traverse the harbor with care. If you're lucky, there may be a Friendship sloop in the harbor. In the late 1800s to early

1900s, these gaff-rigged sloops with elliptical sterns and jaunty bowsprits became the state's renowned workhorse fishing boats. The design was influenced by Gloucester fishing boats, but evolved as Friendship-area builders met the need for a boat that could both carry large loads and be managed by one man to haul lobster traps.

The island's shore is mostly undeveloped, interspersed with homes. Judging by the dates on headstones in a cemetery hidden in the north-end woods, the locals have been here for a couple of centuries. Near the northwest point, a dam across the mouth of a cove forms a 6-acre lobster pound and research facility for the Lobster Conservancy. On the island's east side, much of the area around Lobster Gut develops mudflats at low tide, but lobster boats still pass through at top speed. Also overlooking Lobster Gut is Morse Island, where Warren, Cornelius, and Edward Morse built some of the original Friendship sloops.

South of Friendship Long, homes on Cranberry Island (private) are concentrated around the cove on the north end, facing Minister Gut. A shallow area south of Cranberry is barred at low tide to Cedar Island (private). Black Island (CF) has campsites

Among the chains of closely spaced islands leading south from Friendship, Black Island has public campsites near its north end.

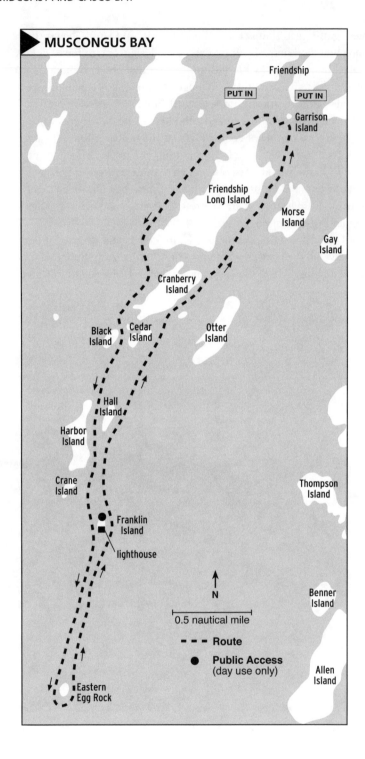

MUSCONGUS BAY

Friendship

PUT IN   PUT IN

Garrison
Island

Friendship
Long Island

Morse
Island

Gay
Island

Cranberry
Island

Otter
Island

Black
Island

Cedar
Island

Hall
Island

Harbor
Island

Crane
Island

Thompson
Island

Franklin
Island

lighthouse

N

Benner
Island

0.5 nautical mile

- - - Route

● Public Access
(day use only)

Allen
Island

Eastern
Egg Rock

near its north end. If no one is already camping there, it's also a good spot for a break. To the south, houses overlook the shallow stretch of water between Harbor and Hall islands; one stone home on Harbor dates back to the mid-1800s.

The light on Franklin Island (MCINWR) has guided mariners since it was finished in 1807. The island is off-limits from April through July due to nesting seabirds; at other times, in calm conditions, there is a challenging landing area among rocks on the north side, beside the remains of a dock.

Read the stretch of water around Franklin Island to get a sense of conditions southward to Eastern Egg Rock (state-owned), where you won't find much shelter. There's plenty of fetch to the south, and seas can get big here. As the tide changes, the current may turn against the prevailing wind and seas, turning conditions rougher. Even if it's a good day, take a bearing before you start just in case the fog rolls in. As you paddle, line up a distant lobster buoy with the island to get a sense of where the current is pushing you. Adjust your ferry angle, if necessary, to avoid paddling a big arc toward the island rather than a straight line. Approach the island slowly, keeping an eye out for birds. If you're lucky, you'll see some puffins or razorbills. These pelagic birds usually go back out to sea by mid-August. Outside of nesting season (April through August) you could land at the northern end of the island.

Once you've had your fill of Eastern Egg's desolate beauty, turn north and follow the route back. If you're up for a longer trip, you could head either east or west to make a big loop back to Friendship.

ALTERNATIVES

Combine this route with a circuit of the islands either to the east or the west for a route of 18 miles or so, or explore east *and* west for a longer multiday trip. For a truly epic journey, venture north into the rivers as well.

The Meduncook River is a relatively sheltered area to paddle, and at higher tides may be followed more than 3.0 miles inland from the Bradford Point launch.

MORE INFORMATION

Chewonki Foundation (chewonki.org; 207-882-7323). Maine Coastal Islands National Wildlife Refuge (fws.gov/refuge/Maine_Coastal_Islands; 207-594-0600). Maine Department of Inland Fisheries and Wildlife (maine.gov/ifw; 207-287-8000). To the west of the described route, Thief Island (state-owned) has sites at the north and south ends. Just south of Thomaston on the St. George River, Saltwater Farm Campground is another overnight option off-route. Several other nearby options are available to MITA members.

LOBSTERS

Lobsters' highly developed sensory abilities help them navigate the rocky ocean floor at night. In addition to two pairs of antennae, lobsters' shells bristle with thousands of tiny hair-like setae, which can sense motion and chemical clues in the water. Their eyes contain around 13,500 mirror-like surfaces, which Trevor Corson's *The Secret Life of Lobsters* describes as "such a novel and ingenious design that it inspires religious faith and scientific admiration alike." All of this complex information is gathered and processed by a very tiny brain. We will probably never know what a lobster experiences, but they certainly have the ability to sift through an amazing amount of environmental information.

For an animal of its size, the lobster is a well-equipped predator. The pincher claw moves quickly; the crusher claw breaks into shellfish or other lobsters and has the ability to snap shut and stay that way. In older males, the claws can account for half of a lobster's total body weight. Much of the lobster's remaining muscle is in the tail, which it uses to propel itself backward quickly and suddenly.

In the first five years of their lives, lobsters molt about 25 times. Then they molt only twice a year until they reach sexual maturity, somewhere between 5 and 8 years; after that, lobsters molt only once a year. This long, difficult process leaves lobsters extremely vulnerable. Lobsters may starve themselves beforehand in order to slip out of their shells. After molting, they fill themselves with water, puffing up to create a larger shell. They can increase their volume by half.

After they molt, lobsters hunker down for a few weeks in a protected area, which they've prepared in advance. They use their claws and legs to build a den of sand and rocks into which they may haul food to store for later. Lobsters eat just about anything, dead or alive, from plankton and sea grasses to shellfish and other lobsters.

Male lobsters deposit sperm packets in recently molted females, who may then store them for up to a year before fertilizing. When she's ready, she releases up to 100,000 eggs and attaches them beneath her abdomen with a sticky substance. She may carry these eggs for 9 to 11 months before they hatch.

The larvae hatch at night and float to the surface in a planktonic state to spend the next month or two at the whim of tide and wind, far more likely to become food for another creature than to grow into a harvester's catch. As the lobsters grow, the molting process begins and they start to resemble their adult counterparts, finally sinking to the ocean floor to begin life as a lobster.

21
DAMARISCOVE ISLAND

*These wild, steep-sided rocky islands are
steeped in history and are a short paddle
from shore.*

Distance ▶	9.0 nautical miles, round-trip
Tidal Planning ▶	9.35-foot mean tidal range on Damariscotta River. Floods north, ebbs south. Fisherman Island Passage floods east.
Cautions ▶	These islands are exposed to the open ocean and whatever conditions it may bring, particularly around the south end of Damariscove Island. The ledges past the southwest tip of Damariscove (labeled "The Motions" on the chart) can have especially rough conditions. Fishermans Passage has plenty of boat traffic, including large tour boats.
Charts and Maps ▶	NOAA chart #13293; Maptech #76; Waterproof Chart #102

LAUNCH

Ocean Point, East Boothbay Hand-carry to beach; drop off gear and park a short distance up the road at a public parking area; no facilities. From the intersection of US 1 and ME 27 in Edgecomb, follow ME 27 south for 10.7 miles to Boothbay. Turn left on ME 96/Ocean Point Road. In 5.9 miles, find the beach as Ocean Point Road curves southwest. *GPS Coordinates: 43° 48.927' N, 69° 35.726' W.*

Other Public Access Landing on Ram Island is permitted by prior appointment only; the island is managed by the Ram Island Preservation Society. Damariscove Island (Boothbay Region Land Trust) has a few areas with possible landings; Woods End is closed for nesting March 15 through August 15.

ROUTE DESCRIPTION

Damariscove Island is a wild, desolate spot exposed to the open ocean, ringed by steep rocks. This is a true "bargain" destination, just a few miles' paddle from the launch, with rich history and a lighthouse on the way.

Habitation on Damariscove goes way back. The Abenaki called it "place of landing," paddling there in canoes to collect eggs and catch fish. Stories of Europeans on the island go back to the 1500s (clay pipes from that era have been unearthed) but the more established history begins in 1608, when the Popham colonists returned to England, leaving one man who chose to stay. Humphrey Damerill settled on the island and set up a store catering to fishing crews, who began using the island as a base. The *Mayflower* stopped here in 1620 en route to Plymouth. By 1622, thirteen fishermen lived on the island year-round. When the starving Pilgrims returned for provisions, the islanders sent them back with a boatload of cod.

Massachusetts Bay Colony laid claim to Damariscove in 1671, establishing government, setting up a military and law enforcement presence, and assessing taxes. There were wars with the Americans Indians and then the American Revolution, during which the island was raided, a house burned, and the livestock commandeered. But the island residents carried on dairy farming, fishing, and harvesting ice from the freshwater pond. In the late 1800s, Damariscove residents sold their wares to nearby summer communities, and in 1897 the Coast Guard established a lifesaving station on the island. By 1917, most of the community had left, but the Coast Guard station was manned until 1959. The Boothbay Region Land Trust now owns the island.

From the cove at Ocean Point, head for the lighthouse on Ram Island, managed by the Ram Island Preservation Society. Keep an eye on the channel markers and cross the channel quickly. The current here floods to the east. According to local lore, in the mid-1800s, a fisherman sailing home after dark came so close to hitting the rocks near Ram Island that he became the area's self-appointed light-keeper. Each evening he hung a lantern so others could find their way. Years later he moved away, but not before another fisherman, saved by his lantern, appointed himself as successor. This tradition continued until the third self-appointed lantern-tender rigged a dory with a lantern that returning boaters would light as they passed by at the end of the day. The next self-appointed light-tender agreed to light a lantern on foggy or stormy nights, but this light was weaker and less visible and failed to prevent wrecks. After a period in which ghosts are reported to have aided sailors past this spot, the government finally built the lighthouse in 1883.

Just southeast of Ram, Fisherman Island (private) has a large home on it. The prevailing winds from the southwest tend to make its west side a bit rougher to paddle. From the south end of Fisherman, head for Damariscove Island. You're likely to start feeling any swell here, if you haven't already. Again, you could paddle on either side of the island, depending upon conditions.

At the north end of Damariscove, Wood End is a seabird nesting area and is off-limits to visitors from March 15 through August 15, although there are several pocket beaches where landing is possible. Landing may be possible in the coves flanking the narrow strip of rocks joining Wood End with the south end, especially at the eastern cove. Just above the eastern cove beach is the freshwater pond and access to the island's trails. The shore from here to the south end is steep with minimal bailout opportunities.

At the south end of Damariscove, deep water quickly gives way to gradual shallows sloping away from the island; expect the swell to get a bit taller here. Be especially

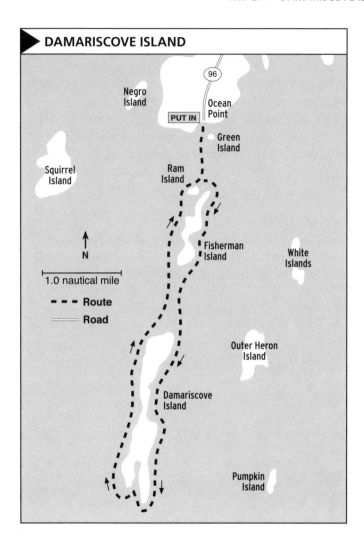

careful south of the west point, where numerous rocks make conditions even livelier. Inside the harbor though, the seas tend to calm down. Make your way to the head of the cove, past the former lifesaving station (private), private cottage, and a tiny museum housed in a former fish house. You're welcome to explore the grounds, but don't use the stone pier, which is leased to commercial fishing operations. It takes about 10 minutes to follow the trail through dense, shrubby vegetation up to the tower. Be careful to avoid poison ivy, which thrives on the island. On a clear day, from the tower you can Metinic and Monhegan islands to the east over to Seguin Island and Cape Small to the west.

For the return trip, if you came out along the east shore, follow the west shore back. With the prevailing southwest winds and swells, you're likely to get some help. If you go that way, be careful going around the southwest point—don't cut it too short.

ALTERNATIVES

Take a side trip out to Outer Heron and the White Islands. Both Outer Heron and Outer White islands are part of the Maine Coastal Islands National Wildlife Refuge and are off-limits during nesting season, but they are dramatic. Outer Heron has the only substantial forest among these islands, while Outer White has tall white cliffs plunging directly into the sea. When it isn't nesting season, land in a tiny pocket beach on the north side of Outer White and follow rocky ledges up to the chimney at the island's high point, where the view is spectacular.

Depending on conditions, head east up the Damariscotta River for a more sheltered paddle.

MORE INFORMATION

Boothbay Regional Land Trust (bbrlt.org; 207-633-4818). No camping is available on the route. West Cuckhold Island, 1.5 miles west, has a small campsite, as does Fort Island, 5.5 nautical miles up the Damariscotta River from Ocean Point.

Damariscove Island's narrow harbor, shown here with the former lifesaving station (private), feels remote, despite the relatively short paddle to get there.

22
GEORGETOWN ISLAND

Paddle past a rocky coast, sandy beaches, rivers, marshes, and the charming Five Islands Harbor.

Distance ▶ Up to 20.0 nautical miles, round-trip

Tidal Planning ▶ 8.48-foot mean tidal range in the Kennebec River. Floods north, ebbs south. Fast currents develop in some constricted areas, developing standing waves and other features that most will want to avoid. Exercise caution in Lower Hell Gate, Goose Rocks Passage, and the mouth of the Kennebec, particularly near Jack Rock. The tide change upriver takes place later than at the mouth: check tide and current charts. The tide change at Mill Point on the Sasanoa River generally occurs about a half-hour later than at Fort Popham.

Cautions ▶ Strong currents. Open ocean conditions at southern end of Georgetown Island.

Charts and Maps ▶ NOAA chart #13293; Maptech #76; Waterproof Chart #102

LAUNCHES

Fort Popham, Phippsburg Hand-carry beach launch; limited daytime parking; outhouse. From the junction of US 1 and ME 209 in Bath, follow ME 209 south for 2.4 miles. Turn left to continue on ME 209/Bridge Street, then left again—in another 8.8 miles—on ME 209 at its junction with ME 216. In 1.7 miles, turn right to stay on ME 209 until it ends at Fort Popham in 3.1 miles. *GPS coordinates: 43° 45.290' N, 69° 47.063' W.*

Reid State Park, Georgetown Hand-carry beach launch; daytime parking with entry fee; bathrooms and water. From the junction of US 1 and ME 127 in Woolwich, follow ME 127 south for 10.4 miles, following signs to the park. Turn south on Seguinland Road. In 2.2 miles (during which you'll enter the park and pay an entry fee), bear left and park in first lot to launch at adjacent beach. *GPS coordinates: 43° 47.066' N, 69° 43.369' W.*

Robinhood Marine, Georgetown Hand-carry fee launch; day and overnight parking. From the junction of US 1 and ME 127, follow ME 127 south for 5.6 miles to Robinhood Road. Turn left; follow signs to that marina over the next 1.7 miles. *GPS coordinates: 43° 51.201' N, 69° 44.032' W.*

Other Public Access Perkins (state-owned) and Castle (Chewonki Foundation [CF]) islands both have campsites. AMC's Knubble Bay Camp and Beal Island are available for overnight use with prior reservations. Wood Island (The Nature Conservancy [TNC]) is open to the public for day use. An additional hand-carry launch at Five Islands is located near Reid State Park at the end of ME 127.

ROUTE DESCRIPTION
When you read a chart of the Midcoast rivers, it can be tough to tell where the islands begin and end. The maze of marshes, rivers, and long, winding inlets end in more marshes or mudflats. Winding roads, connecting islands such as Arrowsic and Georgetown, take drivers over short bridges, making it easy to forget that you're on an island. Tidal rivers with unstopping currents that switch direction every 6 hours or so define these islands, yet it takes some effort to get the whole picture from the water. Following the complex shores in a kayak, you will end up where you began hours earlier; the island identities undeniable.

The Abenaki name for Georgetown Island translates to "good spear fishing," but fishing must not have been good enough. In 1649 a chief commonly known as Chief Robinhood sold the island for a hogshead of rum and some pumpkins. But the Abenaki got it back when the Indian wars of the late 1600s drove European settlers away until the early 1700s. It developed into a summer resort in the late 1800s.

The current is as much an attraction here as it is a force to be reckoned with. Some of the more obvious tidal falls have names, like Lower Hells Gate, but you'll find stacked-up waves and chaotic water at various constrictions and twists and turns, or on days when the wind whips down the river and opposes the current. Some of these could be hazardous to the unprepared paddler, but in many cases they can be avoided.

Tidal timing is crucial on this route. Poor timing will leave you slogging against the current, but time it right and you can get a push—at times a very considerable push—going both ways. Timing the tides should affect your choice of launch and the direction you travel. For instance, if low tide is at 7 A.M., launch at Reid State Park shortly after 7:30 or 8. While you'll run against some minor current for 3.5 miles, the stronger current will push you for the 9.0 miles to Hockamock Bay, where you'll want to be when the tide changes again in early afternoon. Then you'll have ebbing current for the afternoon to get you back to Reid. Or if high tide is at 7 A.M., launch at Robinhood a short time later. You'll encounter some resistance for 2.5 miles to Hockamock Bay, but you'll have the current with you for the 9.0 miles to the south end of the island where you can rest while the tide changes in early afternoon. Ride the flood tide back north to Robinhood. However, odds are good that the tides aren't always going to occur just as you expect. Their mysteries are part of the fun.

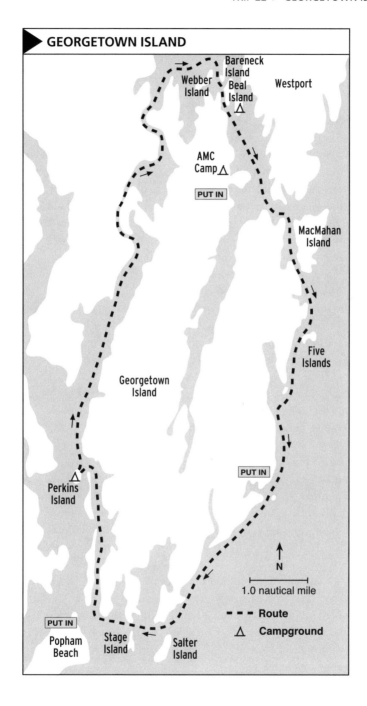

For the simplest route, launch at Fort Popham mid-tide on the flood and go north up the Kennebec. Be cautious as you enter the current. The fort pinches the river just enough create an eddy line. Watch for boat traffic. Or, to start in the sheltered water of Todd Bay, paddle south from the launch and then ferry-glide across the river. Todd Bay has less current and tends to be sheltered from the wind. Its shallowness discourages larger boat traffic, so it can be a quiet, peaceful stretch of water.

Two miles north, pull out on Perkins Island (state-owned; camping) if you need a break. From a small, grassy point near the southeast end, trails lead to a large campsite and the lighthouse, built in 1898. The campsite is up in the woods, but it has nice views down the river toward the fort. Continue up the river, staying near the east shore where the water is deeper and probably faster. The cliffs of Bald Head rise up at the entrance to the Back River. Continue north as the east bank of Back River turns marshy. Eventually, the river turns abruptly west past a small boatyard on Georgetown Island, and passes beneath the green steel and concrete bridge carrying ME 127 onto the island. Soon, a large marshy area appears on the right. Stay with the main current, winding east then west until Hockamock Bay opens ahead.

Pause at the tip of Flying Point and use your compass to get your bearings. Go east (about 90 degrees magnetic), staying south of Berry Island (CF). At the southern end of Castle Island (CF; camping), look for a small path leading into the woods. You could take a breather here or on Beal Island (AMC; camping by reservation only), reached from Castle by paddling south between Webber and Bareneck islands. Again, use your compass to make sure you know what you're looking at: this can be a confusing area. If the high tide hasn't yet come and gone, take a break at Castle or Beal and wait for the change before you start heading south.

You could also pass the time with a visit to Lower Hell Gate. Wind your way east through the small passage at the southern tip of Bareneck Island, continuing to the northeast end of Beal. Be cautious as you approach: a granite ledge rises up here, pinching the current. As the current increases, it drops over a ledge and creates standing waves. Pull your boat up just south of the ledge and eat your lunch as the current increases. Note: if you can't paddle back over the ledge, you're committed to paddling this side of Beal Island. No worries if you are: it works, and the whitewater generally settles down below this point.

If the tide has already changed and the current is with you, paddle south through Little Hell Gate, the scenic narrow gap separating Beal from Georgetown Island with bluffs dropping right into the river and a small island with a big osprey nest. Stay along the Beal Island shore, and at the south end look for the beach, the landing for AMC's Beal Island campsite. There's an AMC sign atop a tiny islet. The beach or the islet make a nice spot for a break.

While following the shoreline is usually more interesting and keeps you out of boat traffic, if you've got the current south of Beal, you might prefer to stay in the middle where the current is strongest. Knubble Bay Camp (AMC; reservations only) is on the Georgetown Island shore on Campbell Cove, just north of where the Knubble reaches

The Five Islands area (pictured here is Wood Island) is one of several enticing areas to paddle around Georgetown Island.

east. Look for two sets of stairs leading up to the cabin. South of the Knubble a large mooring area off of Robinhood Marine is south of the docks at a small cove.

Be cautious as you approach Newdick Point at the entrance to Goose Rocks Passage to the east. If you're not very comfortable negotiating current, cross the channel before turning into the passage, heading for Lowe Point. Current exits Robinhood Cove here as well, so you may find some confusing swirls. Otherwise, watch for boats and head right for the middle, letting the current take you across toward Soldier Point; you may need to point upstream and ferry-glide across the strongest current. Head south, down the Little Sheepscot River, the name given to the gap between Georgetown and Mac Mahan islands. You'll encounter plenty of boats in this area, most of them on moorings. Keep an eye out for the ones underway.

South of MacMahan, the current empties into the Sheepscot River. Follow the shore toward Five Islands; watch for boat traffic in this area. Look for the red Five Islands Lobster building with casual picnic table dining on the deck, a good place for a meal or just an ice cream. A public landing/launch area is just to the south. It's a postcard-pretty spot, but the view seaward takes in the islands the place is named for, each of them with classic summer "camps" hanging over the shore.

But Mink Island (private), the southernmost, has no houses on it. The east side has tall bluffs dropping directly into the sea, while the west side is also steep with a couple of chasms into which you can paddle. Further south, Wood Island (TNC) is barred to Dry Point and is a good spot for a break. Depending on conditions, you may enjoy paddling near the steep southern shoreline of Georgetown Island. With swell from the southeast, the seas along here can feel pretty huge, especially as they hammer into those bluffs.

The northern beach landing in Reid State Park is just north of Outer Head, a tree-less ledge of an island around 5 miles from Fort Popham. The park beach is a good spot for a break if you don't mind a few people. From there, pass the steep shore of Outer Head and Griffith Head (the big granite hump with silver coin-operated binoc-ulars atop it—no landings here) and follow One Mile Beach past the entrance to Little River, where there's a possibility for rough water. Continue down to Indian Point and pass the mouth of Sagadahoc Bay to Kennebec Point. There may be some standing waves at the day marker at Jack Rock; the currents in this area can be confusing. If the tide is still going out, hug the east shore, where you may find an eddy headed north, up to Bay Point and Gilbert Head at the south end of Long Island. Fort Popham is just across the river. Depending on the current, you'll probably need to point upstream and ferry-glide across, back to the beach.

ALTERNATIVES

Odds are, if conditions are dicey on one part of the route, another part of the route will be out of the weather. Robinhood Cove is particularly sheltered. Todd Bay and the upper Back River could also be sheltered.

MORE INFORMATION

Maine Bureau of Public Lands (maine.gov/dacf/parks/about/public_reserved_lands.shtml; 207-287-4960). Chewonki Foundation (chewonki.org; 207-882-7323); the tent plat-forms at the north end of Castle Island are for Chewonki groups. AMC's Knubble Bay Camp and Beal Island (amckbc.org; 603-466-2727). Sagadahoc Bay Campground (sagbaycamping.com; 207- 371-2014) is another overnight option along the route.

23
SEBASCODEGAN ISLAND

Enjoy a variety of environments in one trip—open ocean, rivers, finger-like coves—and the opportunity to use tidal current to your advantage.

Distance ▸ Up to 18.0 nautical miles for a complete circumnavigation

Tidal Planning ▸ 9.12-foot mean range at Portland. Flood tides meet in Long Reach. Good tidal planning is a must for a circumnavigation. Strong currents develop in the rivers and narrow areas—particularly in Gurnet Strait and Ewin Narrows—accelerating enough to make paddling against them impossible and developing steep waves if facing opposing winds or swell. Even if you do catch accelerated currents, allow enough time to complete the trip at your usual paddling speed; a little wind can counteract much of your current assist.

Cautions ▸ The southern end of the island is exposed to open ocean conditions, which will likely be heightened near Gun and West Cundy points, as well as the shallows south of the islands where there are numerous, often submerged reefs. Be aware of changing conditions and how the currents will affect the seas south of the island: you will be committed to paddling these areas when circumnavigating.

Charts and Maps ▸ NOAA chart #13290; Maptech #73 Casco Bay; Waterproof Chart #101E Casco Bay

LAUNCHES
Bethel Point Town Landing, Harpswell Paved ramp; drop off gear and park (fee) about 100 yards up the road at Bethel Point Boatyard (parking at ramp for resident permit holders only); no facilities. From the junction of US 1 and ME 24 in Brunswick, follow ME 24 south for 4.3 miles. Turn left on Cundy's Harbor Road, then in 3.2 miles, turn right on Bethel Point Road. The ramp is at the end of the road in 1.6 miles. *GPS coordinates: 43° 47.459' N, 69° 54.710' W.*

Buttermilk Cove, Brunswick Concrete ramp; roadside parking; no facilities,. From the junction of US 1 and ME 24 in Brunswick, follow ME 24 south for 3.1 miles. Turn right onto Prince Point Road; ramp is an immediate left after the bridge. *GPS coordinates: 43° 51.939' N, 69° 54.906' W.*

Other Public Access The town of Harpswell and the Harpswell Heritage Land Trust (HHLT) manage many public access lands in the area, including the Devil's Back Trail (town) and Doughty Point (HHLT). State-owned Indian Point Island is also open for day use. Strawberry Creek Island (town) offers day use and campsites.

ROUTE DESCRIPTION
On the east side of Casco Bay, spindly interwoven fingers of ocean and land create maze-like passages that generally dead-end in coves and transform into vast mudflats at low tide. How those passages encircle Sebascodegan Island can take some time to see, but route daydreamers will connect dots with ease.

Sebascodegan Island is known locally as Great Island, which may be a near-literal translation of its Abenaki name: "great measure," according to one source. At its widest points, the island is a little over 5 miles long by 3 miles wide, but its amazingly contorted shoreline stretches nearly 50 miles at high tide, if you count every nook and cranny. Still, it can be circumnavigated in less than 18.0 miles of paddling. With tide planning, it could make for a long day trip if you plan well for the tides, but with on-route camping, it is a good multiday route as well.

Planning for current here is crucial, especially for a longer trip or a circumnavigation. On a day with a midday high tide, launch at Bethel Point, and for the most current assist, paddle through Long Reach at slack tide. For a trip with a midday low tide, launch at Buttermilk Cove and be on the southern end as the tide changes. Paddling against it is certainly possible, but some of the scenery is best appreciated with an extra knot or two of current helping you along.

Sebascodegan's shores harbor a variety of environments, from open ocean to tidal rivers to protected coves. While some areas have shoulder-to-shoulder vacation homes, some surprisingly long stretches of schist bluffs topped with gnarled oaks remain undeveloped.

To paddle the route as described, plan for a midday high tide and launch from Bethel Point, proceeding clockwise. Head south across the small channel and follow the west shore of Yarmouth and Little Yarmouth islands (private). Yarmouth is mostly undeveloped, except at the northwest, where there's a concentration of cottages. Pass Raspberry Island (private) and cross the channel over to Gun Point and the collection of small islands off its tip. Gun Point and the shore of Orrs Island to the west are all residential. A small, undeveloped island a mile north of the point is surrounded by ledges frequented by seals and birds.

At the head of Gun Point Cove, a very narrow channel separates Orrs and Sebascodegan islands; the ME 24 bridge passes overhead. Strong currents develop here, so plan to have them push you. Just to the south, on the east shore of Long Cove, the

1.2-mile Devil's Back Trail (town of Harpswell) is open for day use. Cross Long Cove and head north, toward little-used Strawberry Creek Island (Stovers Island; town of Harpswell) near the mouth of Strawberry Creek. Houses are visible along the shores not far away, but it is generally quiet on this island, which is part of the Maine Island Trail. Campsites are in the woods on the north end and in the open grassy area on the southern end. Take care to prevent erosion while ascending the banks.

To the northwest, pass beneath the bridge and head 1.5 nautical miles up Ewin Narrows and follow Prince Gurnet between Doughty and Prince points. Expect some current. The Doughty Point Preserve (HHLT) is open for day use; land on its east side

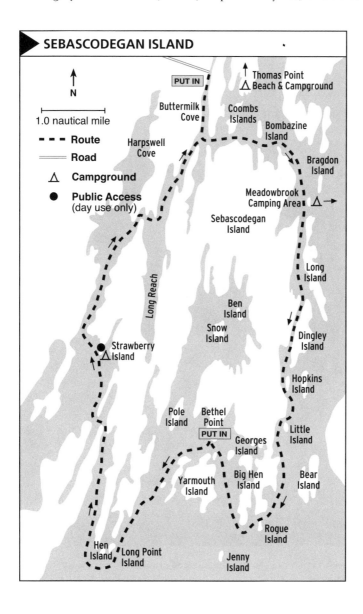

SEBASCODEGAN ISLAND

N

1.0 nautical mile

- - - **Route**
═══ **Road**
△ **Campground**
● **Public Access**
   (day use only)

PUT IN

Thomas Point
△ Beach & Campground

Buttermilk
Cove

Coombs
Islands

Bombazine
Island

Harpswell
Cove

Bragdon
Island

Meadowbrook
Camping Area   △→

Sebascodegan
Island

Long Reach

Long
Island

Strawberry
△ Island

Ben
Island

Snow
Island

Dingley
Island

Hopkins
Island

Pole
Island

Bethel
Point

PUT IN

Georges
Island

Little
Island

Yarmouth
Island

Big Hen
Island

Bear
Island

Hen
Island

Long Point
Island

Jenny
Island

Rogue
Island

The northern shores of Long Reach are fairly undeveloped and it is one of the quieter places along this route. This is where the flooding tide meets (and the area from which the ebbing tide drains). Ideally, cross the Reach at around slack tide to gain the tide's aid through Gurnet Strait where ME 24 again passes overhead. The current will accelerate as high as 7 to 8 knots beneath the bridge, ebbing to the east. A few well-kept Victorian cottages overlook the strait. Back in the late 1800s to early 1900s, steamboats from Portland made their way up the rivers and docked at the Gurnet. According to some sources, gurnet is Abenaki for "place of fast water." From here, the New Meadows River continues north about 6 miles to the salt marshes in Bath where it ends. Though it is called a river, "embayment" would be a more accurate term for this tidal waterway with very little fresh water.

About a mile east of the bridge, tiny Indian Point Island (state-owned) is open for day use. Past Indian Point, the east shore of Sebascodegan Island is generally residential. If you've planned well for the tides, you should be getting some tidal assist, making this stretch a bit more interesting, especially since you'll be able to get through areas that will flat-out later. The narrow gap between Sebascodegan and Dingley islands is fairly

While only about 5 miles long, Sebascodegan Island's contorted shoreline stretches some 50 miles. A close circumnavigation may be done in less than 18 miles of paddling. Shown is Prince Gurnet.

quiet and pretty. You should have just enough space to squeeze through beneath the Dingley Island Road bridge. This quiet stretch continues past Hopkins Island, where you can paddle beneath the pedestrian bridge.

Cundy's Harbor is a small community on the shore of Maine's oldest commercial fishing harbor (since 1841). It is still very busy; keep an eye out for boats as you cross it. There are several restaurants and general stores in town.

Head south around East and West Cundy points and make your way north through Ridley Cove, back to the launch.

ALTERNATIVES

The contorted shoreline creates numerous coves to explore, which you're likely to skip while attempting a one-day circumnavigation, but which might be interesting on a multiday trip, or on a shorter excursion. These could also be good Plan B routes when conditions at the south end are rougher than desired. Trips 24 and 25 are about 5 miles west. Launch from Sawyer Park a few miles up the New Meadows River, or arrive in that area at high tide to add Middle Grounds and the upper river stretches (6.0 to 7.0 nautical miles) to your circumnavigation. Other possible launches include Thomas Point Beach and the Great Island Boatyard.

Depending on the wind and tides, you could usually paddle a smaller portion of this route to do a there-and-back trip from either launch. From Bethel Point, Quahog Bay is a fairly sheltered area, most easily accessed from Great Island Boatyard.

MORE INFORMATION

Town of Harpswell (harpswell.maine.gov; 207-833-5771); no fires are allowed on town property, but camping is allowed on Strawberry Creek Island. Harpswell Heritage Land Trust (hhltmaine.org; 207-721-1121); no fires or camping allowed on trust property. Little Snow Island (state-owned; Maine Island Trail-managed) is nearby in Quahog Bay and offers three campsites. Other overnight options are available for Maine Island Trail Association members.

WHO OWNS THE INTERTIDAL ZONE?

Paddlers generally launch from points of public access, entering the vast plane of the ocean where we are free to go where we choose. Landing possibilities may seem determined primarily by physical barriers such as steep shorelines, but invisible, man-made barriers are often the most limiting.

In most states, including Connecticut, Rhode Island, and New Hampshire, the intertidal zone—the area between mean high and low water—is a common area, owned by the people. This doesn't guarantee access from shore: in most New England coastal areas, parking is an issue, and residents tend to do what they can to keep it that way. For those traveling in a sea kayak in these states, the entire shoreline below the high-tide line is yours to enjoy.

Massachusetts and Maine lawmakers, though, have based their decisions upon a Colonial ordinance enacted in the mid-1600s, when both states were part of the Massachusetts Bay Colony. The ordinance extended private ownership of beaches to the low-water mark, taking away all public rights to that area except for fishing, fowling, and navigation. Today, laws continue to permit shellfish harvesting and bird hunting, but not bird-watching

The term "navigation" in the modern laws, though, may give paddlers more leeway. Both laws have been interpreted as allowing sailing over intertidal lands, mooring a craft upon them, and allowing vessels to rest upon intertidal land when the tide recedes. This privilege extends to incidental uses, such as walking, as long as it has something to do with navigation (carrying your boat is an obvious example). In short, for kayakers, the word "navigating" might just as easily be replaced with "kayaking."

But if you land, get your navigating done and be on your way. The right to travel on intertidal lands does not include the right to stay there for sunbathing or recreational walking. The Maine Supreme Court has further ruled that the law prohibits you from eating your lunch or throwing a Frisbee on privately owned intertidal land. The question on many paddlers' minds, though, is "Where can I pee?" So far there is no legal precedent, so the answer is unclear, but it might be best for all of us if it remains that way.

Not all landowners will understand the subtleties of legal "navigation," and confronting them will help no one. When presented with a legal gray area, act in keeping with Leave No Trace ethics: strive to be respectful of people and their private property, as well as of the land and water. If paddlers were all good ambassadors of the sport, we might be more welcome when we do visit.

24
UPPER CASCO BAY

A chain of beautiful islands with slate cliffs stand over pocket beaches and plenty of public access, usually more sheltered than Casco Bay's outer islands.

Distance ▶ 11.0 to 13.0 nautical miles

Tidal Planning ▶ Average tidal range is 8.9 feet, flooding northeast, ebbing southwest.

Cautions ▶ Although the area is more sheltered than Casco Bay's outer islands, it can still develop some choppy water, especially when the prevailing southwest winds oppose an outgoing tide.

Charts and Maps ▶ NOAA chart #13290; Maptech #73; Waterproof Chart #101E

LAUNCHES

Lookout Point, Harpswell Paved ramp and mud/gravel shore parking for a dozen or so cars; no facilities. From the intersection of ME 24 N/Bath Road and ME 123/Sills Drive in Brunswick, turn right onto ME 123. Follow it south for 8.3 miles to Lookout Point Road. Turn right here and follow it to the end. *GPS coordinates: 43° 48.498′ N, 69° 59.604′ W.*

Mere Point Boat Launch, Brunswick All-tides paved ramp and kayak launching area; daytime-only parking is ample but requires a gear drop or a bit of a carry; outhouses. From the intersection of US 1 and Stanwood Street in Brunswick, turn south on Stanwood Street and continue 0.4 mile to McKeen Street. Turn right, then left in 0.2 mile onto Baribeau Drive. In 0.9 mile, turn left onto Pleasant Hill Road, then right in 0.2 mile onto Main Street/Mere Point Road. Continue to follow Mere Point Road for 5.5 miles, then turn left onto Birch Island Road. The launch is at the end of the street in 0.2 mile. *GPS coordinates: 43° 49.679′ N, 70° 1.028′ W.*

Other Public Access The Maine Coast Heritage Trust (MCHT) manages two preserves in this area—Whaleboat Island and the Goslings (including Irony Island); camping is permitted on both islands; the southern half of West Goslings is closed April through July for osprey nesting. An MCHT easement permits landing on the south end of otherwise private Lower Goose Island. Harpswell's Mitchell Field and the Harpswell Heritage Land Trust's Birch Island South Preserve are open for day use.

Upper Goose Island is protected by The Nature Conservancy (TNC) and is closed March 15 through August 15 for nesting.

ROUTE DESCRIPTION

This part of Casco Bay has a more sheltered, less developed feel than its counterparts. The islands on this route could be reached from either north or south, but the vast stretches of low-tide mudflats exposed in the bay's northern reaches don't inhibit launches on Harpswell Neck. These starting points are also more likely to be semi-sheltered from the prevailing southwest winds. The area is popular with powerboaters and sailors, but the channel crossings are likely to be less traveled than those in the rest of Casco Bay.

At 122 acres, Whaleboat Island—so-named for the upraised "bow" and "stern" one might see in the island's profile—is the largest uninhabited island in Casco Bay, its 3 miles of shoreline alternating between steep slate cliffs and cobble beaches. Recently acquired by MCHT, the Goslings—a pair of idyllic islets, totaling less than 13 acres— are connected by a sandbar at low tide, and have an intimate, sheltered feel that welcomes picnicking on its rocky ledges and sandy beaches.

The best launch may depend on tidal flow. Launches at Basin and Potts points (see Trip 25) are options with a midday high tide, while Mere Point works with a midday low tide. Lookout Point, though, is generally a good spot to launch. This rustic Harpswell town launch isn't the powerboat mecca found at Mere Point or Basin Point, and there is a local harbor nearby where seven or eight lobster boats come and go. Lookout Point is also close to a restaurant and an inn, and it's a pretty little harbor, with a couple of tiny, rocky islets connected to the neck at low tide.

A clockwise route tends to work well, following the shore of Harpswell Neck then crossing to Whaleboat Island (MCHT). The typical southwest winds may be partially avoided, saving them for a stern push on the way home, and if the tides aren't in your favor, the near-shore waters will likely have less current, or even eddies. This shoreline is mostly private, with the densest development south of Whites Point. Just over 2.0 miles from the launch, a crumbling former naval fueling dock juts into the bay at Mitchell Field, a town-owned park; get out for a break, but stay clear of the wharf.

For a perpendicular channel crossing, pick a target on Whaleboat—the birches stand out—and line up with the lobster buoys. Depending on wind and current, cross to Whaleboat Island anywhere between Curtis and Peter coves. Curtis Cove is a shallow indent with a few sailboats moored at its mouth and a sandy, muddy beach at its head. Just south of it, the shore turns steep, rising to a bluff just before Peter Cove where a distinctive midcentury modern home cantilevers over the edge. Built for artist Stephen Etnier in 1948, the home's interior is a three-dimensional tribute to Piet Mondrian's *Broadway Boogie Woogie*, with Mondrian-esque picture windows overlooking Whaleboat Island. The Etnier family owned Whaleboat Island until MCHT acquired it in 2002.

Spruce and fir forests dominate Whaleboat's "bow" and "stern" hills on either end. Once across the channel, head for the central saddle's shrubby, rolling meadows where there are several easy landing areas and a campsite, near the small patch of salt marsh. If you poke around the island's interior you might come across a cellar hole or stone walls, remnants of the island's residents, the last of whom left around 1906. The south end of the island has steep cliffs along its shore and is likely to have somewhat rougher seas, due to its exposure. If you're looking for more docile conditions, head around the north end. Below the light tower at the southwest end you not only get a view down the length of Whaleboat Island, but out to the rest of Casco Bay as well. Another, more sheltered campsite is tucked into the forest on the island's northwest side. From here, head across the channel to Little Whaleboat Island.

Little Whaleboat Island (private) is composed of two uninhabited islands connected at low tide, and is a popular spot for powerboaters who come ashore on its beaches and ledges. Despite sharing a name with its larger neighbor with public access, both parts of Little Whaleboat Island are privately owned. They are fun islands to paddle around though, with plenty of eye-catching vistas.

The Goslings (MCHT) lie a mile to the northeast, just off the southern end of Lower Goose Island. As you make your way there, look out for increased boat traffic

Upper Casco Bay has a more sheltered, less developed feel than the rest of the bay.

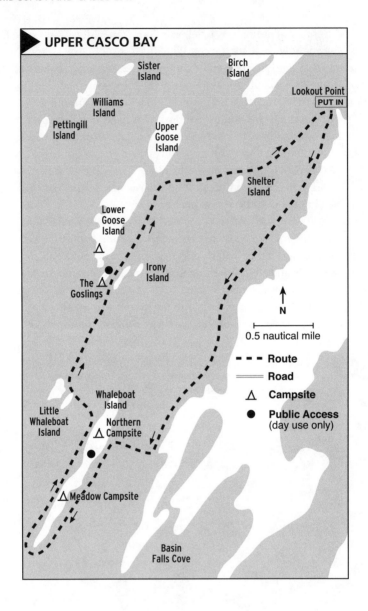

UPPER CASCO BAY

Sister Island
Birch Island
Lookout Point
PUT IN
Williams Island
Pettingill Island
Upper Goose Island
Shelter Island
Lower Goose Island
Irony Island
The Goslings
N
0.5 nautical mile
- - - Route
=== Road
△ Campsite
● Public Access (day use only)
Whaleboat Island
Little Whaleboat Island
Northern △ Campsite
△ Meadow Campsite
Basin Falls Cove

in the north–south channel. A mile and a half to the northeast lies Bustins Island, its shoreline dense with homes. There are plenty of places to land on the Goslings, and odds are good that you'll be sharing them with others; the sheltered water to the north is a popular anchorage. There's much to share though, including (at lower tides) tiny Irony Island (MCHT) to the east, which has steep, darker-colored rocks (perhaps of an iron-y hue?). Until 2014, the Goslings and Irony Island were privately owned, with public use allowed by the owners, including camping at a couple of Maine Island Trail Association sites and exclusive use of one site by L.L. Bean's Outdoor Discovery

School. With the help of L.L. Bean, MCHT purchased the islands, ensuring public access for future generations. The southern half of West Gosling is closed April through July for osprey nesting. If you've brought a dog with you, take particular care to keep your four-legged friend under strict voice or leash control as poorly behaved dogs (and the waste they've left) have led to dogs being banned from these islands in the past.

A 44-acre MCHT easement on the south end of Lower Goose Island expands the public access to the larger island, but don't land elsewhere else on it; the rest is private, with several homes along its shore. If the Goslings are feeling too crowded for your taste, you could check out Grassy Ledge en route to Upper Goose Island.

Much of the shoreline of Upper Goose Island (TNC) is off-limits March 15 to August 15 to provide habitat for birds. You can get a distant glimpse of the shoreline from a tiny islet just off its southeast end, a good spot to pause and get your bearings before heading back to Lookout Point, which is visible to the east. If you're in the mood for more exploring, follow the shore of Upper Goose and cross over into the inlet at the southwest end of Birch Island, and follow it in to the Birch Island South Preserve (HHLT; day use) on the northwest side at the head of the cove.

Otherwise, cross over to Shelter Island (private). Shelter's name is probably derived from its being used by early settlers to escape hostile Indians. Later, local tradition says, it became a haven for smugglers. Now it shelters a discreet cabin tucked into the woods, but the bluffs on the north end are a good spot to pause before paddling the final mile to Lookout Point. En route, you'll probably pass Black Rock, which would be more appropriately named White Rock, due to the cormorants and other seabirds that tend to favor it.

ALTERNATIVES
If you're looking for a longer day, add East Casco Bay (Trip 25) to your plans. If conditions are poor and tide allows, stick to the upper reaches of the bay.

MORE INFORMATION
Town of Harpswell (harpswell.maine.gov; 207-833-5771). Maine Coast Heritage Trust (mcht.org; 207-729-7366). The Nature Conservancy (nature.org/maine; 207-729-5181); no pets are allowed in the preserve. Harpswell Heritage Land Trust (hhltmaine.org; 207-721-1121). Recompence Shore Campground (freeportcamping.com; 207-865-9307) in Freeport offers additional overnight options.

25
EAST CASCO BAY

Paddle idyllic islands with historic sites and multiday route options not far from Portland.

Distance ▶ 4.0 to 16.0 nautical miles, round-trip

Tidal Planning ▶ 9.12-foot mean tidal range in Portland.

Cautions ▶ Heavy boat traffic in the central part of bay, including fishing boats, ferries, and water taxis. Conditions from the open ocean will affect this area, especially on the southern sides of the islands. Be attentive to what the tidal current is doing relative to those conditions, as a great deal of water flows between these islands as it moves in and out of the northern bay.

Charts and Maps ▶ NOAA chart #13290; Maptech #73, Casco Bay; Waterproof Chart #101E, Casco Bay

LAUNCHES

Dolphin Marina and Restaurant, Basin Point, Harpswell Ramp; very limited parking (fee), with preference given to restaurant patrons. From the intersection of ME 24 N/Bath Road and ME 123/Sills Drive in Brunswick, turn south on ME 123. Follow it south for 11.5 miles. Turn right on Ash Pond Road, then turn right again in 0.2 mile on Basin Cove Road/Basin Point Road. The restaurant and marina are 2.5 miles farther, on the left. *GPS coordinates: 43° 44.387' N, 70° 2.479' W.*

Potts Point Public Landing, Harpswell Gravel beach launch; limited parking. From the intersection of ME 24 N/Bath Road and ME 123/Sills Drive in Brunswick, turn south on ME 123. Follow it south for 13.4 miles. Continue straight on Potts Point Road; the launch is about 0.4 mile farther. *GPS coordinates: 43° 43.961' N, 70° 1.459' W.*

Other Public Access Publicly owned islands are plentiful in this area; land managers and permitted uses are noted in the description. Contact land managers for specific restrictions (see More Information).

ROUTE DESCRIPTION

Compared to Casco Bay's urban Portland side, the middle of the bay is quiet and rural. Harpswell Neck juts nearly 10 miles toward the open ocean, giving paddlers fast access to the archipelago beyond. To really appreciate the numerous opportunities for public access here, compare the archipelago's shoreline to the densely settled shores of Orrs and Baileys islands to the east, seen from the road along the neck.

In some years, Harpswell has been one of the busier fishing ports in the state, and along with Portland, sends quite a few fishing and recreational boats into Casco Bay. Stay alert and look both ways (and behind) before going anywhere. But this side of the bay lacks the steady presence of ferries and water taxis buzzing in and out of Portland, as well as the regular, ominous appearance of super tankers, making this a less nerve-wracking route out to the islands. While there are some moderate crossings, the islands are generally arranged in long rows—parts of the same ridge appearing now and again above the water surface.

Your options here vary from a 4.0-mile round-trip excursion to see Admiral Peary's Eagle Island to a 16.0-mile circuit, taking in Little Chebeague. The 6.0- to 7.0-nautical-mile round-trip to Chebeague Island via Bangs and Crow islands is a worthwhile paddle with a little variety. Public access is reliable throughout the route, but some inhabited stopovers are warranted here as well. Chebeague Island in particular has much to offer the traveler; Cliff Island may be interesting to walk around, but has little in the way of services or amenities.

History also abounds here. Allow an hour or two to tour Admiral Peary's house on Eagle Island. To the north, the 1809 pyramidal stone monument on Little Mark Island memorializes shipwrecked sailors and now functions as a navigational aid. Little Chebeague Island was used in World War II as a firefighting training center for the Navy, hosting thousands of sailors; a steel training tower still stands. Jewell Island has a tower and several other fortifications remaining from World War II.

Vertical fins of schist along the shores of Casco Bay's islands form low, steep bluffs with a variety of deciduous trees atop. Breaks in the cliffs are fairly frequent, offering possible landings atop piles of smooth, flat rocks, and some sandy beaches.

For a small fee, launch at the Dolphin Marina and Restaurant to avoid competition for valued parking spaces, even for overnight trips, and to start in a good position to reach the islands. Choose the direction of your route according to conditions or your priorities; this description proceeds counterclockwise.

Paddle out past Basin Point and Little Birch Island. The smokestack on Cousins Island rises behind Chebeague. Directly in front of it, Stockman Island is about 1.5 nautical miles away. Depending on the tide, you'll probably notice some current running through here. Between the numerous lobster buoys and the smokestack, you should be able to sight a range to keep you on a straight course.

Grassy, mostly treeless Stockman Island (day use) is owned by the Chebeague and Cumberland Land Trust (CCLT). Eiders nest here in early summer, so foot traffic is banned from April 15 to July 15. Bangs Island (state-owned; camping) lies to the southwest across a 0.25-mile gap (watch for increased currents). The Maine Island

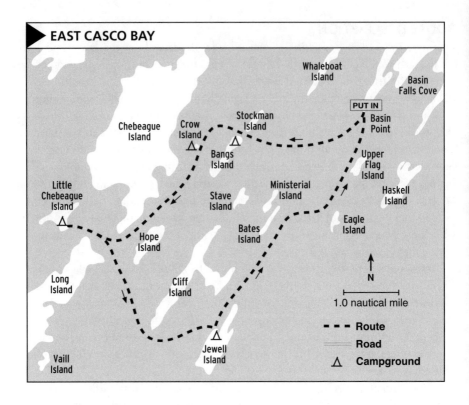

Trail Association (MITA) maintains campsites at the north end's meadow and on the forested south end. The cove pinching the island's middle is a good spot to land for a break except in bigger seas. The aquaculture floats on the northwest side belong to Bangs Island Mussels.

Crow Island (Harpswell Heritage Land Trust; camping) lies 0.5 mile to the northwest, at the edge of a cove on Chebeague Island. Even if you don't plan on camping on this usually busy island, Crow is worth a visit. The northeast-facing pocket beach is about as idyllic as they come. And while you might prefer your own tent to the very rustic cottage nestled behind oaks in the middle of the island, the porch can provide shelter in a storm.

Just 0.25 mile west is Rose's Point (CCLT) and the Chebeague Island Boatyard, both landing points for Chebeague Island. The newest town in Maine, Chebeague Island seceded from Cumberland in 2007 and is home to more than 340 people year-round (2,000 in the summer). First settled in the 1730s, Chebeague is the largest un-bridged island in Casco Bay at about 3 miles by 1.5 miles. Fishing drives much of the island's economy, though a few businesses cater to visitors. A regular ferry runs from Cousins Island to a cove at the northwest side of Chebeague; the Casco Bay Lines ferry docks at the east side of Chandler Cove. If time isn't an issue (for instance, if you're camping on nearby Crow, Bangs, or Little Chebeague islands), take your time exploring Chebeague. A few shops, restaurants, and an inn are scattered about the island. The Chebeague Island Boatyard has restrooms, showers, and a gift shop/café with soups, sandwiches, and baked goods. Walk north on South Road to Doughty's Island Market, the library, and the historical society.

From Crow Island, follow Chebeague's shore southwest. At Deer Point, head into Chandler Cove, which is generally sheltered. Both currents and boat traffic are funneled into this area, however, so be attentive. To get to the beach on Little Chebeague, cross over to the breakwater made up of sunken schooners off the northeast tip of Long Island. From there, aim for the rust-colored tower on Little Chebeague's beach. A beach at the head of Chandler Cove on Chebeague could provide a landing and access to the island's roads.

A sandbar connects Little Chebeague Island (state-owned; camping) and Chebeague at Indian Point; many trek from the larger island on foot at low tide to explore the trails and beaches. MITA maintains campsites along the southeast beach where you can also find trailheads. Ticks and poison ivy thrive on the island, and browntail moth caterpillars have been seen there as well. Little Chebeague was farmed for over a century, starting in the early 1800s, and was also the site of a late 1800s resort hotel. In 1943, the U.S. Navy began using it as a training and recreation site for sailors. The steel tower was a training facility for shipboard firefighting.

Depending on conditions and your skills, cross to Cliff and Jewell islands. This area is a bit more exposed, particularly to the prevailing southwest winds, and the currents squeeze between these islands as well; it pays to consider the forecast and have a good look before venturing across to Cliff Island. You could break up the crossing by going to Hope Island (private), easily recognizable by the bright red roofs atop its large buildings and the trios of large American flags waving near the dock and the house.

Either way, head for the Cliff Island, where houses are clustered along the northwest shore. Cliff was the site of large hotels a century ago, but is now residential with no services for visitors. Head around the undeveloped southwest end and continue to Jewell Island (state-owned), a popular destination in the summer; if you want seclusion, you may want to go elsewhere. MITA maintains a number of campsites along its northwest shore and near its south end where you can explore remnants of World War II bunkers and climb the towers once used to watch for submarines.

From "Cocktail Cove" on the northwest end of Jewell, it's about 4 nautical miles back to Basin Point. Either cross back to the cliffy portion of Cliff Island and head northeast along Bates and Little Birch islands, or head past the Brown Cow and the numerous ledges surrounding it on your way to Eagle Island.

Eagle Island State Historic Site (fee; day use) received its designation in 2014 to honor the summer home of Arctic explorer Admiral Robert Peary. The museum is open June 15 through Labor Day, 10 A.M. to 5 P.M. Land near the dock at the northeast end to visit the island's trails and its well-tended garden.

Heading back to Basin Point, skirt the shoreline of Upper Flag Island, where Peary kept his sled dogs. Now owned by U.S. Fish and Wildlife, Upper Flag is closed from April through August for nesting seabirds.

ALTERNATIVES

Adjacent to the Upper Casco Bay trip (Trip 24), this route also overlaps with the West Casco Bay itinerary (Trip 26), together crossing the stretch of Casco Bay from Portland to Harpswell Neck. A 5.0-mile paddle east from Basin Point links this route with the Sebascodegan Island area (Trip 23). Overnight trips can combine with Trips 24 or 26 or allow time to explore Chebeague Island on foot.

For a shorter trip, paddle either the northern or the southern sections of the bay (Trips 24 and 26, respectively).

MORE INFORMATION

Dolphin Marina and Restaurant (dolphinmarinaandrestaurant; 207-833-5343). Chebeague and Cumberland Land Trust (ccltmaine.org; 207-669-2989). Maine Department of Inland Fisheries and Wildlife (maine.gov/ifw; 207-287-8000). Harpswell Heritage Land Trust (hhltmaine.org; 207-721-1121). Maine Island Trail Association (mita.org, 207-761-8225). Eagle Island State Historic Site (parksandlands.com; 207-624-6080). U.S. Fish and Wildlife Service, Gulf of Maine Coastal Program (fws.gov/GOMCP; 207-781-8364). Besides the camping options noted in the description, there are several other overnight options for MITA members.

An 1809 pyramidal stone monument on Little Mark Island memorializes shipwrecked sailors and now functions as a navigational aid.

26
WEST CASCO BAY

Tour the busiest harbor in Maine to enjoy a Civil War-era fort, views of Portland, and a few quiet and remote coves and beaches.

Distance ▶ 2.0 to 17.0 nautical miles

Tidal Planning ▶ 9.12-foot mean tidal range.

Cautions ▶ Portland Harbor is extremely busy with near-constant ferry and water taxi traffic, along with recreational and fishing boats and very active Coast Guard vessels; tankers and container ships regularly come and go. The south sides of Long and Peaks islands are exposed to open ocean and whatever conditions it may bring. Tidal currents between the islands can accelerate and create lively conditions when opposing swell and wind.

Charts and Maps ▶ NOAA chart #13290; Maptech #73, Casco Bay; Waterproof Chart #101E, Casco Bay

LAUNCH

East End Public Launch, Fort Allen Park, Portland Paved ramp (fee) and adjacent sandy beach (free); daytime parking available in the upper parking area (short walk); restrooms are available in summer. From I-295, Exit 8 (Washington Avenue/ME 26), take the first left onto Eastern Promenade. After 1.0 mile, turn sharply onto Cutter Street. *GPS coordinates: 43° 40.213′ N, 70° 14.496′ W.*

Other Public Access Public landings are available at Fort Gorges and on Long Island's Andrew Beach and its public landing; landing in the intertidal zone on Great and Little Diamond islands is permitted. Public access is permitted on Little Chebeague (state-owned), Cow (Rippleffect), Vaill (state-owned; closed April 15 to July 31), and College (Oceanside Conservation Trust of Casco Bay [OCT]) islands.

ROUTE DESCRIPTION

Maine's largest city, Portland is home to almost a quarter of the state's population and the second largest crude oil port in the Northeast. Regularly landing in the top of various magazine rankings, Portland is usually defined as a progressive city with highly educated, physically active citizens who like to eat well. Also, it may have the most restaurants per capita than any U.S. city (just behind San Francisco), and has developed a reputation for locavore eateries.

On most days at the Promenade, a few people sit in the grass, staring out at the islands. There's a lot to see: Fort Gorges just a mile away across a channel; Peaks and the Diamond islands just beyond. Bright yellow-and-white ferries of the Casco Bay Line make their way back and forth from the harbor, and if you wait long enough, a massive tanker or container ship is likely to appear. Every now and then, someone drops off a kayak, carries it down to the water's edge and leaves the city behind.

For the city dweller, the nearby islands are Portland's quieter neighborhoods. For the visitor more accustomed to paddling in the wild, the urban backdrop is a jolt to the senses. It makes you feel small, especially when you're sharing the water with a supertanker, and it will put your mental boat-tracking devices on high alert. But the heightened senses will settle down after a bit, as you begin to enjoy what feels like an extremely privileged view of the city.

On the shoreline of Little Diamond Island, century-old cottages are tucked into the forest far from the hum of the metropolis. Here and in the islands' secluded coves that could be anywhere on the Maine coast—were it not for the smokestack on Cousins Island across the bay—the rhythmic plunk of paddle strokes takes over. The skyline is perhaps best enjoyed from atop Fort Gorges, a pre-Civil War fort open to the public and a perfect rest stop. Beyond that, much of the island shoreline is private, perhaps even exclusive, but your kayak breaks down those barriers; the water above the intertidal zone is all yours, and a few islands have public access as well. Just remain aware of the regulations and expectations regarding the intertidal zone and private property (see "Who Owns the Intertidal Zone?" on page 142).

Since one of the biggest concerns around Portland Harbor is staying out of the way of all the larger boats, launch at East End Beach. The crossing to Fort Gorges is under a mile across a channel that, while still busy, is less traveled than the more southern passages. To spend the least time in the channel, head along shore to Fish Point and aim for Fort Gorges. The channel here is about 0.5 mile wide, and the current generally floods north and ebbs south. At lower tides, Fort Gorges is surrounded by ledges and it's easy to find a spot to pull up. At high tide, go to one of the small gravel beaches near the entrance on the north side. There are no facilities at the fort. Prominent signs remind visitors that they may tour the fort at their own risk—some parts are in disrepair and could be dangerous. The fort was first proposed following the War of 1812, but work didn't begin until 1857. Constructed of local Maine granite, the fort was finished in 1865, in time for the end of the Civil War. By then, modern weapons had made the fort obsolete.

Climb up the stair tower and make your way along the overgrown top level to a break in trees to get an amazing view of Portland Harbor. Beside this viewpoint, there's an old cannon—a 10-inch Parrott Rifle—just sitting in the weeds. The interior of the fort feels peaceful and insulated, the granite corridors lit by subtle, monastic sunlight seeping through narrow windows that once held large guns. Bring

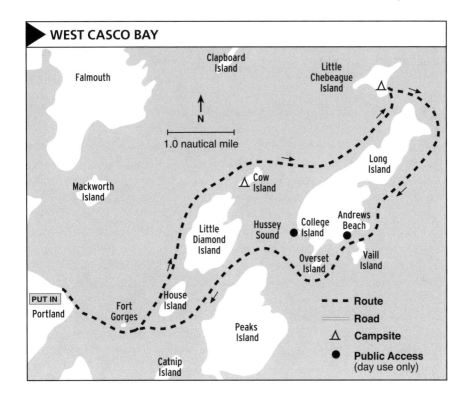

a flashlight if you want to do any serious exploration. Paddle beside the exterior to have a close-up look at those imposing granite walls.

It's less than 0.5 mile with a short channel crossing over to Little Diamond Island, where a cluster of cottages built in the early 1900s overlooks a cove. The island has around 50 homes, mostly concentrated around the south and western sides, but only about five year-round residents. At the southwest end, the communal "Casino" building overlooks a dock; a few golf carts are usually parked nearby (there are no cars on the island). Land here to walk the island's dirt roads.

Great Diamond Island lies across a short gap that is barred at lower tides (people like to walk between the two islands). The west shoreline has a similar feel as Little Diamond: quiet, rocky coves with cottages (some more contemporary than others) hidden behind stately oaks. A gated community dominates the island's northern end, its facilities centered on the former Army base on Diamond Cove. The old brick barracks have been converted to residences, a restaurant, and a general store. There is a public landing at the southwest end.

For a longer break on true public access land, cross the short passage to 26-acre Cow Island. The former land trust island is now owned by Rippleffect Outdoor Leadership Education as a base for youth adventure programs. The west side is open to the public and includes campsites that are on the Maine Island Trail; the island's composting toilets are open to the public.

From Cow Island, cross about 0.75 nautical mile to the varied development along Long Island's shore. Compared to the Diamonds, Long has an overall more utilitarian feel, with its share of stacked lobster traps and the useful clutter needed by those who pull their livelihood from the sea. The ferry docks at a public landing on the north side of the southwest end of the island. With around 200 year-round residents, Long Island is its own town, having seceded from Portland in 1993. Its roads are public and there are a few shops, inns, and restaurants.

Little Chebeague Island (state-owned; camping) lies across a 0.25-mile channel off the north end of Long Island. Part of the Maine Island Trail, Little Chebeague is a good spot for lunch or an overnight. Beaches along the south and east sides make for a good walk, as does the network of trails into the interior. Used by the Navy as a retreat and shipboard firefighting school during World War II, the island is barred to Great Chebeague at low tides, and has frequent visitors. At this point, the route overlaps with Trip 25; see Alternatives for ideas on how to adjoin them for a longer trip.

Head to the northeastern point on Long Island and determine if conditions are favorable for a paddle along the southeastern shore. The difference between this side of the island and the more protected shore can be dramatic: the southeastern shore is dotted with numerous submerged ledges that can make navigating a challenge in any conditions. This shore is also less developed, with its share of larger, more recent bluff-top homes looking out to the bold southern horizon.

A channel just over a mile wide separates Fort Gorges and Portland's busy waterfront.

About 1.5 nautical miles down the shore, just past Harbor Grace, watch for Obeds Rock. Just ahead, a sandy beach extends to a cottage on a point, with Vaill Island (state-owned) to the south. Closed April 15 through July 31 for bird nesting, Vaill's north-facing cove is a good spot for a break at other times. Whatever seas and current squeeze into this area will likely make for lively conditions. Just past this is town-owned Andrew Beach on Long Island, where you may land. To the west, a cottage perches high above the dramatic bluffs on Overset Island, which is connected to Jerry Point by a breakwater. This is also a potentially rough area, especially with a current running through Hussey Sound.

For those with the energy and the skills to deal with whatever conditions the sea is dishing out, this would be the spot to continue on to the south side of Peaks Island, Ram Island, and the Ram Island Ledge Light (private). But this area is no place for the unprepared. In May 2010, two paddlers in 12-foot kayaks set out from Peaks Island and were seen arriving on Ram. No one knows what caused them to later capsize, but south winds blowing against an ebbing tide may have made for rough seas. While they wore lifejackets, their clothing was not warm enough to sustain them in the 48-degree-Fahrenheit water, and they died of hypothermia.

From Overset Island, the route continues north along the southwest end of Long Island. Tiny, treeless College Island (OCT; day use) is in full view of quite a few houses and is barred to Long Island at low tide.

From College Island, minimize your exposure to boat traffic in the channels by first crossing Hussey Sound to Pumpkin Nob, then crossing Diamond Island Pass. Occasional homes tucked into the woods top the schist cliffs, but this is a pretty and quiet spot to paddle, considering that the opposite shore on Peaks Island is dense with homes.

Continue around Little Diamond Island and back to Fort Gorges, where you may want to pause to catch your breath before heading back to the launch.

ALTERNATIVES

This route overlaps Trip 25 at Little Chebeague Island, giving you a logical connection point for a longer daylong or multiday itinerary. Peaks Island is just to the south, and depending on conditions and your skill, Ram Island and Ram Island Ledge Light can be a good addition to the route.

When winds or seas pick up from the south, calmer water is usually found on the north sides of the islands. Back Bay is a sheltered spot to paddle when other areas are not.

MORE INFORMATION

Rippleffect Outdoor Leadership Education (rippleffect.net/cow-island/public-use; 207-791-7870); camping at designated sites with no more than four people per site; fires by permit only. Maine Island Trail Association (mita.org, 207-761-8225). Maine Department of Inland Fisheries and Wildlife (maine.gov/ifw; 207-287-8000). Oceanside Conservation Trust of Casco Bay (Oceanside Conservation Trust; 207-699-2989).

KITTERY TO BOSTON

Southwest of Portland and Cape Elizabeth, the Maine coast is dominated by long stretches of sandy beach, much of it overlooked by private property and tourist amenities. The islands off of Cape Porpoise are good places to paddle at higher tides, when there is ample water.

The Piscataqua River, a 12-mile-long estuary, separates Maine and New Hampshire, flowing between Portsmouth and Kittery, where a network of tidal creeks, navigable only at higher tides, cut off Maine's Gerrish Island (Trip 27) from the mainland; several more sheltered paddles are just upriver on the New Hampshire side. To the east, the Isles of Shoals (Trip 28) split the border between Maine and New Hampshire.

The Merrimack River flows 117 miles from its source in central New Hampshire to where it enters the ocean between Massachusetts's Salisbury and Plum Island beaches. There's plenty of good paddling on the river, but be extra cautious at the mouth, which is notoriously hazardous. Just south are the barrier islands of Plum Island (Trip 29) and Castle Neck (Trip 30), which shelter the Great Marsh, the largest continuous stretch of salt marsh in New England. Extending from Cape Ann to New Hampshire, the marsh spans more than 20,000 acres and is an important area for birds and other wildlife.

Only a few miles from Castle Neck, the Annisquam River makes it possible to circumnavigate Cape Ann (Trip 31), but there are plenty of worthwhile shorter and sheltered routes on the Annisquam. In an area without a lot of offshore islands, Thacher Island stands out, just south of Rockport. Its twin lighthouses are unmistakable from miles away, and you can even climb to the top of one for a view that takes in the Boston skyline.

For an even closer view of Boston's skyscrapers, a trip around Boston's outer islands (Trip 32) offers quiet yet easy-to-reach paddling along bold, rocky shores only a few miles from downtown. There is plenty of good paddling around Boston, including the more sheltered Charles River or Hingham Harbor.

27
GERRISH ISLAND

Varied paddling here includes rocky, wave-pounded shores, winding creeks through salt marshes, placid Chauncey Creek, and historical points of interest including forts, lighthouses, and an old lifesaving station.

Distance ▶ 7.0 to 8.0 nautical miles

Tidal Planning ▶ Mean tidal range in Portsmouth Harbor of 7.8 feet; floods upriver, ebbs to the south. The creek between Chauncey Creek and Brave Boat Harbor is navigable only for an hour or two around high tide. Currents converge at the basin just north of the culvert joining the creeks.

Cautions ▶ The Piscataqua River has very strong currents that may result in increased conditions. The southern and eastern sides of Gerrish Island are exposed to open ocean and can turn very rough, with increased wave heights in the near-shore shallower waters, which are generally rock-strewn. The entrance to Brave Boat Harbor can be difficult to negotiate in bigger conditions.

Charts and Maps ▶ NOAA chart #13283; Maptech #27

LAUNCHES

Fort Foster Park, Kittery, ME Beach launches on Windsurfers' Beach with a short carry from parking (entry fee); fairly ample parking spaces; bathrooms with water. Picnic areas, trails, historic fortifications. Open Memorial Day to Labor Day, 10 A.M. to sunset or 8 P.M., whichever is earlier; pedestrian traffic welcome sunrise to sunset October 1 to April 30 and weekends in May and September, just before and after the regular season. From I-95, Exit 2, follow ME 236 south 1.1 miles. Continue straight on ME 103/Whipple Road/Pepperell Road for 2.6 miles, then bear right on Chauncey Creek Road. In 0.5 mile, turn right on Gerrish Island Lane, then make an immediate right onto Pocahontas Road. Follow this road for 1.4 miles to the park entrance. *GPS coordinates: 43° 4.041′ N, 70° 41.615′ W.*

Frisbee Pier, Pepperell Cove, Kittery, ME Town pier with adjacent ramp (launch fee); limited stickered parking for residents, with public parking at the Horace Mitchell School, 0.25 mile away. From the intersection of ME 236 and ME 103, continue southeast on ME 103/Whipple Road/Pepperell Road for 2.0 miles. Turn right on Bellamy Lane for pier and ramp. For nonresident parking, continue on Pepperell Road 0.4 mile past Bellamy Lane, then turn right on Haley Road. Make the next left on Mitchell School Lane. *GPS coordinates: 43° 4.938′ N, 70° 42.198′ W.*

Chauncey Creek, Kittery, ME At the trailhead for Rachel Carson National Wildlife Refuge (RCNWR), just east of the culvert between Chauncey Creek and the creek leading to Brave Boat Harbor. Higher tides only; very limited parking; outhouse. *GPS coordinates: 43° 20.847′ N, 70° 32.885′ W.*

Other Public Access Seapoint Beach (Kittery Land Trust [KLT]) and Chauncey Creek (RCNWR) both provide public landings and alternative launches from those mentioned above. Cobble Beach also provides a public landing point.

ROUTE DESCRIPTION

Considering its proximity to a large population and more urban waters plied by big ships and countless recreational boaters, the paddle around Gerrish and Cutts islands tours remarkably beautiful and undeveloped coast, with long stretches of rocky, wave-pounded shoreline and a quiet, winding creek through a salt marsh. The seaward stretch has plenty of rocks and potential challenges; if conditions warrant a less challenging trip, opt to stay in more sheltered waters. Time passage through the creek to Brave Boat Harbor for the highest hours of the tide cycle; on a busy day, plenty of pond boaters arrive at the culvert shortly before high tide to make the 3.0-mile round-trip to the harbor and back. You could even time your trip for a meal at Chauncey Creek Lobster Pier.

First known as Champernowne's Island, Gerrish and Cutts are truly one island separated by the end of Chauncey Creek, where it gives way to salt marsh that puckers out to sea, forming the split that separates Seapoint and Crescent beaches. The area has been settled since the early 1600s, but this prime piece of real estate and the Brave Boat Harbor estuary—which stretches inland into the Rachel Carson National Wildlife Refuge—have remained open to the public since the early 1900s.

Frisbee Pier is typically recommended as this route's launch. It's very crowded despite the launch fee, but it may be the best option to avoid open ocean and other uncertain conditions around the outside of Gerrish, or to launch before 10 A.M. when Fort Foster Park opens. Entrance to the park also costs a fee, but parking is closer to the beach launch. Conditions will likely be livelier here than at the town pier, but if you're planning a circumnavigation, you get a glimpse of what the rest of the route will look like. The park's late opening hours are the most obvious drawback to this launch; by the time you get around the island, the conditions may well be a good bit bumpier than when you set out.

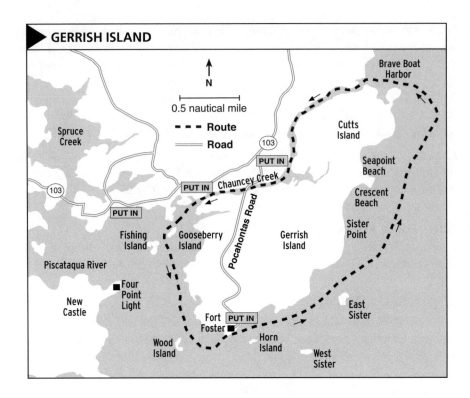

This description starts at Fort Foster and proceeds counterclockwise through the outside section of the route first. It also assumes you'll head up the creek from Brave Boat Harbor within an hour or so of high tide.

Fort Foster—Maine's southernmost point—would be a logical place to start a paddle of the entire Maine coast. The fort's first guns were installed in 1872 to protect the entrance to Portsmouth Harbor and the naval installation on Seavey Island. The fort remained in use through World War II when an antisubmarine net stretched to the New Hampshire side, and soldiers kept a lookout for U-boats from a concrete tower that still remains. The tower is not open to paddlers looking to scout their route. Nearby, the Pocahontas Hotel flourished in the late 1800s, a self-sufficient resort on 200 acres with its own steamboat pier and a golf course. The Army began testing Fort Foster's guns in 1901, however, firing missiles over the resort and damaging one of its buildings. This undoubtedly perturbed guests. Bookings suffered and the hotel closed in 1904.

The launch looks out to the mouth of Portsmouth Harbor: Wood Island Lifesaving Station, Whaleback Island Lighthouse, and the fortifications at Odiorne Point on the New Hampshire side are all in sight. On clear days Isles of Shoals (Trip 28) is visible on the horizon, more than 5.0 miles southeast, where the sub-spotting tower rises over Appledore Island. Plentiful rocks and ledges off this shore tend to keep other boaters away.

Paddle around the point and along the shore of Sewards Cove, past the concrete tower to a cobble beach, another potential launching area that may be more exposed than the southern point. For the next mile or so, paddle past a mix of jagged rocks and small rocky beaches below mostly undeveloped shoreline. To the northeast, look for Cape Neddick Nubble Lighthouse; if the weather is clear and you have a sharp eye, you may see the tall cylinder of Boon Island Lighthouse, 8.0 miles out to sea.

Homes begin just south of Sisters Point and continue to Crescent Beach, a public cobble beach separated by a sand spit from Seapoint Beach (KLT) on the north side. This is a favored spot for local dog walkers; parking in summer is limited to Kittery residents with a few spots along the road for nonresidents. The shore from here to Brave Boat Harbor is privately owned with a few homes. The harbor entrance is barely visible until you arrive there. Look for a steep cobble beach just before you reach the shallow and rocky entrance, which has a reputation as a tough spot to get through. In the right conditions, you might also find a surfable wave.

Inside the harbor, conditions are generally calm and out of the wind. Paddle west and pass through the remains of the railroad trestle that carried the Kittery–Portsmouth–York Trolley (KP&Y), which operated from 1897 to 1923. The creek meanders to the southwest; follow it on a rising tide. The shore on the east side of the creek is part of the RCNWR; you'll see a few houses along the west shore. The creek takes multiple sharp turns through the oxbows, making it a good place to practice edging and turning skills. The water opens into a basin where the road passes just south and the creek squeezes through a culvert where the current increases—probably against you at this point, since the currents meet in this area. This is a good spot for a break. The RCNWR provides a fancy-looking outhouse at the trailhead on the east shore. If paddling against the current in the culvert isn't your thing, carry across the road to a set of steps leading down to Chauncey Creek.

Chauncey Creek is more densely populated than other areas on this route. There's a rowing club on the south bank, and you're likely to encounter all sorts of self-propelled craft along this stretch, but probably not a lot of powerboat traffic until you reach Chauncey Creek Lobster Pier, a dockside restaurant on the north bank. This is another good spot for a break, with a casual enough atmosphere to accommodate paddlers.

Follow the shore back to the launch—most of it along this stretch is developed—or take a side trip out to tiny Fishing Island (private), a popular picnic spot that marks the edge of deeper water, which may well be less choppy than the shallower stretches to the north.

Continue toward the old pier and the Wood Island Lifesaving Station. Built in 1908, the building is owned by the town of Kittery and is slated for demolition; as of 2016, concerned citizens were still raising money to repair it instead. Whaleback Lighthouse is just to the south, where a light has stood since 1829, the current tower since 1872. If you parked above the Fort Foster Park launch, you may be able to see your car from here. Be careful as you approach the beach; there are plenty of jagged submerged rocks just offshore, and the waves occasionally get big here.

The quiet stretch of water between Brave Boat Harbor and Chauncey Creek provides calm paddling just about any time the tide is high enough, making it possible to circumnavigate Gerrish Island.

ALTERNATIVES

On rougher days, launch at Frisbee Pier or the culvert near the end of Chauncey Creek in the RCNWR, paddling the more protected waters of the creeks and marshes leading to Brave Boat Harbor.

MORE INFORMATION

Kittery Recreation Department (kitteryme.gov; 207-439-3800). Kittery Land Trust (kitterylandtrust.org; 207-439-8989). Rachel Carson National Wildlife Refuge (fws.gov/refuge/rachel_carson; 207-646-9226).

EXPLORING TIDE POOLS

Tide pools are excellent places to observe the life that is usually beneath our hulls and to gain a better understanding of how the intertidal ecosystem functions. Remember the Leave No Trace principals when observing tide pools. Merely walking over some small creatures may crush them; return any rocks you move to their original position.

At first glance, tidal pools may appear lifeless. If you sit and closely watch barnacles you'll see the wispy cirri slipping in and out of their shells, filtering particles and pulling in plankton. When the tide goes out, barnacles close the hard plates over the opening and seal themselves off from the elements. Watch for periwinkles, perhaps moving along rockweed branches, their eyestalks waving above in the current. Get near them and they retract into their shells.

Paddlers often encounter what appear to be miniature shrimp when we pull our kayaks onto a pile of tide wrack and they flip into our cockpits like grasshoppers. These are actually members of the amphipod family, with seven pairs of legs. While there are more than 9,500 species of amphipods, the largest in New England—known as scuds—are easiest to spot as they move through the water.

Keep an eye on the bottom long enough and you may see worms undulating through the water or burrowing into the bottom. Ribbon worms are usually 4 to 8 inches long, but one was measured at 177 feet, the longest animal ever found. These carnivorous worms use their needle-like snout to impale their prey. Most common in New England are clam worms, which grow to about 8 inches and use their proboscis to catch and ingest their victims. If they sense your presence, they burrow to escape. Be careful: clam worms have strong jaws, and they will bite.

Anemones are almost floral in appearance, but their "petals" are tentacles that disable prey with a toxic sting. You're most likely to find anemones in the lower intertidal zone on the undersides of rocks. Related to anemones are tiny, plant-like hydroids, which often live as colonies attached to rocks.

Jellyfish, another anemone relative, are less likely to be found living in the intertidal zone. Moon jellyfish are common and easily identifiable by their whitish, nearly transparent pallor; their sting is not harmful to humans. Lion's mane jellyfish are red-hued and mesmerizing to watch, but be wary of their long tentacles (up to 90 feet). Even if they are washed up on shore their sting is painful.

Hermit crabs top the list of charismatic tidal pool fauna, and watching them amble along with periwinkle shells on their backs can pass for entertainment. It's hard not to project personality and even attitude upon the tiny crabs, which are actually more closely related to lobsters. Green crabs are the most common crab species in New England. Rock and Jonah crabs—about twice the size of green crabs—may also be found.

Echinoderms such as sea urchins, sea stars, and sand dollars may seem sedentary, but watch long enough and you may get to see one of these creatures in action. Sand dollars prefer sandy bottoms, where they sift through the grains for the plant life that sustains them. Closely related, sea urchins scrape algae off rocks. Sea stars, found clinging to rocks or hunting along the bottom, are covered in armor-like calcareous plates and tiny tube feet, which enable them to travel. There are a number of species of sea stars in New England, but most common is the northern or common sea star. These carnivorous creatures will eat just about anything, but mollusks make up much of their diet.

28
ISLES OF SHOALS

The only islands around, full of history and bold, rocky scenery.

Distance ▶ 14.0 to 18.0 nautical miles

Tidal Planning ▶ Mean tidal range in Portsmouth Harbor is 7.8 feet.

Cautions ▶ This route requires a long crossing in very exposed water. It should only be attempted by experienced paddlers with solid navigation and rescue skills. In February 2009, a solo kayaker left Smuttynose Island after lunch and was lost at sea.

Charts and Maps ▶ NOAA chart #13283; Maptech #27

LAUNCHES

Rye Harbor State Park, Rye Harbor, NH Ramp (launch fee); parking (fee, in-season); portable outhouse. Park gates are open 8 A.M. to 6 P.M. late May through mid-June and until 8 P.M. mid-June through September. From I-95, Exit 3, take NH 33 east for 1.5 miles then turn right onto Peverly Hill Road. In 1.1 miles, cross US 1 and continue straight onto Elwyn Road. At the Rye traffic circle in 1.4 miles, take the first exit onto Sagamore Road. In 1.5 miles, bear left onto Long John Road, then turn left onto Washington Road in 0.7 mile. Turn right onto NH 1A in 0.8 mile and continue into the park; the ramp and parking are on the left. *GPS coordinates: 43° 0.157′ N, 70° 45.110′ W.*

Odiorne Point State Park, Rye, NH Ramp; parking. Follow the directions above to the traffic circle in Rye and take the second exit for NH 1A. Continue 1.2 miles; after crossing the bridge over the Piscataqua River/Seavey Creek, take an immediate left into the ramp parking lot. *GPS coordinates: 43° 2.921′ N, 70° 43.632′ W.*

Other Public Access Public landings on the Isles of Shoals include Star Island (Star Island Family Conference Center) and Smuttynose Island. Malaga Island, part of the Maine Coastal Islands National Wildlife Refuge (MCINWR), is closed April through August for nesting.

ROUTE DESCRIPTION

The Isles of Shoals may be best known for their history. Writer Celia Thaxter hosted a stream of New England artistic luminaries—including Ralph Waldo Emerson, Nathaniel Hawthorne, and Sara Orne Jewett—on Appledore Island in the late 1800s. The notorious Smuttynose Island ax murders of 1873 also put these islands on the map. For most sea kayakers though, the isles stand out more as a challenging trip to isolated islands exposed to the infinite horizon of the open ocean and whatever conditions it brings.

The crossing isn't for everybody: more than 5.0 miles of open water stand between the Rye Harbor entrance and Lunging Island, and the paddle there takes 2 hours or so on a good day. From the higher ground of NH 1A, it's easy to look to the isles and think, "That's not so far!" But in your cockpit at the mouth of Rye Harbor, they're little more than far-off smudges that are likely to bring you to the opposite conclusion. Good judgment is everything here: understanding the conditions and how they might change while you're out there and a reasonable perspective of your ability to deal with those conditions. If you choose your day well, it should be uneventful, almost boring even, but have a backup plan. If conditions aren't what you want, leave this trip for another day. This is no place for someone without excellent navigation and rescue skills. Even after the crossing, conditions can be a concern: there's likely to be some swell, and when it comes from the depths into the shallows just east of the islands, lively water ensues.

The islands are a stunning, remote place to paddle. Once there, you can see the entire New Hampshire seacoast, from the Seabrook Station nuclear power plant to Portsmouth, where the Picsataqua River Bridge arcs above an otherwise flat landscape. Farther north, Mount Agamenticus rises over the southern Maine shoreline. To the south, wind generators turn in the breeze at Cape Ann. There's a lighthouse, a grand hotel (now a conference center), a marine research station, and a few houses. You'll also paddle across a state border: the nine islands of Isles of Shoals were divided in 1629, with the five northern islands going to Maine, and the four southern islands going to New Hampshire.

Launching from Odiorne State Park adds a couple of miles onto each leg of the trip, but is an option if you would like to leave earlier than the gates open at Rye Harbor. Otherwise, launch in Rye Harbor and proceed out past the breakwater where you will abruptly be in the open ocean. If conditions feel big here, turn back, although waves are likely to turn into more organized swells as you leave the shallower area near shore. Take a good look at your first destination: the Isles of Shoals Lighthouse, 5.5 nautical miles away. Even if it doesn't look foggy, follow a bearing. Look out for boats and start paddling. As you proceed, look back at the shoreline every once in a while to spot landmarks that will help you upon your return and to make sure there isn't a whale-watching boat bearing down upon your stern.

This is a popular area for recreational boats, and they tend to head straight for the "RH" (Rye Harbor) buoy, probably following their chart plotter. Those red lines on your chart might suggest the routes those boats are taking. Your crossing might be

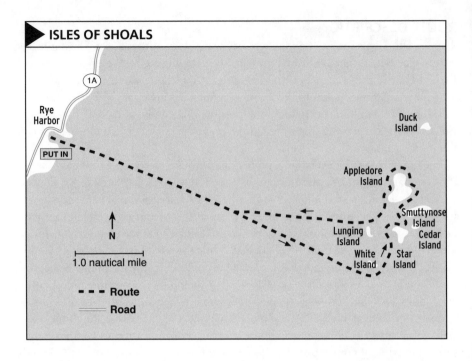

more relaxing if you are clear of those routes. There are a few lobster boats here as well, and their buoys are conveniently placed so that you may take a range on them. Find a distant buoy and line it up with the lighthouse.

As you paddle, you will probably discover that you are being pushed to one side or the other (I seem to get set to the south here, regardless of tides). Adjust your ferry angle so that you can stay on the range, and get to your destination as efficiently as possible. Focus on a good forward stroke and try not to look at your watch too often.

Slowly, the buildings on the islands will become more distinct. White Island (private) is actually two islands connected by a bar. The western one is home to a tern colony, while the Isles of Shoals Lighthouse has stood on the eastern side since 1822 (the present tower dates to 1855). To the northeast, the massive Oceanic House dominates Star Island's skyline amid a dense cluster of other buildings including the stone Gosport Chapel, which rises above the rest. Once an upscale resort, a retreat founded on the ideals of Unitarian Universalism and the United Church of Christ opened here in 1915; present-day events at the Star Island Family Conference Center are attended by those with a variety of beliefs. The island is open to visitors, for a small fee, from mid-June until mid-September, 8 A.M. until sunset. Visitors may also stay for a week-long conference or a personal retreat. Land by the dock on the north side.

Star is connected by breakwater to Cedar Island, which in turn is connected by breakwater to Smuttynose Island. This enclosure creates the calmer waters of Gosport Harbor. As you cross over to Cedar Island, you enter Maine.

Smuttynose Island (private) is open to day visitors. There are no facilities, but stewards can direct you on a walking tour of the island, which includes a couple of small, historical houses. If it's crowded there, pull up on the seaweed on neighboring Malaga Island (MCINWR; closed April through August for nesting).

Head north around the steep and rocky east side of Appledore Island. To the north, you'll see Duck Island (MCINWR; closed to visitors) and Eastern Rocks, the northern end of the island group. As you round the northern end of Appledore, watch for several slots cutting deep into the rocky shore. Continue around to the cove on the west side, where Shoals Marine Laboratory has a dock. Marine lab buildings and a World War II radar tower ring the cove. The research facility is run by the University of New Hampshire and Cornell University. Also on the island is Celia Thaxter's Garden, a reminder of the woman who once presided over the island's thriving artists' salon.

To begin the trip back, paddle southwest to Lunging Island, a privately owned island with a house on it. Your bearing back to Rye Harbor should be about 300 degrees magnetic. If possible, pick some landmarks on shore that will help you follow this bearing. Paddle for a couple of hours, and reenter Rye Harbor.

Isles of Shoals Lighthouse on White Island is usually visible from the New Hampshire shore, providing the more obvious destination while crossing over to the island group.

ALTERNATIVES
Portsmouth Harbor, Great Bay, Gerrish Island (Trip 27). On the other hand, you could catch a ride on one of the tour boats that regularly make the trip to Isles of Shoals from Portsmouth or Rye, and Plum Island Kayak does a guided "mothership" trip.

MORE INFORMATION
Rye Harbor State Park (nhstateparks.org/explore/state-parks/rye-harbor-state-park.aspx; 603-227-8722). Odiorne State Park (nhstateparks.org/explore/state-parks/odiorne-point -state-park.aspx; 603-227-8722). Star Island Family Conference Center (starisland.org; 603-430-6272). Maine Coastal Islands National Wildlife Refuge (fws.gov/refuge/Maine _Coastal_Islands; 207-594-0600).

29
PLUM ISLAND

This 7-mile-long barrier island is a refuge for more than 300 species of resident and migratory birds, including the endangered piping plover.

Distance ▶ 17.0 to 18.0 nautical miles to circumnavigate, or choice of distance for one-way routes

Tidal Planning ▶ Mean tidal range is 8.3 feet. Much of the areas west of Plum Island and south of Sandy Point drain at low tide, revealing many square miles of mudflats. In the Plum Island River, the tide enters from north and south, with a shifting tidal divide; it is unlikely that you'll completely avoid paddling against current, but plan to be in this area at roughly high tide to have plenty of room to navigate with minimal current. The mouth of the Merrimack River develops a strong current. Plan to avoid paddling against it and avoid this area when the ebbing tide stacks up against on-shore winds.

Cautions ▶ The mouth of the Merrimack River can be a treacherous stretch of water, attaining 2-knot currents off of Newburyport and faster between the granite block jetties extending from the river's entrance. Recreational boaters, many challenged by the currents and waves, also complicate matters for kayakers. Fishing lines cast from jetties can foil attempts to stick close to shore and eddy-hop. The shallow mouth of Plum Island Sound can also get a bit dicey when wind and current oppose each other. Greenhead flies can be a menace from mid-July to mid-August.

Charts and Maps ▶ NOAA chart #13282 and #13274; Maptech #7

LAUNCHES

Plum Island Bridge, Plum Island, MA Crude launch on southeast side of bridge; parking area on southwest side of bridge; no facilities. From the US 1 traffic circle in Newburyport, take Parker Street east. In 1.0 mile, turn right on MA 1A/High Road.

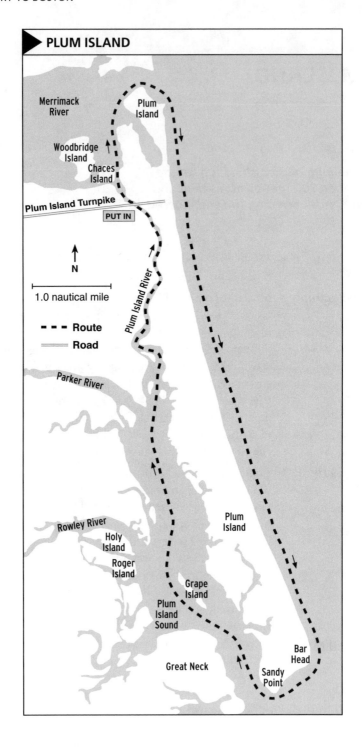

PLUM ISLAND

Merrimack River

Plum Island

Woodbridge Island

Chaces Island

Plum Island Turnpike

PUT IN

N

1.0 nautical mile

- - - Route

Road

Plum Island River

Parker River

Rowley River

Holy Island

Roger Island

Plum Island

Grape Island

Plum Island Sound

Great Neck

Bar Head

Sandy Point

Make a left 0.1 mile beyond at Rolfe's Lane/Ocean Avenue. In 0.7 mile, turn right on Water Street, which turns into the Plum Island Turnpike just 0.1 mile after the turn. Continue on the turnpike for 1.3 miles. The turnoff for the launch is 0.1 mile before the bridge, on the right. *GPS coordinates: 42° 47.840' N, 70° 49.355' W.*

Other Public Access Though the Parker River National Wildlife Refuge has conserved much of Plum Island, landings are sparse April through August due to nesting season. Sandy Point State Reservation is open throughout the season. An additional public boat launch is at Pavilion Beach on Great Neck; see Trip 30 for directions.

ROUTE DESCRIPTION

A barrier beach island stretching 7 nautical miles from the mouth of the Merrimack River to the mouth of Plum Island Sound and the Ipswich River, Plum Island offers protected creek and river paddling through salt marshes and wild stretches of sandy beach, backed by graceful dunes. For much of the summer, efforts to protect the piping plovers that breed here in abundance close most of the beach to human traffic, which only adds to the quiet, faraway feeling the place inspires. The downside: you'll need to stay in your boat, rather than land on the beach.

Named for wild beach plums that grow in its dunes, Plum Island is dominated by the Parker River National Wildlife Refuge (PRNWR), which attracts more than 300 species of birds. Sandy Point State Reservation (SPSR) occupies the southern tip, overlooking the shallow inlet to Plum Island Sound, and is open to the public even when the rest of the beach is not. During spring and fall migrations, Plum Island is on the flyway, attracting hundreds of species of birds. On the north end, a small community with a couple of restaurants, an inn, and a historic lighthouse overlooks the mouth of the Merrimack.

Protected from open ocean by the island, Plum Island Sound is a tidal estuary fed by the Parker, Rowley, and Eagle Hill rivers, as well as countless shorter passages that wind through the salt marsh. Toward the north end, the Plum Island River narrows and passes beneath a drawbridge before joining the Merrimack River.

The ideal launch site and direction for this route are dependent on tide and conditions. Ideally, plan to travel through Plum Island Sound with the current and arrive at the mouth of the Merrimack River close to slack current. If unsure of conditions, scout them by car from the north end of Plum Island. Launch from the bridge almost an hour before low tide to reach the mouth of the Merrimack around slack low, break at Sandy Point at mid-tide, and travel up Plum Island River on a rising tide. Launch at Pavilion Beach on a rising tide to reach the mouth of the Merrimack close to slack high tide. This route will assume a bridge launch on an early low tide and a clockwise direction.

North of Plum Island, across the mouth of the Merrimack River, Salisbury Beach State Reservation hosts the only overnight option on-route. While it is possible to launch from the paved ramp at Black Rock Creek, the risks associated with crossing the Merrimack outweigh the reservation as a practical launch if you aren't camping there.

From the launch, pass beneath the drawbridge and follow the creek, bearing right where it forks and heading generally north along the Plum Island shore. An inlet called the Basin divides the north end, past which you'll pass the Plum Island Lighthouse. The first tower was built here in 1788, when Newburyport was an important port and mariners needed guides through the dangerous mouth of the river. The current tower has stood since 1898.

Pass the dock for tour boats and follow the shore out toward the breakwater. Even at slack current, you will likely encounter some currents and eddies. You'll probably find less current near shore, but be attentive to fishing lines. Give the end of the breakwater a wide berth and head back in toward the beach.

Your route for the next 7.0 nautical miles is obvious: keep the beach on your right. In the distance, Cape Ann (Trip 31) stretches out to sea, with wind turbines towering near the Annisquam River. On your right there's just beach and more beach stretching into the distance. Waves along Plum Island tend to break near shore; it may be possible to paddle just out of the breaking zone, but this will change as you progress, so be alert. A stretch of homes overlooks the first 1.5 miles, slowly dwindling as the beach erodes.

The beach immediately below the PRNWR parking area and visitor center remains open during piping plover breeding season, but south of that, the beach is closed from April 1 through late summer. Be ready to stay in your boat for a while. This is a good stretch of paddling to have a friend with whom to chat. Otherwise, there's not much to differentiate one stretch of beach from the next. The sand dunes rise behind the beach and take on individual characteristics: a Matterhorn of sand, followed by a mound with sensual curves. The wind turbines gradually grow closer, and at some point Castle Hill appears, rising behind the dunes up ahead. You may find a surfing wave or two, but they are generally steep and dumping, breaking too close to the beach to provide much of a ride. As you near the end of the island, you could spot a birder up on a platform in the dunes (these are not connected to the beach) and eventually Emersons Rocks come into view, followed by Bar Head Rocks just before the beach starts curving westward.

The south end of the island is encompassed in SPSR, where you'll get a good view of the dunes on Castle Neck and the Crane Estate on Castle Hill (Trip 30). To the west rise the two mounds of tightly clustered houses on Great Neck (and the Pavilion Beach launch between them). The near-shore waters here are very shallow, the site of numerous shipwrecks, and you may see swimmers wading far from shore

If you've planned well, the tidal current is with you as you head north through Plum Island Sound, passing an old house on a point called Ipswich Bluff, site of the Ipswich Bluffs Hotel. Along with the Plum Island Hotel at the north end, this was a tourist destination into the early 1900s. To the east of Ipswich Bluff is Stage Island Pool, site of an ambitious but short-lived salt production venture in the 1830s.

To the north is Grape Island (PRNWR; no landing), which was inhabited for nearly two centuries, home to clammers, anglers, and farmers, supporting a school and a hotel. After the population dwindled in the 1920s, the government took possession and it became part of the wildlife refuge. John Kilborn and his son Lewis refused to leave and paid the government $10 a month to stay. After John Kilborn died in 1946, Lewis remained another 38 years, until his death in 1984.

Follow the sound north. On the west side, the Hog Islands and Nelson Island are high spots in the salt marsh with a few cabins on them. Where the Parker River enters from the northwest, bear right (north) into the Plum Island River, which winds through the marshland for 3.5 miles, an area popular with clammers. Shortly before the bridge, as the river bends eastward, there is a launch in the wildlife refuge—another launch option.

ALTERNATIVES

Castle Neck (Trip 30) could be added for a longer trip.

For more sheltered paddles, head to the Plum Island Sound or the Parker River. If paddling isn't possible, walk on the PRNWR's paths and boardwalks.

MORE INFORMATION

Parker River National Wildlife Refuge (fws.gov/refuge/parker_river; 978-465-5753). Sandy Point State Reservation (mass.gov/eea/agencies/dcr/massparks/region-north/sandy-point-state-reservation.html; 978-462-4481). Salisbury Beach State Reservation (mass.gov/eea/agencies/dcr/massparks/region-north/salisbury-beach-state-reservation.html; 978-462-4481).

From April through late summer you'll need to admire Plum Island's dunes from the water; much of the beach is closed to protect crucial breeding habitat for piping plovers.

30
CASTLE NECK

Paddle in relatively sheltered creeks that wind
through salt marshes to remote beaches.

Distance ▶ 8.0 to 9.0 nautical miles

Tidal Planning ▶ Fox Creek dries out 1 to 2 hours on either side of low tide; Pavilion Beach also dries out considerably at low tide. If you launch or return at lower tides, be prepared to carry your boat over mudflats.

Cautions ▶ When wind is from the south, the ebbing current from Plum Island Sound and the Ipswich River can cause waves to stack up and turn particularly choppy over shallow areas. This can also occur at the mouth of the Essex River.

Charts and Maps ▶ NOAA charts #13279 and #13282; Maptech #7

LAUNCH

Pavilion Beach, Great Neck, Ipswich, MA Designated small-boat launch area at north end requiring 50-yard carry over mud at low tide; limited parking; no facilities. From the intersection of US 1 and MA 133 in Rowley, drive east on MA 133 for 4.1 miles. Where MA 133/MA 1A bear right, leave left on High Street. Continue onto East Street in 0.4 mile. In 0.6 mile, bear left on Jeffery's Neck Road, then bear right in 1.7 mile on Little Neck Road. Follow Little Neck Road for 1.4 mile to beach parking on the right. *GPS coordinates: 42° 41.941' N, 70° 47.529' W.*

Other Public Access Public access here is all on land owned by The Trustees of Reservations (TTOR). Landings are possible on Choate (Hog, Round, Long) Island and on the southwestern reaches of Crane Beach.

ROUTE DESCRIPTION

Facing the ocean, Castle Neck has more than 3 miles of sandy, dune-backed beach paddling, with a maze of salt marsh creeks winding through its backyard. At the higher end of the tide cycle, Fox Creek and Fox Creek Canal turn it into an island, creating a paddler's route through placid, historic scenery with rest stops on Choate Island and Castle Neck's remote beaches.

At the north end of the neck, Castle Hill rises over Crane Beach, a popular spot on warm summer days. Castle Hill's first inhabitants called it "Agawam," referring to the abundant fish. European habitation began there in 1637 and the property passed through a series of owners until plumbing magnate Richard Crane bought it in 1910. In 1928, Crane built the 59-room mansion that still overlooks Ipswich Bay. The Trustees of Reservations (TTOR) owns the mansion, grounds, the Inn at Castle Hill, the rest of Castle Neck, and Choate Island—a total of 2,100 acres open to the public. The southern part of the neck is mostly wild and undeveloped, site of the Massachusetts North Shore's largest pitch pine forest and home to a significant nesting area for piping plovers.

The dunes of Castle Neck protect the salt marsh, islands of Essex Bay, and the Castle Neck River to the west, creating sheltered routes that wind through hundreds of acres of waving grasses encompassed in the TTOR's Crane Wildlife Refuge, part of the 25,000-acre Great Marsh that stretches from Hampton, New Hampshire, to Gloucester, Massachusetts. Encompassing seven islands in the Essex River estuary, the refuge includes Choate Island (formerly Hog, Round, and Long islands), which may be visited on foot by boaters who land at its public dock and beach. Visitors may view the island's historic buildings via 3.5 miles of trails.

When deciding which way to go around Castle Neck, your top concerns are the conditions in Ipswich Bay and having enough water to get through Fox Creek and Fox Creek Canal. With an early or midday low tide, you won't have much choice but to paddle clockwise, passing Crane Beach first, perhaps even taking a break at Castle

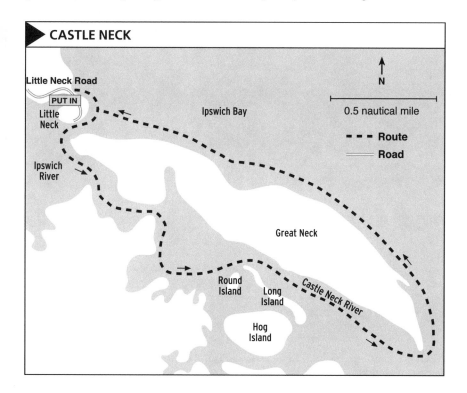

Neck's southern end or on Choate Island while the tide fills the creeks. With an earlier high tide, you'll need to go counterclockwise, getting through the creeks while you can. The counterclockwise route is described here.

From Pavilion Beach, follow the shore south to the mouth of the Ipswich River, where the tightly packed cottages on Little Neck, now a private condominium association, occupy the hillside overlooking the river mouth. Cross over to the undeveloped south side and follow the sandy shore of Castle Neck west to the entrance of Fox Creek.

The mouth of the creek offers the last sandy landing areas before the banks turn muddy and marshy. After about 0.5 mile, pass a stretch of rotting wooden posts along the west shore, which is the remains of Robinson's Shipyard, where wooden minesweepers were built during World War II.

The creek narrows as it curves eastward, then takes a couple of oxbow turns south before the unnaturally straight Fox Creek Canal (Hay Canal) takes a right-angle turn southward. (Continuing straight here would put you in a narrow creek that eventu-

At the north end of Castle Neck, the Crane Estate on Castle Hill rises over Crane Beach, a popular spot on warm summer days.

ally disappears—an amusing paddle if you don't mind backing out of it.) The oldest tidewater canal in the United States, the Fox Creek Canal was begun in the late 1600s, but wasn't completed until 1820. Schooners carrying logs from Maine and New Hampshire anchored at the mouth of the creek and floated logs through, en route to the shipbuilding capital in Essex. Follow the canal beneath the Argilla Road bridge and onward until it merges with the Castle Neck River. (If you're doing a clockwise circumnavigation, look for the "no wake" signs that mark the creek entrance.) Follow the river east, passing a couple of small creeks leading north. Ahead to the east is Wigwam Hill. A home built at the hill in 1726 is now completely buried beneath a sand dune, the result of deforestation and the erosion that followed. All that protrudes now is the top of a chimney.

To the south is Choate Island (TTOR), listed on most charts by its former designations as Hog, Round, and Long islands. Go south and circle the island, passing below the historical buildings, or continue southeast through the Castle Neck River, where you'll soon see a dock and landing area on Choate's shore. Land here to explore the island.

Continue along the inside shore of Castle Neck to its southeast end, at the mouth of the Essex River. Land for a break before you round the point; depending on tide and conditions, the vast shallow areas there can be a bit choppy. On a calm day, anywhere along the less-traveled southern end of the beach could be a good spot to land. Since this is a prime habitat for the threatened piping plover, avoid fenced nesting areas and the high-tide wrack line, where the birds often feed and hide.

Continuing north, you'll know when you arrive at the busy part of the beach, near the parking area and concessions. Kayaks aren't generally welcome where swimmers congregate, so stay well offshore and aim for Little Neck. Return close to shore along Steep Hill Beach before crossing the Ipswich River to Little Neck.

ALTERNATIVES

This route is adjacent to Plum Island (Trip 29), which could be added for a longer day. The Annisquam River (Trip 31) is a 2.0-mile paddle away, southeast.

At higher tides, explore Plum Island Sound or launch in Essex and explore the more sheltered upper reaches of the Essex River. Go for a hike among the 5 miles of hiking trails on Castle Neck. Take a tour of the Crane Estate or just hang out on the beach.

MORE INFORMATION

The Trustees of Reservations (thetrustees.org; 978-356-4354 [Crane Beach]; 978-356-4351 [Castle Hill and Crane Wildlife Refuge]); entrance fees are required from nonmembers.

THE GREAT NEW ENGLAND SEA SERPENT

At Cape Ann in 1638, two Englishmen and two American Indians encountered the first re-corded sea serpent in New England waters.

But the area's native people were already familiar with the creature (John Josselyn, *An Account of Two Voyages to New England*). A petroglyph beside the Kennebec River depicts a serpentine creature that may represent the serpent killed by Wabanaki folk hero Klose-kur-beh. The beast is said to have stuck its tongue out at him in a threatening manner. Klose-kur-beh shot six arrows at it, all of them bouncing off, until the seventh penetrated, breaking the serpent's spine and killing it.

In her book *The Great New England Sea Serpent* (Downeast Books, 1999), J.P. O'Neill doc-uments more than 250 credible sightings, often consistent in their substance, over the next 359 years. Witnesses estimate the serpent's length at anywhere from 40 to 150 feet, occa-sionally longer. Its head is often compared to that of a horse, in size and shape, carried atop a sinuous neck angling 4 to 6 feet out of the water. Humps or fins break the water's surface along its back. And though differences in details occur in various accounts—including its length, coloring and patterns, fins, humps, horns, scales, and a ball at the end of the tail—separate and unrelated accounts often list the same anomalies, suggesting that there have been multiple serpents, perhaps of different genders or species.

Most of the sightings have been between May and October and have coincided with the arrival of large schools of mackerel or herring. The movement of the animal has usually been described as vertical, like that of a caterpillar, rather than horizontal like a snake. Everyone who has seen the serpent agrees that it moves quickly, at 10 to 15 knots, if not faster. When it goes underwater, it drops straight down like a seal.

After several reports of sea serpent sightings in August 1817, visitors flocked to Gloucester Harbor in hopes of glimpsing the creature for themselves. Most were not disappointed. The Linnaean Society of New England recruited Essex County Justice of the Peace Lonson Nash to interview witnesses, providing historians with numerous sworn statements. Though some of these testimonies differ in particulars, overall they create a credible story from all manner of witnesses.

Sightings continued every summer in various parts of New England and eastern Cana-da, but in decreasing frequency. Some who stepped forward with their testimonies were ridiculed, so some sightings may have gone unreported. In *Cape Cod*, Henry David Thoreau relates the story of Daniel Webster (the well-known orator) who, having seen the serpent on a fishing excursion, told his companion, "For God's sake, never say a word about this to anyone, for if it should be known that I have seen the sea serpent, I should never hear the last of it, but, wherever I went, should have to tell the story to everyone I met."

Sightings of the serpent dwindled as the large shoals of herring and mackerel disappeared. Many witnesses also fired upon the serpent, which had little effect but to make it go away. The only report of its aggression toward humans occurred when it was tangled in ropes and some men in a small boat were capsized by its thrashing tail. From this point on, it became increasingly less eager to engage with humans.

Sightings continued infrequently into the twentieth century. In 1947 the steamer Santa Clara collided with a "marine monster" off of Cape Hatteras, recording the event in red in

This drawing of the first American sea serpent, reported from Cape Ann om 1639, shows the classic vertical movement and horse-like head typical of sea serpent reports of the early colonial period. Image courtesy of Mgiganteus, distributed under a CC-PD Mark liecense. https://upload.wikimedia.org/wikipedia/commons/0/04/Sea_serpent_Cape_Ann_1639.jpg

the ship's log. Brought on deck by the impact, several crew and passengers witnessed a 45-foot creature "with an eel-like head and body approximately 3 feet in diameter, thrashing in a large area of bloody water and foam" before it sank in the ship's wake. Following an article in the *New York Times,* the report was predictably criticized by skeptics with the usual explanations: porpoises, oarfish, alcohol, etc.

The most recent known sighting occurred in 1997, and though there is ample conjecture about what people have seen, the lack of a specimen relegates this and other serpents, including those at Loch Ness and Lake Champlain, to the realm of cryptozoologists. It remains unknown if the creature is a mammal or a reptile, but thousands of witnesses have undeniably seen something.

There have so far been no recorded kayak–sea serpent encounters, but historical evidence suggests that we are not on its menu.

31

CAPE ANN

*Get a push from the current in the Annisquam
to help you cover the same route of the
famed Blackburn Challenge, taking in six
historic lighthouses, Gloucester's busy
fishing harbor, wild marshland, and quaint
Rockport Harbor.*

Distance ▶ Around 20 nautical miles, round-trip, to circumnavigate; options to shorten

Tidal Planning ▶ 8.9-foot average range in Gloucester Harbor. Current in the Annisquam River meets and divides somewhere between the town ramp and MA 128 bridge.

Cautions ▶ Depending on where the wind and swell originate, any of the seas around Cape Ann may be big and difficult, prone to rapid changes with the tidal current, with long exposed stretches with minimal bailouts. Cape Ann is known for numerous shipwrecks for a reason; plan well and monitor conditions carefully. See additional cautions for each area.

Charts and Maps ▶ NOAA chart #13279; Maptech #7

LAUNCHES

Long Wharf Landing, Gloucester, MA Crude ramps requiring a muddy walk at low tide; parking on the west side of the lot is less prone to high-tide flooding; no facilities. From MA 128, Exit 13, take Concord Street north about 0.75 mile and turn right on Atlantic Street. In 0.9 mile, turn right onto Long Wharf; watch for a Jones River Salt Marsh sign on the right. Parking is at the end. *GPS coordinates: 42° 38.482′ N, 70° 41.640′ W.*

Gloucester Town Ramp, Gloucester, MA Ramp (fee); plenty of parking for vehicles with boat trailers but little parking for cars; no facilities. Formerly known as the Dunfudgin Public Boat Ramp and is still labeled that way on many maps. Drop off gear and park. From MA 128, Exit 11, take Washington Street south for 0.3 mile. Turn right on Centennial Avenue, then in 0.2 mile, turn right on Commonwealth Avenue. Continue straight onto Emerson Avenue, then turn left in 0.2 mile and follow the road to the ramp. *GPS coordinates: 42° 36.839′ N, 70° 40.661′ W.*

Pavilion Beach, Western Gloucester Harbor, MA Beach launch usually shared with swimmers; ten or so parking spaces at a tiny lot (unloading can be tricky without a parking space there) with street parking nearby; portable toilets. From MA 128, Exit 11, take Washington Street south for 0.3 mile. Turn right on Centennial Avenue, then left on Stacy Boulevard/Western Avenue in 0.6 mile. Continue 0.2 mile to the beach. *GPS coordinates: 42° 36.606′ N, 70° 40.084′ W.*

Granite Pier, Rockport, MA Town ramp; parking; fee. From MA 128, Exit 10, follow MA 127 N/Eastern Avenue/Railroad Avenue 4.1 miles to Wharf Road and Granite Pier. *GPS coordinates: 42° 40.028′ N, 70° 37.437′ W.*

Lanes Cove Landing, Gloucester, MA Small ramp protected by massive seawalls, mudflats at low tide; limited parking; no facilities. From MA 128, Exit 11, take MA 127/Washington Street for 4.5 miles. Turn left onto Duley Street to the launch. *GPS coordinates: 42° 40.750′ N, 70° 39.579′ W.*

Other Public Access Public lands are plentiful in this area and a few private lands offer intertidal landings and bailouts; land managers and permitted uses are noted in the description. Contact land managers for specific restrictions (see More Information).

ROUTE DESCRIPTION

There's a lot to see around Cape Ann. The Annisquam River twists through salt marshes. Countless boats pack Gloucester Harbor, the epicenter of New England commercial fishing. Half a dozen lighthouses guide mariners around the cape, past outer shores lined with sandy beaches and solid granite ledges and into Sandy Bay, with often-painted Rockport Harbor—the epitome of nautical quaintness—at its head. Twin lighthouses on Thacher Island beckon paddlers to stop for lunch or a night at the campsite to savor the island's history and outstanding views. All this is concentrated on a peninsula small enough to be circled in a day, but perhaps best appreciated in shorter trips.

With a great variety of features comes great potential for vastly varied conditions: from sheltered marshes to the volatile waters that have wrecked countless ships. Good planning is essential, whether you hope to circumnavigate the cape or just check out birds in the marshes. If you plan your trip right, you can get a big push from the current; plan it wrong and you may face currents against which you can't paddle or conditions that leave you wishing you'd stayed on shore. The conditions on the north shore can be completely different from those along the south, and they may change quickly, especially with a changing tide. Scout conditions by car before you launch; keep your plans flexible to stack the odds in your favor.

Described here is a circumnavigation of Cape Ann presented in stages, each with a launch/takeout; choose a section, make backup plans, or shoot for the entire route. Weigh the decision of which way to navigate by conditions and current. Clockwise follows the lead of the Blackburn Challenge (see "The Blackburn Challenge" on page 191), catching the current north through the Annisquam before circling the cape. Counterclockwise gives you a chance to paddle the more exposed south side before the conditions you've scouted have had a chance to drastically change. This description follows the route counterclockwise from Long Wharf Landing, but some comments on clockwise route-planning are given.

The Annisquam River to Gloucester Harbor (3.7 nautical miles)

Combined with the Blynman Canal, the Annisquam River effactually turns Cape Ann into an island. Tidal planning is important, whether you hope to get a push through the river on a circumnavigation or you're exploring the marshes and coves at higher tides.

The two most obvious launches on the Annisquam are Long Wharf Landing and the Gloucester Town Ramp (Dunfudgin). While tidal timing will play a role in your choice (currents meet somewhere between the ramp and the MA 128 bridge), the town ramp's launch fee won't secure you a parking space unless you're pulling a trailer, and the ramp starts you in an area with plenty of powerboats. Rustic and undeveloped

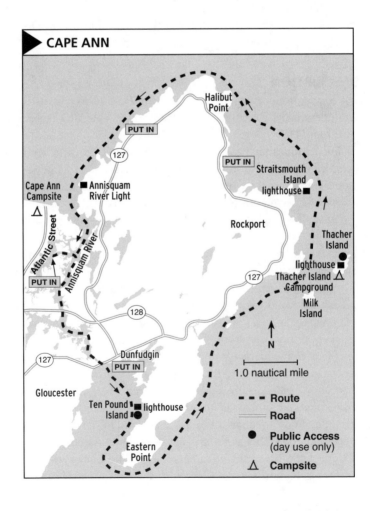

Long Wharf Landing might be the easier launch for paddlers, but be aware the higher tides may flood the parking spots closest to the ramps, and at low tide much of the area flats out, leaving a shallow, muddy creek and a short carry to the launch. Additional high tide-only launches are described along the route.

Most circumnavigators will probably plan for max current in the Annisquam and cruise through in under an hour. For a quick trip like this, the most noticeable landmarks are the bridges: the soaring arc of the MA 128 bridge and the narrow gap beneath the railroad bridge. It helps to have current behind you to get through beneath the Blynman Canal drawbridge; watch for other boaters before entering. At lower tides, monitor the channel markers and don't stray too far from deep water.

At the higher half of the tide cycle, the Annisquam offers relatively sheltered paddling with plenty to explore. On a slower trip, avoid the channel and its boat traffic, opting for the edges of the river, the marshes, and coves. Most of the river winds past densely populated shorefront; the commuter trains and traffic on MA 128 are just part of the background.

The soft white sand of Wingaersheek Beach (town of Gloucester) draws large crowds on warm summer days. As you paddle past on the Annisquam, people appear to be walking on water as they follow the sandbar far from shore. Exorbitant parking fees may partially account for the hordes of powerboats that anchor just offshore in the river to the south. Across the river on Babson Point is Quattro Venti (Italian for "Four Winds"), a red-roofed Mediterranean Revival home with stucco walls and arches. It was built in 1914 for a vice president at Bethlehem Steel named Quincy Bent, whose forbears used the property to load granite from river barges to schooners.

Around the point, Lobster Cove reaches inland. Pass a marina before ducking beneath a wooden pedestrian bridge toward the shallow head of the cove where there's a hand-carry launch (higher tides only) with limited parking. Near the mouth on the north side of the cove, pull up to the Market Restaurant, a laid-back, chef-owned eatery with a daily-changing menu.

Goose Cove is mostly cut off from the Annisquam by a causeway, and the opening beneath the road bridge develops strong whitewater currents with standing waves. If you ride the current into the cove, be prepared to wait a while to get out; carrying over the road would be challenging. You can land at the 26-acre Goose Cove Reservation (Essex County Greenbelt Association [ECGA]) along the southern shore, a nice quiet spot for a break, but there are more dramatic paddling destinations, and the waves below the bridge, while challenging and entertaining, aren't the best for surfing.

Higher tides create hours worth of channels through the salt marshes along the west side of the Annisquam. Just south of the MA 128 bridge, the Little River enters from the west. At the northwest bend of the river the tidal shoreline is encompassed in ECGA's Stoney Cove and Presson Point Reservation. There's a high tide-only launch area at Stanwood Point, on the south shore of the Little River, with another high tide-only launch known as Stubby Knowles Landing at the head of the river.

A busy marina sits south of the railroad bridge; the town ramp is below the high school on the east shore. The Blynman Canal leads beneath a drawbridge into Gloucester Harbor.

Gloucester Harbor to Cape Ann's Southeast Side (2.0–3.0 nautical miles)

If you're headed around Cape Ann, you'll probably want to take the express route across Gloucester Harbor. You could just point straight for the end of Dog Bar, 1.5 miles away, but it would be wiser to try to avoid at least some of the boat traffic going in and out of the harbor. From the canal entrance, follow the seawall and Pavilion Beach, passing the Greasy Pole (a horizontal pole mounted on a platform over the water) toward Fort Point before crossing the busy channel en route to Ten Pound Island.

Ten Pound Island has had a lighthouse on its northwest end since 1821, the present tower since 1881. Winslow Homer boarded at the lighthouse during the summer of 1880, producing about 50 scenes of Gloucester Harbor. The gravel beach on the east side of the island is a popular destination for boaters. From Ten Pound, arc south toward Eastern Point, away from the heaviest boat traffic, for a better view of the palatial homes along shore. Just south of Niles Beach (summer parking for residents only), the enclave of Eastern Point was created in the 1880s by wealthy Bostonians, and includes Beauport, a sprawling gothic mansion that is now a museum, open to the public. Make your way through the anchorage off the Eastern Point Yacht Club to the end of Dog Bar, a 0.5-mile breakwater popular with anglers. (If you're arriving at Dog Bar after a clockwise circumnavigation, you could arc around the west side or east side of the harbor, depending on larger boat traffic and conditions. The decorative white tower atop the high school is a good landmark toward which to navigate, whether you're returning to Blynman Canal or Pavilion Beach.)

The oldest fishing port in the western hemisphere, Gloucester Inner Harbor is a hub of nautical activity and is worth checking out if you're able to stay out of the way. Venturing there would be a bad idea for a group that can't maintain a tight formation. Be on your toes, attentive to the comings and goings of boats, and on the lookout for nearly invisible fishing lines hanging from above. Landings are difficult to find among the seawalls and piers. The harbor has several sub-harbors. On the north side, you'll find Gloucester's public docks at the head of Harbor Cove. The Cape Pond Ice facility, Coast Guard Station Gloucester, and all manner of fishing boats flank the entrance to the cove. To the east are home ports for whale-watching and harbor tour boats, as well as the Adventure, a 122-foot Gloucester fishing schooner built in 1926, now restored as a floating classroom. Cruiseport Gloucester hosts about a dozen cruise ship port calls a year, mostly in the fall.

The State Fish Pier divides the east end of the harbor. You may encounter several large fishing boats tied up here, including the trawlers *Challenger*, *Endeavor*, and *Voyager*, all owned by Western Sea Fishing and each nearly 150 feet long. These ships make the 10- to 16-hour trip to Georges Bank to trawl for herring, returning usually after a few days to land the catch with Cape Seafoods, where the fish are processed.

At the head of the South Channel, Cripple Cove Landing is a public dock—another possible launch with limited parking. Smith Cove separates East Gloucester from Rocky Neck, a renowned art colony that has drawn numerous well-known artists for over a century and a half.

Cape Ann's Southeast Side to Rockport and Thatcher Island (6.0 nautical miles)

Because of the lack of public launches along Cape Ann's southeast shore, the stretch is most likely only paddled as part of a longer trip or a circumnavigation. A near-shore paddle from Dog Bar to Lands End is 6 miles. Don't underestimate the potential difficulty of this section: with wind or seas coming from the south—especially if combined with mid-tide currents—and with little opportunity to rest or bail out, this can be a rough bit of paddling. Much of this coast is visible from Atlantic Avenue, just above; scout conditions from here before committing to the trip.

Dog Bar Breakwater extends about 0.5 mile from Eastern Point, covering what were once the dangerous Dog Bar Reefs. The Eastern Point Lighthouse, along with a rambling assemblage of red-roofed keeper's buildings, was first established in 1832, but rebuilt in 1890.

A few large homes dominate the western stretch of shoreline along Eastern Point. The beach at the head of Brace Cove is rocky and private, a potential bailout in rough conditions, but likely to be a difficult landing. The stretch between there and Good Harbor Beach is all rocky and exposed. While the beach might present a possible emergency bailout in rough conditions, it is one of the most popular beaches around (with limited, paid parking) and not a good place to plan on stopping. Just east of the beach though, Salt Island is likely to have a patch of calmer water where you might take an on-the-water breather. Landing here could be difficult.

Past Brier Neck and below a concrete seawall, sandy Long Beach will appear very uninviting with dumping surf at high tide in rough conditions. But in more favorable conditions it is a popular beach, with rocky Cape Hedge rising from the waves at its northeast end. Lands End and Emerson Point have a rough, rocky shoreline, below which the Milk Island Bar extends to Milk Island. Expect rougher conditions here. Treeless Milk Island (state-owned) is open to the public, with gravel beach landings. Thacher Island's lighthouses are just to the north.

Rockport and Thatcher Island to Cape Ann's North Shore (4.0–5.0 nautical miles)

Thacher Island, probably the most popular Cape Ann kayaking destination, has not one but two lighthouses, rising 166 feet above sea level. The pair were deemed necessary back in 1771 when they were first built, due to rough seas and nearby ledges that had caused numerous shipwrecks. They were the first lighthouses built to mark a dangerous spot rather than a harbor entrance, and they are the only operating twin lighthouses in the U.S. When the pair of towers come into view, they command your attention—and the attention of many other visitors. On busy August afternoons, so

Just off the Annisquam River, the entrance to Goose Cove develops strong mid-tide currents.

many kayakers have arrived that caretakers report they have run out of places to stack the boats. Land at the Thacher Island Association's wooden ramp below the old life-saving station on the north side. Caretakers collect a per-person fee and provide a map of the island that includes 3 miles of trails (maintained by the Thacher Island Association and the Thacher Island National Wildlife Refuge) and a camping area. You can even climb the stairs to the top of the north tower, one of the few New England lighthouses regularly open to the public. Carry your kayak to an area behind the boathouse.

(If Thacher is your midpoint break, again assess conditions before leaving the island. It's more than 6.0 nautical miles for clockwise circumnavigators to Gloucester Harbor, and if conditions are rough the stretch along the cape's southeast side can be slow and difficult; there are few bailouts along the way. It may make sense to return via the northwest side of the peninsula in foul conditions.)

The 50-yard gap between Gap Point and Straitsmouth Island (Mass Audubon) can get rough, particularly when wind and current oppose each other, or when you share the tight space with powerboaters. Going around the northeast side of the island adds about 0.75 nautical miles. Straitsmouth Island has had a lighthouse on its east end since 1835, with the present tower standing since 1896. The buildings are owned or leased by the town of Rockport, but the rest of the island is a wildlife sanctuary.

Cut straight across Sandy Bay to Andrews Point or consider a side trip along Rockport's shores that will likely add less than a mile to the route and is far more interesting.

Artists have flocked to Rockport for a long time, drawing yet more visitors to its narrow streets and shops. The most obvious place to launch here is at Granite Pier, but in the off-season you might find parking to launch at the cobble beach to the north. If tackling only this section, a round-trip of the harbor from Granite Pier could be done in 6.0 miles.

The sandy beach in Back Harbor is for swimmers only. Just east of Back Harbor, poke into an opening between seawalls to reach an intimate harbor overlooked by some shops. East of that, Bearskin Neck encloses Rockport Harbor, busy with fishing boats. Aside from Pigeon Cove, the residential shore between Granite Pier and Andrews Point is generally steep with granite block riprap.

Cape Ann North Shore to the Annisquam River (3.5 nautical miles)

The northwest shore of Cape Ann is generally rocky, residential shoreline and several coves and beaches. The Isles of Shoals (Trip 28) are often visible on the northern horizon, 16.0 miles to the north, while the dunes of Plum Island (Trip 29) mark the western shores of Ipswich Bay.

Launch at Lanes Cove and explore in either direction. Lanes Cove is enclosed by large granite breakwaters built in 1842 to load granite onto schooners and protect the harbor. In addition to the boat ramp, it is now the home port for a few lobster boats. The other coves present somewhat more challenging launching and landing opportunities. Plum Cove has a small beach, popular with families, with locals-only parking. Hodgkins Cove has a high tide-only launch ramp with street parking.

Steep, rocky Halibut Point encompasses Halibut Point State Park, Halibut Point Reservation (The Trustees of Reservations; no landings) and Sea Rocks (town of Rockport). You're likely to see visitors hiking and sunning among the rocks, including a large grout pile of cast-off granite blocks from the nearby quarries. Most of the shoreline is a bit rugged for landing a kayak, particularly in angry seas. A probable bailout lies just to the west, at the head of Folly Cove where there's a small beach popular with divers.

The Annisquam Harbor Light comes into view from the end of Davis Neck, the site of a former lifesaving station that often tended to vessels run aground in the constantly shifting sands at the mouth of the Annisquam. A lighthouse has stood on Wigwam Point since 1801, the current tower since 1897.

ALTERNATIVES

Castle Neck (Trip 30) is only about 2 miles from the mouth of the Annisquam River, with Plum Island (Trip 29) just beyond that; consider connecting northern segments of this route to those itineraries for a longer day.

The Annisquam River is likely to be somewhat sheltered when other areas aren't. On a rising tide, the river offers miles of marshy exploration, as do the marshes west of Plum Island and Castle Neck (Trips 29 and 30).

MORE INFORMATION

Town of Gloucester (gloucester-ma.gov; 978-282-3012 [harbormaster]; 978-281-9785 [Public Works]). Essex County Greenbelt Association (ecga.org; 978-768-7241). Knight Wildlife Reservation (Milk Island), Massachusetts Division of Fisheries and Wildlife (mass.gov/eea/agencies/dfg/dfw; 508-389-6300). Thacher Island Association (thacherisland.org; 508-284-0144 [camping reservations]); per-person fee to camp in addition to landing fees; outhouse available, but no water is available. Thacher Island National Wildlife Refuge (fws.gov/refuge/Thacher_Island; 978-465-5753). Mass Audubon (massaudubon.org; 781-259-9500). Halibut Point State Park (mass.gov/eea/agencies/dcr/massparks/region-north/halibut-point-state-park.html;   978-546-2997). Town of Rockport (townofrockport.com; 978 546-9589 [harbormaster]). Camping is also available nearby at Cape Ann Campsite (Capeanncampsite.com, 978/283-8683) in West Gloucester, just south of Long Wharf Landing; no water access is available.

THE BLACKBURN CHALLENGE: CIRCUMNAVIGATING CAPE ANN

Thanks to the Blackburn Challenge, circumnavigating Cape Ann looms in the imaginations of many New England paddlers. Every July, up to 300 small oar- and paddle-powered craft race the 20-or-so-mile circuit around the peninsula via the Annisquam River and a short canal that connects it to Gloucester Harbor.

The race is a tribute to Howard Blackburn, a Gloucester dory fisherman who became separated from his schooner during an 1883 squall. In the five-day ordeal that followed, Blackburn's dory mate gave up hope and died, while Blackburn froze his hands to the oars and rowed for his life, almost 60 miles to the nearest land. Though he lost most of his fingers, Blackburn went on to set transatlantic sailing records and became known as "The Fingerless Navigator." Appropriately, the Blackburn race route is known for treacherous conditions resulting in many capsizes.

A Cape Ann circumnavigation need not be such an ordeal, but the surrounding seas offer plenty of potential for difficult and dangerous paddling. The race course is subject to change to a there-and-back trip on either the north or south sides of the peninsula, and paddlers planning their own trip should be prepared to do the same. Before attempting a circumnavigation, familiarize yourself with shorter sections of the route, each of which is detailed in the Trip 31 description.

Aside from its function as a race course, the Cape Ann shoreline is a beautiful place to paddle, with great variety and much to see for those preferring to take their time. Thacher and Milk Islands are popular day trips for kayakers, but also provide the added option of camping. The Salvages, a group of ledges about a mile off the route, are popular with rock enthusiasts. Several launches provide access to the Annisquam River, which has miles of marshy shoreline to explore at higher tides, and is a good place to find more sheltered paddling.

32
THE BOSTON OUTER ISLANDS

These wild and dramatic islands offer public access—even camping—within sight of Boston's skyscrapers.

Distance ▶ 11.0 to 13.0 nautical miles, round-trip

Tidal Planning ▶ Mean tidal range is 9.5 feet, flooding west and ebbing east.

Cautions ▶ Currents in Hull Gut can be quite strong, creating turbulent conditions. The gut is also a nexus for boat traffic and at peak times can turn downright chaotic. Ideally, pass through the gut at times with less current and boat traffic. Around the outer islands, expect open ocean conditions and plenty of boat traffic, including high-speed ferries and whale-watching boats. Most large ships follow the channels north of this area into President Roads, but they will also follow Nantasket Roads on their way into Quincy Bay.

Charts and Maps ▶ NOAA chart #13270; Maptech #12

LAUNCH

Hull Gut, Windmill Point, Hull, MA Paved ramp and beach launch; adjacent street parking; no facilities, but adjacent to water taxi pier and takeout restaurant with portable toilets. *GPS coordinates: 42° 18.200′ N, 70° 55.232′ W.*

Other Public Access Boston Harbor Islands National Recreation Area encompasses 34 islands and peninsulas. Contact the Boston Harbor Islands Partnership for the most current information about access, closures, and restrictions (see More Information). Private lands in the area are noted.

ROUTE DESCRIPTION

With more than 4.6 million inhabitants, one of the country's busier airports, and the oldest continually active seaport in the Western Hemisphere, the Greater Boston area wouldn't sound like an obvious place to get away from it all in a sea kayak. But its rocky outer harbor islands have steep, dramatic shorelines with exposure to the bold open ocean and an amazing sense of quiet removal from the urban hubbub only a few miles away. Pitch your tent and spend the evening watching lights come on in the skyscrapers, and in the morning see the sun rise over the open Atlantic. For more rural-minded paddlers, the roar of jets and distant views of Boston's skyline might be all the city they wish to take in.

Amazingly, most of the islands here are publicly owned. The Boston Harbor Islands National Recreation Area comprises 34 islands and peninsulas, providing ample public access, interpretive tours of historic sites, hiking trails, beaches, and camping. Twelve of the islands are improved in some manner; the rest are preserved as wilderness areas. History abounds; you'll come across crumbling fortifications on many of the islands, the oldest lighthouse in the U.S., and a fort you can tour.

Boat traffic can be lively here. Plan routes to avoid the busiest channels, and keep a sharp eye out for approaching boats. High-speed ferries, whale-watching boats, and water taxis are a constant presence. And with such abundant opportunities available on the city's doorstep, one might expect to fight crowds to get to it, but with abundant launches throughout the area for powerboaters, the kayak-friendly launches in Hull,

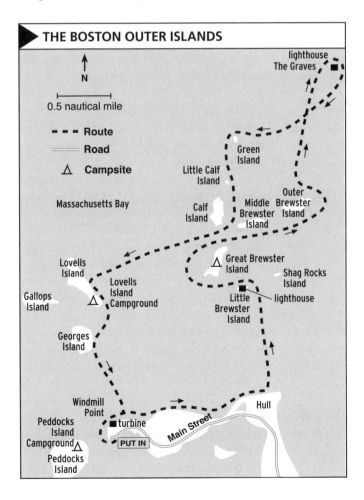

THE BOSTON OUTER ISLANDS

N

0.5 nautical mile

- - - Route
——— Road
△ Campsite

lighthouse
The Graves

Green Island
Little Calf Island

Massachusetts Bay

Calf Island

Outer Brewster Island
Middle Brewster Island

Lovells Island
Lovells Island Campground

Gallops Island

Great Brewster Island
Shag Rocks Island
Little Brewster Island   lighthouse

Georges Island

Hull

Windmill Point
turbine
Peddocks Island
Campground △
Peddocks Island

PUT IN
Main Street

Hingham Harbor, and City Point in South Boston are generally manageable. This route focuses on the outer islands, launching from Windmill Point in Hull to gain the quickest access.

Despite the strong currents and boat traffic in Hull Gut, the ramp offers an easy-to-manage launch area, parking, and even a takeout restaurant next door for après-paddle refreshments. When returning to the launch, the huge wind turbine is a convenient landmark. As noted elsewhere, time passage through Hull Gut with slack currents; getting through along the edge shouldn't be a problem if the current is against you, but if currents are brisk it may be rough and difficult to paddle near shore. Since the wind and waves often pick up in the afternoon, get out to the most exposed islands first, saving Lovells and Grape for later.

Once through Hull Gut, follow the densely populated north shore of Hull east about 1.5 nautical miles toward Point Allerton. Line up red nun #4 with Boston Harbor Light, take a good look both ways for larger ship traffic, and proceed. Be especially on the lookout for approaching traffic as you near the channel markers, but you're just as likely to encounter recreational boat traffic outside of the channel. The total crossing to Little Brewster Island from Point Allerton is just over a mile.

Little Brewster's Boston Light is America's oldest continually used lighthouse site, dating back to 1716, and the second oldest working lighthouse. The British blew up the first tower when they retreated in 1776; the current tower was built in 1783. The lighthouse also has the distinction of being the last in the country to be automated (1998) and the only one to still be staffed by Coast Guard staff, who live and work on the island, maintaining the light and conducting tours. The 7-acre island is open to visitors at certain times; lighthouse tours may be scheduled for groups by arrangement.

At low tide, Little and Great Brewster islands are nearly connected by a rock-strewn bar. If tide allows, land on the southwest point, just above where another long, meandering spit extends almost to Lovells Island. Great Brewster is composed of two drumlins, the northern one rising to 105 feet with tall, eroding bluffs spilling into the sea. Crude paths lead around the island, past a World War II bunker to the hilltop. Avoid the edges of the eroding bluffs—a concrete gun emplacement appears ready to tumble into the ocean at any time—but the views of the Boston skyline make this hike a must-see feature.

From the mid- to late 1800s, workers' huts and wealthy Bostonians' retreats dotted Middle Brewster Island, but it has been uninhabited for the last century or so. Reaching Middle Brewster along its craggy shoreline is difficult. The gut between Middle and Outer Brewster has been called "The Flying Place" because of the wave action during storms. Outer Brewster was quarried in the nineteenth century and was home to 125 soldiers who manned the gun batteries during World War II. A sheltered cove on the north side is a good spot for a break, with landing possible on the cobble beach surrounded by steep rocks.

From the north cove on Outer Brewster, cross 1.5 nautical miles north to the Graves, a pile of rocky ledges that would be hardly noticeable if it were not for the Graves Light (private) rising to 113 feet, the tallest lighthouse in Boston Harbor. Built in 1905 and named for British Rear Admiral Thomas Graves, killed in a 1653 battle against the Dutch, the lighthouse was sold in 2013 at auction to buyers who envision creating an inn. Kayakers and other boaters often float near the light to snap photos. The faraway feeling one gets among these rocks belies the proximity to Boston, only 7.0 miles away, and it is warranted: the island's exposure to open ocean ensures that you will certainly feel the conditions out here.

Circle back toward the Brewsters via Green Island, a lightly vegetated ledge outcropping where one might take a break in calm seas; beware of aggressive nesting gulls. Little Calf and Calf Island are just south. On the south end of Calf Island, you could land at the cobble beach to explore the sparse remains of a summer estate built in 1902.

To the north of President Roads, the wind turbines and huge white orbs at the Deer Island Waste Water Treatment Plant are a constant presence, looking like something from a science fiction movie. About 1.5 miles to the southeast, a plethora of power-

In addition to a dramatic archipelago, paddling among Boston Harbor's Outer Islands offers views of the city's skyline and the constant activity around it. Photo by Matt McCambridge.

boats often anchor off Lovells Island's visible beach. From this popular, long, sandy beach, trails extend to explore the ruins of fortifications scattered about the island. Shuttles run from nearby Georges Island. Camping is allowed at six sites, including two group sites; reservations are recommended.

Between Lovells and Georges islands, the Narrows is a busy thoroughfare for all manner of boat traffic, including high-speed ferries. Look for incoming vessels before proceeding across; boat wakes can turn the shallow, near-shore areas quite rough. Expect strong currents here, as the tide is funneled into the gap between Hull and Brewster Spit before being further squeezed between the islands.

Georges Island is the site of Fort Warren and is the hub for ferries coming from Boston and boats taking visitors to the other islands. Land near the pier on the west side. The government began using the island for coastal defense in 1825, but the fort wasn't completed until 1847, after its design was already obsolete. It was used as a training ground and perhaps most famously as a Civil War prison with a reputation for humane treatment of its Confederate prisoners. The island is open May through October with rangers leading interpretive tours.

From Georges Island cross back toward Windmill Point a little to the east, lining up green can #11 with a spot east of the wind turbine to the west, or lining up red nun #10A with the west side of Peddocks Island. (A direct route back to Hull would only take a mile-long paddle, but half of that would be spent in the busy channel.)

Peddocks Island, with the most shoreline of the Boston Harbor islands, is a worthwhile trip in itself. Farmed since 1634, the island was a strategic location for the military as well. During the Revolution, 600 militiamen were stationed there to guard against the return of British forces. From 1904 until the end of World War II, Fort Andrews, much of which still stands, protected the harbor. Campsites and yurts (reservations recommended) are near the northeast end, under a half-mile from the launch at Windmill Point.

ALTERNATIVES
South of Hull, Hingham Harbor has several islands, including Bumpkin and Grape, which are part of the recreation area and offer campsites; launch from Hingham Harbor Park on MA 3A. A longer version of this trip may also be done from City Point Park in South Boston, which could encompass Thompson, Spectacle, and Long islands; the park and launch are off Day Boulevard.

These alternate launches also offer opportunities for shorter trips.

MORE INFORMATION
Boston Harbor Islands National Recreation Area (nps.gov/boha; reserveamerica.com [campsite reservations]). Boston Harbor Islands Partnership (bostonharborislands.org; 617-223-8666). Inland camping in Hingham is available at Wompatuck State Park (mass.gov/eea/agencies/dcr/massparks/region-south/wompatuck-state-park.html; 781-749-7160).

CAPE COD AND MARTHA'S VINEYARD

Cape Cod offers paddlers miles of sandy beaches backed by undulating sand dunes, waters warmed by Gulf Stream currents, and networks of estuaries, salt marshes, and rivers to explore, but paddling along miles of unpopulated sandy beaches may become monotonous. Bring along a beach blanket, a swimsuit, some good reading, and plenty of drinking water and keep your plans flexible to ensure you have more fun. Allow time to make mistakes. Taking wrong turns in salt marshes or discovering that your chart is out-of-date may not be  big problems if you've set aside some time to enjoy the unexpected.

On charts, areas shown with one shade of green or another indicate flats that, in areas such as Cape Cod, might never actually be navigable. Some are salt marshes with peaty soil topped by spartina and only navigable at higher tides via creeks that run through them. Flats may also be shallow, sandy, mucky areas, difficult to traverse in a boat or on foot. In some cases they may be charted as islands, but don't count on them for a rest stop. Maneuvering from a boat up a muddy bank to the top of these flats could be quite a challenge. Paddling among them can be akin to finding your way through a maze that can change from season to season as storms rearrange the topography.

Trips in large areas of flats will be easier to paddle in at high tides. Getting lost in a creek can be fun with plenty of time and a rising tide on your side; not so with darkness coming and the tide going out. Tide tables reflect big differences between locations. For example, high tide reaches the northern fingers of Little Pleasant Bay almost 2 hours later than it reaches the harbors along Nantucket Sound. Sea conditions may also be drastically different from one side of the Cape to the other, with warmer waters found on the south side. Keep all of this in mind as you plan your routes.

Cape Cod becomes extremely crowded in July and August. If you don't get a parking space near your launch site early in the day, you may be out of luck. Cape Cod has much more public access than is apparent, but parking is often reserved for locals with resident stickers.

Both Nantucket and Martha's Vineyard have beautiful beaches, charming towns, and some good places to get out in a kayak, but getting to and staying on Nantucket can be pricier and harder to plan. You could carry a kayak onto the passenger ferry from Hyannis (more than a 2-hour trip), go for a paddle, and take the ferry back at the end of the day. In summer, the vehicle ferry to Nantucket is cost-prohibitive for most day trips. There's no camping, but there is a hostel about 3 miles from the ferry terminal by road, or about 14 miles of exposed and potentially rough paddling. Getting to Martha's Vineyard is more within reach of most paddlers. If you plan well in advance, you could car-top kayaks via the ferry and stay in the island's only campground. Both the campground and the island's hostel are far from any launch, so you will need a vehicle to get around. If you choose to stay at a hotel or rental on either island, your options may differ.

Experienced paddlers may consider paddling to Martha's Vineyard from the Elizabeth Islands or the mainland, but keep in mind that the currents in Vineyard Sound can be strong and conditions pick up quickly. Think of Nantucket Sound as a large tidal basin that fills and empties through three openings: Vineyard Sound to the west, Muskeget Channel to the south, and Great Round Shoal Channel, stretching between Monomoy and Nantucket. The current floods into Nantucket Sound and empties out the way it came in.

However you get there, the islands have plenty of paddling opportunities. The islands' ponds and more sheltered areas make for less challenging trips and easy opportunities to see the landscape, but paddling beneath the cliffs at Gay Head (Trip 40) is spectacular and the Chappaquiddick circumnavigation (Trip 39), following quieter shores past miles of wild beaches, is not to be missed.

LOBSTER FISHING

Despite the present-day dominance of lobster fishing along the New England coast, the crustacean was slow to gain popularity as a food source. Native peoples used lobster as bait and fertilizer, only eating it when they couldn't get fish. In the Colonial era, lobsters were so plentiful they could be gathered from the beach after storms and were easily caught with bare hands or a gaff. The fishing industry was instead centered on the Grand Banks and its more profitable catch: cod.

After the 1790s, New Yorkers' newly developed taste for lobster quickly depleted what seemed an endless supply of lobsters off Cape Cod. With the introduction of well smacks—boats with live wells to transport lobsters—the market expanded. As lobster catches diminished in Massachusetts, the smack captains began going to Maine. To keep up with demand, harvesters also began using baited hoop nets, which they lowered to the bottom to collect whatever lobsters they lured in during a short time. A crew would work a series of these nets, rowing from one to the next, hauling each several times an hour.

A lobster boom ignited when canning lobster solved problems with both preservation and transportation. By 1880, there were 23 lobster canneries along the coast of Maine. Canning's inefficiencies drove the industry to evolve. As many as 30 lobsters were needed to fill a one-pound can that sold for a nickel, so traps took the place of hoop nets, allowing crews to work large areas, claim territory, and bring in bigger hauls.

Soon enough, Maine's lobster population diminished too. By the late 1890s the lobster harvest reached its peak, and for the next 90 years there were no assurances that lobster populations would ever return to their former numbers. Regulations were gradually enacted—though they were largely ignored in early years. Massachusetts established size limits in 1874, followed by other states. Maine closed fishing grounds during summer months and restricted canneries from using small or egg-bearing lobsters. With the devastation caused by crews on sailboats and hand-hauled traps, consider the effect motorized lobster boats and pot haulers might have had, were it not for regulations and improved enforcement. By the 1940s, lobster landings began to increase, and over the next 40 years, landings made an amazing comeback.

Today lobster harvesters pride themselves on some degree of self-regulation, even beyond state laws. In all coastal New England states, lobster harvesting licenses are limited in number to regulate the number of traps. All states also impose roughly the same size limits, with a few local anomalies. In addition, egg-bearing females must be returned to the water with a V-shaped notch out of the tail to identify egg-bearers even after the eggs are gone.

The industry is further regulated by unwritten territorial rules that go back to the 1890s. Crews claim certain waters for their town or their port, further dividing the ocean floor. The right to fish in certain areas is usually inherited; some families have worked the same territory for generations. Violators are likely to get a warning—a knot tied in their line, or perhaps even traps cut off from buoys. When these conflicts heat up, the consequences can be extreme. Trap cutting has led to vandalizing, sinking, or even burning boats. In 2009, a territorial dispute on Matinicus resulted in a near-fatal shooting.

So, while lobster harvesters don't own a piece of the ocean, some understandably protect their watery "turf" as if they do. Paddle enough in one place and you're likely to develop some feelings for it as well.

33
DUXBURY

Wind through Duxbury Marsh, then paddle past miles of sandy beach to views of Gurnet Point and Saquish Neck.

Distance ▶ 14.0 to 15.0 nautical miles round-trip

Tidal Planning ▶ 9.89-foot mean tidal range. Access through the Cut River is possible only close to high tide.

Cautions ▶ Many areas flat-out or become impassible at low tide, especially the marsh north of the bridge. If attempting the circumnavigation of Duxbury Beach/Gurnet Point, the creek can only be paddled for an hour or so around high tide. The beach is subject to open ocean conditions, particularly Gurnet Point, which is likely to be exposed to most winds and seas. The area west of Saquish Head can develop strong currents and steep waves when opposed by the wind.

Charts and Maps ▶ NOAA chart #13253; Maptech #20

LAUNCH

Powder Point, Duxbury Gravel and mud beach with a short carry at low tide; limited parking; no facilities. From the intersection of MA 14 and MA 3A in Duxbury, take St. George Street east for 1.1 miles. Turn left onto Powder Pointe Avenue. Parking is ahead in 1.1 miles, just south of the Powder Point Bridge. *GPS coordinates: 42° 2.787′ N, 70° 39.099′ W.*

Other Public Access Duxbury Beach (town; fee or sticker parking, vehicular access only with permit) provides a potential pit stop or bailout point, but the carry from the beach park headquarters makes this a tough spot to launch or land unless conditions make it necessary.

ROUTE DESCRIPTION

Halfway between Boston Harbor and the Cape Cod Canal, the shoreline dips westward, forming Plymouth, Kingston, and Duxbury bays. Almost as if by design, long barrier beaches jut south and northward across the mouth, sheltering the shallow bays from open ocean conditions and leaving a mile-wide gap between them through which the Mayflower sailed before anchoring in Plymouth Harbor on December 16, 1620.

Nearly four centuries later, the shores of Plymouth, Kingston, and Duxbury are lined with development with a few prominent landmarks. The Standish Monument towers over Captains Hill. The stacks of Pilgrim Nuclear Power Station rise just south of Rocky Point and mark the south end of the bay. As if in counterpoint, wind turbines spin atop the hills, just inshore. Aside from a road and a few signs visible from the water, the thin cape running from Gurnet Point northwest is about as wild as it was when the Pilgrims arrived—just much more crowded. The seaward side is a long, gently sloping stretch of sand upon which the inhabitants of Duxbury drive all manner of off-road vehicles and park for the day. Separated by a thin layer of dunes with a few stands of cedars and beach roses, the Duxbury Bay side is marshy and muddy, frequented by kite boarders and windsurfers and a slow progression of SUVs winding along the road to the beach, Gurnet Point, and Saquish Neck.

When French explorer Samuel de Champlain first visited the region, Saquish Head was still an island, a drumlin like Gurnet Point and adjacent Clarks Island, which were formed when the last glacier retreated. Within a couple of centuries, sand had filled the gap between Saquish Head and Gurnet Point. Now, the area has more than 200 cottages, but is reachable only by boat from Powder Point or over the off-road vehicle trail (permit required), making the place feel far more remote than it is.

The potential for circumnavigation enables paddlers to explore plenty of interesting shoreline. You would need enough water to get through Cut River and comfortable enough conditions to get around Gurnet Point and Saquish Head. It could be wise to get around Saquish earlier in the day, but your tidal timing needs to be spot-on to get through Cut River. This description will take the clockwise strategy, launching not long before an early high tide at Powder Point to take advantage of conditions, to secure a parking spot, and to have the most time to complete the trip. If you don't have a high tide or favorable conditions outside Gurnet Point, there's plenty of good paddling to be found in the marsh and in Duxbury Bay.

From the launch, paddle beneath the Powder Point Bridge. Originally built in 1888, the half-mile-long bridge held records as the world's longest and oldest wooden bridge until it was rebuilt in the 1980s. The Back River winds westward for 0.5 mile before the Great Wood Island River branches northward through the marsh grass. (For a shorter excursion, follow any of these channels inland and explore the myriad passages through the marsh. It helps to have good turning and reverse-paddling skills.) Bear right just east of Great Wood Island (private). The main channel takes a few oxbow turns on its way to the Canal Street bridge. Beyond, the creek begins to widen again with more tidal influence from the Green Harbor side. It widens considerably before passing beneath another bridge; keep an eye out for swimmers who like to jump off. From here to the mouth of the Green Harbor River you'll be paddling past homes built close to the water.

At the mouth of the river, take a good look at the conditions and decide whether or not you want to continue with the circumnavigation. Conditions beyond Gurnet Point and Saquish Head are likely to be quite a bit bigger than they are here, especially in a couple of hours when the outgoing current is stronger. More protected water is about 7 miles away (depending on conditions), north of Saquish Head. If this isn't your day to circumnavigate, you should still have time to get back through the Cut River, but don't dilly-dally or you may find a muddy slog waiting for you.

If conditions agree, exit the breakwater and curve back toward the beach. For the first mile you'll have some homes along the shore to look at. About 0.5 mile after the

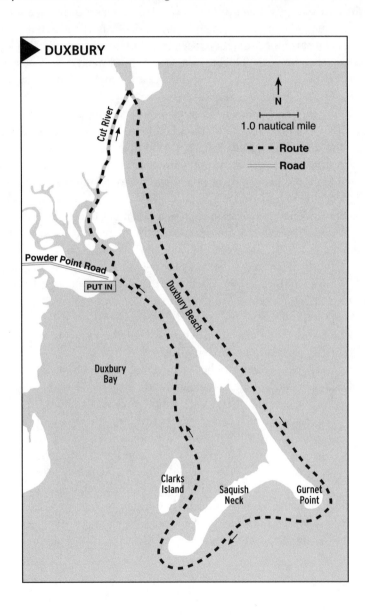

The Cape Cod area offers a great variety of paddling opportunities, from sheltered salt marshes to exposed, sandy beaches (pictured: Nauset Marsh).

houses end, a beach-side restaurant offers casual fare. From there, the beach park headquarters near the Powder Point Bridge is less than 0.5 mile farther. Don't plan on carrying across here to the parking lot, but in a pinch (including deteriorating conditions) it could be an emergency bailout.

Beyond the park headquarters, pass a short pedestrian-only beach before the off-road vehicle access area, which goes on for about 1.5 miles, to just south of High Pines (where there are restroom facilities). Beach paddling isn't always interesting, but keeping an eye on the shore will probably keep you mildly entertained.

By the time you arrive at Gurnet Point (private), you'll most likely be ready for the change of scenery. You get a good view of the hillside cottages and the Plymouth Light (Gurnet Light), up on the bluff. The first lighthouse stood on Gurnet Point in 1710, with the present, red-roofed tower built in 1843. During the Revolution, local militia protected the harbor from Fort Andrew, which stood atop Gurnet Point. American Indians inhabited the headland, and human history here may have included a visit from the Vikings in 1004. Be careful as you paddle around Gurnet Point. With any wind or seas from the south, the outgoing tide is likely to stack up the waves here; in addition, waves tend to steepen before dumping into the shallows south of Saquish Neck.

Despite its otherworldly charm, Saquish Neck (private) remained unpopulated until ditching the salt marshes reduced the mosquito population. During the Civil War, Fort Standish guarded the harbor entrance from atop Saquish Head. After World War II, off-road vehicles made getting to Saquish Neck more feasible, resulting in the construction of about 50 cottages over the next decade. Use caution while venturing around Saquish Head, where currents and conditions tend to increase. If you went through Cut River at high tide there's probably a fair amount of outgoing current by now. Look for near-shore eddies to make progress against it.

North of the head, follow the channel east of Clarks Island, one of the Pilgrims' first landing places. Truman Capote spent time in a cottage on the island while he worked on *Breakfast at Tiffany's*.

The main channel heads north, angling toward the backside of Duxbury Beach. With a falling tide, stick to the channel, approaching the east shore. Just south of the bridge, cross back over to the launch.

ALTERNATIVES
To the north of Powder Point, the Back River leads to the Duxbury Marsh, which is laced with a network of twisting creeks and can be a sheltered paddle, tide permitting. Cut River, which leads to Green Harbor, can only be paddled for an hour or two around high tide.

MORE INFORMATION
Project Gurnet and Bug Lights is a non-profit group that perserves, maintains, and conducts tours of these lights, as well as Fort Andrews and the Keeper's Cottage, which is available to rent (buglight.org). No camping is permitted on the route. Wompatuck State Park and Scusset Beach State Park are each a little over half an hour away by car.

34
BARNSTABLE HARBOR

*Take a short, usually sheltered paddle to
Sandy Neck, a 7-mile barrier beach with
campsites and trails through the dunes.*

Distance ▶ 2.5 to 12.0 nautical miles round-trip

Tidal Planning ▶ 9.5-foot mean tidal range.

Cautions ▶ Vast areas of Barnstable Harbor flat-out at lower tides. Significant boat traffic travels between the inner harbor (just south of Blish Point) to the bay via a channel that hugs the southeast end of Beach Point.

Charts and Maps ▶ NOAA chart #13251; Waterproof Chart #64

LAUNCHES

Barnstable Town Landing Beach launch (fee); most parking is for vehicles with boat trailers, but kayakers may park at northwest end of lot where trailers won't fit (leave a note inside the windshield that reads "kayaker") or drop off gear and park elsewhere; portable outhouses. From US 6, Exit 6, take MA 132/Iyannough Road northwest 0.8 mile. At MA 6A, turn right. Continue 2.6 miles to The Mill Way and turn left. The lot is on the left in 0.6 mile. *GPS coordinates: 41° 42.489′ N, 70° 17.966′ W.*

Scudder Lane Town Landing, Barnstable Town-issued sticker required for parking in one of about six spaces; no facilities. From the junction of MA 132 and MA 6A, take MA 6A east for 1.4 miles to Scudder Lane. Turn left and drive 0.4 mile to landing. *GPS coordinates: 41° 42.585′ N, 70° 19.354′ W.*

Other Public Access Sandy Neck Beach Park (town of Barnstable) permits landings at a high-tide take-out on the marsh side of the neck, on the beach of Beach Point, and on the beach side of the neck. Camping (permit only) is allowed at five primitive sites. Beach access for off-road vehicles (permit) and hikers is at the west end of the neck (bathrooms, water, parking). Mass Audubon's Long Pasture Wildlife Sanctuary (fee) covers 101 acres on Barnstable Harbor's south shore, about 1.25 nautical miles east of Blish Point. A beach landing is adjacent to the visitor center, trails, boardwalks, and beachfront.

ROUTE DESCRIPTION

Barnstable's Sandy Neck is a 7.0-mile long barrier beach, piled with 30-foot dunes and mixed forests sheltering the 3,000-acre Great Marsh, Cape Cod's largest salt marsh and most diverse habitat. Decide whether you want to explore the more sheltered and ecologically dynamic waters on the harbor side or the beach on the north side, open to whatever conditions Cape Cod Bay may bring. The two worlds meet near the east end of Sandy Neck, where the Sandy Neck cottage colony and the restored Sandy Neck Light adorn the shore. In addition, you can pitch a tent in a remote camping area nestled among Sandy Neck's dunes and pines.

Tidal timing is crucial on the harbor/marsh side; an outgoing tide can strand you in the mud- or sand flats. Armchair navigators will undoubtedly ponder the possibility of circumnavigating Sandy Neck via Scorton Creek; this would have been possible in the past, but development and MA 6A have rendered this impractical at best.

Your route through the marsh could skirt the edges, or if tide allows, venture up one of the creeks. While a few homes overlook the southern shore and a short stretch of MA 6A, most of the marsh is undeveloped, wild, and full of life. Saltmeadow and smooth cord grasses wave in the breeze over semi-solid peat that has built up over the years, providing ideal habitats for insects (which you'll notice most midsummer) and the swallows that dart back and forth, eating them. The marsh is an important stop for migrating birds, especially in the fall. In addition to the usual marsh-dwelling birds, you may get a glimpse of a northern harrier or a woodcock. Diamondback terrapins also live in the marsh, the northernmost extent of their range, leaving the water only once a year to climb the dunes to lay eggs.

It can take a little effort to find a creek that gets you close to solid land on the Sandy Neck side of the marsh (a particular one is suggested later in this route description). Unless the tide is rising, be attentive to depth, since some of these creeks dry out well before low tide. Getting from your boat onto land can also be challenging, since the creek banks are steep and muddy. If you do manage to get out to walk on Sandy Neck, only follow marked trails and roads; the dunes are fragile. While most of the land on the neck is part of a Barnstable town park, several portions are private and have rustic cabins overlooking the marsh. The cottage colony and the lighthouse are all private, but landings are allowed anywhere along Beach Point.

From the Barnstable Town Launch on Blish Point, head south out of the inner harbor and west toward Salten Point. A channel leads from the harbor out to Beach Point, and you may avoid most of the boat traffic if you remain west of it.

For the most direct route to the campsites, head straight across Barnstable Harbor, aiming for Great Thatch Island. The islands in the harbor, Great Thatch included, are hard to see as they are patches of peat and grass that barely rise above the water surface. From Salten Point your bearing is just west of true north, roughly 350 degrees magnetic for the crossing of a little over 1.0 nautical mile. With a pair of binoculars, you may be able to identify the Handy Cabin on Sandy Neck, which is about a hundred yards east of the trail junction, and is the only cottage on the marsh side of the off-road vehicle trail.

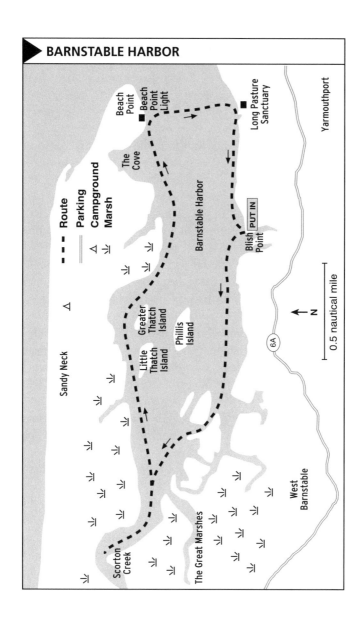

BARNSTABLE HARBOR

Route

Parking

Campground

Marsh

Beach Point

Beach Point Light

Long Pasture Sanctuary

Yarmouthport

The Cove

Barnstable Harbor

Blish Point

PUT IN

6A

N

0.5 nautical mile

Sandy Neck

Greater Thatch Island

Phillis Island

Little Thatch Island

West Barnstable

The Great Marshes

Scorton Creek

There are some possible landing spots just east of the cabin, but to get closest to the trail junction (at higher tides) venture into the creeks to the west. Look for the blue boxes on stilts—put there to trap greenhead and deer flies—and count over to the fourth blue box west of the Handy Cabin (there's one other cabin between the Handy Cabin and the trail junction). Near that box is the creek that gets closest to the trailhead.

If you're camping, you may want to unpack your boat here, haul your gear to the campsite, and then store your boat beyond the trail junction, well above the high-tide line. Notice the tidal wrack gets very close to the trail, and on the highest tides it floods in some areas.

The campsites are a 5- to 10-minute walk from the landing and are more commonly used by hikers who make the 3-mile trek on the beach or on the sandy off-road vehicle trail that follows the marsh side. Allow plenty of time, since navigating the creeks can be confusing and because arriving at lower tides could mean half an hour walk from your landing. (If exploring the north side of the neck, you could land on the beach to the north for a 3- to 5-minute walk, but conditions can change overnight and you may prefer to have your kayak on the more sheltered marsh side. The distance between the beach and the marsh requires a long carry.) Five sites, each with a picnic table and a shared privy, are available on a first come, first served basis through the park office at the west end of Sandy Neck in West Barnstable. The nightly fee can include delivery of drinking water and firewood.

If you're not camping, and especially if you have a rising tide, head west from Salten Point and follow the Barnstable shore. Pass a few homes, a boat builder, and the Barnstable Yacht Club before reaching the Scudder Lane landing, just before the point. At lower tides, the beach here turns into parking for oyster harvesters. Off to the west, the tall smokestack well beyond the marsh is at the Sandwich power plant. The Great Marsh begins just after this point, with passages leading off here and there. Explore if you have a little time and the right tide. An efficient reverse stroke will help if you find yourself at a dead end with no turning room.

The edge of the marsh to the east follows a broad expanse of peat flats that extend from the Sandy Neck shoreline. Continue between the flats and the low islands in the harbor, passing the Handy Cabin as you continue toward Green Point. In addition to being an easily identifiable, prominent landmark, the Handy Cabin has a long history, documented in Edward O. Handy's book, *The Little House at Sandy Neck*. Often photographed, the rustic cabin may look a bit isolated and forlorn, but many are drawn to it, perhaps inspired by a sense of simplicity and connection to the place that few people experience.

To the east, the flats extend farther south from Sandy Point. Follow the edge south to Green Point past Bass Creek, another inlet worth exploring if tide allows. After Mussel Point, head in toward the cove and follow the shoreline past the cottage colony. This small community of weathered, seasonal homes can be reached only by boat or the off-road vehicle trail. Unlike almost any waterfront property in these parts, there's nothing fancy about these cottages; they maintain a simple, weather-beaten

Just across the harbor from Barnstable, the cottages and lighthouse on Sandy Neck have a rustic, weather-beaten charm.

charm seen only in places that have stayed in the same hands for a while. Enjoy them from the water, though; the land is private.

For years after Sandy Neck Light was decommissioned and the top story razed, the light stood as a decapitated landmark, identifiable largely by the light that was missing. Now, though, thanks to the owners, the light has been returned to its former postcard-worthy glory.

The beach just east of the lighthouse is a good place for a break. You'll notice the buoys marking a near-shore channel here that develops a brisk mid-tide current. Be careful here: there's plenty of boat traffic, including whale-watching boats out of Barnstable.

If conditions permit, poke out around Beach Point. The sandbars north of the point shift occasionally and may not match your chart. In spring and early summer, these beaches and dunes are roped off to protect nesting birds. If you're in the mood for a beach paddle, it's about 2.0 miles from here to the northern camping area access, identified by a sign marking Trail 4 at a break in the dunes and probably by a number of off-road vehicles on the beach. Kayaks may be left at roped-off areas beside the trail entrance. The walk to the campsites takes only a few minutes.

To get back to Blish Point, retrace your steps back toward Green Point, where you can head south to Salten Point, or cross directly south from Beach Point; either route avoids the channel. From Beach Point look for an area on the shore, a little under 1.0 mile south, where a road descends to a small parking area with several interpretive signs along the shore of Long Pasture Wildlife Sanctuary (Mass Audubon; fee). Aim for the sanctuary for a quick crossing into shallower water.

The sanctuary's beach landing offers a good spot for a break. From there you may follow the residential Barnstable shore about 1.5 nautical miles back to the launch at Blish Point.

ALTERNATIVES

If you have more time than you'd expected, perhaps return in your car to Long Pasture Wildlife Sanctuary to learn more about the birds and wildlife in the area.

MORE INFORMATION

Sandy Neck Beach Park (town.barnstable.ma.us/sandyneckpark; 508-362-8300 [gatehouse]; 507-790-6272 [office]); self-contained off-road vehicles may camp on the beach; campsites (fee) available first come, first served; purchase permits at the gatehouse. Long Pasture Wildlife Sanctuary (massaudubon.org/get-outdoors/wildlife-sanctuaries/long-pasture; 508-362-7475).

35
WELLFLEET

Sandy bluffs, dunes, and beaches are a short paddle from the heart of Wellfleet Harbor.

Distance ▶ Up to 9.0 nautical miles, round-trip

Tidal Planning ▶ 10-foot mean tidal range. Large areas flat out at lower tides.

Cautions ▶ Boat traffic in Wellfleet Harbor

Charts and Maps ▶ NOAA chart #13250; Waterproof Charts #64

LAUNCHES

Wellfleet Town Pier Multiple launch/dock areas, including a dedicated sandy beach for launching kayaks; plenty of parking (and plenty of demand); public restrooms. From the intersection of US 6 and Main Street in Wellfleet, go west on Main Street for 0.3 mile. Take the second left onto East Commercial Street and continue 0.7 mile to the pier complex. The kayak launch is at the west end, right in front of Mac's Seafood. *GPS coordinates: 41° 55.754′ N, 70° 1.832′ W.*

Other Public Access Great Island (Cape Cod National Seashore) extends south from the park entrance, parking lot, and trailhead, just west of the Gut on the Herring River. The beaches provide easy landing spots, while trails follow some of the shoreline and venture inland.

ROUTE DESCRIPTION

To many, it may not seem like a grand gesture for the town of Wellfleet to designate a dedicated kayak launching area on its own sandy beach with nearby parking, but after you've encountered enough "trailer only" parking areas adjoining large paved ramps emptying into high-traffic channels, you become accustomed to second-class citizen status and you don't expect much in the way of help or empathy from the locals. So when the Wellfleet harbormaster directs you to the sign that reads "Kayak Launching Area," right on the beach, you may feel welcome enough to stick around this friendly town and soak up the vibe.

From the head of Wellfleet Harbor, the long strip of land to the west draws curious paddlers and separates this relatively sheltered stretch of water from Cape Cod Bay. From the beach along Great Island and Little Beech Hill, sandy bluffs rise steeply to tall pine forests, tapering as it points southward, giving way to undulating dunes and a sandy spit that merges with the horizon. When the dunes and bluffs catch the light just so, they seem to glow, drawing paddlers to the shores beneath. As paddling routes go, the trip out along the islands is neither long nor complicated: this simple there-and-back itinerary gives you a chance to hang out on idyllic stretches of sand.

Well before 1644, when seven families from Plymouth settled in the Nauset area, the Punonakanit, members of the Wampanoag Federation, lived along the shores of Wellfleet Harbor. French explorer Samuel de Champlain called it Port aux Huitres (the oyster port) due to the abundance of oysters the explorers encountered. Whales

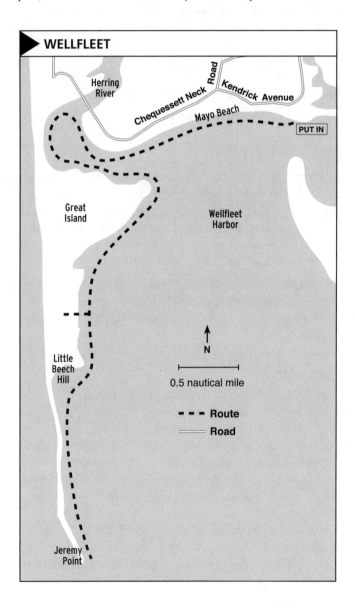

occasionally beached themselves on the shoal sands of the harbor, sometimes in great numbers, which provided subsistence for the Punonakanits.

Later, both whales and oysters spurred industry for European settlers, but the consequences were steep. They drove whales into the shallows where they could be killed and their blubber boiled down for lamp oil, and they burned oyster shells to make lime for mortar. Only after oysters disappeared here in the mid-1800s did it become clear that oyster larvae need the hard substrate of old shells to attach to and develop. The mollusks were later reintroduced using southern stock. The area was once covered with tall, dense, old-growth forests, but the trees were harvested to build boats and to fire the tryworks that boiled down whale fat. As Great Island began to erode in the wake of deforestation, the sand threatened to choke Wellfleet Harbor, putting businesses at risk. By the late 1800s, new forests were planted atop Great Island.

These days, the harbor is full of oyster harvesters and oyster cultivation cages, but whale-watching excursions and recreational fishing boats have long since replaced whaling ships.

If you arrive early enough in the day, you may be lucky enough to get a parking spot near the kayak launch; otherwise drop off gear and park elsewhere. From the launch, follow Mayo Beach west, coasting over the submerged cages where oysters are cultivated. Some of the classic, gray-shingled homes overlooking the beach have been around long enough that Edward Hopper painted them back in the 1920s.

One house stands out from the others: a dark-shingled cottage known as the Elephant House, which features an octagonal turret rising from a corner, and a room-like porch tucked into the structure. The house was built for Captain Lorenzo Baker, a pioneer of the banana industry.

Following the shore west, approach the mouth of the Herring River, which flats-out at lower tides. Head south to the sandy eastern point of Great Island (Cape Cod National Seashore) and follow the shore toward the bluffs. Though Great Island is now connected to Griffin Island to the north, shifting sands attached both islands to the Cape proper, making one big peninsula. Back in the late 1600s and early 1700s, Great Island became a whaling center, and local legend has it that whalers would wait at a tavern high on the bluffs where whales could be spotted.

Depending on tide height, follow close to shore or swing farther out to avoid sandbars exposed at lower tides. A low area with grassy, shifting dunes connects Great Island to Little Beech Hill, and at very high tides you may be able to paddle into the marsh. Otherwise continue south along the beach below Little Beech Hill's bluffs. The trees give way to dune grasses, which extend to a long, narrow point. At the southern end of the peninsula, Jeremy Point tapers into the ocean, its location changing with shifting sands. This is a good spot to pull up your boat and consider the scenery. If you go far enough west around the point you should be able to see the Pilgrim Monument in Provincetown, while far in the southwestern distance you may be able to make out the smokestack in Sandwich. It's a unique vista, taking in much of Cape Cod Bay.

Great Island and Little Beech Hill separate the calmer waters of Wellfleet Harbor from Cape Cod Bay. A low area with grassy, shifting dunes connects these landforms and at very high tides you may be able to paddle into the marsh.

To the south is Billingsgate Island, which is under water at higher tides. At one time, the island occupied about 50 acres of dry land and included 30 homes, a school, and a lighthouse. By 1872, the lighthouse keeper's log noted that a seawall was built to protect the lighthouse from ongoing erosion. There was no stopping it, though, and the lighthouse fell into the sea in 1910. By 1912, all the families had moved away, and by World War I, the island had shrunk to 5 acres. It submerged completely by the 1940s. At lower tides you may land at Billingsgate and look for the circular foundation of the lighthouse. Be aware that the tide quickly uncovers the island and may leave your boat a long carry from the water. It can also come in quickly and carry away unmonitored boats.

Head back the way you came; odds are, the light on the dunes and the water over the sandbars will have shifted enough to give the place a different feel. If there's enough water in the Herring River, detour along Great Island's northern shore and the marshy tombolo joining it to Griffin Island before heading back to the launch.

ALTERNATIVES

Armchair navigators will ponder the possibility of a circumnavigation at the highest tides, with a carry over the tombolo that joins Great Island to Griffin Island. The route is possible, but for most paddlers the effort outweighs the experience. The same is true for the east shore of the harbor across the busy channel, which requires crossing the 2.0-mile-wide mouth of Wellfleet Harbor from Jeremy Point to circle Lieutenant Island and following the residential east shore back to the launch. Most paddlers would prefer not to tackle the long stretch of open water, thick with motorboats, and several miles of residential shoreline, but it would provide a more varied route.

If conditions here aren't favorable and the tide is high enough (or rising), check out Nauset Marsh. From US 6 in Wellfleet, continue south on US 6 for 9.3 miles and turn left on Hemenway Road to reach the Eastham Town Dirt Boat Ramp. The north side of the marsh, near the Coast Guard Station, is the least developed area, and you may follow creeks out to a breach in the barrier beach where they meet open ocean. Expect strong currents near the breach and plan to paddle with the tide.

MORE INFORMATION

A favorite spot for birders is Mass Audubon's Wellfleet Bay Wildlife Sanctuary. Located at 291 State Highway, Route 6, South Wellfleet, the sanctuary boasts 937 acres of protected land overlooking the stunning shoreline of Wellfleet Harbor. It is well worth the trip to experience the 5 miles of trails and many programs Mass Audubon offers.

36
PROVINCETOWN

The view of Provincetown from the water, three lighthouses, and miles of sandy beach.

Distance ▶ 2.4 to 14.5 nautical miles, round-trip

Tidal Planning ▶ Mean tidal range 9.1 feet.

Cautions ▶ Expect heavy boat traffic in the harbor and open ocean conditions with strong currents outside the harbor, especially off Race Point.

Charts and Maps ▶ NOAA chart #13249; Waterproof Chart #64

LAUNCHES

Provincetown Town Ramp Sandy beach and paved ramp; metered parking (accepts cash or credit; bring cash just in case); no facilities. From the intersection of US 6 and Conwell Street in Provincetown, turn southeast on Conwell Street and follow it 0.4 mile to MA 6A/Bradford Street. Turn right (west) and continue 0.9 mile to Franklin Street. Turn left, continue about 500 feet, then continue straight onto Commercial Street. The road turns right and continues another 0.3 mile to the West End Boat Parking Lot on the left. *GPS coordinates: 42° 2.509′ N, 70° 11.613′ W.*

Other Public Access All waterfront described in the route is encompassed by the Cape Cod National Seashore. Obey all posted signs, including those regarding shorebird nesting, sensitive cultural resources, and private property within the seashore.

ROUTE DESCRIPTION

Provincetown is a busy place; here the traffic on Cape Cod reaches the end of the road. Even on the not-so-busy days, the narrow streets are crowded, and parking—especially near a launch—is at a premium. The water affords paddlers a privileged view of the waterfront and remote beaches, but it's hardly the place to get away from it all. Plenty of boat traffic fills the water and foot traffic keeps the beaches busy. Maybe the crowds are part of what Provincetown is all about.

Kayakers may go to the Monomoy Islands (Trip 37) for the gray seals, but people are drawn to Provincetown by human wildlife. Beginning almost a century ago when artists began flocking here, the town has been *the* gay hot spot in New England, which

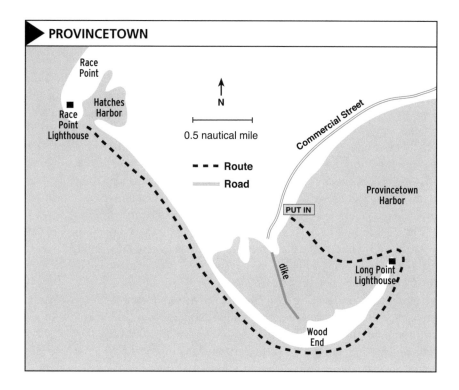

▶ **PROVINCETOWN**

Race Point

Hatches Harbor

■ Race Point Lighthouse

N

0.5 nautical mile

- - - Route
=== Road

Commercial Street

Provincetown Harbor

PUT IN

dike

■ Long Point Lighthouse

Wood End

is evident everywhere, especially if you stick around for the nightlife. Even in Provincetown Harbor, which in summertime is thick with recreational boats on moorings, you're likely to encounter numerous visitors soaking in the "P-town" ambiance from sailboats, stand-up paddleboards, and even a houseboat or two. From here, downtown is a muffled din, and it feels like you've come to a quiet, outer room of a party.

The 253-foot-tall Pilgrim Monument—its design taken directly from a similar tower in Sienna, Italy, and built with granite from Stonington, Maine—presides over the scene. As strangely out of place as the tower might appear, it is oddly fitting in such a diverse town whose harbor first sheltered the Mayflower Pilgrims as they searched for a less conventional haven from a constricting society.

The parking area at the launch can be a bit tricky to negotiate. Unless you arrive early in the day, you may need to wait for a spot, but it seems that plenty of visitors just stop here for a quick look around before they leave. Don't forget to pay the meter enough to ensure that you don't have to hurry back.

The sandy peninsula of Long Point outlines Provincetown Harbor, the lighthouse at its tip making it an obvious first destination for anyone in a small boat, most of whom will not venture farther. To bypass the busier traffic in the harbor, follow the shoreline southwest and paddle along the dike that separates the harbor from a salt marsh, for about 2.3 nautical miles. If you're planning a long day, a more direct route is about a mile shorter. Be careful of traffic in the harbor; the motorboats seem to buzz around at high speeds in just about every direction.

Landings are permitted on the beaches to the west and east sides of the lighthouse. Be wary of steep powerboat wakes hitting the shallows off the point and of the lines of anglers, who favor this spot. Pull your boat well beyond the reach of bigger than usual wake waves, and look out for poison ivy, which grows here in abundance. Long Point was a fishing community from 1818 until the late 1850s. When the settlers left, they floated their homes—about 30 of them—across the harbor to Provincetown, where many still stand. Long Point Lighthouse has a 38-foot-tall square brick tower built in 1875, which you may walk around but may not enter. Just to the west is a grassy mound with the remains of a Civil War battery, a World War II memorial cross atop it.

In favorable conditions, skilled paddlers may make the fairly featureless trek past sandy beaches toward Race Point. The 5.0-mile stretch between points is punctuated only by the Wood End Light. Strong near-shore currents gave Race Point its name. To avoid them, plan to follow the beach, and stick close to shore. Having these currents behind you along the way back may be helpful.

The sandy beach stretching 1.7 nautical miles between Long Point and Wood End is probably the least populated area you'll encounter on this trip. If you want to get away from it all, this is your best bet. As you near Wood End Light, you may begin to encounter swimmers and sunbathers. Beyond, recreational fishing boats are likely to patrol the edge of the bars, where depths plunge abruptly more than a hundred feet from the shallower waters. Whales are sometimes spotted in this area, mostly in springtime. A trail leads to the square brick 39-foot-tall lighthouse, built in 1873.

North of Wood End, the dunes turn a little steeper and continue another 1.7 nautical miles to the parking area for Herring Cove Beach, part of the Cape Cod National Seashore. Earlier charts illustrate a breach between the salt marsh and Cape Cod Bay, but the sands have shifted and as of 2014, this is no longer the case. This stretch of beach is an unofficial clothing-optional area. The atmosphere is friendly enough if you stash the camera and don't gawk, but if this isn't your scene, just paddle farther from shore.

As you approach the parking area, you'll probably want to stay in deeper water to avoid swimmers. The crowds will again diminish beyond the parking area. This is another place where the sands shift, creating openings into Hatches Harbor, which may be explored at higher tides. If you'd like to avoid the strong currents off the point, land on the beach south of it. Trails lead to the Race Point Lighthouse, a 45-foot-tall cast iron cylinder, built in 1876. The keeper's house and whistle house are available for overnight guests.

Now to head back. If you have a rising tide, you might prefer to take a direct, offshore line from Race Point to Wood End. At this point in the paddle, you might appreciate whatever extra push you get more than the scenery along the beach. Retrace your steps back to Provincetown Harbor. If you have enough energy left and the tide is high enough, follow the dike around the harbor. If it's later in the day and you're heading straight back from Long Point Light to the launch, take care: the sun will be

While the 5-mile trek from Long Point to Race Point may be fairly geographically featureless, paddlers may encounter plenty of human activity along the sandy beaches—perhaps more than desired.

right in your eyes—as it will be for other boaters approaching from behind, who may find it difficult to see you.

ALTERNATIVES

With the boat back on your car—or if conditions prove too rough for a paddle—there's plenty to do in Provincetown, but you may want to drive out to Race Point Beach, one of the few places in the U.S. where you can see both the sunrise and sunset from the same beach.

MORE INFORMATION

Provincetown Harbor & Pier (provincetown-ma.gov/index.aspx?nid=79; 508-487-7030). Cape Cod National Seashore (nps.gov/caco; 508-771-2144). The Race Point Lighthouse offers overnight accommodations (mybnbwebsite.com/racepointlighthouse; (855-722-3959). No camping is available on the route, but nearby The Trustees of Reservations' Dunes Edge Campground (thetrustees.org/places-to-visit/places-to-stay/dunes -edge-campground) and privately owned Coastal Acres Camping Court (76R Bayberry Avenue, Provincetown; 508-487-1700) offer drive-in camping.

37
MONOMOY ISLANDS

Thousands of seals and birds pack onto miles of sandy beaches.

Distance ▶ 17.0 nautical miles, round-trip

Tidal Planning ▶ Mean tidal range is 5.77 feet in Chatham. Vast areas flat-out at lower tides; plan on paddling over them with adequate water. Two very different currents—both averaging about 2 knots at their fastest—converge at Monomoy Point and may produce very dangerous conditions. Just west of the point the flood moves south, while current to the south in Pollock Rip Channel floods northeast. If you're going around the point, plan for slack tide. Currents around the shifting sands may be very confusing. (At 0.2 mile west of Monomoy Point, the max flood averages 1.7 knots at 170 degrees and the max ebb averages 2 knots at 346 degrees. Just south of the point, in Pollock Rip Channel or "Butter Hole," the max flood averages 2 knots toward 37 degrees and the max ebb averages 1.8 knots toward 226 degrees.)

Cautions ▶ Shifting sand and vast shallow flats can make navigation tricky, especially at lower tides; check at Monomoy National Wildlife Refuge headquarters for updates, and allow plenty of time. Open ocean conditions occur outside the bar; stop at Chatham Light to assess. Strong currents occur around breaches and off Monomoy Point. In recent years, the increased population of gray seals has drawn more sharks to the area.

Charts and Maps ▶ NOAA charts #13248 and #13244; Waterproof Chart #64; Google Earth. Due to the dynamic nature of Monomoy's shifting sands, it is prudent to rely more on local knowledge. Staff at the Monomoy National Wildlife Refuge headquarters can provide up-to-date information.

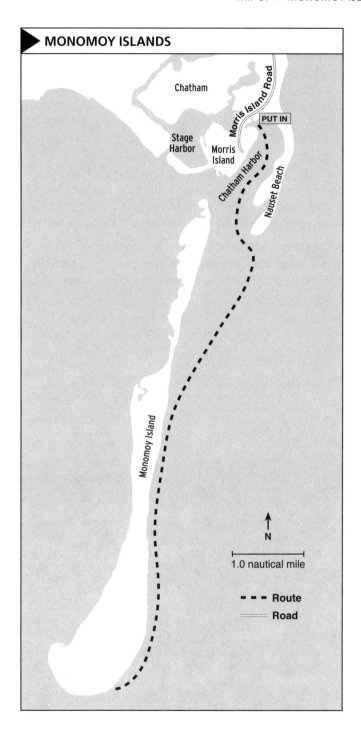

LAUNCH

Monomoy National Wildlife Refuge, Chatham A 100-foot carry from the causeway via any one of several paths to the very shallow water; parking permitted on the pavement on the east side of the road; no facilities at launch; visit the refuge headquarters for up-to-date information and restrooms. From the traffic circle on MA 28 in Chatham, follow Main Street east for 0.8 mile to the Chatham Light; this is a good spot to scout conditions outside the bar. From the lighthouse, continue right (south) on Main Street for 0.4 mile and bear left onto Morris Island Road. In 0.2 mile, turn right to remain on Morris Island Road. Causeway parking begins in about 0.5 mile. (To reach the refuge headquarters: continue 0.2 mile, take a left on Tisquantum Road, then another left on Wikis Way in another 0.2 mile. The headquarters is a few hundred feet farther on the left.) *GPS coordinates: 41° 39.837' N, 69° 57.538' W.*

Other Public Access Except for parts of Morris and Stage islands (noted in the description), the entire route lies within Monomoy National Wildlife Refuge. In nesting season, some areas will be closed and roped-off to protect nesting birds; obey all posted signs.

More than 10,000 gray seals have been observed hauled-out on the Monomoy Islands. Law dictates that we give them a 100-yard berth, but they may not always do the same for us.

ROUTE DESCRIPTION

The Monomoy Islands, a spit of ever-changing sands stretching some 7 miles between Nantucket Sound and the open Atlantic, hang from the elbow of Cape Cod. The islands have formed over the last 6,000 years as long shore currents carried sediment southward from cliffs to the north forming a long, constantly evolving sandspit from Nauset to Monomoy Point. Currents and storms continue to re-form and alter the islands, often enough that charts are often outdated by the time they're printed. Even online satellite maps may not be current; visit the Monomoy National Wildlife Refuge headquarters for the most up-to-date information.

Though it is now uninhabited, Monomoy Island had a tavern for sailors on Wreck Cove (Hospital Pond) as early as 1710. On the west side of the southern end, Powder Hole once housed a fishing community called Whitewash Village, which had a tavern, a school, and about 200 residents. An 1860 hurricane washed away the harbor, and the town was abandoned for three years until a new harbor could be reconstructed. The village thrived until 1876 when a series of murders made mainland living more attractive. During World War II the island was used as an Air Force gunnery range until it was designated as a National Wildlife Refuge in 1944. Now, the only sign of human habitation is the cast iron tower of the Monomoy Point Light, built in 1849. The Cape Cod Canal diverted most ship traffic from the area, and the light was deactivated in 1923.

The Monomoy Islands, as well as 40 acres on Morris Island, are part of the 7,604-acre Monomoy National Wildlife Refuge, established to provide habitat for migratory birds, including the piping plover and roseate tern. More than 8,000 pairs of common terns nest in the refuge, the second largest nesting colony on the Atlantic seaboard.

Miles of sandy beach seems like it ought to be interesting enough, but few features distinguish one stretch from the next. If it weren't for the wildlife—in particular, the thousands of gray seals that haul out in the area—the shoreline might easily seem a bit monotonous.

Keeping an eye on the tides is essential around Monomoy, especially if you plan on paddling on the western side, where vast areas empty at low tide, leaving sand flats and mudflats far from any shore. In addition, strong currents may develop at the breaches and around the southern end of South Monomoy. To ensure that you're prepared with the best information possible, visit the refuge headquarters. The refuge requests that boaters land at preferred landing areas, which are updated on an annual basis; maps with GPS coordinates are available online and at the headquarters. Refuge staff camp on both islands full-time in summer months to monitor wildlife and visitors.

Your best route will depend on conditions and current topography. If there is a breach to paddle through into the Atlantic side (see map), you might prefer to do it on the way out, in case the seas are rougher than you anticipated and you choose to shorten your trip or limit it to the west side. Getting through the breach will be easier with the current behind you. Expect conditions at the breach to be more volatile than elsewhere. Without a rising tide, you can keep plans simple and paddle only the east side, stopping short of the full 8.5 nautical miles to Monomoy Point to avoid the most volatile conditions. Unless the seas are small and you have good surf skills, however, don't expect to land on the eastside beaches: most of them are steep and produce dumping waves close to shore.

Another tactic: follow the western side of the islands south on a rising tide (the current should be with you, at least near South Monomoy), arriving at Monomoy Point at around slack high. Proceed north along the Atlantic side, hugging the shore, where there should be less current, perhaps even eddies. Or instead of rounding the point you could head back north along the west side. Either trip totals approximately 17.0 nautical miles. Due to the extensive flats, avoid the shallow water west of the islands at lower tides.

Be flexible when paddling around Monomoy; be ready to change your plans if tides and conditions (or even topography) aren't what you expected.

ALTERNATIVES

Shorten this route by paddling to North Monomoy Island (5.0 to 6.0 nautical miles round-trip) or circumnavigating Stage Harbor and Morris Island (3.0 nautical miles). The north end of Nauset Marsh is also a good alternate route; for directions to that launch, see Trip 35.

MORE INFORMATION

Monomoy National Wildlife Refuge (fws.gov/refuge/Monomoy; 508-945-0594). No camping is available on-route.

MONOMOY'S GRAY SEALS AND GREAT WHITE SHARKS

After the Marine Mammal Protection Act passed in 1972, seal populations quickly rebounded from near-devastated lows. The Muskeget Island population of gray seals soared from only 19 adults in 1994 to 3,500 in 2011, when the overall gray seal population in Massachusetts reached nearly 16,000. In that year, more than 10,000 gray seals were observed hauled-out on Monomoy Island alone.

(Remember: As kayakers, our role is to stay away from seals, giving them a 100-yard berth when we can; in fact, the MMPA explicitly forbids us from harassing any marine mammal, which includes "pursuit, torment, or annoyance." See "Seals" on page 56 for more information.)

Compared to smaller harbor seals that tend to flee anytime we draw near, the gray seals that flock to the Monomoy Islands are large and curious, and their behavior may reflect your own. If you're loud and aggressive they may be less likely to swim near you; sit still, or even pull your boat up on shore (far from any hauled-out seals) and they may gather around to watch for your next move. At first, being near a group of 20 to 30 seals is impressive and a bit unnerving. Their size and power is unmistakable as they surface and dive, sometimes slapping the water with a massive splash. Their numbers may also grow, and you may find yourself surrounded by a large pack of seals as you paddle. Take this behavior as a reminder for you to go your own way. Paddlers should not try to get near the seals. However, they may join you out of curiosity; try not to encourage them to follow.

The explosion of the seal population at Monomoy has attracted predators to the area, including great white sharks. The Monomoy National Wildlife Refuge monitors some sharks with acoustic tags, and injured seals are noted, but there's no way to keep track of how many seals the sharks actually eat, or how many sharks inhabit the surrounding waters. Assume that the sharks are there, whether you see them or not. Don't expect the tell-tale dorsal fin advancing to the sound of ominous theme music. In most areas, great whites tend to approach from below, swimming up from depths and hitting their prey with great force. At Monomoy Island, they have been observed hunting in shallow water, close to shore, sometimes lurking near a sandbar until a seal ventures close enough to strike.

Great whites have an unearned reputation as indiscriminate man-eaters, but according to the International Shark Attack File, as of 2015 there had been only 1,100 unprovoked attacks by great white sharks on humans, including 13 fatalities, documented in the United States since 1837; only three of these attacks occurred in New England. Humans are not appropriate prey for great whites (and the sharks know this) but most incidents are probably either "test bites," in which the shark grabs an object to discover what it is, or cases of mistaken identity, often in waters with low visibility, in which the shark believes it is attacking a seal. In 2014, a great white shark bit a kayak in Plymouth, garnering plenty of media attention. The paddlers were in short boats, close to a number of seals, but after the initial bite, the shark left the area, despite a capsized paddler in the water.

It is admittedly creepy to paddle along, one moment accompanied by a hundred or so splashing seals, and the next second the water turns quiet; then after a few minutes, the seals start popping their heads out of the water near shore, looking back at you. You can't help but wonder what they're waiting for and in the moment, speculation is easy. It may be wise to stay closer to shore than the seals.

For all the drama of these potentially close encounters, the book and movie *Jaws* has probably contributed more than anything to the great white's PR problems. Despite the hype, little is really known about the status of the species. A 2010 study estimated the world population at 3,500; another, published in 2014, countered that California's population may be as high as 2,000. The International Union for Conservation of Nature has listed great white sharks as "globally vulnerable to extinction." It is now illegal to land a great white shark.

38
WAQUOIT BAY

Camping in the heart of wild Waquoit Bay National Estuarine Reserve after less than 1.5 miles of semi-sheltered paddling.

Distance ▶ As little as 3.0 nautical miles to reach the campsites; as much as 14.5 nautical miles to circumnavigate the island and the bay

Tidal Planning ▶ Mean tidal range 3.19 feet at Hyannis Port.

Cautions ▶ Fast-moving recreational boat traffic in marked mid-bay channel. Currents and conditions increase at both openings from bay to Vineyard Sound. South end of island is exposed to open ocean conditions.

Charts and Maps ▶ NOAA chart #13229; Waterproof Chart #64

LAUNCHES

Childs River Public Landing, East Falmouth Paved ramp; plentiful parking spaces in dirt lot near highway, with overnight parking allowed; no facilities. From MA 28 in Falmouth, turn on White's Landing Road (between Seacoast Shores Boulevard and Bosun's East Falmouth Marina). Ramp is at end of road on the left. *GPS coordinates: 41° 34.738′ N, 70° 31.905′ W.*

Great River Launch, Mashpee Public landing; 24 parking spaces for vehicles with boat trailers with more parking on roadside; no facilities. From the MA 28 rotary in Mashpee, head south on Great Neck Road. After 4.0 miles, take first right after Little Neck Bay subdivision (sign for Town Landing) and follow road 0.5 mile to the end. *GPS coordinates: 41° 33.838′ N, 70° 30.356′ W.*

Other Public Access Waquoit Bay National Estuarine Research Reserve (WBNRR) is headquartered at the north end of the bay. You may not launch here, but you may land here and check out the informative displays inside or walk the shoreline. Washburn Island and South Beach State Park are part of the reserve and provide several public landings in the area. Obey all posted signs and take care around areas closed for nesting birds.

ROUTE DESCRIPTION

The shores of Waquoit Bay and Washburn Island are exceptional for what they don't have: shoulder-to-shoulder canal-front homes and upscale subdivisions full of trophy houses, docks lined with powerboats, and brilliant green lawns further fertilizing the warm, algae-infested waters. In the 1980s, a group of citizens urged the state to protect the area from developers by taking the property by eminent domain, which it did in 1987, creating the Waquoit Bay National Estuarine Research Reserve (WBNRR). Not only does the 2,500-acre reserve protect South Cape Beach State Park and the forested uplands along the Quashnet River, but it also offers visitors eleven primitive campsites on 330-acre Washburn Island. From the headwaters of the estuary, paddling options follow some 15 miles of reserve shoreline through salt ponds and marshes, on out to the beaches on Vineyard Sound.

Well before the arrival of Europeans, Waquoit Bay was home to the Wampanoags. The area remained sparsely settled until the 1870s when the railroad came to Falmouth, bringing summer visitors from cities who enjoyed the warm waters along Cape Cod's south shores for sailing and sport fishing. Hotels and summer homes clustered along the shore, and the relative nearness to Boston made it extremely popular.

To be sure, the paddling in Waquoit Bay is docile compared to most routes in this book, but it earns its spot on most paddlers' go-to lists by offering the chance to pull your kayak up onto your own personal sandy beach and pitch your tent. From either launch, the trip to the Washburn Island campsites (reservation only; fee) is under 1.5 nautical miles, and the island is destination enough for many. Some visitors reserve their favorite site months in advance and treat it as a vacation getaway, relaxing in the sand, hiking the island's trails, and taking short paddling excursions. The campsites are all excellent, but #7 and #8 have the most gradual grades to the beach; some of the others have steps over short but steep bluffs. Composting toilets are available; water and additional facilities are not. At night, the only residential lights visible illuminate the northeast shore of the bay with a faint glow in the sky beyond. The rest of the bay remains dark, save for a pair of blinking red buoy lights marking the channel where recreational traffic continues well after dark.

Getting to Washburn Island (1.5 nautical miles)

From the Childs River launch, head south, where you'll get a sense of what Waquoit Bay would have looked like had no one halted development. After about 0.5 mile, take a sharp left, following the Seapit River northeast. Washburn Island is on your right, with shellfish-growing equipment lining the shallow water just off the bank. Soon the river opens into the north end of Waquoit Bay, a popular mooring area for recreational boats. Take a right and follow the east shore of Washburn Island south to the campsites.

From Great River Landing, follow the Great River southwest to where it joins the Little River and enters Waquoit Bay beside a prominent osprey nest platform on the point. You should be able to see the campsites to the west, a little less than a mile away. Look for the big signs that greet visitors, and probably a boat or two along shore. Paddle

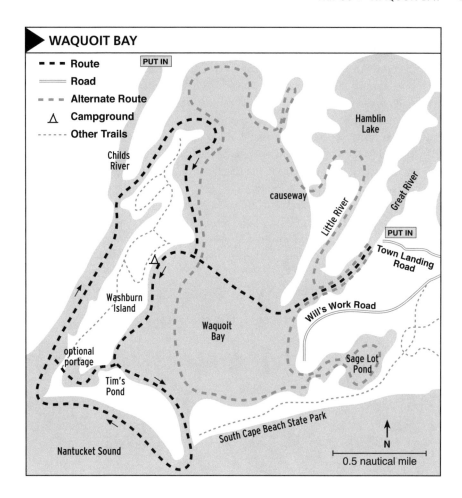

directly there if you like, but be on the lookout for fast-moving boat traffic, particularly in the marked channel in the middle of the bay. If you don't mind a longer paddle and a shorter crossing, follow the shore north to a point where the crossing is less than 0.5 mile and the boat traffic is more confined to the channel.

If you're interested in exploring, a trail runs north to south through the island's interior, shaded by pine and oak forests where lady slippers bloom in the spring. The path occasionally skirts the western shore, looking over the narrow channel to the Seacoast Shores neighborhood. About a mile south from the campsites, a short portage trail joins Tim's Pond and Eel Pond. From there, the barrier beach is only a short walk along Eel Pond; much of the beach is roped off in spring and early summer to protect nesting terns. Occasionally, the trail runs over the remains of crumbling pavement, a remnant of the 1940s when Washburn Island was used as a training facility for amphibious craft.

Circumnavigating Washburn Island (3.0 to 4.5 nautical miles)

If you're extending your paddle, the odds are you won't have current behind you all the way around Washburn Island. The most significant features that affect tidal planning for the circumnavigation are the inlets, where currents increase, and the ponds, where shallow water at low tide makes access difficult (especially if you plan to portage through Tim's Pond).

If you circumnavigate Washburn Island at the higher end of the tide cycle you'll be able to paddle into Tim's Pond, a shallow inlet at the head of the southeast cove. From the pond, you can walk a short trail over to the beach and get a look at conditions on Vineyard Sound. If you'd prefer to stick to protected waters, look for a path on the west side of the pond (most recently marked by a buoy on a stick); a short carry leads to Eel Pond.

If you don't paddle through Tim's Pond, continue to the channel between Washburn Island and Dead Neck. Fishing and clamming boats often anchor in the area north of the opening. Clammers wade the shallow waters near their boats, pushing

Not only does the 2,500-acre Waquoit Bay National Estuarine Research Reserve protect South Cape Beach State Park and the forested uplands along the Quashnet River, but it also offers visitors eleven primitive campsites on 330-acre Washburn Island.

and pulling their clam rakes like a lawn mower over a particularly weedy patch of lawn. You may land just north of the jetty on Dead Neck, the barrier beach on the east side of the inlet, which is part of South Cape Beach State Park.

If you opt to venture out of the channel and into the sound, be aware of the tidal current and how it interacts with conditions; this could be a lively spot when current opposes wind or swell. Boat traffic and the gauntlet of fishing lines near the jetty may add to the challenge. Follow the beach (public) west for a little over a mile. If surf permits, land on the beach, but be aware of areas closed for bird nesting; endangered least terns and piping plovers nest here through midsummer. Keep an eye out down below as well; you may see schools of striped bass.

At the west end of the beach, a small inlet beside the village of Menauhant leads to Eel Pond, where you're likely to see more clammers in the shallows. If you're in the mood to critique architecture, follow the Eel River, the western arm of this inlet; otherwise, stay to the east. A sign on Washburn Island marks the Portage Trail. Follow the west shore of the island. After about a mile, pass a marked trailhead. If you take a break along here, avoid walking on the eroding bluffs and the poison ivy that does very well here. The west shore of Eel Pond is fairly dense with homes, and you're likely to encounter a powerboat or two.

Just past a point, the densely populated Childs River continues north and the Seapit River comes in from the northeast. The Childs River can be followed north to the public landing and a marina. A low narrow opening beneath the MA 28 bridge leads to a less developed, quieter stretch.

But you may as well stick to Washburn Island, which is plenty quiet and has public access besides. As you follow its shore north along the Seapit River, watch for shellfish cages in the shallows. Round the point to the north and follow the shore back to the campsites. Along the way, you may enjoy poking into a small pond, reachable at higher water.

Exploring the Neighborhood (5.0 to 7.5 nautical miles)

On the north shore of Waquoit Bay, WBNRR headquarters is based in the main house of the former Sargent Estate. Built in the 1880s atop a bluff overlooking the bay, the shingle-style house is open to the public with organized programs and exhibits about area ecology. You may land at the boathouse just east of the headquarters or along the beach stretching west from the boathouse; the beach to the east is posted as private.

Following the shore east, Meadow Neck stretches southward to the mouth of the Mounakis River. Ideally, arrive at the river at the higher end of the tide cycle. If you can't, you should still be able to paddle against it, especially if you seek out slower water and eddies along the edges. Beyond the bridge, the upper reaches of the Mounakis is thick with birdlife. Swans frequent the banks, and as you proceed upriver, ospreys swoop left and right before you. At the north end, the river turns shallow, choked by thick, impassable foliage. Beyond this the estuary blends with the freshwater Quashnet River, also part of the reserve. If you'd like to see the Quashnet, it's easier to get there in your car and hike the 2.8-mile loop trail (see directions in Alternatives).

South of the Mounakis, the shoreline is private with a few homes overlooking the beach. On a rising tide, follow Red Brook through a metal culvert beneath the road into Hamblin Pond. These shores are developed, but it's a fun detour to take, circling Seconsett Island, and returning through the Little River. Little River Boat Yard is on the north shore of the river; watch for boat traffic here.

At the head of Great River, much of Jehu Pond's shoreline is encompassed by the Jehu Pond Conservation Area and remains undeveloped (though a few especially large homes overlook it). Best seen at higher tides, this marshy wetland with a couple of islands is a likely place to spot osprey and wading birds.

Just south of where the Great and Little rivers enter the bay is a beach (public) where you may notice a few cars. This is the end of Wills Work Road, part of the state park, reachable by an extremely bumpy dirt road (not recommended for cars with low clearance).

At the southeast corner of the bay, water flows through a narrow inlet into Sedge Lot Pond (Sage Lot on some maps), which is worth exploring when tide allows. Flanked by marsh on the north and South Beach on the south, the undeveloped pond widens at the east end where it almost reaches the parking area for Mashpee Town Beach. One could almost paddle through the creeks to the beach, but not quite; a low bridge blocks the way before the creek tapers into marshland.

The southeast portion of the bay is bordered by Dead Neck, the state park's public barrier beach, forested on the west end. You may land just about anywhere along this beach, just be careful of areas closed for bird nesting.

ALTERNATIVES

If you'd like to add a hike along the Quashnet River to your itinerary, continue along MA 28 S, 1.4 miles from its intersection with White's Landing Road. Turn left onto Martin Road and continue about 0.25 mile for trailhead parking. Trail maps are available at waquoitbayreserve.org.

MORE INFORMATION

Waquoit Bay National Estuarine Research Reserve (waquoitbayreserve.org; 508-457-0495); Washburn Island campsites available by reservation only (fee). South Cape Beach State Park (mass.gov/eea/agencies/dcr/massparks/region-south/south-cape-beach-state-park.html; 508-457-0495).

39
CHAPPAQUIDDICK ISLAND

Paddle miles of public access shoreline, including five uninterrupted miles of undeveloped beach.

Distance ▶ 13.0 nautical miles, round-trip

Tidal Planning ▶ Mean tidal range at Edgartown is 2.13 feet. While it is prudent to try to paddle with the tides, prioritize arriving at the more volatile areas—the breach and Wasque Point—when currents are slower. Currents in the breach could be difficult to paddle against when they're at their fastest. Launching a little before low tide could provide some current assist on your way out the breach, and for a chance at less volatile conditions there and around Wasque Point. At 0.6 nautical mile north of Katama Point, average max flood moves at 0.6 knots toward the north (325 degrees) and floods south at a similar speed. At Edgartown Inner Harbor, average max flood moves at over a knot toward 75 degrees and ebbs at the same speed westward. So the currents meet somewhere between these two points, in the northern end of Katama Bay. The Muskeget Channel passes 1.5 nautical miles southeast of Wasque Point with an average max flood current at 3.8 knots; stay near shore and avoid this.

Cautions ▶ Strong currents at the Norton Point/Wasque breach interacting with swells can create lively and dangerous conditions. Open ocean conditions for most of the route.

Charts and Maps ▶ NOAA chart #13233; Maptech #85; Waterproof Chart #10

LAUNCH

Katama Point, Edgartown Public ramp and beach launch; paved parking; no facilities. From the four-way intersection of Peases Point Way South, Pease Point Road, Herring Creek Road, and Katama Road in Edgartown, follow Katama Road south for 1.6 miles to Edgartown Road (Edgartown Bay Road). The left turn for the landing is another 0.4 mile farther. *GPS coordinates: 41° 21.402′ N, 70° 30.132′ W.*

Other Public Access The Trustees of Reservations (TTOR) protects almost 1,000 acres of land on Chappaquiddick Island. Nearly 10 miles of public access shoreline are contained along the outer shores of Norton Point Beach (TTOR), Wasque Point (TTOR), Leland Beach (state-owned), and Cape Poge Wildlife Refuge (TTOR); the opposite sides of these barrier beaches and the ponds are also public. Obey any posted signs, taking care to avoid areas closed for nesting birds. The Edgartown Lighthouse is open to the public (fee), and is surrounded by a public beach. A small public beach just south of Chappy Ferry landing provides a pit stop when avoiding ferry traffic.

ROUTE DESCRIPTION

For many years, Chappaquiddick Island and Martha's Vineyard were connected by a narrow barrier beach at Norton Point; if you wanted to circle the smaller island (known locally as "Chappy") you could carry over the beach. A 2007 storm wore a breach through the barrier sands, making it possible to circumnavigate without carrying your boat. The breach continues to shift, as do the sands of Wasque Point (pronounced "Way-skwee").

While you're unlikely to be alone on a trip around Chappaquiddick—anglers flock to the beach in SUVs to cast for stripers and bluefish—the shore from Wasque Point to Cape Poge is undeveloped, and you can paddle along the beach for hours, lost in your thoughts and the crash of surf. Dumping waves are a normal occurrence here, along with riptides that discourage swimmers. Be prepared to stay in your boat for a while.

Much of this route lies outside Chappaquiddick's barrier beaches and is subject to open ocean conditions, including the 3- to-4-knot currents in nearby Muskeget Channel. Venturing beyond the breach or around Cape Poge is a commitment, and it's tough to know just what you're getting into beforehand. The most likely place to scout conditions without taking a ferry ride is from South Beach, at the end of Katama Road. However, you can expect bumpier seas at Wasque Point than you'll see here. More sheltered options are still plentiful (see Alternatives).

It may be preferable to head counterclockwise, exiting the breach into open ocean conditions soon after you've scouted them, before they've had much chance to change. Tidal current will also affect your choice, but you will probably paddle against it at some point. Since the breach and Wasque Point will most often be the most volatile areas, try to launch near slack tide and get past those areas before currents have a chance to make conditions more complicated.

From the launch, head south toward the Norton Point barrier beach. Large areas flat-out at lower tides, so you may need to keep your distance from shore. Oyster cultivators use Katama Bay for their operations; their boats are often anchored along the eastern shore where several large homes overlook the bay. The location of the breach may change, but in 2014, it was at the far eastern end of Norton Point, and had two openings; look for the Wasque parking area on Chappaquiddick, just above the breach. If the current is taking you out through the breach, pull to the side and look

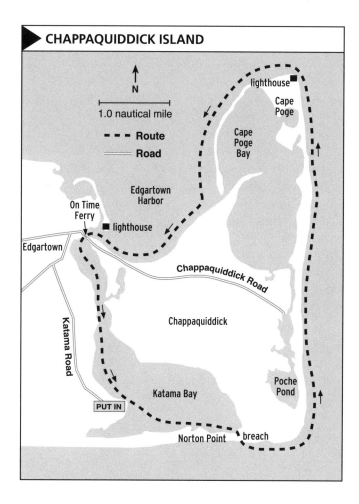

things over, agreeing on a strategy with those in your group. It may be necessary to get some distance from the rough water at the opening before turning to the east.

Be mindful of where the current is moving you as you paddle east toward Wasque Point. One large home divides the state properties, but from here on, the shoreline is public for most of the next 7.0 miles. To the south, you'll probably be able to see the bumpy water where the Muskeget Channel passes offshore. Watch your compass to determine how far you are around the point—the curve is subtle and soon you'll be pointed north, following Leland Beach with Aruda's Point visible about 3.0 miles distant.

This shore is reputed to be one of the best surf-casting spots on the East Coast, and you'll probably see at least a few anglers here, especially as you near the park entrance for vehicles after about 2.0 miles, near Dike Bridge. After another mile or so a hundred-year-old cedar forest dominates the shore before dwindling near Aruda Point. It's not much of a point, but from here you'll be able to see as far as Wasque Point to the south, and Cape Poge to the north, where the lighthouse roof should just be visible through the trees. Ahead, the remains of an old jetty extend into the water; from here it's about 1.0 mile to the lighthouse.

The Cape Poge Lighthouse, a cylindrical wooden tower built in 1893, sits well inland atop a bluff. The shore around the lighthouse and to its west is gradual and should be an easier place to land than the previous beaches.

Follow the Cape Poge Elbow—a strip of sand that narrows to as little as 25 yards—south into Edgartown Harbor, passing a lone rustic house with a skeletal windmill tower. At the sound end, Cape Poge Gut is the entrance to Cape Poge Bay, maybe a hundred yards wide. Beyond is the shore of Chappaquiddick proper, where a row of houses sits atop tall, eroding bluffs.

Follow the mostly developed shoreline back to the launch via the western point. Across the channel to the north is the Edgartown Lighthouse and its public beach. At the point, a pair of small car ferries run constantly back and forth between Chappaquiddick and Edgartown. Pull up at the beach and wait for them to land to give yourself several minutes to get past as they load and unload.

On Chappaquiddick, the shore from Wasque Point to Cape Poge—about 7 miles—is undeveloped sandy beach, usually with dumping waves. The Cape Poge Lighthouse (pictured) sits well inland, atop a bluff.

Beyond the ferry crossing, boats on their moorings fill this narrow, northern stretch of Katama Bay, overlooked by shoreline packed with homes. Just south, Caleb Pond is shallow and relatively quiet. Follow the Edgartown shore back to Katama Point.

ALTERNATIVES

Wasque Point could be an alternate launch (admission and parking fee required). Expect some confused seas here; Muskeget Channel, where max currents may rise over 4 knots, is only 1.5 miles away. Combine this with swell and strong currents heading around the point and through the breach, and one can expect lively conditions here, even on a calm day.

If conditions on the outer beaches are more than you'd like to contend with, Katama Bay, Edgartown Harbor, Cape Poge Bay, and Poucha Pond may be better options.

MORE INFORMATION

Norton Point Beach (thetrustees.org/places-to-visit/cape-cod-islands/norton-point-beach.html; 508-627-7689 [office]; 508-267-8390 [beach closures]). Wasque Point (thetrustees.org/places-to-visit/cape-cod-islands/wasque-reservation.html; 508-627-3599). Cape Poge Wildlife Refuge (thetrustees.org/places-to-visit/cape-cod-islands/cape-pogue.html; 508-627-7689 [office]; 508-267-8390 [beach closures]); lighthouse tours are available (fee). Edgartown Lighthouse (mvmuseum.org/edgartown.php; 508-627-4441); tours available (fee). No camping is available on-route. Camp nearby at Martha's Vineyard Family Camping in Vineyard Haven (campmv.com; 508-693-3772).

40
GAY HEAD CLIFFS

Multihued clay bluffs rise over a sandy beach for exquisite paddling.

Distance ▶ 5.0 to 7.5 nautical miles, round-trip

Tidal Planning ▶ 1.59-foot mean tidal range in Vineyard Haven. Current in Vineyard Sound floods to the east. In the middle of the sound, 3.0 nautical miles northeast of Gay Head, the average max flood is 0.9 knots toward 81 degrees, with average max ebb reaching 1.3 knots toward 238 degrees. This should be of little consequence near the shore. Anticipate strong currents in the inlet to Menemsha Pond.

Cautions ▶ Open ocean conditions. Current between Menemsha Pond and Vineyard Sound can be difficult to paddle against and may create lively conditions.

Charts and Maps ▶ NOAA chart #13233; Maptech #85; Waterproof Chart #10

LAUNCHES

Chilmark Town Ramp, Menemsha Basin Ramp and beach launches; parking; restrooms. From the intersection of State Road and North Road in Vineyard Haven, continue 6.4 miles on North Road to Chilmark's village of Menemsha. Take a right just before the end. *GPS coordinates: 41° 21.067' N, 70° 45.932' W.*

Nashaquitsa Pond Launch, Chilmark Ramp; limited parking; no facilities. From Chilmark Center (Beetlebung Corner), take South Road southwest for 1.3 miles. Parking is on the right, just over the bridge between Nashaquitsa and Stonewall ponds. *GPS coordinates: 41° 19.716' N, 70° 45.602' W.*

Menemsha Pond, Aquinnah Boat ramp; limited parking; no facilities. From Chilmark Center (Beetlebung Corner), take South Road southwest for 3.5 miles. Turn right onto East Pasture Road. Continue on East Pasture Road/East Pasture Shore Road for 1.3 miles, then make a sharp right onto Lobsterville Road. *GPS coordinates: 41° 20.648' N, 70° 46.988' W.*

Other Public Access The beach below the cliffs is part of the Wampanoag trust lands; landings are permitted, but do not touch the cliffs and obey all posted signs and directions of officers patrolling the beach. Lobsterville Beach (town of Aquinnah) is also public and may be used for landings.

ROUTE DESCRIPTION

At the west end of Martha's Vineyard, the iconic Gay Head Cliffs have drawn visitors for years. The clay bluffs rise from a sandy beach, exhibiting bands of color that seep in rivulets down the beach when it rains (the popular advice is to see them on a clear day, for the best colors, but they're spectacular in the rain as well). Most visitors see them from the viewing platform above, but quite a few also make the trek down to the beach, including sunbathers seeking the clothing-optional experience at the far east end. Since the area is shallow and rocky, most boats keep their distance, but sea kayakers have a unique and privileged perspective. Try not to gawk at the nude sunbathers and keep on paddling.

Since the cliffs are only about 3 miles from the inlet to Menemsha Pond, you could just give in to the laid-back Martha's Vineyard vibe and plan on some beach time or plan to paddle farther around Gay Head to make a longer day of it.

The Chilmark town ramp at Menemsha is the easiest launch in terms of parking, distance, and tidal planning, but launching from Nashaquitsa Pond (locally known as "Quitsa") adds almost 2 miles of sheltered paddling to the route. Both Menemsha, Nashaquitsa, and Stonewall ponds are shallow and tidal, with a number of homes overlooking them. Anglers frequent the north end of Stonewall Pond near the bridge,

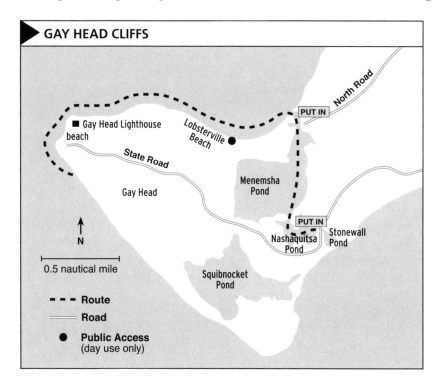

and you'll usually see plenty of wading birds along the banks. At its south end is Stonewall Beach, a steep gravel barrier beach with dumping surf. You'll likely hear the tantalizing crash of surf beyond a prominent No Trespassing sign; circumnavigating Gay Head via this route would otherwise be tempting. The ponds develop mild currents, especially where they join each other, but as always, look for more relaxed currents and eddies along the edges.

From the Chilmark town ramp, head out between the breakwaters; the inlet and the area just south develop strong enough current that some paddlers may not be able to advance against it. At mid-tide during the ebb there may be some turbulent water beyond the opening. This could be avoided by sticking to the side or launching from town-owned Menemsha Beach just east instead, being aware of swimmers and lifeguards present.

One could head straight across Menemsha Bight, but it's more interesting to follow the sandy, undeveloped shore along Lobsterville Beach to the west. Beyond that, intermittent houses overlook the privately owned shoreline for the rest of the way to Gay Head.

Approaching the cliffs, look for a boulder just offshore, white with guano and usually covered with cormorants. The public beach starts here. In busy months, you'll probably start to see people along shore, an area known as "Jungle Beach" for the lack of clothing worn. From the beach you may gaze across Vineyard Sound to the Elizabeth Islands, 5.0 miles distant. The gradually sloping topography produces gently spilling waves that wash in through near shore waters dotted with rocks and boulders. With big conditions, this could be tricky, if not hazardous, paddling. The most remote stretch of beach lies between the white boulder and a concrete bunker just offshore. This bunker once perched atop the cliffs, where it was used during World War II to monitor the west entrance to Vineyard Sound. Beginning in 1958 it slowly slid down the eroding cliffs until it came to rest in the intertidal zone.

Beyond the bunker, the Gay Head Light and a viewing platform become visible atop the cliffs, and the beach turns busier as you progress around the head toward the trailhead. The first lighthouse, a 47-foot octagonal tower, was built in 1799, near the site of the present brick tower, which was built in 1856. Since erosion continues to diminish the land around the lighthouse, the light was relocated farther from the cliffs' edge in mid-2015.

It's well worth following the cliffs to the end. The cliffs were named Gay Head for their brilliant colors, and the town shared this name until 1997, when the name was changed to Aquinnah, which means "land under the hill" in Wampanoag. The Wampanoag inhabited this area, hunting whales from small boats long before English colonists arrived in 1669, and the cliffs feature prominently in their history and lore. The cliffs now belong to the Wampanoag. It is forbidden to climb on or touch the clay, which is enforced by officers who patrol the beach.

If you wish to keep paddling, this southwest corner of the island is minimally developed, cliffs giving way to gently sculpted dunes along town-owned Moshup's Beach. A stretch of smaller bluffs called Zack's Cliffs is followed by private shoreline along

Named for their brilliant colors, Gay Head Cliffs and the Gay Head Light draw plenty of tourists, but the kayakers are treated to a privileged view.

Squibnocket Beach. If there's any swell, as there often is from the southwest, this area could develop considerable waves, especially in the shallow area stretching south from Squibnocket Beach.

To the south, Nomans Land Island and the waters around it are off-limits due to un-exploded ordnance. Nomans was the original Martha's Vineyard, named by explorer Bartholomew Gosnold for his daughter, and was inhabited until 1943, when the Navy began using it for bombing practice, which continued until 1996. The present name probably evolved from being named for the Wampanoag sachem, Tequenoman. The island is now a National Wildlife Refuge.

ALTERNATIVES
Should conditions prove too rough, Menemsha, Nashaquitsa, and Stonewall ponds are a worthy, sheltered paddle on their own.

MORE INFORMATION
Gay Head Lighthouse (gayheadlight.org; 508-645-2300). No camping is available on-route. Camp nearby at Martha's Vineyard Family Camping in Vineyard Haven (campmv.com; 508-693-3772).

BUZZARDS BAY TO LONG ISLAND SOUND

Paddling Massachusetts's Buzzards Bay—separated from Vineyard Sound by the Elizabeth Islands to the south and cities and towns along the I-195 corridor to the north—is less straightforward than it might first appear on a chart.

Public access is limited. Parking at most launch areas requires a resident sticker or is signed ambiguously enough to cast doubt on whether your vehicle will be there when you return from a paddle. The bigger state launches tend to favor parking for vehicles with trailers.

If you ask around, locals might divulge an unofficial favorite launch site with parking for a couple of cars. Some of these areas may be best paddled by locals: much of the Falmouth and Bourne shoreline is private and developed, with heavy motorboat traffic. On the north shore, the paddle from Marion Harbor to Bird Island can be enjoyable, but the island (one of the few around) is closed for bird nesting for much of the summer. The Elizabeth Islands are almost entirely privately owned, despite being an enticing destination. A trip to Cuttyhunk Island would be possible, but only with strong planning and advanced skills (see more in Trip 42, Alternatives).

You can circumnavigate West Island (Trip 41) from an easy launch and a few public access landings. A little west of Buzzards Bay, you can spot countless osprey on the Westport River (Trip 42) and enjoy Westport's many amenities.

Continuing southwest along the coast, Narragansett Bay is tucked into New England's smallest state. The region's largest estuary, it covers more than 120 square miles with 256 miles of shoreline and is home to a diverse and dense population of animal and human life. About 1.8 million people live in the Narragansett Bay watershed, which includes fifteen rivers. The largest of those rivers—the Pawtuxet, Blackstone, and Taunton—flow into the heavily populated northern end of the bay. There, fresh water mingles with the tide from Rhode Island Sound and flows among some 30 or 40 islands as it makes its way to the mouth of the bay. Aquidneck, Conanicut, and Prudence islands offer ample public access along miles of varied shoreline, including sandy beaches, stretches of rocky cliffs, and privileged views of Newport's Gilded Age mansions.

Unlike Maine and Massachusetts, Rhode Island guarantees public access to the shore and even publishes *Public Access to the Rhode Island Coast*, a guide to 344 of the most popular public access sites that makes it easier to find kayak launches and landing areas.

As you head west from Narragansett Bay, the shoreline changes drastically. From Point Judith to the end of Napatree Point, the southern Rhode Island shore is composed of 20 miles of barrier beach. Three breachways and the entrance to Point Judith Pond link more sheltered and shallow ponds to the open ocean. The breachways develop strong, dangerous currents. Eight miles offshore, you might see Block Island, a summer tourist hub that takes planning and much skill to reach.

At the head of Little Narragansett Bay, the Pawcatuck River forms Rhode Island's border with Connecticut. From here it's about a hundred miles to Greenwich and the New York border, and the coast is generally developed and populated. More than 4 million people live along the shore of Long Island Sound, with over 9 million people in its watershed. And many of them like to go to the beach. Fortunately, there are a few good access points for paddlers in some of the less developed areas, giving sea kayakers privileged access to beaches, salt marshes, and even a few islands.

The swells in Long Island Sound are generally smaller than in Maine or Massachusetts, but keep in mind that it can still turn quite choppy, and the current going in and out of the sound creates the sort of lively conditions sought after by adrenaline junkies. There are, however, a few out-of-the-way areas where you can usually find some relatively calm water.

41
WEST ISLAND

Circumnavigate an island with a variety of salt marshes and rocky shores.

Distance ▶ 8.0 nautical miles, round-trip

Tidal Planning ▶ Mean tide range of 3.7 feet. Aside from the obvious flow in and out of Nesketucket Bay, current floods northeast into Buzzards Bay and ebbs southwest. Some areas flat-out at low tide, especially around the launch in Little Bay. Pass beneath the West Island bridge with the current or within an hour of slack.

Cautions ▶ Buzzards Bay can get choppy, especially when an afternoon sea breeze kicks up, and even more so when that wind opposes tidal current.

Charts and Maps ▶ NOAA chart #13232; Maptech #5

LAUNCHES

Edgewater Street, Fairhaven, MA Crude ramp; dirt lot with a few parking spaces that could flood at high water; no facilities. From I-195, Exit 18, follow MA 240 for 1.0 mile. Cross MA 6 and continue straight on Sconticut Neck Road. In 1.0 mile, turn left on Booney Street/Edgewater Street. The ramp is at the end in 0.2 mile. *GPS coordinates: 41° 37.818' N, 70° 51.965' W.*

Seaview Avenue, Fairhaven, MA Paved state boat ramp and adjacent beach; day parking for vehicles with trailers (fee); no facilities. From the intersection of Sconticut Neck Road and Booney Street/Edgewater Street, continue 0.8 mile and turn left on Seaview Avenue. The ramp is 0.4 mile farther at the end of the road. *GPS coordinates: 41° 37.219' N, 70° 51.361' W.*

Other Public Access Pea Island, a bare ledge, provides a good mid-bay spot for a break. West Island State Reservation is intended for passive recreation and preserving natural resources; there are no facilities but several trails to the island's developed western shore.

ROUTE DESCRIPTION

The shore of Sconticut Neck in Fairhaven, Massachusetts, has three public landings that launch boaters into semi-sheltered Nasketucket Bay. The 350-acre West Island State Reservation allows a pleasant circumnavigation around a mix of salt marsh,

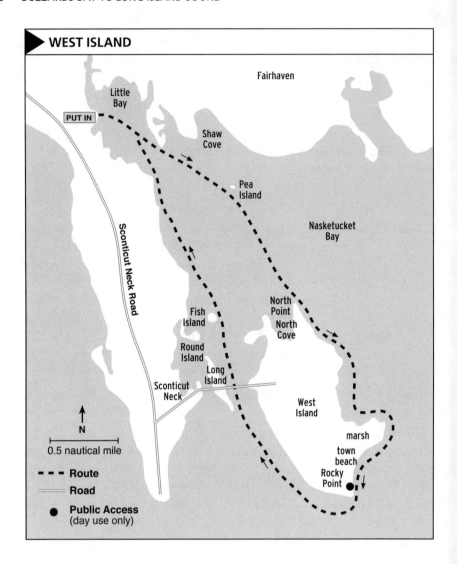

beach, and a few rocks. Much of the bay is shallow and boulder-strewn, asterisks dotting the chart, which might help reduce the motorized recreational boat traffic, but poses little hazard to paddlers in calm seas.

Buzzards Bay is known for its chop, which often increases with the afternoon sea breeze. Keep this in mind as you venture south, and be prepared to forgo circling the island if the winds and chop have picked up more than you would like.

The Seaview Avenue state boat ramp, while far more popular and a little closer to West Island, is more oriented to powerboaters and vehicles with trailers, and charges a fee. The Edgewater Street ramp on Little Bay, while crude, is simpler for kayakers to negotiate; just be careful where you park as it may flood at high tide.

Launch and head southeast past a low-lying island and aim for Pea Island, a group of ledges with a gravel beach. To the south, head for Puppy Rocks en route to North

Point on West Island. Be aware of the channel crossing here: boats pass this way while going to and from the marina and anchorage north of the West Island causeway.

At West Island, follow the east shore to the gravel beach at the south end of the cove, beside the inlet to a marsh—another good spot for a break. If you're here around high tide, follow the marsh's narrow passages all the way to the back side of West Island Beach.

Go around the point and follow West Island Beach to Rocky Point. The black-and-white-striped concrete tower was built in 1943 to spot enemy submarines and ships during World War II. Follow the shore north toward the causeway, which crosses to Long Island and joins West Island to Sconticut Neck. Just south of the bridge is Hoppy's Landing, a town landing and another possible launch site (fee).

Pass beneath the bridge and continue north through the mooring field for Earl's Marina, following the shore of Sconticut Neck back to the launch.

ALTERNATIVES

For a longer route, head to Westport River (Trip 42).

MORE INFORMATION

West Island State Reservation, Fort Phoenix Planning Unit (508-866-2580 x122). No camping is available on-route.

The 350-acre West Island State Reservation allows a pleasant circumnavigation around a mix of salt marsh, beach, and a few rocks.

42
WESTPORT RIVER

Paddle a relatively sheltered, pastoral river with plenty of osprey and the lure of ice cream at the head of the river.

Distance ▶ 7.0 to 12.5 nautical miles, round-trip

Tidal Planning ▶ 3.46-foot mean tidal range at Newport. Floods north, ebbs south. Average max flood current at the entrance is 2.2 knots, average max ebb is 2.5 knots.

Cautions ▶ Strong currents at mouth of river; shallow areas become impassable at low tide.

Charts and Maps ▶ NOAA chart #13228

LAUNCH

MA 88 Bridge Landing, Westport, MA Paved ramp; parking (fee); no facilities. From I-195, Exit 10, follow MA 88 south toward Westport Harbor for 11.1 miles. Turn right just south of bridge and park on the right. *GPS coordinates: 41° 30.872′ N, 71° 4.095′ W.*

Other Public Access Spectacle Islands, owned by the Westport Land Conservation Trust (WLCT), offer public landings along the route; camping is not permitted.

ROUTE DESCRIPTION

The Westport River passes 8.0 miles of residential and quiet, pastoral shores from Head of Westport to the mouth where it empties into Rhode Island Sound. Since the river is tidal for this entire stretch, launch in Massachusetts's Westport Harbor before high tide to get an extra push all the way to the public landing at Head of Westport, where you can stop in at a local outfitter or stroll across the street for an ice cream. After the tide turns, the current will help you back downriver.

Keep this trip in mind for those days when open ocean conditions are rougher than you'd like. Remember, though, that you'll still feel north or south winds as they funnel along the river. While it's possible to paddle against the current, your day will be more difficult; if this happens, stay to the edges and look for eddies. The Westport

Harbor bridge also creates currents that may be tough to paddle against, as do a few challenging features around the rocks and ledges.

While most of the islands east of the Westport Harbor bridge are marshy flats, a couple of the small ones to the north of Big Ram Island, including Little Ram Island, have steep granite humps rising from them that are reachable at all tides—although it may be a steep landing at very high tides.

Mass Audubon maintains 88 osprey nest platforms on both branches of the Westport River. By the 1970s, after ingesting pesticides like DDT for years, local osprey laid eggs with shells so thin they wouldn't last through incubation. Volunteers began

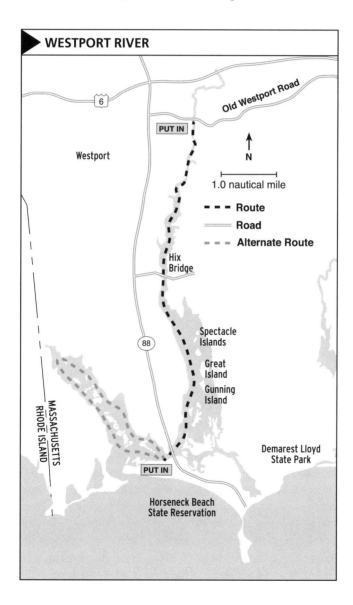

WESTPORT RIVER

building the platforms and brought healthy eggs from the Chesapeake, which local osprey hatched and raised as their own. Ten pairs of ospreys nested here in the 1970s; now their numbers have grown to more than 70.

Since there are numerous shallow areas in the Westport River, launch from the MA 88 bridge on a rising tide, especially if you plan on seeking out ice cream in Head of Westport. If need be, efficient paddlers may certainly get away with paddling against the current. Head beneath the bridge, keeping an eye out for boats. Make your way north, either toward the western shore, or east toward the flats. The granite humps of tiny islands will begin to appear to the east. Private navigational markers track the deeper water northward through the tidal flats toward Gunning and Great island, where there's a house on the north end of Great. The Spectacle Islands (WLCT) have several easy landing areas beneath a mix of hardwoods. Despite the homes lining nearby shorelines, the Upper and Lower Spectacle feel quiet and wild.

Osprey nesting platforms seem to be built on just about every island point, and in the spring to early summer most seem to be occupied by osprey parents that begin fretting if you stray too close. The large raptors are often seen carrying fish in their talons.

Northwest of the Spectacle Islands, the river narrows and is divided by Lakes Island. Beyond this, low Hix Bridge and its landing on the east bank come into view. The location first served as a ferry landing. Between 1738 and 1871, a toll bridge connected traffic crossing the river until the town of Westport bought the bridge and made it public.

North of the bridge, the banks turn marshy and development becomes sparse. The church steeple in Head of Westport comes into view, rising through the trees, and the river continues to narrow to the width of a winding country lane, finally emerging at the grassy, park-like landing just south of the bridge. Land at the public landing beside Osprey Sea Kayak or continue beneath the bridge, where the Head of Westport Country Store also has a take-out.

ALTERNATIVES

Keeping tidal currents in mind, you could continue southward to the river's mouth, where you may get out at Horseneck Point or the Knubble to scout conditions in Rhode Island Sound. Horseneck Beach stretches 2.5 nautical miles east to Gooseberry Neck. Following the beaches about 8 miles west would take you to Sakonnet Point.

The West Branch of the Westport River is also a good alternate or add-on to this route, reaching about 3.5 nautical miles to the northwest from the launch. Since a series of flats stretches down the center of the river, stay close to either the west or east bank. The east shore is relatively quiet with sparse development, as is the head of the river, which narrows into marshy fingers winding toward Adamsville. A public landing is on the west side, where a bend in the river nears Old Harbor Road.

Another possibility in the area would require a good deal of planning and skill to reach. Cuttyhunk Island, the farthest out in the Elizabeth Island chain, is open to the public and has a couple of inns. Tidal planning offers the first challenge. Buzzards Bay and Vineyard Sound both flood to the east, but fill and drain at different rates.

At higher tides, the water drains from the bay into the sound; at mid-tide the current reverses. The "holes" between the islands can generate strong currents, reaching an average maximum of 3.4 knots in the strait off of Woods Hole. Slack current doesn't last long here. Wind or swell off the sound and high-speed ferries can all complicate conditions in a hurry. Keep in mind, Buzzards Bay is also known for its chop, particularly when the afternoon sea breeze picks up. Opting for the 5.5-mile crossing to Cuttyhunk Island from Gooseberry Neck, while possible, would only be safe for experienced paddlers.

MORE INFORMATION
Westport harbormaster (508-636-1105). Westport Land Conservation Trust (westportlandtrust .org; 508-636-9228). No camping is available on-route. Horseneck Beach State Reservation (mass.gov/eea/agencies/dcr/massparks/region-south/horseneck-beach-state-reservation .html; 508-636-8816) and Westport Camping Grounds (westportcampinggrounds.com; 508-636-2555) both offer camping nearby.

The Westport River is a good trip to keep in mind for days when conditions on the open ocean are rougher than you would like. Paddle past its pastoral shores and plan on an ice cream at Head of Westport.

43

PRUDENCE ISLAND

Circumnavigate Narragansett Bay's third largest island and its miles of undeveloped shoreline.

Distance ▶ 16.0 nautical miles, round-trip

Tidal Planning ▶ Mean tidal range of 4.07 feet at Bristol Ferry. Floods north, ebbs south. For ideal timing, launch from Weaver Cove a few hours before high tide, rounding the northern tip of the island around slack and having current assist while heading back. Be aware that this means you'll return across the eastern channel closer to mid-tide, when the prevailing southern winds can work against the current, making for rough conditions.

Cautions ▶ The channel between the launch and Prudence Island is a popular route for powerboaters and a high-speed ferry. When current turns against wind, the area can get fairly rough.

Charts and Maps ▶ NOAA chart #13221; Maptech #18

LAUNCH

Weaver Cove, Portsmouth, RI Paved ramp, adjacent beach; ample parking; no facilities. From the intersection of RI 114 and Stringham Road in Portsmouth, head west on Stringham Road for 0.8 mile. Turn left on Burma Road. The turn-off for the launch is 0.5 mile ahead on the right. *GPS coordinates: 41° 34.431' N, 71° 17.241' W.*

Other Public Access The Narragansett Bay National Estuarine Research Reserve (NBNERR) encompasses Dyer Island, Hope Island, Patience Island, and much of the shore of Prudence Island. Hope Island is closed to public access in summer months for nesting season. A composting toilet is available on the south end of Prudence Island.

ROUTE DESCRIPTION

The Narragansett Indians called Prudence Island Chibchuwesa, "a place apart," which seems appropriate even today: despite its proximity to the large population liv-

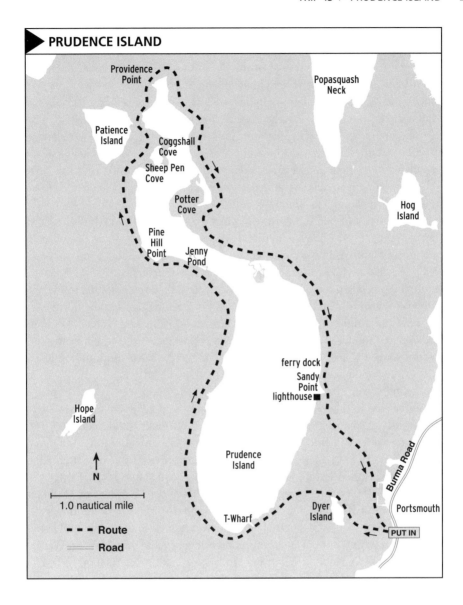

PRUDENCE ISLAND

Providence Point

Popasquash Neck

Patience Island

Coggshall Cove

Sheep Pen Cove

Potter Cove

Hog Island

Pine Hill Point

Jenny Pond

ferry dock

Sandy Point

lighthouse■

Hope Island

N

1.0 nautical mile

Prudence Island

Burma Road

Portsmouth

T-Wharf

Dyer Island

PUT IN

- - - Route
———— Road

ing around Narragansett Bay, Prudence Island is largely undeveloped. Rhode Island's founder, Roger Williams, later renamed Prudence and its neighbors Patience and Hope after virtuous ideals. But perhaps more influential than names, the Narragansett Bay National Estuarine Research Reserve encompasses 2,353 acres of land on Prudence, Hope, Patience, and Dyer islands, protecting a degree of their wildness. Prudence Island's 150 year-round residents have fought development and commercialism on their island, and with 60 percent of the island included in the reserve, it seems destined to retain its laid-back, unpretentious charm, despite the population multiplying tenfold in the summer.

Prudence Island is home to one of the densest herds of white-tailed deer in the northeast, and as a result, there are plenty of ticks as well.

Since Prudence Island lies in the middle of upper Narragansett Bay, it could easily be approached from several launches, but Weaver Cove works well. The launch itself is easy to manage, with plenty of parking, and for the crossing to Prudence Island, the densest boat traffic is relegated to the channel west of Dyer Island. Tidally, it works well with a midday high tide. (For a midday low tide, launch from Warwick or Bristol, but the busy launches and boat traffic in those places might make it preferable to work against the current and eddy-hop.)

From Weaver Cove, head across to low-lying, wooded Dyer Island (NBNERR) with its few gravel beaches. The 28-acre island is ecologically significant as one of the last remaining salt marshes in Narragansett Bay without mosquito ditches and as a nesting area for coastal shorebirds, including the American oystercatcher.

In the shipping channel west of Dyer Island expect all manner of water traffic, often moving very quickly. The shortest crossing (about 0.5 mile) is from the north end of Dyer. Look carefully before entering the channel and choose a target on Prudence Island to make a short, perpendicular crossing. Follow the shore south toward a large, unused T-shaped wharf, known as T-Wharf. Formerly a Naval ammunition loading wharf, T-Wharf now has an adjacent state-owned dock and a small beach with restrooms nearby.

Continue around the south end of Prudence along wild, reserve-protected shoreline with long stretches of slate bluffs—probably the most rocks you'll encounter in the area. To the south, Pell Bridge joins Aquidneck and Conanicut islands, home to the towns of Newport and Jamestown, respectively; the northern tip of the latter is about 2.0 miles away, with Wickford Harbor and Quonset Point acting as a backdrop.

To the north of Conanicut Point, Hope Island lies about 1.5 miles from Prudence. Also part of NBNERR, the forested island is off-limits to visitors during summer since it is a rookery for herons and egrets. The island was farmed in the 1800s, and bunkers still remain from its tenure as an ammunition storage facility during World War II.

About 2.0 miles beyond T-Wharf on Prudence Island's western shore is a settled area known as Prudence Park, where a few well-preserved Victorian homes overlook Stone Wharf, a favored fishing spot. The wharf dates to 1875, when steam ferry service from Providence helped establish a thriving summer resort with inns, a casino, and bathing pavilion. Farther north, a sandy beach curves northwest toward Pine Hill Point. If waves permit, this can be a good spot for a break. Near the middle of the beach, an inlet leads into Jenny Pond, which is navigable at high tide.

As you pass around Pine Hill Point, the more densely settled shores of Greenwich Bay come into view, along with a lighthouse marking Warwick Point. Continue along the shore, passing between Patience Island and the north end of Prudence. Sheep's Pen and Coggeshall coves are popular anchorages with several sand/mud beach areas that make for easy landings. The salt marshes here are feeding areas for a variety of wading birds, including several types of herons, snowy egrets, and glossy ibis. Patience Island was farmed from the mid-1600s to the 1960s, with a respite during the American Revolution after the British burned it. Most of the uninhabited island is included in the reserve.

Continue to Providence Point, the north end of the island. To the west, Warwick Lighthouse marks Warwick Point. Just north of that, the Aldrich Mansion overlooks Narragansett Bay, which narrows northward as it merges with the Providence River. Round Providence Point and follow the shoreline southward; it remains undeveloped to Potter Cove, an extremely popular anchorage and destination for day-trippers in powerboats.

Most of Prudence Island's east shore, from Potter Cove to Bullocks Wharf, is developed, with cottages lining the shoreline. Just southeast of Potter Cove, an inlet leads to a salt marsh and Nag Pond, which is reachable at high tide. To the northeast, the fat, cylindrical cooling towers at Fall River's coal-burning Brayton Point Power Station

Despite its proximity to a large population, Prudence Island is largely undeveloped, with 60 percent included in the Narragansett Bay National Estuarine Research Reserve. The Sandy Point Lighthouse (pictured) is the oldest lighthouse in the state.

will likely catch your eye, along with the Mount Hope Bridge, spanning the entrance to Mount Hope Bay. After the shore curves again southward, pass the ferry landing and a small store. About 1.0 mile later, Sandy Point Lighthouse is located on a low, sandy spit. Originally built on Goat Island in 1823, it was moved to Prudence in 1851 and is the oldest lighthouse in the state. The keeper's house washed away during the New England Hurricane of 1938, taking five people with it.

From the lighthouse, continue along the shore and reverse the crossing to Dyer Island. If current and wind is an issue, however, make a longer crossing to the marina and yacht companies north of the launch. This longer crossing would lessen your exposure to the restricted currents of Dyer and let you cross more quickly, before the strongest mid-tide currents develop (assuming you rounded Providence Point at high tide). The dock and parking area help identify the launch.

ALTERNATIVES
For a longer route, add a trip around Jamestown (Trip 45).

To shorten the route, paddle from the launch to Pine Hill Point and Jenny Pond; paddle up the inlet and carry over to the other side of the island. The Westport River (Trip 42) is a good backup route. You can also reach Prudence Island via ferry from Bristol and eliminate the crossing from Portsmouth.

MORE INFORMATION
Narragansett Bay National Estuarine Research Reserve (nbnerr.org; 401-683-6780). No camping is available on-route. Nearby campgrounds include at Melville Ponds Campground (melvillepondscampground.com; 401-682-2424), operated by the town of Portsmouth.

44
NEWPORT

Paddle past Newport's historic mansions, rocks, and ledges between Brenton Point and Lands End and along Sachuest Point.

Distance ▶	13.0 to 14.0 nautical miles, one-way
Tidal Planning ▶	3.46-foot mean tidal range at Newport. In the East Passage, just west of Castle Hill, the current floods north with an average max speed of 0.7 knots and ebbs southwest at an average max speed of 1.2 knots. The mouth of the Sakonnet has weak and variable currents.
Cautions ▶	Newport's south side is subject to open ocean conditions. Even on days with small seas, swells will grow into sizable waves as they roll over the shallow water and rocks. There are long stretches with few or no easy bailouts; have solid rescue skills before attempting this route and be prepared to be in your boat for a while. Expect heavy boat traffic in the Newport Harbor area.
Charts and Maps ▶	NOAA charts #13223 and #13221; Maptech #18

LAUNCHES

Fort Adams, Newport, RI Paved ramp, beach nearby; drop off gear and park; restrooms nearby. From the intersection of RI 138A/America's Cup Avenue and Thames Street in Newport, head southwest on Thames Street for 0.5 mile. Turn right onto Wellington Avenue/Halidon Avenue. In just over 0.8 mile, turn right onto Harrison Avenue. At the four-way intersection with Beacon Hill Road in 0.4 mile, turn right to stay on Harrison Avenue. Enter Fort Adams State Park on the right in 0.5 mile. Follow Fort Adams Drive and bear right. You'll pass restrooms on a hillside on your right, and take another right when you arrive at the water, passing west of a long building before arriving at the launch after 0.4 mile. *GPS coordinates: 41° 28.241' N, 71° 20.217' W.*

Kings Beach, Newport, RI Fishing access with hand carry (100 feet) to gravel beach; about 20 parking spaces; no facilities. Launches directly into area that may be rough, especially as afternoon winds increase. From the intersection of RI 138A/America's Cup

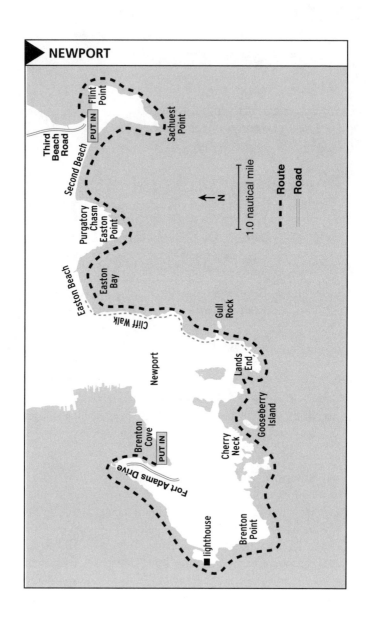

NEWPORT

Flint Point
Sachuest Point
PUT IN
Third Beach Road
Second Beach
Purgatory Chasm
Easton Point
Easton Beach
Easton Bay
Cliff Walk
Gull Rock
Newport
Lands End
Gooseberry Island
Cherry Neck
Brenton Cove
PUT IN
Fort Adams Drive
lighthouse
Brenton Point

1.0 nautical mile
N
- - - Route
——— Road

Avenue and Thames Street in Newport, head southwest on Thames Street for 0.5 mile. Turn right onto Wellington Avenue/Halidon Avenue. In just over 0.8 mile, continue straight on Breton Road. Continue on Breton Road for 1.2 miles then stay right on Ocean Avenue. In 0.3 mile, look for a small sign for the launch on the left and follow the dirt road to the end. *GPS coordinates: 41° 27.222′ N, 71° 20.552′ W.*

Third Beach, Middletown, RI Public ramp and beach; plenty of parking that fills midsummer, plus paid parking at Peabody's Parking at north end of beach; portable outhouses. From the intersection of RI 138 and Mitchell Lane in Portsmouth, head south on Mitchell Lane for 1.9 miles. Turn right on Third Beach Road and continue for another 2.0 miles to the parking on the left. *GPS coordinates: 41° 29.205′ N, 71° 14.763′ W.*

Other Public Access There are several potential landings for breaks and bailouts on-route (see description). Sachuest Point National Wildlife Preserve has mostly rocky shoreline that makes for difficult landings, but there are a few spots reachable by the right paddler in the right conditions. North of Fort Adams, Rose Island (Rose Island Lighthouse Foundation) has a lighthouse and paths around the island.

ROUTE DESCRIPTION

Hundreds of thousands of visitors flock to Newport, Rhode Island's Cliff Walk each year, strolling the mostly paved, 3.5-mile path to peek at the Gilded Age mansions perched along the dramatic stretch of cliffy shoreline. It's a great walk, and certainly recommended. But if you'd like to get away from the crowds and enjoy the view from the ocean, get in your kayak and try the "Cliff Paddle" instead.

In addition to its mansions, Newport has long stretches of gradually sloped sandy beach, where swells roll in and form gently-spilling waves. Rock gardens dot the shores between Brenton Point and Lands End. In the steep rock face beside Second Beach, Purgatory Chasm cuts a deep cleft that you can explore in your kayak, if conditions allow. More than 200 bird species annually visit Sachuest Point National Wildlife Refuge and its rocky shoreline, and some of the world's most impressive yachts anchor in Newport Harbor.

More than 13 miles of shoreline stretch between the launch at Fort Adams and Third Beach. Setting up a shuttle between launches would halve the trip, but most paddlers are more likely to explore either one end or the other—or explore the middle from Kings Beach. The choice between the sides may have more to do with conditions than attractions. Take a drive along Ocean Drive or out to Lands End and have a look before you launch. Presented here is a one-way route followed by a couple of round-trip suggestions.

Tidal current is most significant between Fort Adams and Castle Hill, and in the area around Rose and Goat islands. You should, however, be able to paddle the route just about any time, with minimal resistance from the tide.

Fort Adams to Lands End (5.0 to 6.0 nautical miles)

From the launch at Fort Adams, follow the shore north around the fort. This is a busy area, so watch for boat traffic. Established in 1799, the present fort was built from 1824 to 1857 and remained in use until 1953. Aside from being a popular state park, the fort is now best known as the venue for the Newport Folk Festival and the Newport Jazz Festival, which have been held on the grounds since 1981.

There's a lot to take in as you linger in the water north of the fort. The Pell Bridge soars over Eastern Passage, with the Rose Island Lighthouse marking one side of the channel. Over in Jamestown, an unusual, century-old home known as Clingstone perches on a rocky islet rising directly from the water.

Head southwest past a few large homes, the U.S. Coast Guard Station Castle Hill at the end of a narrow inlet, and the Castle Hill Lighthouse, which stands 40 feet over the water. Continue south; Ocean Drive follows the shoreline atop low bluffs with smooth, polished rocks. When conditions allow, a few small pocket beaches here make for good rest stops. As you round Brenton Point the seas are likely to increase, especially as swells reach the shallower areas around rocks. At Kings Beach—a good landing if conditions allow—Ocean Drive continues inland as Price Neck juts southward.

As you round Price Neck, a large mansion called Seafair comes into view on Cherry Neck. A Louis XIII-revival mansion built in 1935, it is now divided into two condominiums. If you like shopping for mansions, it's worth venturing into the cove to the northwest, where you'll be surrounded by historic residences, including the castle-like Indian Spring at the head of the cove. The result of a collaboration between landscape architect Frederick Law Olmsted and Richard Morris Hunt, the house was completed in 1892 and is still a seasonal private residence.

Just west of Seafair, you could stop for a break at a small public access beach with limited parking. East of Seafair, Gooseberry Island was the site of an exclusive men's club that was swept away by the Hurricane of 1938; it is now the site of a small home.

The shoreline curves northward toward Hazard's Beach, past several historic and newer homes. Hazard's Beach is a private club, but just east is Gooseberry Beach, a public beach with a private club. There are several groups of rocks and ledges to paddle through here.

Just past a smaller point is a rock formation in the intertidal zone called Spouting Rock that sends a spout of water into the air when the waves hit it just right. At the head of the next cove, Bailey's Beach is private, but just to the east, roped-off Rejects Beach is open to the public. From here, Lands End juts southward; the 1927 mansion known as the Waves (now divided into condos) faces out to sea.

Ledge Road reaches its terminus just past the Waves, with a small gravel beach sheltered by a small island just offshore. There is no parking here, but it's a good bailout to keep in mind. Just to the east, shoreward of a rocky area, is a beach of smooth cobbles just beneath the Cliff Walk and Lands End, a summer residence that once belonged to author Edith Wharton.

While hundreds of thousands of visitors stroll Newport's Cliff Walk each year, you can get away from the crowds and see the mansions from the water instead.

Lands End to Third Beach (7.0 nautical miles)

The shore curves northward, and for the next 2.5 miles is followed by the Cliff Walk, which passes over a rocky chasm via a stone pedestrian bridge, which, depending upon tide and conditions, may be paddled beneath. A small gravel beach just below the Cliff Walk may be reachable in calm conditions. Beyond stands Rough Point, the 1887 mansion built for Frederick Vanderbilt. The Cliff Walk real estate gets a bit dizzying in scale and scope, but a few landmarks stand out. Just inside Gull Rock, the Cliff Walk passes through a tunnel on Sheep Point and passes mansion after mansion, among them the Chinese Tea House in the backyard of the Marble House. Approaching Ochre Point, there's a Tudor-style mansion called Fairholme, and then Anglesea with its copper-roofed gazebo just above the Cliff Walk.

Rounding Ochre Point, you can't miss the largest and most-visited mansion: The Breakers. Built for Cornelius Vanderbilt II in 1893, the 65,000-square-foot home has

70 rooms and usually a big green lawn full of visitors. Just past Ochre Court, on the grounds of Salve Regina University, a stairway known as the Forty Steps descends from the Cliff Walk down to the seaside rocks. If you linger, you'll undoubtedly end up in the background of someone's vacation photos.

From here it's under a mile to the end of the Cliff Walk, passing a few more mansions along the way to Easton Beach, or First Beach as it's known locally. Stay a bit offshore here and avoid getting dashed against the rocks at the west end. It may be interesting to paddle past this beach, but the water will likely be full of swimmers and other obstacles, and you may as well continue past it to Easton Point, which has a few rocks along its western shore, overlooked by houses humbler than those across the bay, but by no means humble. At the southern end, the Clambake Club, a private dining club, perches upon the rocky point.

Follow Easton Point northward toward Second Beach, where you may land if there are no swimmers or lifeguards present. Shortly after some offshore rocks, the coastline turns steep, with a rock face rising 50 feet up from the water. Purgatory Chasm, a dark cleft about 10 feet wide, divides the face in two. If seas are calm enough, consider backing into the chasm (it helps to have some decent reverse-stroke skills). You can follow it about 120 feet inland. Overhead, the rock rises about 50 feet and is further shaded by trees rising above it. You may even see a face or two cautiously peering over the edge, since this is a popular stop on the tourist trail.

Follow Second Beach over a mile to Sachuest Point National Wildlife Refuge. On the east side, at the mouth of the Sakonnet River, Island Rocks can be a lively spot, with a view to Sakonnet Point, easily visible just 2.0 miles to the east. The take-out at Third Beach is just around Flint Point.

ALTERNATIVES

Rose and Goat islands, just north and northeast of Fort Adams, are good Plan B routes or could be a 3.0-mile bonus paddle en route to returning to Fort Adams. You could also add Jamestown (Trip 45) to your itinerary or head to Westport River (Trip 42) if conditions here seem too rough.

MORE INFORMATION

Fort Adams State Park (riparks.com/locations/LocationFortAdams.html; 401-847-2400). Sachuest Point National Wildlife Refuge (fws.gov/refuge/Sachuest_Point; 401-364-9124). Rose Island and the Rose Island Lighthouse (roseislandlighthouse.org; 401-847-4242). There is no camping available on-route.

45
JAMESTOWN

Enjoy cliffs, rocks, and ledges; a good surfing beach; lighthouses; and the chance to ogle at several architectural curiosities.

Distance ▶ 7.0 to 10.0 nautical miles, round-trip

Tidal Planning ▶ 3.46-foot mean tidal range at Newport. The shallows off of Beavertail Point can develop tall, dumping seas that collide with reflecting waves and create especially chaotic conditions. Newton Rock can quickly multiply the size of incoming swell and dump it quite suddenly, which would be unfortunate for any small boat in its way. If in doubt, scout this area before launching and steer south of the "NR" buoy. The area around Fort Wetherill and its steep cliffs also gets its share of swell from the open ocean. Outside of the protected coves, there are few, if any, bailouts. The current between Dutch Island and Fort Getty may also create steeper seas, particularly when opposing the wind.

Cautions ▶ The southern end of Jamestown is subject to whatever conditions the open ocean may present, as well as the effects of tidal current splitting around the island as it moves in and out of Narragansett Bay. Both channels that flank Jamestown accommodate large, swiftly moving ships on their way to and from Narragansett Bay's industrial ports. Ferries, tour boats, and one of the busiest yachting harbors in New England all make the rock-strewn near-shore waters look relatively safe.

Charts and Maps ▶ NOAA chart #13221; Maptech #18

LAUNCH

Fort Wetherill State Park, Jamestown, RI Short carry to beach; modest parking area; restrooms and outhouses elsewhere in the park. A ramp is also on the southeast end of the island if preferred. From the Conanicus Avenue/East Shore Road, Exit RI 138 (west of the Pell Bridge), go south on Conanicus Avenue for 1.2 miles to Walcott

Avenue. In 0.6 mile, turn left onto Fort Wetherill Road. In 0.2 mile, bear right into the park, then immediately bear left. At the next fork, bear right and continue 0.3 mile to the parking area. *GPS coordinates: 41° 28.669′ N, 71° 21.867′ W.*

Other Public Access With a lighthouse at its southern end and the ruins of a Civil War fort at the northeast end, Dutch Island (state) has plenty to see beyond the easy landings along its gravel beaches. It is unclear whether access is allowed above high water line. The island is a good spot for a break, but it is not much more than a quarter-mile from sure access and facilities at Fort Getty Park (town of Jamestown). At Jamestown's southern end, the shoreline along Beavertail State Park is mostly steep with difficult landings (see description for more).

ROUTE DESCRIPTION
Conanicut Island, or as most know it, the town of Jamestown, Rhode Island, lies at the mouth of Narragansett Bay, flanked by two busy shipping channels spanned by soaring bridges. Despite its proximity to large populations and dizzying boat traffic, the 8-mile-long island has ample stretches of shoreline where you can escape both.

The most dramatic (and potentially hazardous) shoreline lies along the southern end, where open ocean conditions and tidal currents collide with steep, rocky cliffs. The lighthouse, crumbling fortifications on Dutch Island, and the village of Jamestown offer plenty to look at on shore mid-island. From the Newport Bridge northward, the island is more residential, with only one stretch of undeveloped shoreline along the northwest end.

Despite the proximity of shipping lanes and abundant recreational boat traffic, there's plenty of room for kayakers near shore. In bigger seas, particularly along the southern end, this may be more of a challenge. Check out conditions at Beavertail Point before you launch.

Layers of history are evident all over the island, from the neatly laid stone walls to military fortifications that once guarded the mouth of Narragansett Bay. The American Indian burial site at West Ferry—the largest known in New England—dates back at least 3,300 years. European settlement began in the 1630s when fur traders used Dutch Island as a base and the British began grazing sheep. By the time of the Revolutionary War, the town was home to more than 500 people, but British troops destroyed many of the buildings and forced the evacuation of more than 200 residents. As steam ferry service brought visitors from Newport in the late 1800s and hotels were built, some wealthy visitors chose the island for their summer homes, preferring its quieter, less pretentious lifestyle over that of Newport. The Spanish-American War and World War I prompted the construction of Fort Getty, Fort Wetherill, the military fortifications on Dutch Island, and various other gun emplacements. By the end of World War I, these installations were abandoned, but many were later reactivated during World War II.

Without investigating the coves or other details, a circumnavigation of Jamestown would take a paddler around 18 nautical miles (see "Jamestown Circumnavigation

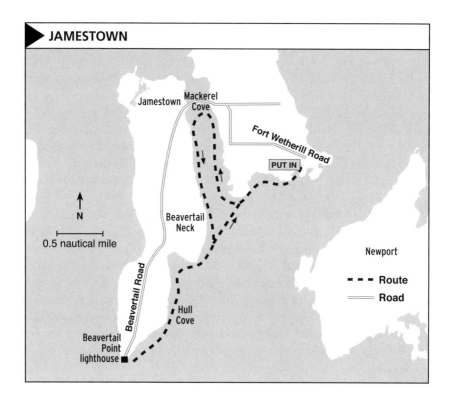

Tips," page 269). It's worth doing, but for most paddlers, this more leisurely out-and-back route along the southern end will be far more satisfying and less tiring.

There are several potential launches in the area, including Fort Getty Park at the northernmost point of Beavertail Neck and the University of Rhode Island's Bay Campus in Narragansett. Depending on the tides, conditions, and your preferred itinerary, any of these could work well. The Fort Wetherill launch, however, gives you immediate access to some of the most spectacular, steep, cliffy shoreline this side of Maine. You'll likely be sharing the water here with divers; watch for their red flags.

South of Jamestown (7.0 to 8.0 nautical miles)

From Fort Wetherill take a right, closely following the shoreline for a little under a mile. Pass steep, rocky bluffs with numerous ledges and boulders beneath them. With any kind of a sea running, waves build over these ledges, crashing into the cliffs, an area with great potential for either fun rock play or great danger; bailouts here are difficult at best. Gauge the conditions and choose your route accordingly; the paddling is plenty awe-inspiring well outside of the surf zone.

After following the shore for nearly a mile, Southwest Point juts southward. Atop the cliffs, the large shingle-style summer home Marbella stands on a property known as Horsehead, for the horse-like rock formations just west of the point. Built between

1882 and 1890 for Philadelphia industrialist Joseph Wharton, the house is visible for miles around (though best viewed a good distance from shore), its fifth-story belvedere noted on charts. Wharton, a founder of Bethlehem Steel, started the Wharton School of Finance at the University of Pennsylvania, and was a cofounder of Swarthmore College. A Philadelphia Quaker, he found Newport's grandiose social scene too frivolous and sought a quieter location on Jamestown. At first, architect Charles L. Bevins intended to build a more modest home than those of Newport that lacked large gathering areas for entertaining, but the size slowly increased. Built of local stone and shingles and set back modestly from the cliff with natural landscaping, the house earned its place on the National Register of Historic Places as the house that set the tone for Jamestown's more laid-back summer community.

The rocky shores continue much of the way around Mackerel Cove, a mile-long gap separating Beavertail Neck from the rest of Jamestown, with Mackerel Cove Beach at its head. In morning, evening, or non-summer months—anytime lifeguards aren't on-duty—the beach can be a good alternate launch (from the intersection of Southwest Avenue and Beavertail Road in Jamestown, paid parking is 0.2 miles west on Beavertail Road, on the left). Play in the surf, which develops gently spilling waves over the gradual, shallow bottom, or carry over to a shallow, tidal cove leading to Dutch Harbor to circumnavigate Beavertail Neck to shorten the trip around the rest of Jamestown Island by 7.0 miles. If swimmers or lifeguards are present, give them some space and continue south along the east shore of Beavertail Neck.

If seas are running outside of the cove, conditions among the rocks in the cove can be a bit less intimidating, increasing southward toward Short Point and Hull Cove, a potentially hazardous area where modest swells can quickly grow into large dumping waves. The beach at the head of Hull Cove is a potential bailout or break area, but big dumping waves may make landings there difficult. The west shore of Hull Cove is pocked with numerous indentations that open to the northeast. One particular cleft extends well inward, a long, narrow sea cave well worth venturing into in calm conditions. Paddle into the cave backward to monitor incoming waves and to make exiting easier. Depending on conditions, this cave or Lion Head might be a good spot to turn back. Seas coming in over the shallow, boulder-strewn near-shore waters east of the point can be tricky and hazardous.

On calm days, stay close for a look at Beavertail Light, which was first established on the point in 1749, with the present tower built in 1856. On bigger days, stay well offshore around Beavertail Point. Newton Rock lies underwater a short distance from the point, and turns even small swells into steep waves that dump into the near-shore rocks; stay well south this volatile spot except on smaller days. The coast here is all part of Beavertail State Park; depending on conditions, tide height, and your own skills, you'll find spectacular picnic spots among the beautiful pocket beaches below its bluffs.

Return the way you came, following the point back past Lion Head and across the mouths of Hull and Mackerel coves to the fort.

Exploring the Dumplings (up to 2.0 nautical miles)

For a bonus mile or two after your return to the launch, continue past the launch cove and Bull Point to a group of small, rocky islets called the Dumplings.

On one of these islands is a historic house called Clingstone, known to locals simply as the House on the Rock. J.S. Lovering Wharton (nephew of Marbella's owner) completed the house in 1905 after the government seized his land for Fort Wetherill. The 23-room, three-story house was built directly on the rocky islet so that it seems to rise directly from the sea. Artist William Trost Richards helped design the home with a circular orientation so all of the windows frame idyllic views. Since the frequent cannon practice at Fort Wetherill cracked plaster walls, the interior walls were shingled. A 1904 society item in the *Philadelphia Press* stated, "Everyone is of the opinion here that Mr. Wharton will not stay in the house more than one season, and they say one nor'easter will settle it." He stayed there every summer until his death in 1938.

Jamestown's most dramatic (and potentially hazardous) shoreline lies along the southern end, where open ocean conditions and tidal currents collide with steep, rocky cliffs.

The notorious New England Hurricane hit shortly after and did little damage despite extensive destruction not far away. The house stood empty for twenty years until 1961 when a Boston architect and distant relative of Wharton bought the building and began a lifelong project of restoring and maintaining it. Keep a respectful distance: weary of curious kayakers and people gawking from tour boats, the owners have resorted to mooning visitors.

ALTERNATIVES

Jamestown can be circumnavigated in at least 18.0 nautical miles (see more in "Jamestown Circumnavigation Tips" on page 269). Newport (Trip 44) is just across East Passage and could be added to extend this route; the shortest crossing is between Bull Point/Fort Wetherill and Fort Adams.

If conditions on the south end are bigger than desired, launch from Fort Getty Park's beach launches at the end of Fort Getty Road to quickly reach Dutch Island and Dutch Harbor with Round Swamp at its head. In addition, Jamestown Harbor or Taylor Point could be starting points for abbreviated but more sheltered excursions.

MORE INFORMATION

Fort Wetherill State Park (riparks.com/Locations/LocationFortWetherill.html; 401-423-1771). Mackerel Cove Beach (jamestownri.gov; 401-423-7260); fee to park. Beavertail State Park (riparks.com/Locations/LocationBeavertail.html; 401-423-9941). Beavertail Light (beavertaillight.org; 401-423-3270). Dutch Island Lighthouse (dutchislandlighthouse.org). Fort Getty Park (jamestownri.gov/town-departments/parks-rec/fort-getty; 401-423-7211) has 115 campsites, including fifteen for tents, which are within a moderate carry to the park's launch; reservations are recommended.

JAMESTOWN CIRCUMNAVIGATION TIPS

Without venturing into the coves, circumnavigating Conanicut Island requires about 18 nautical miles of paddling, all certainly made easier if you plan to paddle with the current. Perhaps more important: conditions at Beavertail Point may change quickly, especially with tide changes. Scout conditions before you launch to make sure the trip is within your abilities.

In most conditions, the safest scenario is to launch from Fort Wetherill a little before low tide and round the point soon after, near slack tide (you could also launch from Fort Getty and go counterclockwise). Follow the western shore north—about 8 nautical miles to Conanicut Point. Along the way, stop at Fort Getty or Dutch Island for a break before passing beneath the Jamestown Verrazano Bridge. The last mile or so before the point is undeveloped shorefront with a view across West Passage toward North Kingstown and the industrial shorefront along Quonset Point, a former Navy base. At the northern end, the former Conanicut Point Light, built in 1886, is now a private home.

Depending on when you launched and how long the west side took, you may have a little current against you on the east side. You'll find less current near shore, and if you take your time, you could even wait for the tide to change again. Another good spot for a break is a small gravel beach, less than a mile from the north end of the island at the end of Broad Street, followed by the end of a road where there are signs and garbage cans. From here Taylor Point is another 3.0 nautical miles or so beyond, just before the Pell Bridge, an excellent spot to pull out on the ledges and pose for a photo.

Beyond the bridge, you'll encounter plenty of boat traffic in Jamestown Harbor. Stick close to shore or hopscotch between moored boats as you make your way toward Clingstone. Fort Wetherill is just around Bull Point.

46
LITTLE NARRAGANSETT BAY

Paddle along undeveloped salt marsh, check out gorgeous boats in Watch Hill Cove, and hang out on a sandy beach.

Distance ▸ 6.0 nautical miles, round-trip

Tidal Planning ▸ Average tidal range is 2.7 feet. Trip may be done at any tide, but there's more to explore around the salt marshes at higher tides. The stretch between Napatree Beach and Sandy Point, while partially sheltered, may still get a little rough. Currents and conditions may increase exponentially just outside Napatree Point.

Cautions ▸ There's plenty of boat traffic here; stick to the edges and avoid channels.

Charts and Maps ▸ NOAA chart #13214; Maptech #86; Waterproof Chart #60

LAUNCHES

Randall Neck, Barn Island Wildlife Management Area, Stonington, CT
Designated kayak beach launch area beside paved ramp; large parking area, mostly for trailers but with several car sites; portable toilets. From US 1 and Greenhaven Road in Pawcatuck, Connecticut, go south on Green Haven Road, then take an immediate right turn onto Palmer Neck Road. The launch is at the end of the street in 1.7 miles. *GPS coordinates: 41° 20.246' N, 71° 52.548' W.*

Other Public Access Besides its kayak launch and ramp, Barn Island Wildlife Management Area (state of Connecticut [CT]) also offers hiking trails, wildlife observation, and hunting; wear blaze orange when on-trail during hunting seasons. Napatree Point (Watch Hill Conservancy and Watch Hill Fire District [WHC/WHFD]) offers landings and trails; obey all posted closures for nesting birds in summer and stay on trails at all times. Landing on Sandy Point Nature Preserve (Avalonia Land Trust and U.S. Fish and Wildlife [ALT/USFW]) in summer requires a permit or a small day-use fee (see More Information); obey all closures for nesting birds.

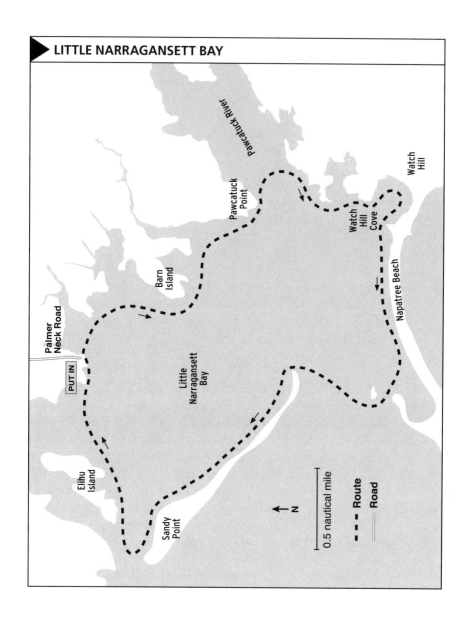

LITTLE NARRAGANSETT BAY

Pawcatuck River

Pawcatuck Point

Watch Hill

Watch Hill Cove

Barn Island

Napatree Beach

Palmer Neck Road

PUT IN

Little Narragansett Bay

Elihu Island

Sandy Point

0.5 nautical mile

← N

▪ ▪ ▪ Route

— Road

ROUTE DESCRIPTION

From its source in South Kingstown, Rhode Island, the Pawcatuck River flows 30 miles before it starts blending with tidal salt water in Westerly, Rhode Island. From there, it flows (subject to the tides) another 4 miles before it reaches Little Narragansett Bay, a shallow corner of the ocean, largely separated from Fishers Island Sound by a pair of sandy spits.

The north shore is dominated by Barn Island Wildlife Management Area (CT), a 1,013-acre tract of upland hardwoods jutting into grassy marshes laced with winding creeks and its state's largest coastal wildlife conservation property. The somewhat remote beaches on Napatree and Sandy points (both in Rhode Island) make up the south end of the bay, making the area a good escape from the coastal sprawl. But as far as sprawl goes, Rhode Island's Watch Hill is an eye-catching stretch of developed coastline, and worth a visit for a privileged, watery glimpse of a pretty town.

From the ramp on Randall Neck, head southeast. If the tide is high enough, explore the wildlife management area's marshes; otherwise head for Barn Island. Avoid the marked boat channel to the south, though powerboats are not relegated to traveling its confines.

Pass Barn Island, continuing out of the wildlife management area to residential Pawcatuck Point. Before you is the mouth of the Pawcatuck River, and the Connecticut–Rhode Island border. On a rising tide, you could take a side trip up the river, reaching Westerly's Main Street Boat Ramp in approximately 4 miles, where the water transitions to a freshwater river.

Otherwise, look for approaching boat traffic and cross the channel quickly, aiming toward the houses on Rhode Island's Rhodes Point. Head south, passing more upscale houses until you reach Watch Hill Cove. Named for its strategic use as a lookout during the Revolutionary War and the French and Indian War, Watch Hill rose to prominence as an exclusive summer resort in the late 1800s. The five-star Ocean House hotel overlooks the harbor from the hillside, along with upscale homes. Eye-catching boats float beside the harbor's docks and moorings.

Leaving the cove, follow the shore of Napatree Point (WHC/WHFD) west. Boaters often anchor near shore to enjoy this popular beach; pull up anywhere along the beach for your own leisure time. Marked trails cross over the dunes to the south side; stay on-trail if you venture over on foot. At the end of Napatree Point are the remains of Fort Mansfield, an artillery post that guarded the entrance to Long Island Sound.

Exercise great care if you choose to poke your bow out around Napatree Point for a look at Fishers Island Sound. As seas move in and out of Long Island Sound, they squeeze through the gap between here and East Point on Fishers Island, which is just under 2.0 miles wide and is a recipe for increased currents. A series of underwater ledges stretching from Watch Hill Point to Fishers Island further restricts the flow, creating a long series of features that tend to get especially rough during mid-tide currents. In the right situation with the right skills, you could have some fun in these features, but in the wrong situation it could be quite dangerous.

Little Narragansett Bay is a shallow corner of the ocean, largely separated from Fishers Island Sound by a pair of sandy spits, including Napatree Point. Here, a group of paddlers take a break on Napatree Point.

Use your compass to get a bearing on the south end of Sandy Point, and head across. This area is very shallow, which helps regulate the motorboat traffic, but could also result in choppy conditions. Sandy Point (ALT/USFW), now a conserved island with beaches all around it, was connected to Napatree Point before the hurricane of 1938. In summer a steward may ask for a small fee or to see your permit to visit the island (see More Information). At Sandy Point's north end (which is in Connecticut), a breakwater extending from Edwards Point relegates boat traffic and current to a narrow channel, which makes a quick crossing easy. Head toward the south end of Elihu Island. The cove to the north is a pretty spot, worth checking out, but don't expect to get through to the north side; a low bridge makes this unlikely.

Follow the southeast shore of Elihu Island and cross the mouth of Wequetequock Cove. If you're lucky, you may see an Amtrak train speed over the bridge, a ubiquitous feature along the Connecticut shoreline. Randall Point and the launch are just to the east.

ALTERNATIVES

Depending on conditions and your skills, you could paddle around the south side of Napatree Point to Watch Hill Point to get a closer look at the lighthouse (and the lifestyles of the rich and famous); check conditions first by landing on Napatree Beach and crossing the dunes on foot (stay on-trail). A trip up the Pawcatuck River to Westerly could also be added. Mystic (Trip 47) is only a few miles west.

In rough conditions, stay in the more sheltered areas of this route, including the marshes of Barn Island Wildlife Management Area or the Pawcatuck River. For drier options, hike on the 4 miles of trails in the wildlife management area, or check out Mystic Seaport.

MORE INFORMATION

Barn Island Wildlife Management Area (ct.gov/deep; 860-424-3000). Napatree Point Conservation Area (thewatchhillconservancy.org; 401-315-5399). Napatree Beach (watchhillfiredistrict.org/beaches.html; 401-348-6540). Sandy Point Nature Preserve (avalonialandconservancy.org/preserves/sandy-point-nature-preserve; 860-884-3500); purchase day-use permits from the Stonington Community Center at 28 Cutler Street (thecomo.org; 860-535-2476). No camping is available on-route.

47
MYSTIC

*Paddle near historic boats at Mystic Seaport,
beneath mechanical bridges in action, and up
to your own patch of beach on an island.*

Distance ▶ Up to 15.0 nautical miles, round-trip

Tidal Planning ▶ Mean tidal range is 2.3 feet. Aside from the more predictable north–south flood and ebb, tidal current floods west into Long Island Sound and east out of it. Fishers Island Sound is known for strong currents. Midday high tide works well; plan to have an outgoing tide help you on your way out, negotiate the potentially stronger currents of Fishers Island Sound around slack tide, and ride the incoming tide back up the river.

Cautions ▶ Boats waiting at the drawbridge have limited maneuvering ability and are subject to the current; steer clear. There's also plenty of boat traffic elsewhere on the river and in the sound. Fishers Island Sound is subject to open ocean conditions, and steeper waves when the current opposes wind. Be aware of tide changes and anticipate changing conditions.

Charts and Maps ▶ NOAA chart #13214; Maptech #86

LAUNCHES

Mystic River State Boat Launch, Groton, CT Dirt ramp; limited parking on-site; no facilities. From I-95 South, Exit 89, turn right onto Mystic Street/CT 614. In 0.2 mile, turn right onto Cow Hill Road. Continue 0.4 mile then turn left onto Bindloss Road. At the T intersection in 0.2 mile, turn left on River Road. The launch is 0.4 mile ahead on the right. *GPS coordinates: 41° 22.441′ N, 71° 57.963′ W.*

Other Public Access Much of the area is private. Enders Island is home to a retreat center owned by the Society of Saint Edmund; visitors are welcome and a gravel beach landing is reachable on the east side. Additional public launches include the Stonington town ramp on Isham Street, the Mystic YMCA on Williams Beach, and the town dock in Groton on Main Street.

ROUTE DESCRIPTION

The scenic Mystic River is sheltered from open ocean conditions, making it a good place for paddlers of all levels. There's really not enough time to enjoy Mystic Seaport's maritime museum and get in a good paddle in the same day. At least allow yourself some time to paddle among the scores of well-preserved old boats as well as the more urban claptrap of mechanical bridges and speeding trains.

Well before the Mystic River became best known for its maritime museum, the area had been a shipbuilding center. Between 1784 and 1919, more than 600 vessels were built along its shores. Mystic Seaport began preserving this heritage in 1929, when steamships and railroads began replacing sailboats, and over the next 50 years the museum became home to nearly 500 historic watercraft. From a kayak, you will get an especially good perspective of some of these boats.

While launching at points farther south puts you closer to the ocean, the Mystic River State Boat Launch is easier to contend with and gives you more river to explore. Head south below the I-95 bridge and continue past the park-like Elm Grove Cemetery on the east shore toward the auspicious concentration of tall-masted sailboats and other unusual boats in Mystic Seaport.

About 0.5 mile south, the Mystic River Bascule Bridge spans the river. Built in 1920, the bridge uses massive concrete counterweights to open an 85-foot span for boat traffic. Boats line up to wait for the bridge to open; in summer months, the drawbridge raises 40 minutes after every hour. Be careful around waiting boats, especially sailboats: although they may be attempting to stay stationary, they are still subject to the current and don't always have great control over their movements. Fortunately, kayaks easily fit beneath the bridge and don't need to wait, but you may want to stick around to see the bridge go up and down at least once. Around the next bend, a swing bridge carries the railroad across the river.

After the railroad bridge, stay west of the channel as you head south through Mystic Harbor. To the east is Mason Island, the site of the 1637 Mystic massacre, when English forces led a retaliatory attack on the Pequot settlement here. With the help of Narragansetts and Mohegans, the group set fire to 80 homes, killing 600 to 700 Pequots in an hour, most of them women and children. If you prefer a shorter trip, cross over to the island at the narrow spot between Sixpenny Island (private) and Clam Point and continue south around the island.

Otherwise, follow the western shore to Noank, a historic village with several boatyards, a marina, and two waterside restaurants. South of town, privately owned Morgan Point Light occupies the point. A stone house with a light tower at its peak, the lighthouse operated from 1868 until 1921, when it was replaced by an automated light on a nearby ledge.

Head southwest, passing the tiny cottages just over the water on Mouse Island (private), and continue across the mouth of the large cove to Groton Long Point. The shoreline in this area is completely residential. From the point, North Dumpling Island (private) and its lighthouse are a little over a mile to the southwest. As you cross, monitor your movement by the current. Keep a range by lining up two fixed objects

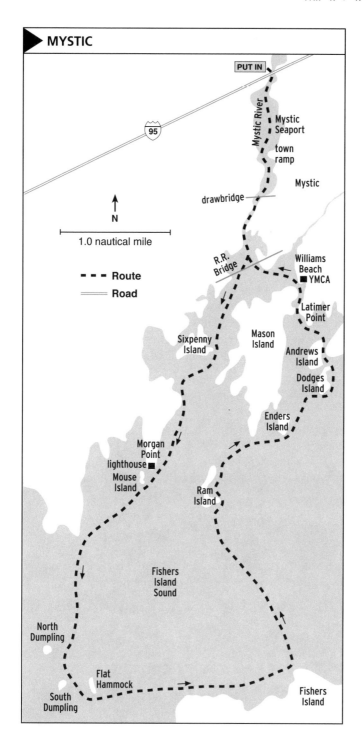

MYSTIC

PUT IN

Mystic River

Mystic Seaport

town ramp

Mystic

drawbridge

N

1.0 nautical mile

- - - Route

═══ Road

95

R.R. Bridge

Williams Beach ■ YMCA

Latimer Point

Sixpenny Island

Mason Island

Andrews Island

Dodges Island

Enders Island

Morgan Point

lighthouse ■

Mouse Island

Ram Island

Fishers Island Sound

North Dumpling

Flat Hammock

South Dumpling

Fishers Island

and adjust your ferry angle accordingly so that you don't end up paddling much farther to achieve the same distance. Also, be sure to look both ways: this area has plenty of boat traffic, including a Block Island ferry from New London.

A lighthouse has stood on North Dumpling Island since 1849. The current tower, which is built into a house, was built in 1871. The light was deactivated in 1959 and replaced with an automated beacon. The 2-acre island has been owned by Dean Kamen, inventor of the Segway Human Transporter, since 1986. After Kamen was denied permission to build a wind turbine, he joked that he was seceding from the United States. The island eventually became powered by wind and solar power, and though its secession is not legally recognized, Dumplonians have their own constitution, flag, currency, and national anthem. There's also a replica of Stonehenge standing over the island's north shore.

Continue south past South Dumpling (Audubon New York; landings not permitted) to Flat Hammock (private), a gravel pile that rises only a few feet above the water surface, and take a break below the high-tide line before paddling east to Clay Point on Fishers Island. Be attentive to boat traffic coming and going from West Harbor, to the south. At Clay Point follow the shore, attentive to the current and possible near-shore eddies.

To start the journey back upriver, cross from just about anywhere along here; in the interest of keeping a shorter, safer crossing, leave from Brooks Point. From there you can line up the navigation buoys with Ram Island and keep a range throughout the 1.5-

The Mystic River area can accommodate paddlers of all levels.

mile crossing, if you don't let the current push you off course. Again, be attentive to the current, establishing a ferry angle so that you paddle a straight line instead of a big arc.

Ram Island (private) was once known as Mystic Island, and was the location of a Victorian-era resort hotel with steamship service from New York and Boston. More recently it has been a home and farm, but both were destroyed by fires. There's a beautiful cove on the east side, a popular anchorage. Paddle past this en route to the two tiny, undeveloped islets just to the north: Quirk and Ahoy islands. Both islands are barred to Ram Island, and are private, but have a long history of public use. Again, we may legally land below the high-tide line. Ahoy, the northern islet, has a sandbar on the west side that makes for easy landings. This is a very popular spot, so expect company. Quirk Island made it onto the literary map when Arthur Henry—best known for his connection to Theodore Dreiser—wrote *An Island Cabin* about his time on the island. The cabin is long gone; like many structures in the area, the last vestiges were taken away by the Hurricane of 1938.

Head northwest across the channel to Mason Point. Again, this is a busy channel, so watch for boats and monitor the current. Continue to Enders Island (St. Edmund's Retreat). At high enough tide, you can paddle beneath the causeway joining Enders to Mason Island; otherwise, paddle beneath the vertical stone walls protecting its south shore. You may land on the gravel beach near the chapel on the east side.

Depending on your energy level, head straight north along the shore of Mason Island to the causeway and bridge, or paddle a little farther, around Dodges and Andrews islands (private) and then angle northwest toward the bridge. North of the bridge pass the YMCA on Williams Beach as you wind your way west toward the marina at Murphy Point. Just ahead is the railroad swing bridge, where you reconnect with the outgoing route. With any luck or good tidal planning, your final 1.5 miles to the launch will be aided by the incoming tide.

ALTERNATIVES

Add the Little Narragansett Bay (Trip 46) for a much more comprehensive trip around Fishers Island Sound. Be attentive to potentially rough areas, like the tide race between East Point and Napatree Point.

More sheltered routes include heading upriver to Old Mystic or paddling Little Narragansett Bay (Trip 46) instead. For a less-challenging trip, make a circuit around the river and Mason Island (7.0–8.0 nautical miles), perhaps with a lunch break on Ahoy Island. This partial-day trip would be perfect for those looking to build skills without tackling open water conditions.

MORE INFORMATION

Mystic River State Boat Launch, Connecticut Department of Energy & Environmental Protection, Boating Division (ct.gov/deep; 860-434-8638). Mystic Seaport (mysticseaport.org; 860-572-0711); hours and ticket prices online. Enders Island (endersisland.com; 860-536-0565).

48
OLD LYME

Enjoy marshes, tributaries, and abundant birdlife near the mouth of the Connecticut River.

Distance ▶ 5.0 to 9.0 nautical miles, round-trip

Tidal Planning ▶ Mean tidal range is 3.5 feet. In the river, tidal current floods north and ebbs south. In Long Island Sound, current floods west and ebbs east. Ideally, launch on a rising tide and head south after the tide turns.

Cautions ▶ The shallow river mouth can get choppy, especially when winds oppose current. The main channel of the river is extremely popular with powerboaters, and gets very churned up from their wakes.

Charts and Maps ▶ NOAA chart #12375; Maptech #17

LAUNCHES

Great Island Wildlife Management Area Boat Launch, Old Lyme, CT Paved ramp; plenty of parking; portable toilet. From I-95, Exit 70, take CT 156 south for 1.8 miles and turn right on Smith Neck Road. The ramp is 0.8 mile farther at the end of the road. *GPS coordinates: 41° 17.249' N, 72° 19.435' W.*

Other Public Access Landings are not permitted on Great Island Wildlife Management Area (CT Department of Energy & Environmental Protection [CT DEEP]) outside of the official boat launch; obey any posted signs regarding osprey nesting. Griswold Point Preserve (The Nature Conservancy [TNC]) is reachable by kayak from the launch; please stay on-trail and obey all posted signs, especially during nesting season.

ROUTE DESCRIPTION

The Connecticut River is New England's longest river, running 410 miles from its source at the Canadian border to the Long Island Sound. Thanks to shifting sandbars at its mouth—the result of large amounts of silt washing downstream during spring snowmelt—the Connecticut is the only major U.S. river without a port at its mouth. Instead, it has the communities of Old Saybrook and Old Lyme, with the marshes of Great Island buffering the east side from development. Great Island is a beautiful

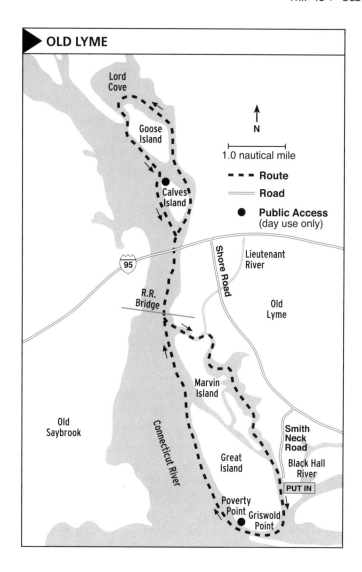

area, popular with birders and anglers. Back in the 1960s when the ospreys were endangered by DDT, Old Lyme resident Roger Tory Peterson erected the first osprey nesting platform on Great Island, and many more followed. Now you can't paddle far in the area without seeing or hearing an osprey. The Nature Conservancy listed Connecticut's tidelands as one of the Western Hemisphere's 40 Last Great Places.

North of Great Island are a massive bridge for I-95 and US 1 and a drawbridge that frequently lowers to allow Amtrak trains to pass. Powerboaters abound; take great care to stay out of their way. But north of the interstate, a couple of marshy islands create sheltered channels where boaters tend to slow down.

Launch and head south, toward Griswold Point Preserve (TNC) and the south end of Great Island (CT DEEP). Odds are good that you'll encounter a few anglers around here. Apparently the choppy water over the river mouth's shallows tends to confuse baitfish, which attracts the bigger fish. If you paddle a decked touring kayak with no apparent fishing apparatus, a common question at some of these southern New England launches is a puzzled, "Are you fishing or just sightseeing?"

Pass around the southern end of Great Island. To the southwest is the Saybrook Breakwater Lighthouse and the breakwaters protecting the channel into the river. North of that are the marinas along the Old Saybrook waterfront. There are a couple of mud/sand beaches along Poverty Point on Poverty Island, at the southwest end of Great Island, where landing is possible among piles of large driftwood logs. Just north of Poverty Point, a narrow creek cuts through the marsh and can be explored at higher tides, along with other such passages. No landings are permitted in this wildlife management area.

Follow Great Island's shore northward. Just before the Back River angles back toward the launch, dividing Great Island, a rocky, forested island rises from the marsh offering another possible landing. A little farther north is the entrance to the Lieutenant River. If you're opting for a shorter (4-5 nautical miles) trip, turn here. Otherwise, continue northward, beneath the railroad bridge. The boardwalk along shore here is popular among anglers, and you'll probably need to stay some distance from it. The drawbridge tends to stay in the up position to allow boats through, but every now and then drops into place before a train passes.

Pass a municipal dock and a town-access beach before passing a marina. There are plenty of nice homes along this route, and the railroad bridge is certainly an engineering feat, but as architectural marvels go, the I-95 highway bridge is massive and a bit daunting. Officially known as the Raymond E. Baldwin Bridge, it was completed in 1993 and is crossed by more than 80,000 vehicles daily.

North of the bridge, follow the channel to the east of Calves Island, past a marina. A popular landing area at the north end of Calves Island has mostly vegetated sand dunes rising behind the shore—the spoils of dredging channels in the river.

Follow the channel east of Goose Island toward Lord Cove. Each year from late August to early October, Goose Island (no landings) is a nightly roost for the swallow migration. Each day, hundreds of thousands of swallows arrive from all directions and gather in the air over the island. After they've all arrived, the birds organize themselves and spiral downward where they disappear into the reeds. Half of the island is also home to the Potapaug Gun Club; the other is part of TNC's Lord Cove Preserve. No Trespassing signs are posted across the island, but the shore is generally too marshy and muddy to get out of your boat anyway.

Continue around the north end of the island, returning to the main river channel through a narrow passage, and turn south, reconnecting with the northward route at Calves Island (you could pass either east or west of it). Most of Calves Island is private, but the dune-like hills at the north end (the result of dredging spoils) are land trust-owned and a popular landing spot. Return to the railroad bridge following the eastern shore, then turn east into the Lieutenant River, which winds through reedy banks. The main river curves southward before straightening somewhat and pointing north, where it passes beneath a railroad bridge. Just south of the bridge, however, a smaller channel heads eastward, which is where you will ultimately proceed back to the channel.

Follow the channel eastward, then southward before it enters a wider stretch of water. Follow the main channel south behind Great Island, eventually arriving back at the launch.

ALTERNATIVES

If, however, you have plenty of time and energy left after you've crossed back under the railroad bridge, take a 4.0-mile side trip up to Old Lyme on the Lieutenant River, winding through quiet, wooded scenery. You could continue farther up the river, past Goose Island, to Nott Island, Essex, or Selden Island to camp (10.0 miles from the launch). The Black Hall River, east of the launch, is also a nice change of pace.

MORE INFORMATION

Great Island Wildlife Management Area (ct.gov/deep; 860-424-3000). Griswold Point Preserve (nature.org/Connecticut; 203-568-6270). No camping is available on-route. Selden Neck State Park (ct.gov/deep; 860-526-2336), on an island 10 miles upriver from the launch, offers primitive campsites for boaters; reservations are required. Sites at Rocky Neck State Park (ct.gov/deep; 860-739-5471) in East Lyme are located well inland from the beach.

Fiddler crabs, like these on the bank of the Black Hall River, are a common sight in salt marshes.

49
THIMBLE ISLANDS

*Paddle among beautiful pink granite islands
topped with an intriguing array of houses.*

Distance ▶	4.0 to 5.0 nautical miles, round-trip
Tidal Planning ▶	Mean tidal range is 6.14 feet in New Haven. Floods west, ebbs east.
Cautions ▶	Plenty of boat traffic.
Charts and Maps ▶	NOAA charts #12372 and #12373; Maptech #1

LAUNCH
Stony Creek Town Landing, Branford, CT Paved ramp/beach launch beside town dock; adjacent on-street parking is limited in summer; portable toilets. Adjacent park and swimming beach (no kayak launching from beach). From I-95 South, Exit 56, turn left onto East Industrial Road. In 0.3 mile, turn left onto Leetes Island Road. In 1.7 miles, continue straight on Thimble Island Road. The launch is on the left in 0.7 miles. *GPS coordinates: 41° 15.973' N, 72° 45.120' W.*

Other Public Access Only two areas are open to the public on this route: Veddar Preserve, owned by the Branford Land Trust (BLT), and Outer Island, which is part of the Stewart B. McKinney National Wildlife Refuge (SBMNWR). All other islands and features described are private.

ROUTE DESCRIPTION
The granite archipelago of the Thimble Islands is scattered just off the coast of Stony Creek. Depending on how you define an island, there's anywhere from 100 to more than 300 Thimble Islands, named for the thimbleberries that once grew there. Perhaps this was before the Revolutionary War, when all the islands' trees were cut down to minimize hiding places for British ships. Now the islands are known by their pink granite bedrock and the homes that perch on them. Twenty-three of the islands are inhabited—a total of 81 houses; fourteen of the islands have only one house. Only one island is open to visitors.

Any number of routes through the islands could be paddled. Try to travel with the tidal current and plan for a stop on Outer Island; otherwise thread a path among the islands according to whim. A decent circuit of the islands might only take you 4.0 to 5.0 nautical miles.

From the launch, arc northwest toward Pleasant Point, passing a tidal inlet with a railroad bridge at its head. Beyond the homes on Pleasant Point is Veddar Preserve (BLT); it may be close to the launch, but it's one of the few opportunities in this area to get out of your boat.

Ahead on Juniper Point is a barge-loading facility, used to load crushed stone carried there by railroad from a quarry about 5 miles away. Continue to Lewis Island, much of which is dominated by a well-proportioned stone and shingle home with a view of the barge-loading facility. Head south to Rogers Island, which has a newer home landscaped with stone walls and steps between terraces of well-kept gardens and a few potted palm trees. Rogers Island is one of ten Thimble Islands owned by Christine Svenningsen, who paid more than $36 million for her acquisitions over a period of 21 years. Her personal elm tree flag flies over the islands she owns.

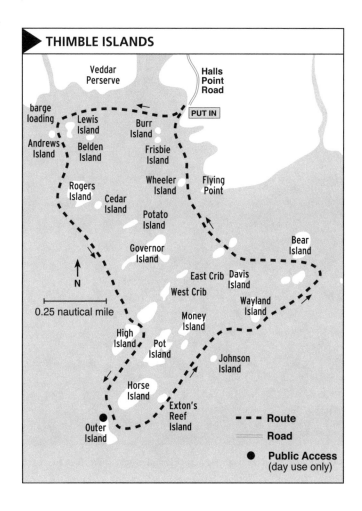

To the southeast, tiny Cedar Island has only a gazebo on it; the town of Branford denied, permission to build more. Continue past Potato and Governor islands to High Island, where you could paddle beneath the bridge at higher tides, right through the gap between the two islands. Or head around the southwest end of High Island and continue toward Horse Island. Horse is the largest island in the Thimbles and is used as an ecological laboratory by Yale's Peabody Museum of Natural History.

Just southeast of Horse is Outer Island (SBMNWR), your one opportunity to get out of the boat and stretch your legs. Aside from its status as a National Wildlife Refuge, the island is used by Southern Connecticut State University for ecological studies. If you're lucky, an intern will welcome you to the island and offer a tour. Aside from that, there's an outhouse and a picnic area.

Continue along the southern side of Horse, Pot, and Money islands. Part of the fun here is just checking out the houses. Some are parts of tiny island communities. Others, like the one built atop stilt-like concrete columns on a ledge, are barely even on islands. Wind your way around the islands however your spirit and the current moves

For more of a full-day adventure, head out to Falkner Island, where you're likely to see terns and interns (no landing here during nesting season).

you. Mid-tide currents do pick up as the tide squeezes between the islands, and it will help to have the current behind you.

At Smith and Bear islands, circle back westward. Bear Island is the site of a granite quarry that exported stone to such monuments as the Lincoln Memorial and the base of the Statue of Liberty. From Cut in Two Island, head back for Flying Point, following the shore back to the launch.

ALTERNATIVES

If you want a little mileage, continue on to Sachem Head for an 8.0-nautical-mile round-trip. If you're up for more of a full-day adventure and conditions warrant it, continue from Sachem Head out to Falkner Island Lighthouse (a round-trip of 15.0 nautical miles) where the sky is thick with nesting terns; no landings here in nesting season. Be attentive to currents and the effect that tide changes will have on conditions.

If you prefer to add some landbound miles instead, walk on the Trolley Trail to Branford Land Trust's Jennie Vedder Preserve, where you can look out over the Thimble Islands from a high, rocky outcrop. From Thimble Island Road, turn west on West Point Road and park in front of West Point Field.

MORE INFORMATION

Stony Creek Town Landing (branford-ct.gov/parks; 203-488-8304). Vedder Preserve (branfordlandtrust.org; 203-483-5263); a trail map is available online. No camping is available on-route. Stewart B. McKinney National Wildlife Refuge (fws.gov/refuge/stewart_b_mckinney; 860-399-2513).

50
NORWALK ISLANDS

Chain of islands has great public access—and camping—and a (distant) view of Manhattan's skyscrapers.

Distance ▶ 9.0 to 10.0 nautical miles round-trip

Tidal Planning ▶ Mean tidal range in South Norwalk is 7.07 feet. Aside from flooding into the Norwalk and Saugatuck rivers and ebbing back into Long Island Sound, the tide floods west up the sound toward New York and ebbs eastward.

Cautions ▶ Heavy motorboat traffic at times.

Charts and Maps ▶ NOAA chart #12368; Maptech #16

LAUNCH

Calf Pasture Beach, Norwalk, CT Gravel beach launch (entry fee); parking nearby; bathrooms nearby. From I-95, Exit 16, go south on East Avenue. After 0.5 mile, turn left onto Cemetery Street/CT 136, then keep right on Cemetery Street, and right again onto Gregory Boulevard. In 0.5 mile, go left around the monument before taking a right (third exit) onto Marvin Street/Calf Pasture Beach Road. Follow Calf Pasture Beach Road for 0.7 mile to the beach entrance. The launch is 0.5 mile around the park on the right. *GPS coordinates: 41° 4.962' N, 73° 23.688' W.*

Other Public Access Publicly owned islands are plentiful in this area and a few private lands offer public access; land managers and permitted uses are noted in the description. Contact land managers for specific restrictions (see More Information). Other public launches include the Saugatuck River State Boat Launch beneath the I-95 bridge on Underhill Parkway and the Five Mile River on Rowayton Avenue in Rowayton, Connecticut.

ROUTE DESCRIPTION

Less than 40 miles from Manhattan, the Norwalk Islands are a group of at least 23 islands, ranging from tiny, rocky islets to a 59-acre island with thick forests and diverse bird populations. Generally less than a mile from the mainland, the islands are easily reachable by kayak and half are open to the public. The cities of Norwalk and Westport manage campsites at three of the islands, which all require advance reservations. Several other islands have good landings for day use. For a more in-depth tour around the islands, David Park's *Kayaking in and Around the Norwalk Islands* is a valuable resource.

You can also just find yourself a stretch of beach and relax. The beaches in the area are terminal moraines shaped by glaciers and tend to be more gravel than sand, but they're great places to pull up for a lunch break or to watch for birds. The Stewart B. McKinney National Wildlife Refuge (SBMNWR) parcels on Peach, Chimon, Sheffield, and Goose islands are closed during nesting season, but provide habitat for the birds you may see in the area, including various herons, ibis, and egrets, as well as osprey.

Despite the easy access to landings, you'll never quite get away from it all in this neighborhood, but perhaps part of the attraction is how close to "it all" you are. Besides distant views of Manhattan, the Norwalk Harbor Power Station dominates the northern shoreline on Manresa Island. The oil-burning plant is shut down for the most part and its future is in the balance. Like it or not, the plant is a useful land-mark, and some may find it weirdly exotic. Paddling along the south of the islands, the view stretches across 6.0 miles of Long Island Sound to Port Jefferson, New York, where the four red-striped smokestacks of yet another power plant counter the one on Manresa Island.

Calf Pasture Beach, while not an inexpensive option, is probably the easiest launch. The Norwalk city beach offers the quickest access to the heart of the Norwalk Islands. From the launch, head south toward green can #9 and the east end of Betts Island. Take a careful look around before crossing the channel; this is a very busy spot. The safest course could be to arc over to Calf Pasture Island and follow the shallow, rocky area through Grassy Hammock Rocks, where you are less likely to encounter power-boats. Past that, the channel is fairly narrow and quick to cross.

South of Betts Island (private) is 7-acre Grassy Island (city of Norwalk) with four campsites and portable restrooms in-season. The gravel shores provide easy landings. Head west, following the north shore of Chimon Island (SBMNWR). Most of Chi-mon is closed from spring through August 15 for nesting season. The beach on the west side, however, is always open and is popular.

Continue to Shea Island (city of Norwalk), with sixteen campsites and restrooms. At the west side is Ram Bay, an area sheltered by the thin gravel spits that join Shea and Sheffield islands at most tides. Ram Bay is a pleasant, out-of-the-way place to paddle. There's a house on Wood Island (private), while L'Hammock (private) is a man-made island—essentially a foundation for the trio of houses on it.

On the northern point of Sheffield Island (SBMNWR and Norwalk Seaport Associ-ation) are the crumbling remains of an old estate, including the granite and concrete pavilion that was once the end of a dock. During the 1930s, visitors arrived at this dock for extravagant parties at the estate of Robert L. Corby, an executive at Fleischmann's Yeast. Boats of partygoers went back and forth between here and Tavern Island where Billy Rose, a Manhattan club owner, threw his own extravagant parties. Earlier, the

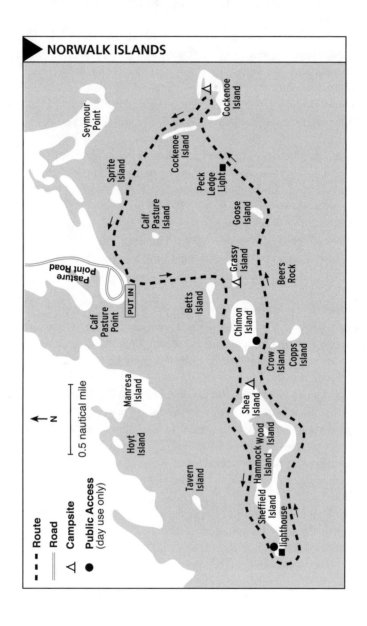

two island estates had been speakeasies, where rum runners dropped off liquor, and customers came from the mainland to buy it. In the 1940s and '50s, the Sheffield Island estate was owned by weapons manufacturer Remington Rand, which used it more as a secretive think tank, drawing scientists and high-level government officials for covert conferences. The refuge now maintains facilities including a sanitation station, a trail system, and an observation platform.

Follow the shore to the Sheffield Island Lighthouse and if desired, land at the adjacent gravel beach. There may be a small landing fee, but the lighthouse is sometimes open to visitors. A light has stood on the point since 1828, with the present limestone block structure built in 1868. In 1902, the Greens Island Light to the west replaced the Sheffield Island light, which was then deactivated. Harbor seals may sometimes be seen around the lighthouse and the ledges to the southwest.

Continue around the point and begin the trip east, first along the shore of Sheffield and Shea. The gravel beach on the south shore of Shea is a good spot for a break; a few of its campsites overlook Long Island Sound. Continue back to Chimon Island, crossing over the sandbar linking it to Copps Island (private).

Pass by the south side of Grassy Island en route to Goose Island (SBMNWR), another potential stopping place that tends to attract plenty of birds—and rumors. The small stone structure is reputed to be a former yellow fever research facility and a World War II spy lookout, but now it belongs to the birds. From here, aim for the lighthouse and behind it, Cockenoe Island. The channel here is a busy spot; be cautious and cross quickly.

The semi-enclosed harbor contained in Cockenoe Island (pronounced "kah-KEE-nee"; town of Westport; camping) is popular among anglers and boaters. Float into the horseshoe-shaped cove, claim your own stretch of sheltered, inward-facing beach, and perhaps scout for treasure rumored to have been buried here by Captain Kidd.

In the 1800s, 27-acre Cockenoe was a working farm, and in 1870 the government raided a whiskey distillery there. In the 1960s, local citizens thwarted efforts to build a nuclear power plant on the island. Cormorants, herons, and egrets now nest on the island; sustained exposure to their guano has killed much of the vegetation, but a few thick stands of trees remain. Plan ahead if you'd like to reserve one of the four campsites. At higher tides, check out the pond at the northeast corner.

The route back to Calf Pasture Beach is less than 2.0 miles. Powerboats dominate here with little regard to channel markers, but be aware of an unmarked channel leading between the lighthouse and the inlet to the north, west of Seymour Point. Head for the shallower water near Sprite Island and on toward the east end of Calf Pasture Beach. Follow the beach, past the wharf, back to the launch.

ALTERNATIVES

For more sheltered paddling, travel along the Goodwives River via the launch at Pear Tree Point Beach Park in Darien, Connecticut.

MORE INFORMATION

City of Norwalk Island Parks (norwalkct.org/index.aspx?nid=580; 203-854-7806 [Department of Recreation and Parks]; 203-886-8810 [harbormaster]); permits for camping on Grassy and Shea islands must be purchased in advance at the Veteran's Park Boating Center on Seaview Avenue or the harbormaster's office at city hall 14 days prior to stay. Stewart B. McKinney National Wildlife Refuge (fws.gov/refuge/ stewart_b_mckinney; 860-399-2513); guided tours are available from U.S. Fish and Wildlife staff on summer weekends. Norwalk Seaport Association, Inc. (seaport.org/ page-872480; 203-838-9444); lighthouse tours are available in-season. City of Westport Conservation Department (westportct.gov/index.aspx?page=56; 203-341-1170); permit (fee) required for camping on Cockenoe Island.

Less than 40 miles from Manhattan, the Norwalk Islands attract a great variety of boaters. Here, paddlers on surf skis leave Cockenoe Island.

Appendix A: Information and Resources

National Oceanic and Atmospheric Administration (NOAA)
Weather: weather.gov
Tides and currents: tidesandcurrents.noaa.gov
Charts: nauticalcharts.noaa.gov
Marine Mammal Stranding Hotline: 866-755-6622

United States Coast Guard
National Response Center: 800-424-8802
24 Hour Emergency Response: 800-410-9549
Eastport, ME: 207-853-2845
Jonesport, ME: 207-497-2200
Southwest Harbor, ME: 207-244-4200
Rockland, ME: 207-596-6667
Boothbay Harbor, ME: 207-633-2661
South Portland, ME: 207-767-0320, 207-767-0303 (after working hours)
Portsmouth Harbor, NH: 603-433-7324
Merrimack River, Newburyport, MA: 978-465-0731
Gloucester, MA: 978-283-0705
Point Allerton, Scituate, MA: 781-925-0166
Cape Cod Canal, Sandwich, MA: 508-888-0020
Air Station Cape Cod: 508-968-6800
Provincetown, MA: 508-487-0077
Chatham, MA: 508-945-3829, 508-945-0164 (emergency)
Woods Hole, MA: 508-457-3254
Menemsha, Martha's Vineyard, MA: 508-645-2662
Brant Point, Nantucket, MA: 508-228-0398
Castle Hill, Newport, RI: 401-846-3675
Point Judith, RI: 401-792-0306
New London, CT: 860-442-4471
New Haven, CT: 800-774-8724
Burlington, Vermont: 802-951-6792

Shellfish Information

Maine Red Tide and Shellfish Sanitation Hotline: 800-232-4733

Maine Marine Patrol (for details on shellfish closures).

Division 1 (New Hampshire border to western shore of St. George River): 207-633-9595

Division 2 (eastern shore of St. George River to Canadian border): 207-667-3373

New Hampshire Clam Flat Hotline: 1-800-43-CLAMS

Massachusetts Division of Marine Fisheries: 617-626-1520

Rhode Island Office of Water Resources: 401-222-2900

Connecticut Bureau of Aquaculture: 203-874-0696

Fire Permits

Maine Forest Service

East of Penobscot River: 207-827-1800

West of Penobscot River: 207-624-3700, 1-800-750-9777

First Aid Instruction

Appalachian Mountain Club (AMC): activities.outdoors.org

Stonehearth Open Learning Opportunities (SOLO): soloschools.com, 603-447-6711

National Outdoor Leadership School (NOLS): nols.edu, 866-831-9001

Wilderness Medical Associates: wildmed.com, 207-730-7331

Kayaking Instruction

American Canoe Association: americancanoe.org

Appalachian Mountain Club (AMC): activities.outdoors.org

Organizations and Publications

Appalachian Mountain Club (AMC): outdoors.org

Maine Island Trail Association (MITA): mita.org

Southern Maine Sea Kayaking Network: smskn.org

North Shore Paddlers Network: nspn.org/

Rhode Island Canoe and Kayak Association: ricka.org

Northeast Paddlers Message Board: npmb.com

Connecticut Sea Kayakers: connyak.org

Paddling.net: paddling.net

Atlantic Coastal Kayaker: atlanticcoastalkayaker.com

Adventure Kayak magazine: rapidmedia.com/kayaking.html

Ocean Paddler magazine: paddlepressmedia.com/

Canoe and Kayak magazine: canoekayak.com

Coastal Access Guides

Maine Coastal Public Access Guide, published by the state of Maine (maine.gov/dacf/mcp)

Massachusetts Coast Guide to Boston Harbor and the North Shore, published by the Massachusetts Office of Coastal Zone Management, plus an online guide for the whole coast (mass.gov/eea/agencies/czm/program-areas/public-access-and-coast-guide/coast-guide)

Rhode Island Public Saltwater Boat Launching Sites, managed by the Rhode Island Division of Fish and Wildlife (dem.ri.gov/programs/bnatres/fishwild/boatlnch.htm#salt)

Connecticut State Boat Launches, managed by the Connecticut Department of Energy & Environmental Protection (depdata.ct.gov/maps/boating/boatingmap.htm)

United States Fish & Wildlife Service

Maine Coastal Islands: fws.gov/refuge/Maine_Coastal_Islands/about.html, 207-594-0600

Appendix B: Float Plan

If we do not report by _____ A.M./P.M. on _____ (date),
please call _____ (agency/phone)
and report me/us overdue/missing and provide the following:

TOTAL NUMBER OF PADDLERS IN GROUP _____

KAYAKERS

Names _____

Ages/genders _____

Phones _____

Kayak colors (deck/hull) _____

PFD colors _____

Clothing _____

Skill levels _____

Medical info _____

GEAR CARRIED

Signaling and communications gear _____

_____

Tent descriptions _____

_____

LAUNCH SITE _____ DATE _____ TIME _____ A.M./P.M.

FINAL LANDING SITE _____ DATE _____ TIME _____ A.M./P.M.

VEHICLE(S), LICENSE # _____

_____

SHUTTLE VEHICLE(S) (IF ANY), LICENSE # _____

_____

PROPOSED ROUTE, CAMPSITES, ALTERNATIVES _____

_____

_____

_____

_____

Appendix C: More Reading

Sea Kayaking Manuals

Brown, Gordon. *Sea Kayak: A Manual for Intermediate and Advanced Sea Kayakers.* Pesda Press, 2006.

Dowd, John. *Sea Kayaking: A Manual for Long Distance Touring.* 5th edition. Greystone Books, 2004.

Hutchinson, Derek. *The Complete Book of Sea Kayaking.* 5th ed. Falcon Guides, 2004.

Johnson, Shelley. *The Complete Sea Kayakers Handbook.* 2nd Edition. International Marine/Ragged Mountain Press, 2011.

Robison, John. *Sea Kayaking Illustrated: A Visual Guide to Better Paddling.* International Marine/Ragged Mountain Press, 2003.

Navigation and Safety

Broze, Matt. *Sea Kayaker's Deep Trouble: True Stories and Their Lessons from* Sea Kayaker *Magazine.* International Marine/Ragged Mountain Press, 1997.

Burch, David. *Fundamentals of Kayak Navigation.* 4th edition. Falcon Guides, 2008.

Cunningham, Christopher. *Sea Kayaker's More Deep Trouble.* International Marine/ Ragged Mountain Press, 2013.

Ferrero, Franco. *Sea Kayak Navigation: A Practical Manual, Essential Knowledge for Finding Your Way at Sea.* 2nd edition. Pesda Press, 2007.

Local Guidebooks

O'Connor, Michael. *Discover Cape Cod: AMC's Guide to the Best Hiking, Biking, and Paddling.* Appalachian Mountain Club Books, 2009.

Park, David. *Kayaking In and Around the Norwalk Islands.* Self-published, 2009.

Sinai, Lee. *Discover Martha's Vineyard: AMC's Guide to the Best Hiking, Biking, and Paddling.* Appalachian Mountain Club Books, 2009.

Wivell, Ty. *Discover Maine: AMC's Outdoor Traveler's Guide to the Pine Tree State* Appalachian Mountain Club Books, 2006.

INDEX

ABOUT THE AUTHOR

Michael Daugherty is a Registered Maine Guide and an ACA-certified sea kayaking instructor at Pinniped Kayak. He writes for *Sea Kayaker, Ocean Paddler,* and *AMC Outdoors* magazines and documents his sea kayaking experiences online at seakayakstonington.blogspot.com. He lives in Stonington, ME.

ABOUT AMC IN NEW ENGLAND

Each year, AMC's eight New England chapters—Berkshire, Boston, Connecticut, Maine, Narragansett, New Hampshire, Southeastern Massachusetts, and Worcester—offer thousands of outdoor activities including hiking, backpacking, bicycling, paddling, and climbing trips, as well as social, family, and young member programs. Members also maintain local trails, lead outdoors skill workshops, and promote stewardship of the region's natural resources. To view a list of AMC activities in New England and across the Northeast, visit activities.outdoors.org.

AMC BOOK UPDATES

AMC Books strives to keep our guidebooks as up-to-date as possible to help you plan safe and enjoyable adventures. If after publishing a book we learn that trails have been relocated or route or contact information has changed, we will post the updated information online. Before you hit the trail, check for updates at outdoors.org/bookupdates.

While hiking or paddling, if you notice discrepancies with then trail descriptions or map, or if you find any other erros in a book, please let us know by submitting them to amcbookupdates@outdoors.org or in writing to Books Editor, c/o AMC, 5 Joy Street, Boston, MA 02108. We will verify all submissions and post key updates each month. AMC Books is dedicated to being a recognized leader in outdoor publishing. Thank you for your participation.

APPALACHIAN MOUNTAIN CLUB

t AMC, connecting you to the freedom and exhilaration of the
utdoors is our calling. We help people of all ages and abilities to
xplore and develop a deep appreciation of the natural world.

MC helps you get outdoors on your own, with family and friends,
nd through activities close to home and beyond. With chapters
om Maine to Washington, D.C., including groups in Boston,
Jew York City, and Philadelphia, you can enjoy activities like hiking,
addling, cycling, and skiing, and learn new outdoor skills. We offer
dvice, guidebooks, maps, and unique lodges and huts to inspire
our next outing. You will also have the opportunity to support
onservation advocacy and research, youth programming, and
aring for 1,800 miles of trails.

Ve invite you to join us in the outdoors.

YOUR CONNECTION
TO THE OUTDOORS

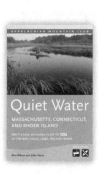